D1701972

EILEAN
A CLASSIC
YACHT

MAY FIFE KOHN
FRANÇOIS CHEVALIER

EILEAN
A CLASSIC
YACHT

Flammarion

We wish to thank Mr Giampiero Negretti, whose book *Panerai*, published by Flammarion in 2008, was the inspiration for the text relating to the founding of the Panerai firm.

François Chevalier is a naval architect and journalist for various international publications, including the magazine *Voiles & Voiliers*. He has written many reference books on yachting in France and abroad, in particular on the America's Cup, pleasure boating in the United Kingdom and the United States in the nineteenth century and the first research study of the French pleasure yacht, *Velox*. He has also written illustrated books about round-the-world voyages, safety at sea, manoeuvring sailing boats and spinnaker handling. Although an eclectic architect, he has a preference for beautiful sailing yachts and has collaborated with the restoration of classic yachts since 1973.

Dr May Fife Kohn is a descendant of the Fife family and was born in Fairlie. She is the author of *Fast and Bonnie, A History of William Fife & Son Yachtbuilders*. Over many years she has researched archival material and drawn on local knowledge and reminiscences to tell the story of the Fife yard. The book was regarded as a most valuable contribution to the industrial history of Scotland. A sailing enthusiast, she is passionate about all Fife yachts and as a scientist is delighted that the history and restoration of *Eilean* is preserved in written form for posterity.

EXECUTIVE DIRECTOR
SUZANNE TISE-ISORÉ

DESIGN
LUDOVIC DROUINEAUD

DESIGN ASSISTANT
CLAUDE-OLIVIER FOUR

EDITORIAL COORDINATION
NATHALIE CHAPUIS

FRANÇOIS CHEVALIER'S TEXT TRANSLATED FROM FRENCH BY
JACQUES REDON

COPYEDITOR
HELEN WOODHALL

PROOFREADER
MARC FEUSTEL

PRODUCTION
ÉLODIE CONJAT-CUVELIER

COLOUR SEPARATION
LES ARTISANS DU REGARD, PARIS

© Flammarion SA, Paris, 2011

All rights reserved. No part of this publication may be reproduced in any form or by any means, electronic, photocopy, information retrieval system, or otherwise, without written permission from Flammarion.

Flammarion SA
87, quai Panhard et Levassor
75647 Paris Cedex 13
editions.flammarion.com

ISBN 978-2-08-030163-5
Dépôt légal: May 2011
Printed by Gruppo Editoriale Zanardi (Maniago, Italy), in April 2011.

PAGES 6–7 *Eilean*'s name, gilded on the transom, reflects in the ripples of her wake.

PAGE 8 *Eilean* was designed by William Fife in 1936, the year Panerai created the first Radiomir watch for the commandos on Royal Italian Navy assault crafts.

PAGE 9 Wooden blocks, restored hatches identical to the originals, varnished cap rail, classic teak deck, and bronze winches: the authenticity of the restoration of this great ketch was of paramount importance.

PAGES 10–11 The dragon, which adorns all yachts designed and built by William Fife from the early 1890s, originated from the famous and successful *Dragons* built for Mr. Hill.

PAGE 12 Louis Fulton (1879–1934), the father of James and Robert Fulton, and his wife standing on the stern of *Ian*, a steam yacht built in 1898. His father-in-law, Robert Waterston is at the helm and his sister Margaret – married to Peter MacCallum Lang – is sitting in front wearing an eccentric hat. *Ian* belonged to Louis's father, who gave her to his son-in-law Peter.

PAGE 13 All the deck gear underwent X-ray resistance tests before being totally restored and stamped with the yacht's name.

PAGE 14 Nowadays, the sails of classic yachts benefit from modern cloth, which faithfully reproduces the colour of the old sails but with a much reduced weight.

PAGE 15 *Eilean* cruising in 1937. Her bow spray shows the power of the yacht in the choppy waters of the Clyde.

PAGES 16–17 When classic sailing yachts gather for the Panerai Classic Yachts Challenge the beauty of the display is in their reflection on the water as much as in the yachts themselves.

PAGE 18 With the wind behind her and mainsail sheeted out, the ketch *Eilean* runs down the white-capped seas of the North Channel between Scotland and Ireland.

PAGE 19 Seventy-eight years later, *Eilean*, with all sails aloft, faces the choppy seas of the Mediterranean under the autumn sun.

PAGES 20–21 On *Eilean*, the cockpit stretches from the mizzenmast to the helmsman's seat. The running backstays' bronze levers are visible along the bulwark on each side of the yacht.

PAGE 22 In 1936, halyard drum winches were commonly used on sailing boats of that size. *Eilean*'s were restored meticulously.

PAGE 23 James Louis Vandalle Fulton at the helm of *Eilean* in 1937 during one of the yacht's first outings from the Fife shipyard. The sportswear is '*de rigueur*'. In flat, calm weather, the ketch is motoring with sails furled.

CONTENTS

FOREWORD BY ANGELO BONATI	25
PREFACE BY WILLIAM SHAWCROSS	27
THE HISTORY OF *EILEAN* BY MAY FIFE KOHN	33

1. THE BIRTH OF A LEGEND

HORA ITALICA, PANERAI AND THE SEA BY GIAMPIERO NEGRETTI	47
EILEAN, FIRST RACES	63
NEW OWNERS, NEW FITTING-OUT	73
JOHN SHEARER, ARCHITECT AND NAVIGATOR	79

2. PANERAI AND *EILEAN*

THE DISCOVERY OF *EILEAN*	91
THE RESTORATION OF *EILEAN*: A PASSION FOR AUTHENTICITY	107
THE PANERAI CLASSIC YACHTS CHALLENGE	139
FACTS AND FIGURES	161
BIBLIOGRAPHY	190
ACKNOWLEDGEMENTS	192

LILLE

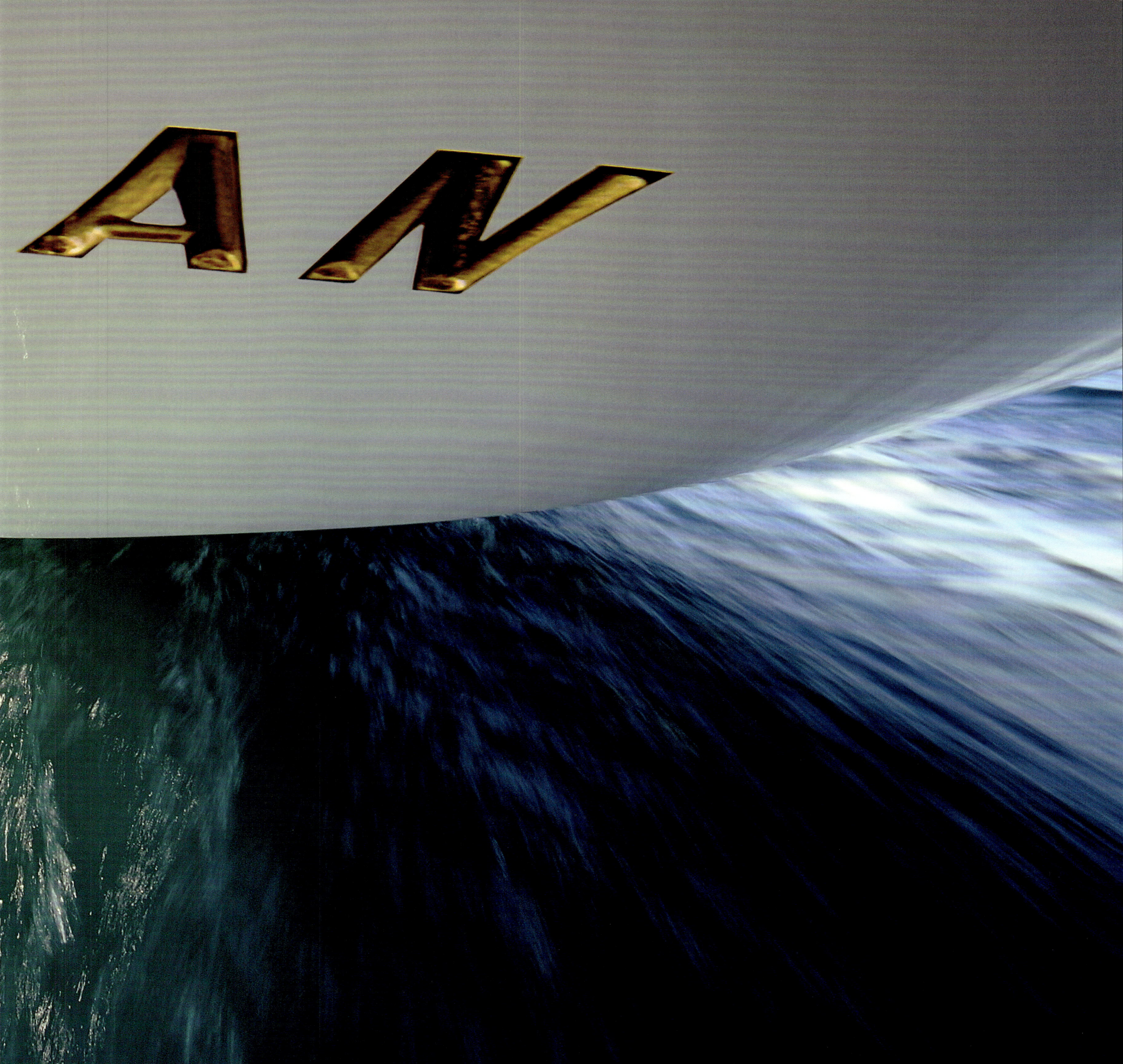
AN

EILEAN 1936

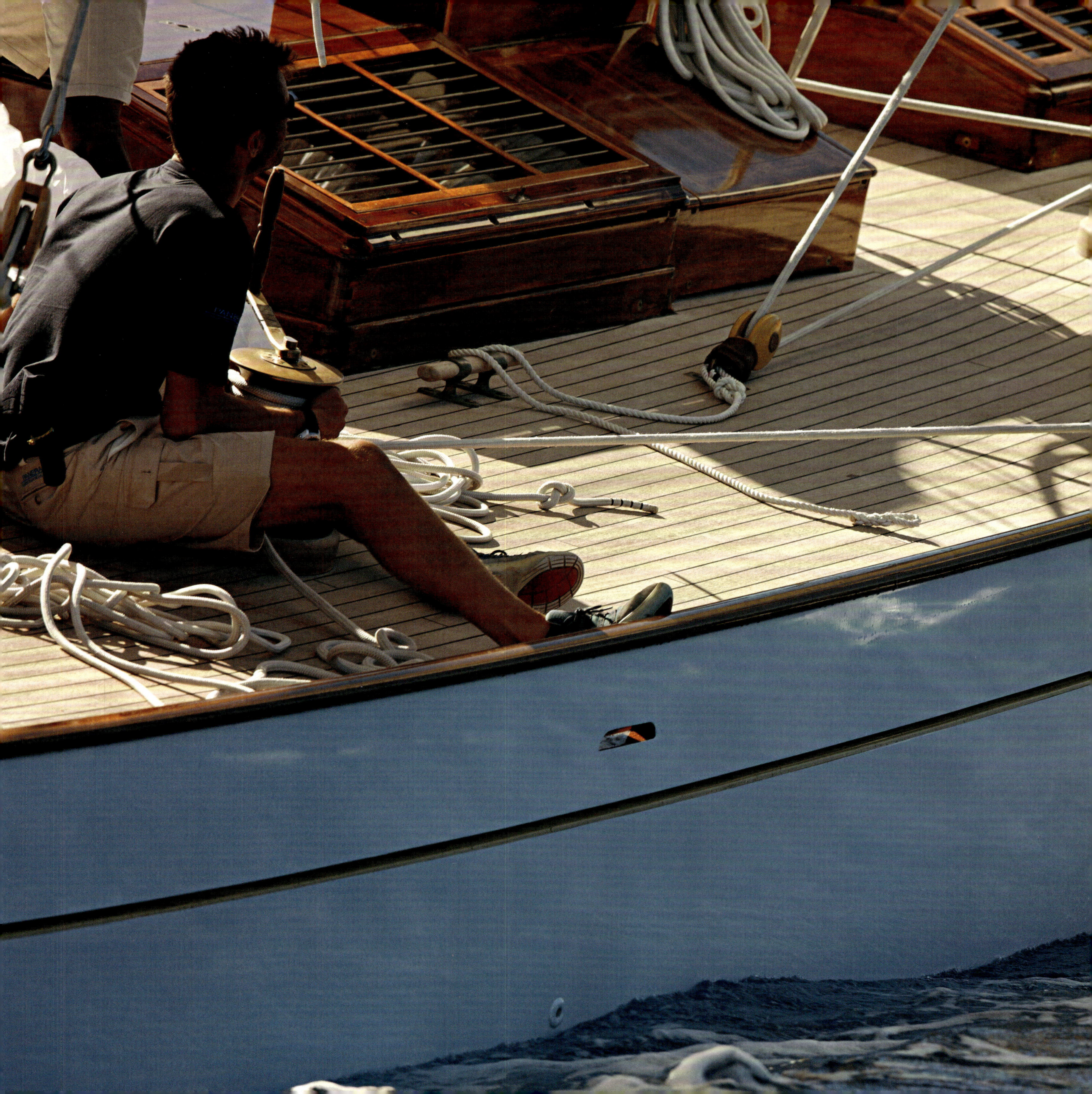

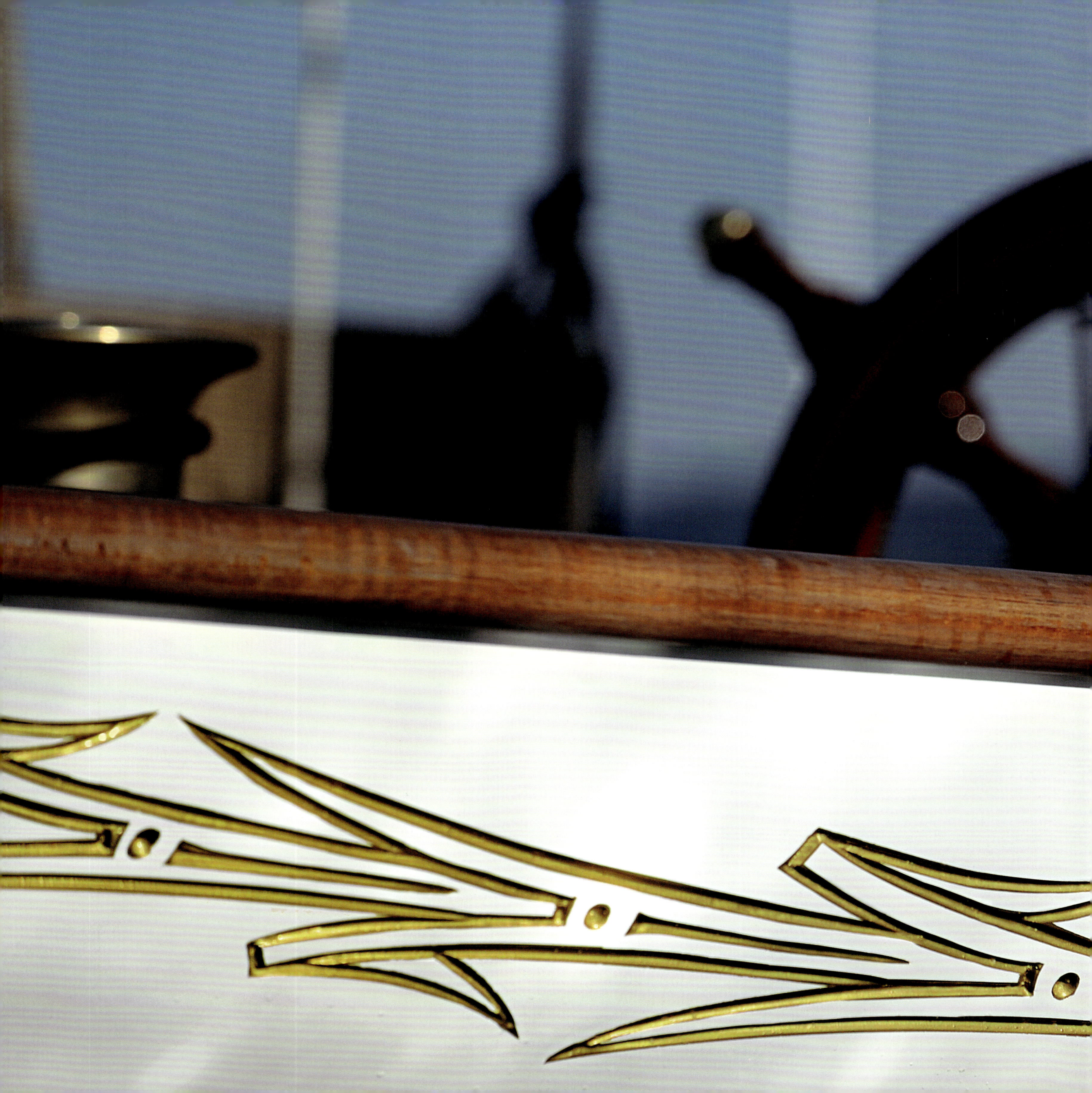

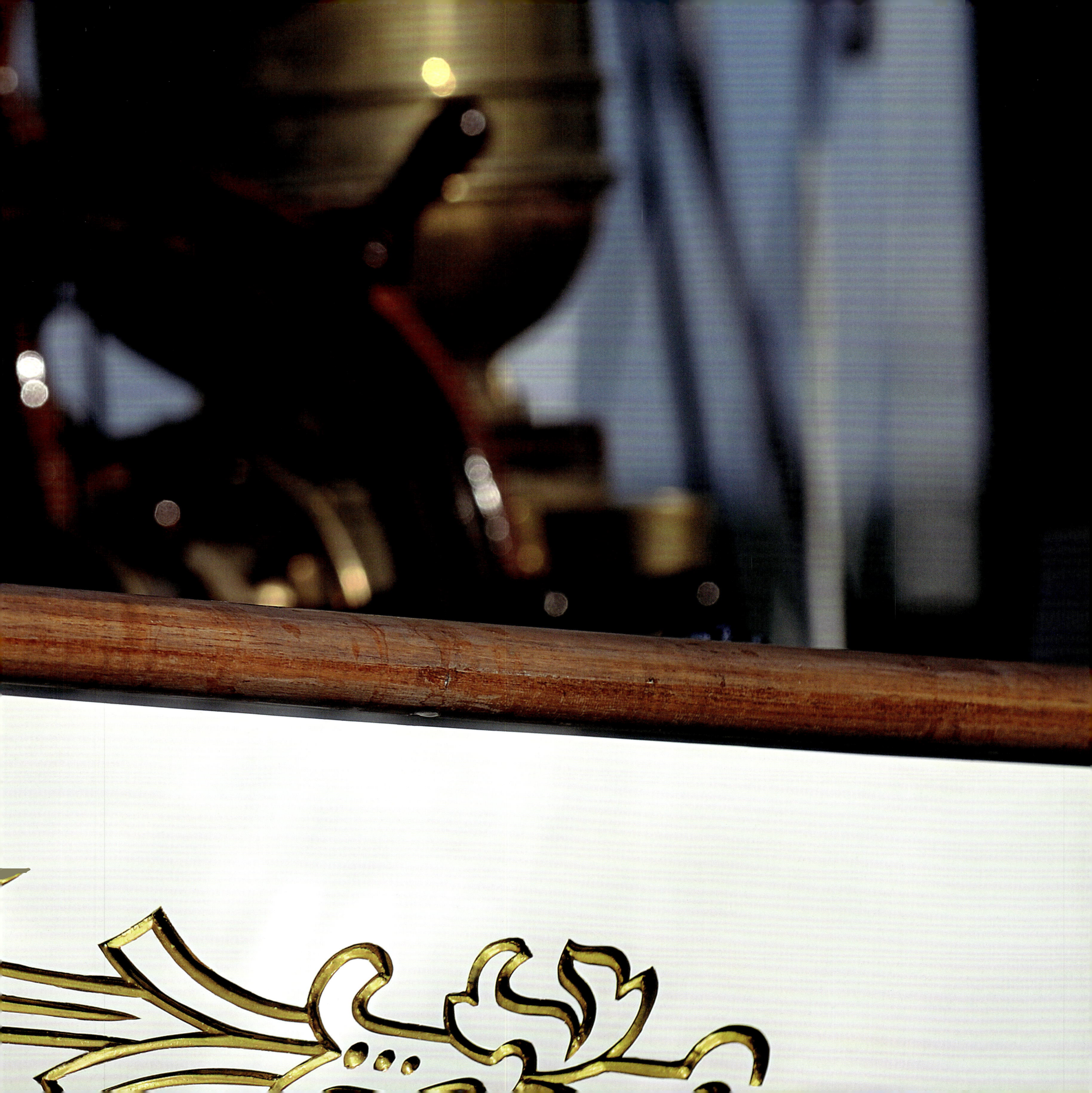

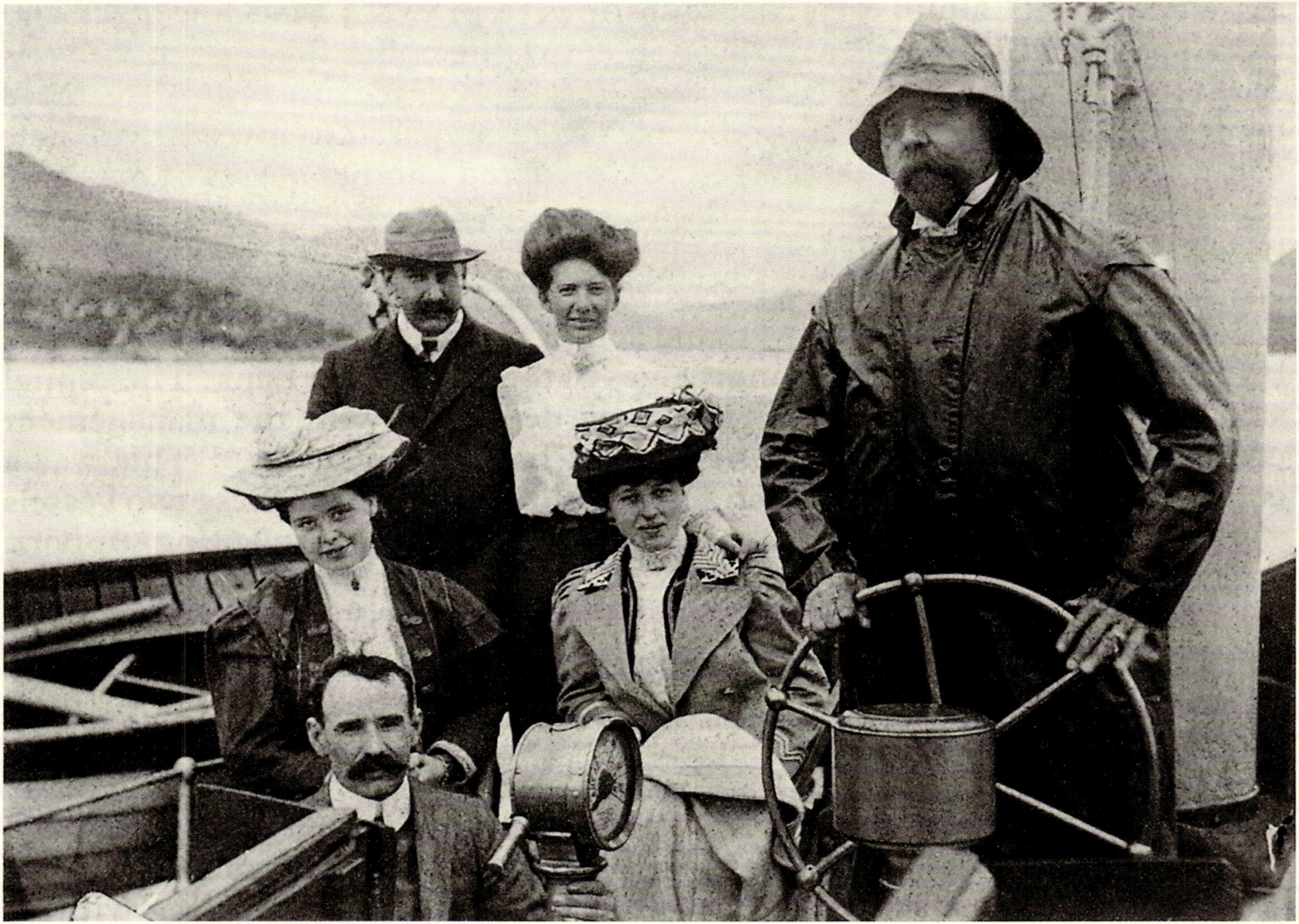

EILEAN
· 1936 ·

180 C

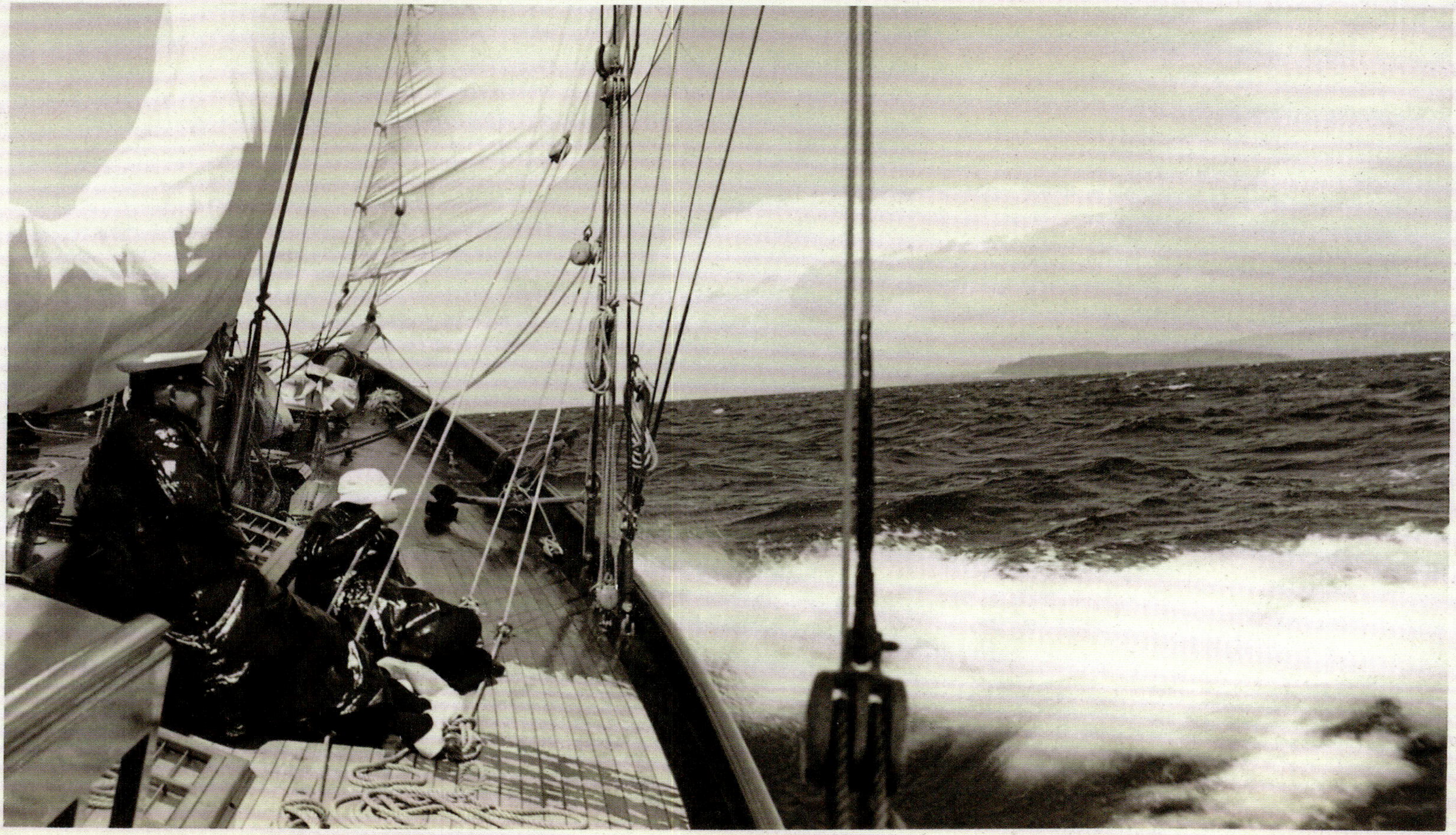

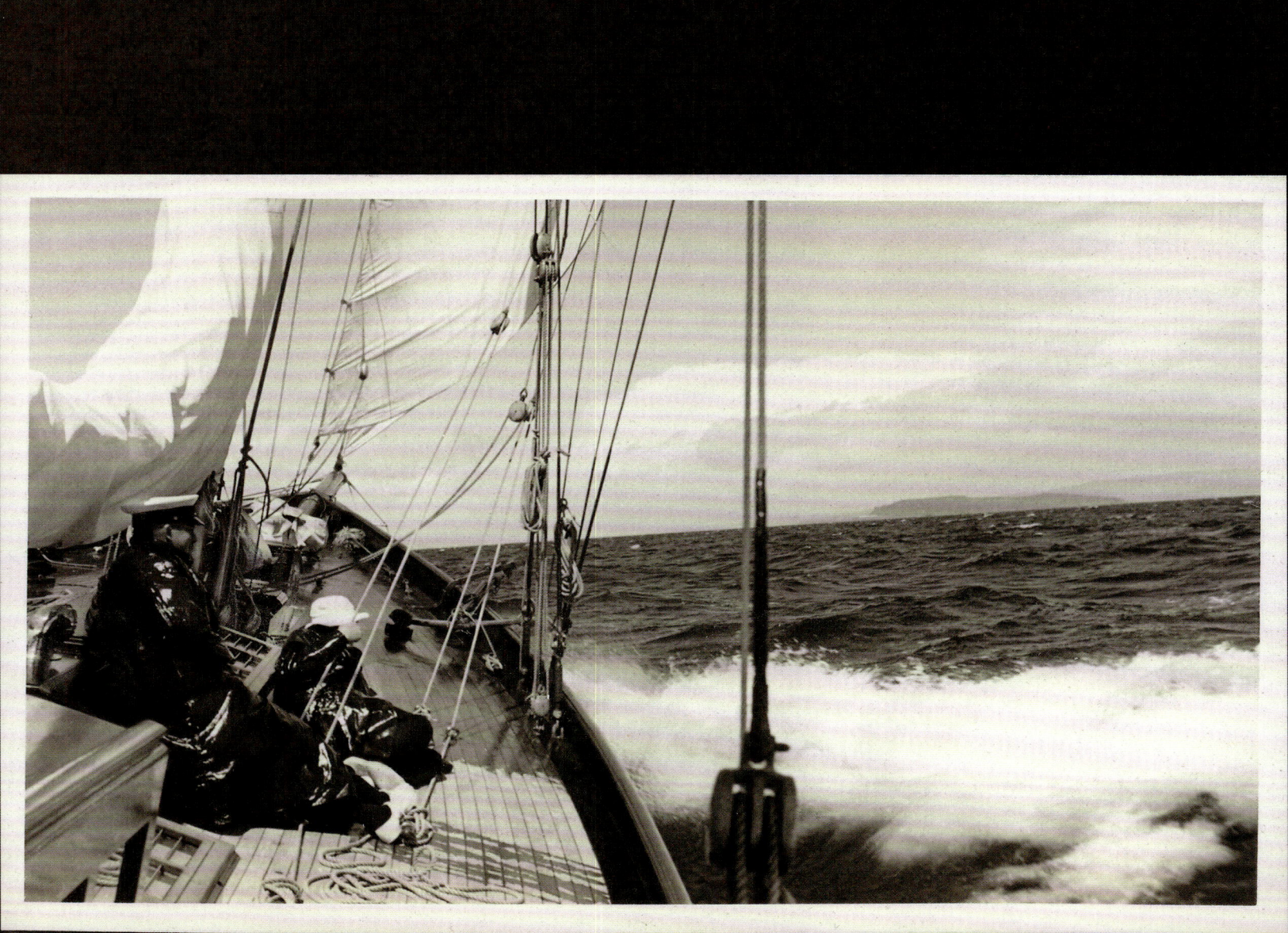

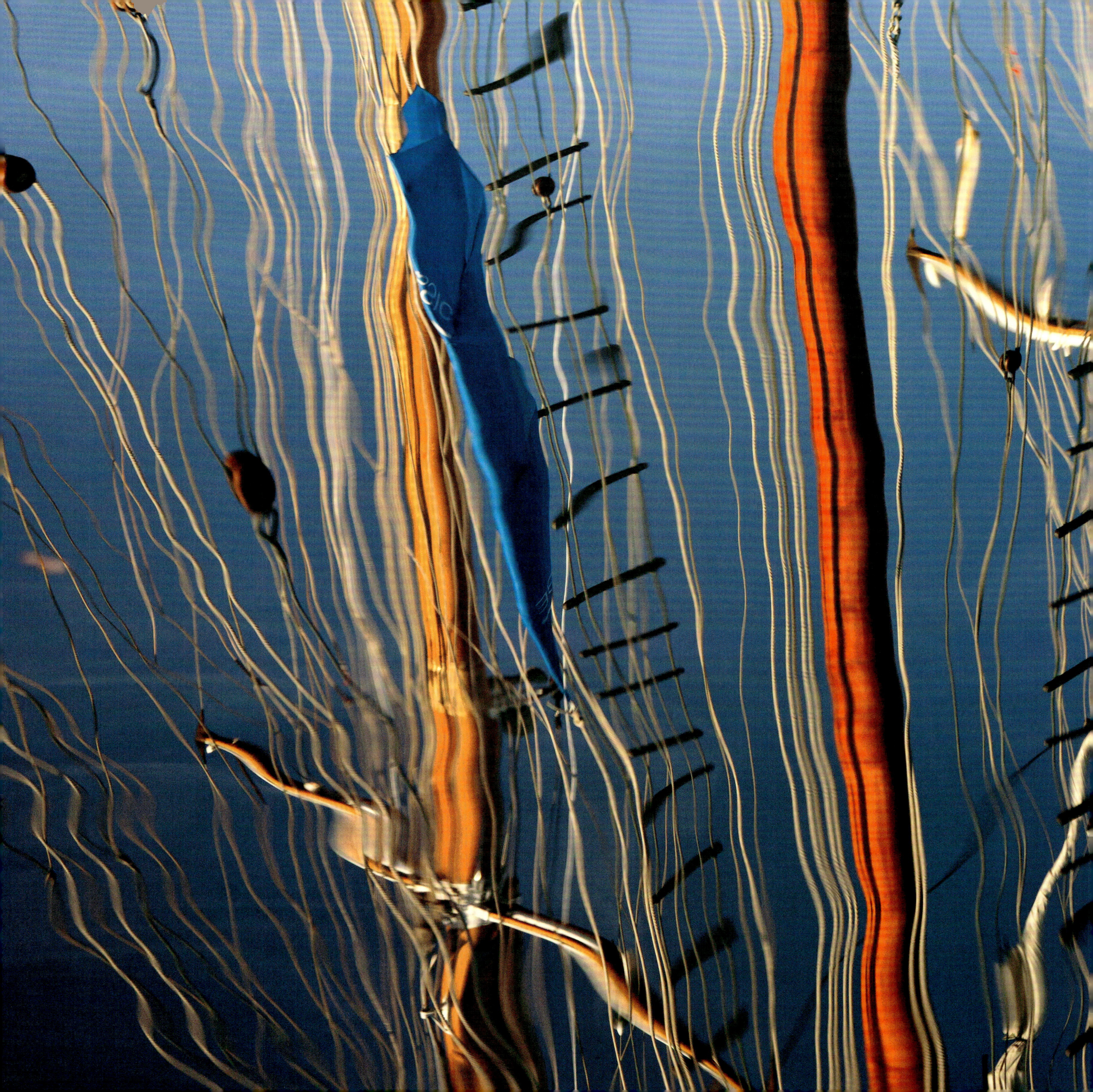

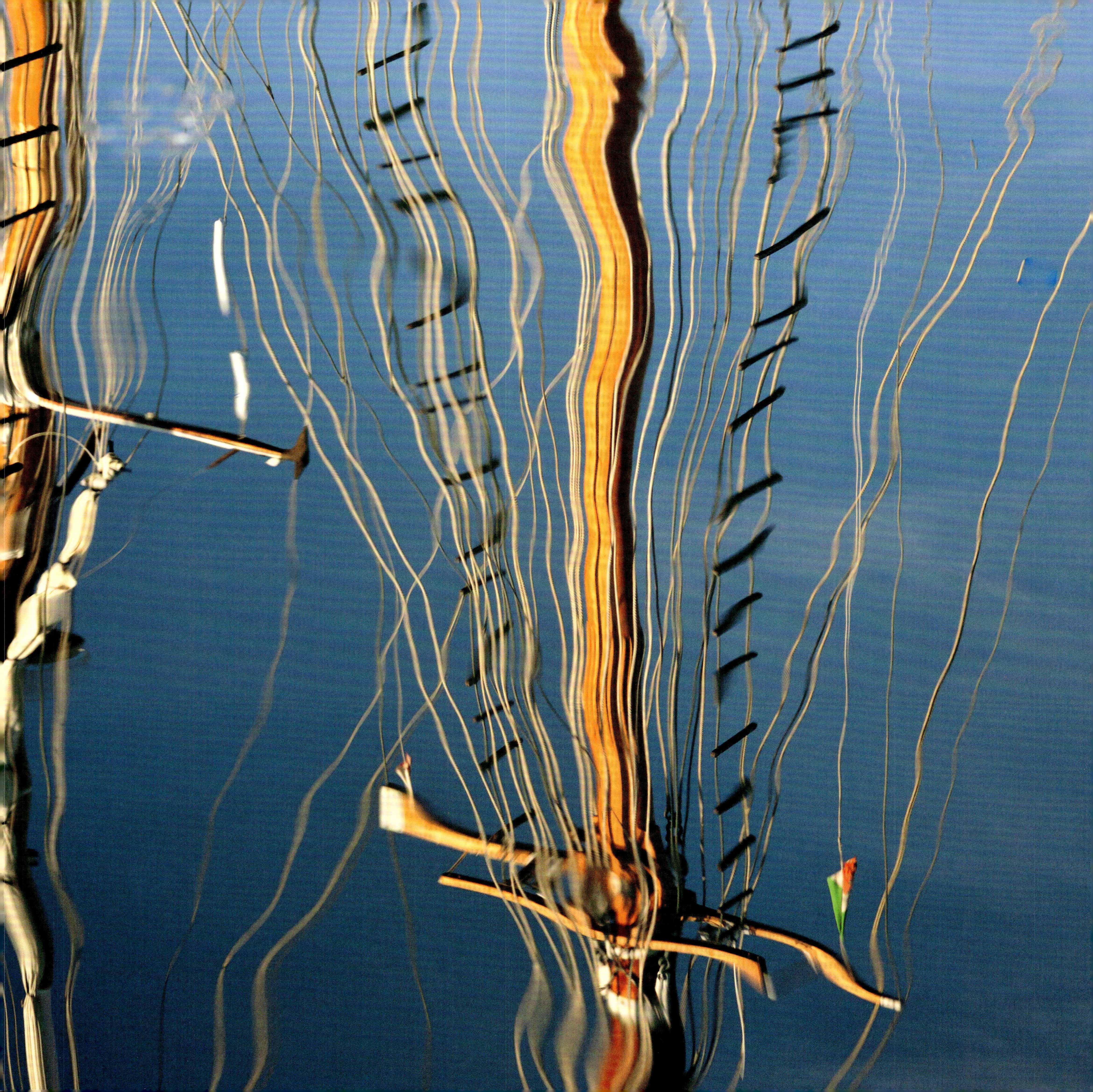

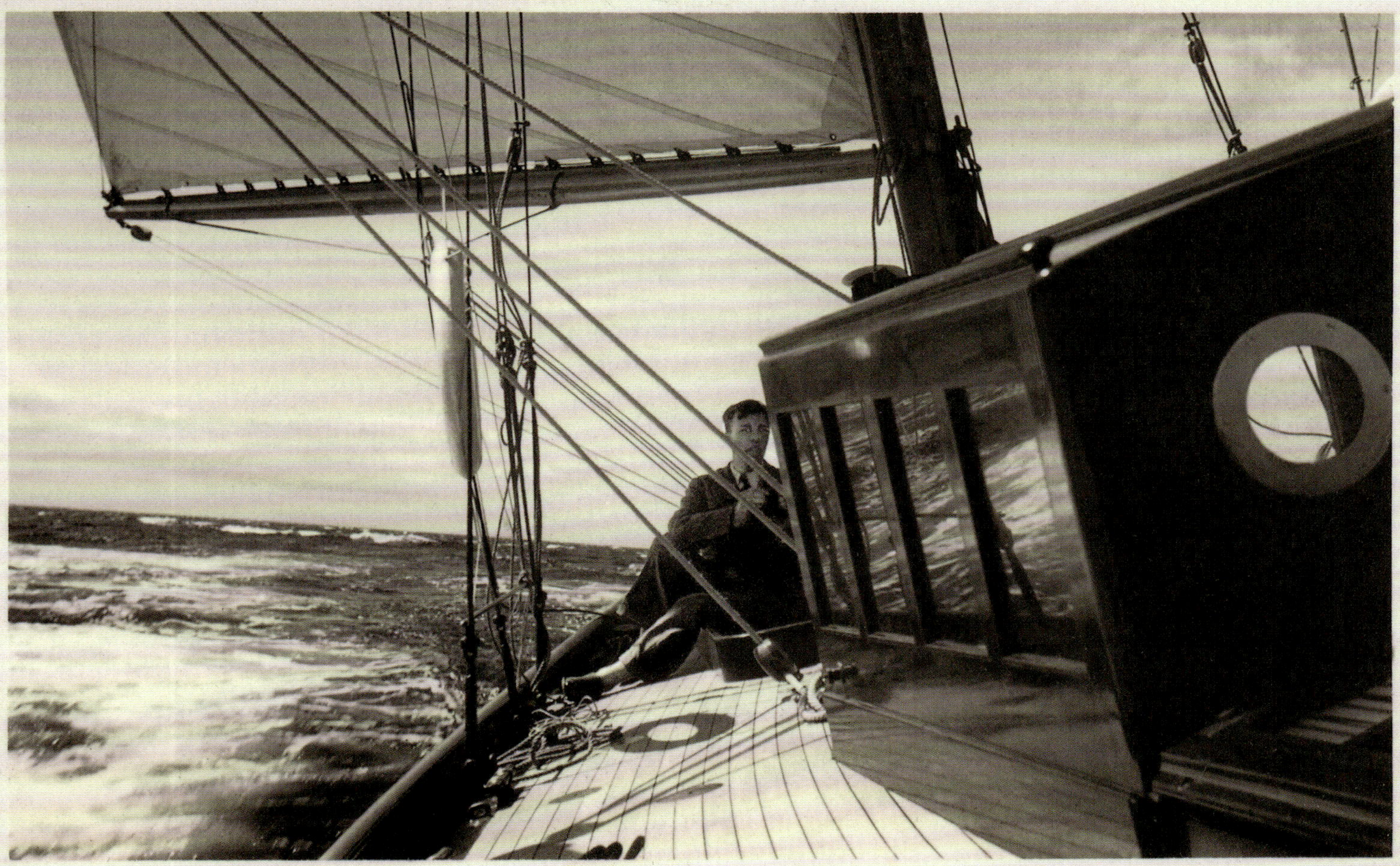

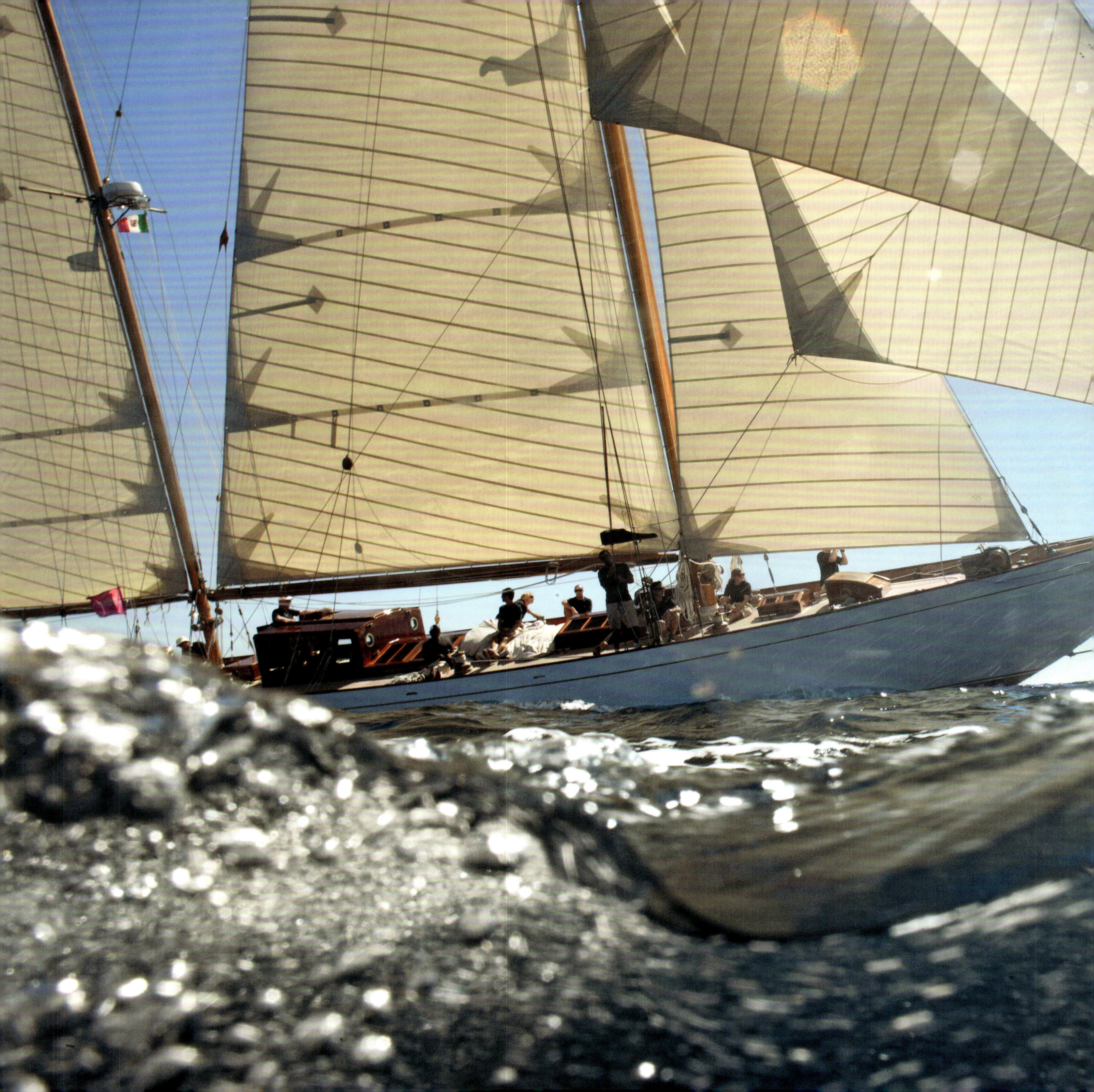

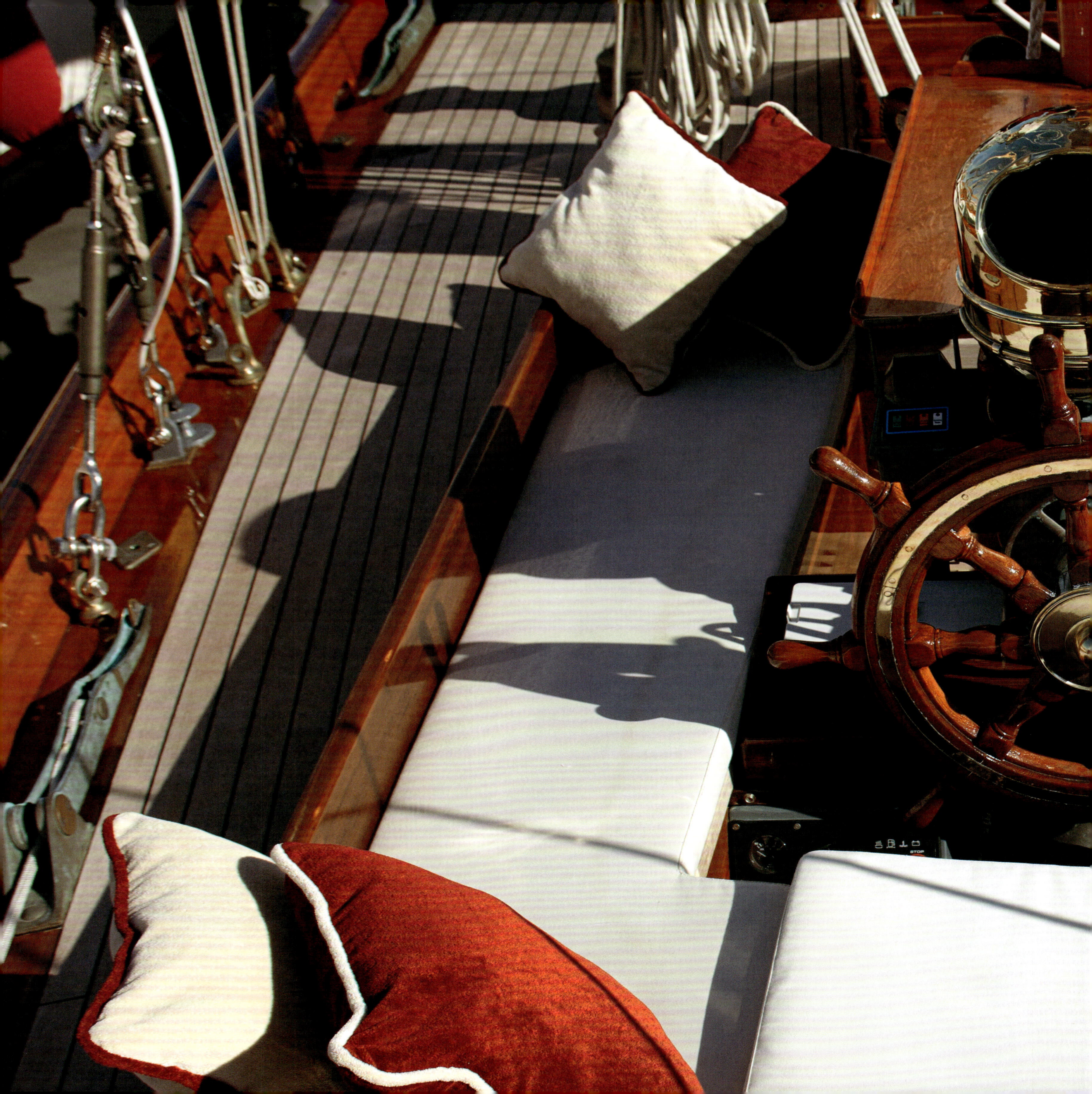

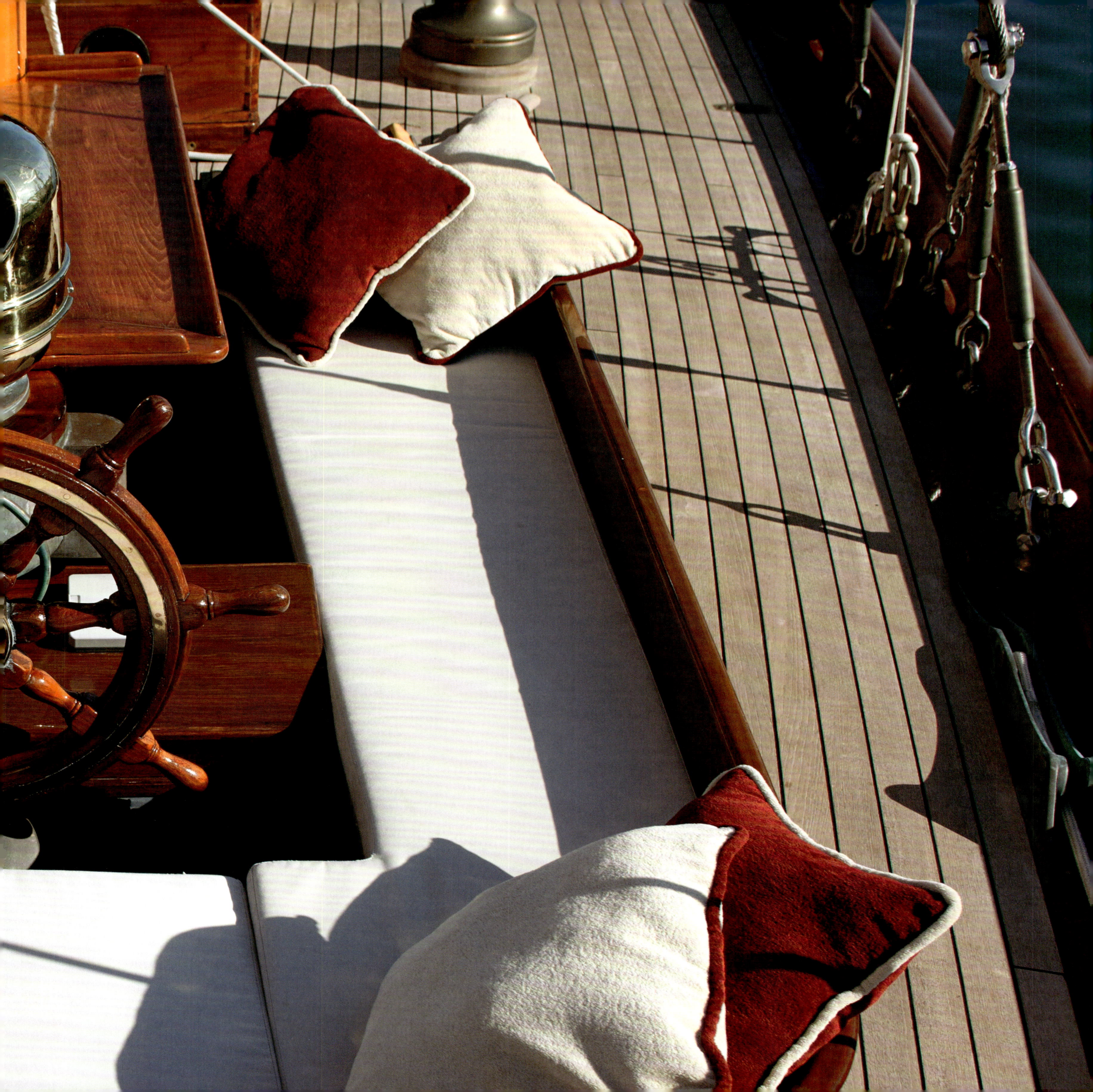

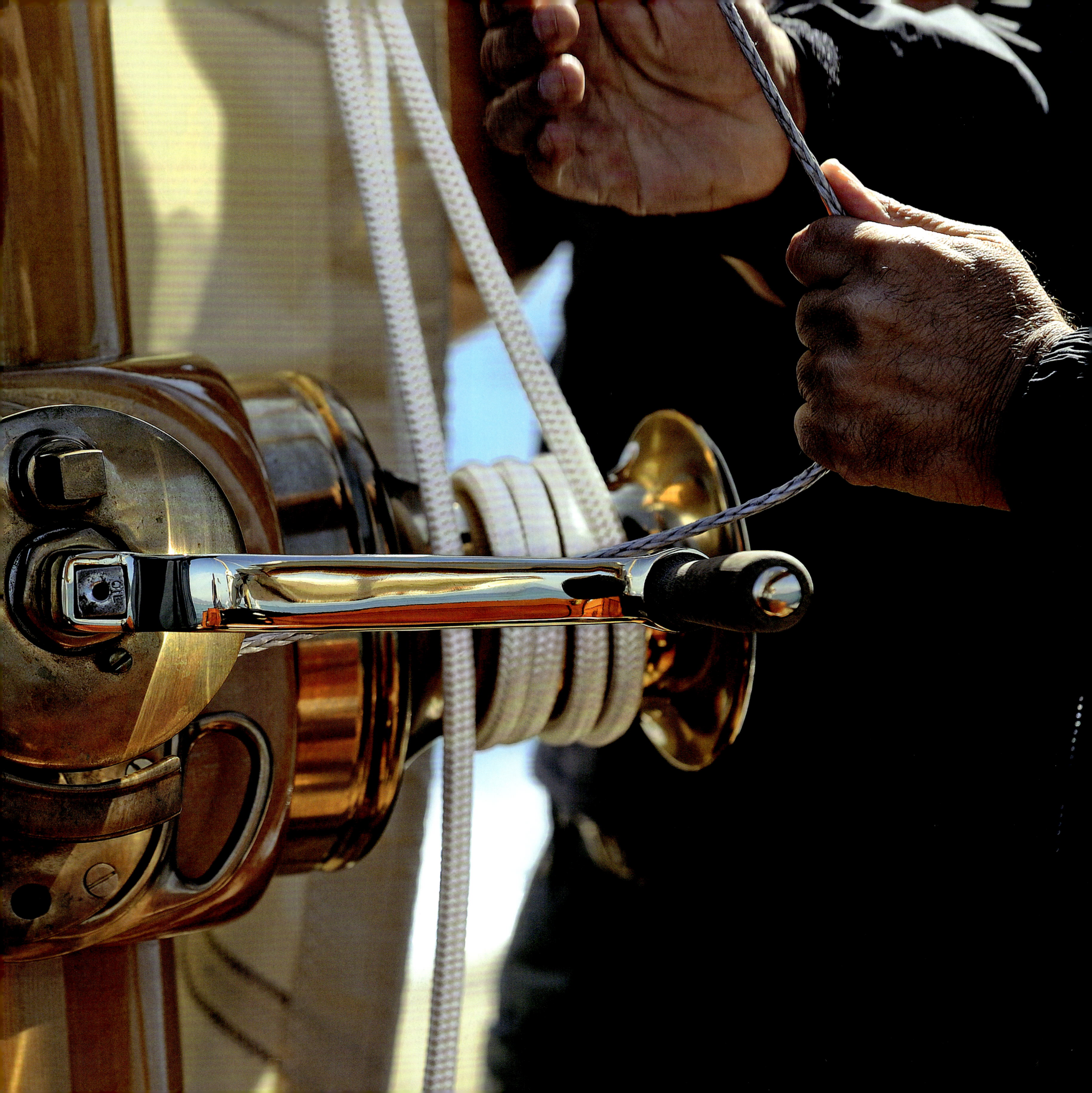

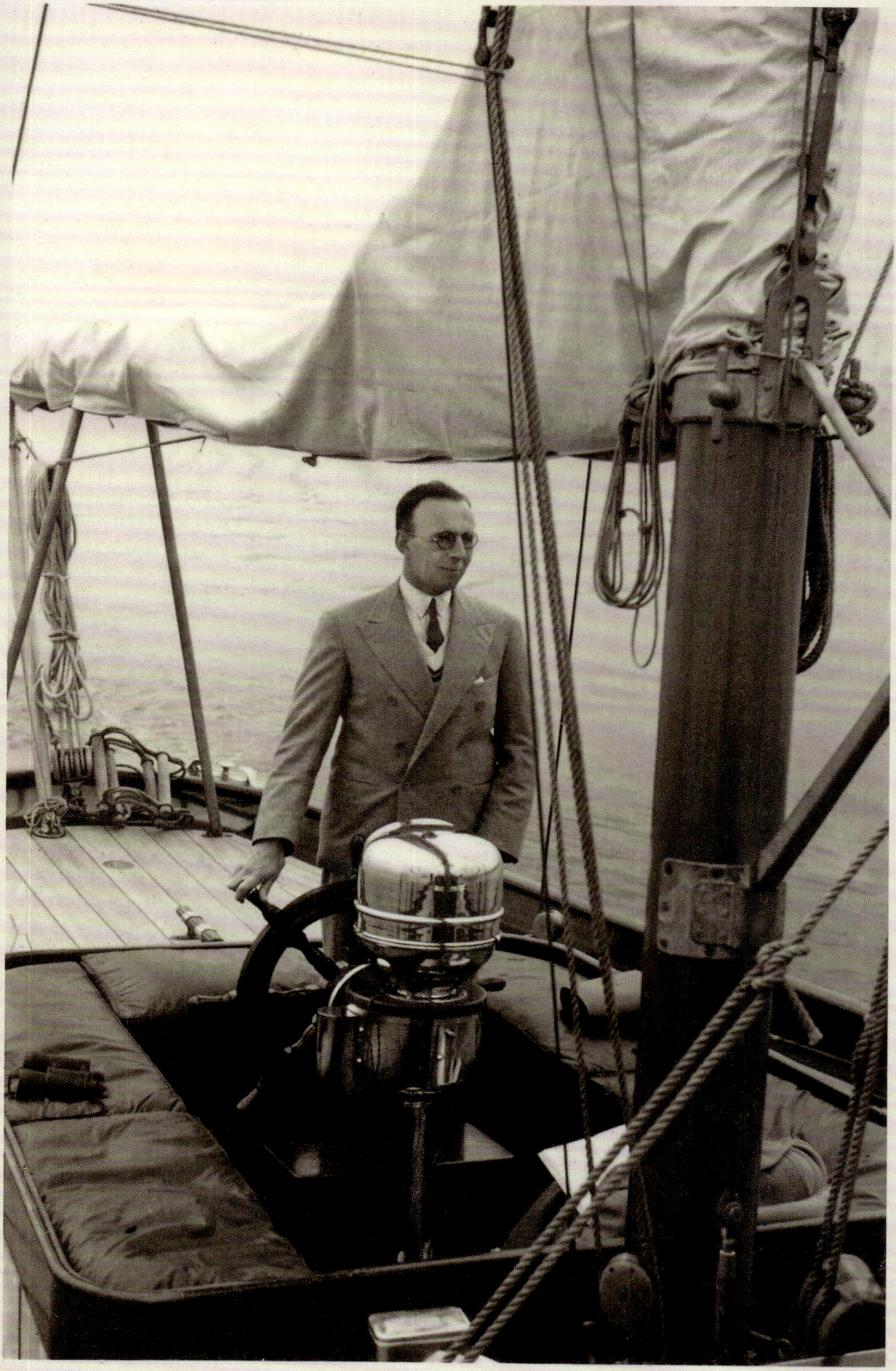

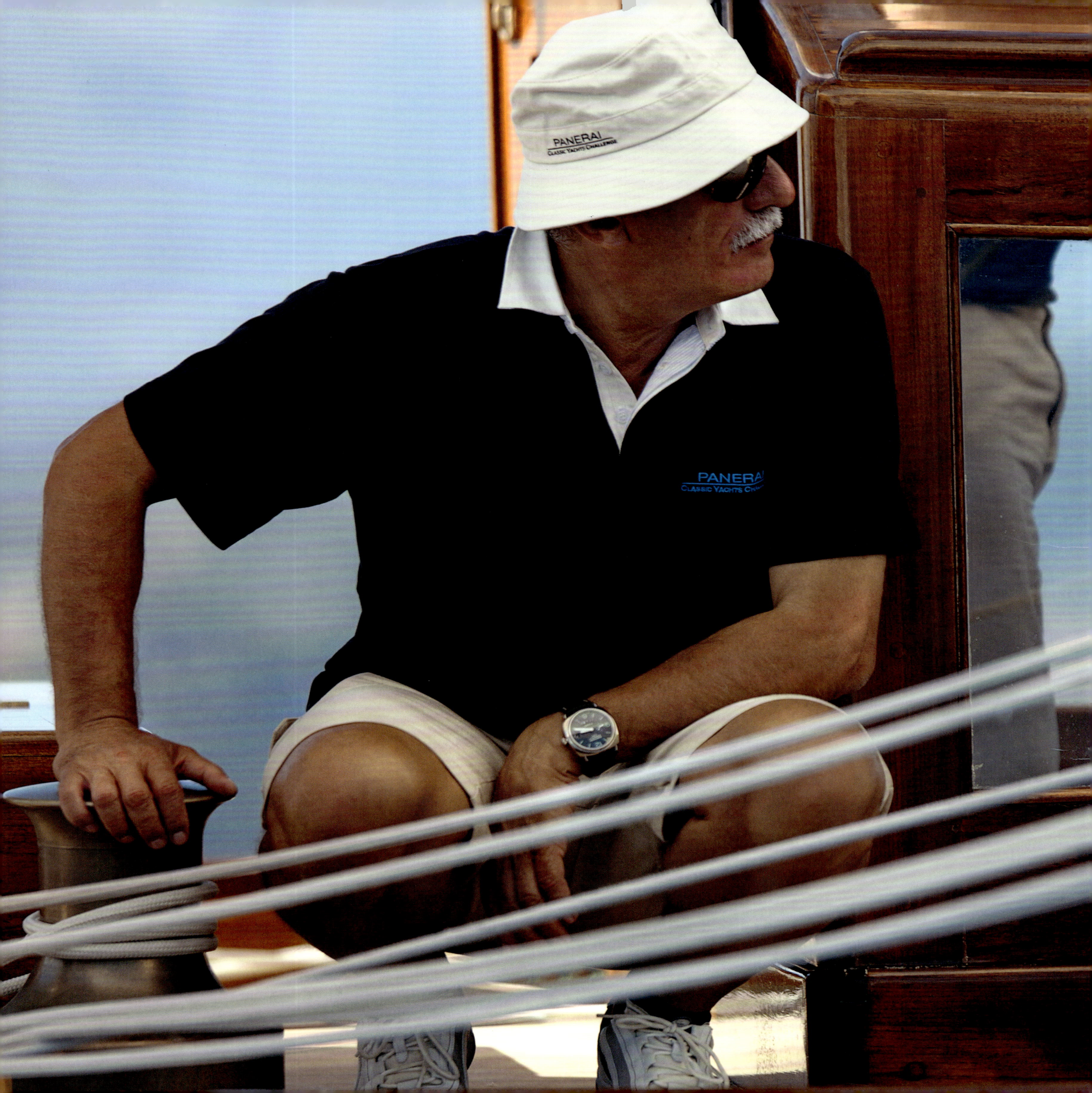
PANERAI
CLASSIC YACHTS CHALLENGE

FOREWORD

I saw *Eilean* for the first time in April 2006. I was in Antigua for the first stage of the Panerai Classic Yachts Challenge and during an interval between the regattas, I happened to catch a glimpse, almost hidden between the mangroves close to English Harbour, of the hull of a splendid vintage sailing boat that had clearly seen better days. Drawn to her unmistakeable waterline, I realised that this was a Fife when I saw the well-defined dragon, still recognisable despite the boat's poor general condition.

It was immediately clear to me that what I was seeing was living heritage, a legacy that could be recovered. *Eilean* turned out to be one of the last projects designed and built by William Fife III at the Fife boatyard in Fairlie, where some of the yachts that have marked the history of sailing were created. The vessel was undoubtedly in poor condition, but it would be possible to restore her while preserving a substantial part of the original materials. *Eilean*'s year of construction, 1936 – the same year in which Panerai created the first watch prototype for the Royal Italian Navy – confirmed my intuition. What I could see before me was the perfect medium by which to communicate a company such as Officine Panerai, already committed to promoting the culture of classic yachting for a number of years.

Transferring *Eilean* to Italy and piecing together her history in order to carry out a restoration that was as historically faithful as possible represented a highly stimulating endeavour. A team of experts and extraordinary craftsmen took on this challenge, bringing to the project all the passion and time-honoured know-how that always characterizes excellence in artistic crafts, nautical science, and in fine watchmaking.

This passion and pursuit of excellence has enabled us to bring the project to fruition successfully, and makes us proud, today, to share the timeless beauty of *Eilean* with all of you. In conclusion, I would like to express my special thanks to Johann Rupert, who through his support and encouragement has made a fundamental contribution to the rebirth of *Eilean*.

Angelo Bonati – CEO Officine Panerai

FACING PAGE Angelo Bonati insists on personally supervising every operation that contributes to *Eilean*'s seaworthiness, as he has done with every detail of her restoration since 2006.

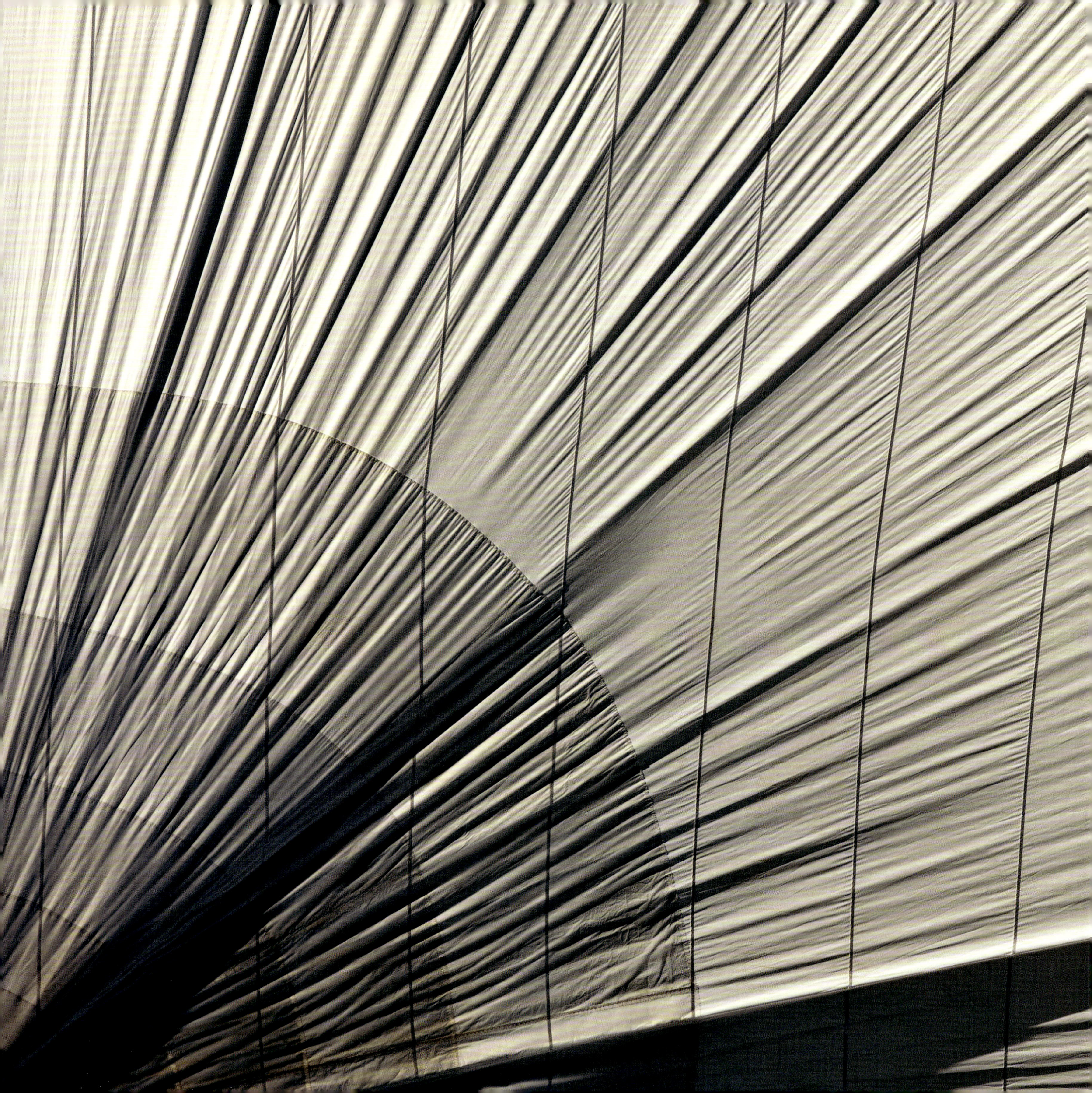

PREFACE

The great English poet John Keats famously wrote, 'A thing of beauty is a joy for ever'. Thanks to Angelo Bonati, that is true of *Eilean*, the loveliest of Fife yachts and a happily lingering dream of my own youth. One of the happiest aspects of my childhood was that I came to appreciate at an early age the glorious achievements of William Fife.

My father, Hartley, was a lawyer – as Britain's Attorney General in 1945 he was the Chief British prosecutor at the Nuremberg War Crimes Tribunal. He was also a keen yachtsman and used to spend his summer holidays in Cornwall. From the 1930s onwards his passion was for Fife yachts. He and his long-serving Cornish skipper Walter Paull (who taught me to sail) were agreed that the *crème de la crème* of yachts were those built at Fairlie on the Clyde by the great Scottish boat builder. There was simply no argument; anyone on the sea with an eye to see could understand that Fife yachts were in a class of their own – more fine, more elegant, with more exquisite sheer than those of any other designer and builder around. I picked this up fairly quickly and while still quite young I learned to spot other Fife boats on the sea – and not just by their proud and distinctive dragons carved on the bows. We had a game – 'I bet that's a Fife' – 'No, no, impossible – not quite elegant enough'. He started in the 1930s with a relatively small Fife – a 6 Metre named *Finvola*, progressing through an 8 Metre, *Caryl*, to the yacht which defined my childhood, *Vanity V*. She was a 12 Metre – the class that till recently duelled with great elegance and verve for the America's Cup. We lived on this exquisite sleek machine for two months every summer. In the early 1950s she had no engine and no safety rails even though my brother and sister and I were all very young. In those days it was much easier to take risks and the seas and harbours were much less crowded. I remember entering Cherbourg, St. Malo and other French ports under sail and coming up into the wind to drop the sails smartly and using the boat's remaining speed to glide alongside the dock. Fifes, I knew, were so beautifully balanced that a mere whisper of wind would push them through the water. Then in the 1960s my father suddenly decided to exchange his racing Fife for a cruising yacht – *Eilean* came into our lives. I remember well my first sight of her in Falmouth harbour in Cornwall. She was so much larger than any yacht we had owned and sailed before. We quickly became used to her different needs and her charms – both as a sailing yacht and as a family home. I used to love her ketch rig and the infinite variety of sails that enabled one to hoist – the mizzen staysail I liked in particular.

The greatest summer we had on *Eilean* was in the early 1960s when my father had her taken to Majorca; we spent idyllic weeks cruising through the Balearic islands, a holiday which was made all the lovelier for me because

FACING PAGE The reinforced tack patches on *Eilean*'s balloon jib form concentric patterns and the radial shape of the sail is crisscrossed by the vertical seams of the cloth. This foresail is the most important in the whole wardrobe. It is tacked right at the end of the bowsprit and overlaps more than half the sail plan. It is used off the wind.

FACING PAGE Slightly distorted on the surface of the deep blue Mediterranean Sea, the reflection of *Eilean*'s varnished hull shines in the midday sun.

PAGE 30 Once the balloon jib has been hoisted and trimmed to the wind, the bowman drops the flying jib, the most forward of the foresails, on deck.

PAGE 31 An emotional and historic moment: the launch of the ketch *Eilean* on 24 April 1937 at the William Fife and Son shipyard in Fairlie on the Firth of Clyde. The workers assembled forward are busy pulling the cradle from under the hull. Opposite the shipyard, one can see the shore of Little Cumbrae Island.

I had on board a beautiful girlfriend, Nicky, to whom I became very close. We lived on deck and slept under the stars. *Eilean*, the Mediterranean and love – a summer for a young man to remember always. Sadly, my father decided then to sell *Eilean* and it was many years before I saw her again. I heard that she was owned by a Frenchman and that she was being chartered in the Caribbean, but that was all. Then, about ten years ago, my wife and I were invited by friends to Antigua. We went, of course, to English Harbour, Admiral Nelson's beautiful and strategic hidden port on the south of the island. I looked around all the gleaming new yachts and then suddenly under the mangrove trees across the harbour I saw a beautifully elegant stern that looked to me unmistakably a Fife. I took a dinghy across the harbour and there was beloved *Eilean*. She was in an unhappy state of disrepair but she still retained her irresistible classic Fife lines. I met with her owner, John, and he invited me on board. I was rather horrified by the state into which *Eilean* had fallen but I was also struck by John's obsession with his yacht. Standing on her filthy decks and looking into her interior (all ripped out), I remembered those carefree youthful sailing days of forty years before and I listened for the call of my mother, cooking in the galley, and of my father, asking me to change the sails.

I thought of how wonderful it would be for me to try and buy *Eilean* from John and bring her back to her former glory. He said that in view of my father's ownership of the boat, he would consider selling *Eilean* to me. I even consulted Fairlie Restoration, the English yard which has beautifully restored many Fife yachts. But it was an absurd dream for me and, sadly, I left *Eilean* rotting under the trees. Imagine, then, my delight, when I heard that Angelo Bonati had seen *Eilean* there and had bought her and was taking her to Italy for a total restoration! I was thrilled to think that she would be brought back to life and sail again. Mr Bonati kindly invited me and my wife Olga (an Italian, of course) to the unveiling of newly restored *Eilean* in La Spezia at the end of 2009. I had no idea what to expect but I found myself enormously moved, first by Mr Bonati's words on his discovery of *Eilean* and his passion for her, by the film of her meticulous, loving restoration, and then by the sight of her gently bobbing on the water. So many memories rushed back! Her restoration has been absolutely faithful to the original created so many decades ago by William Fife and is a great and lovely triumph. She will be a superb ambassadress for Panerai – Mr Bonati has really achieved a miracle. If I may return to the words of the poet John Keats, *Eilean* was always 'a thing of beauty', but that beauty had faded away. Now, thanks to Angelo Bonati and Panerai, *Eilean*'s beauty is restored for all to see. She will be a joy for all who sail in her, all who see her, everywhere across the seas.

William Shawcross

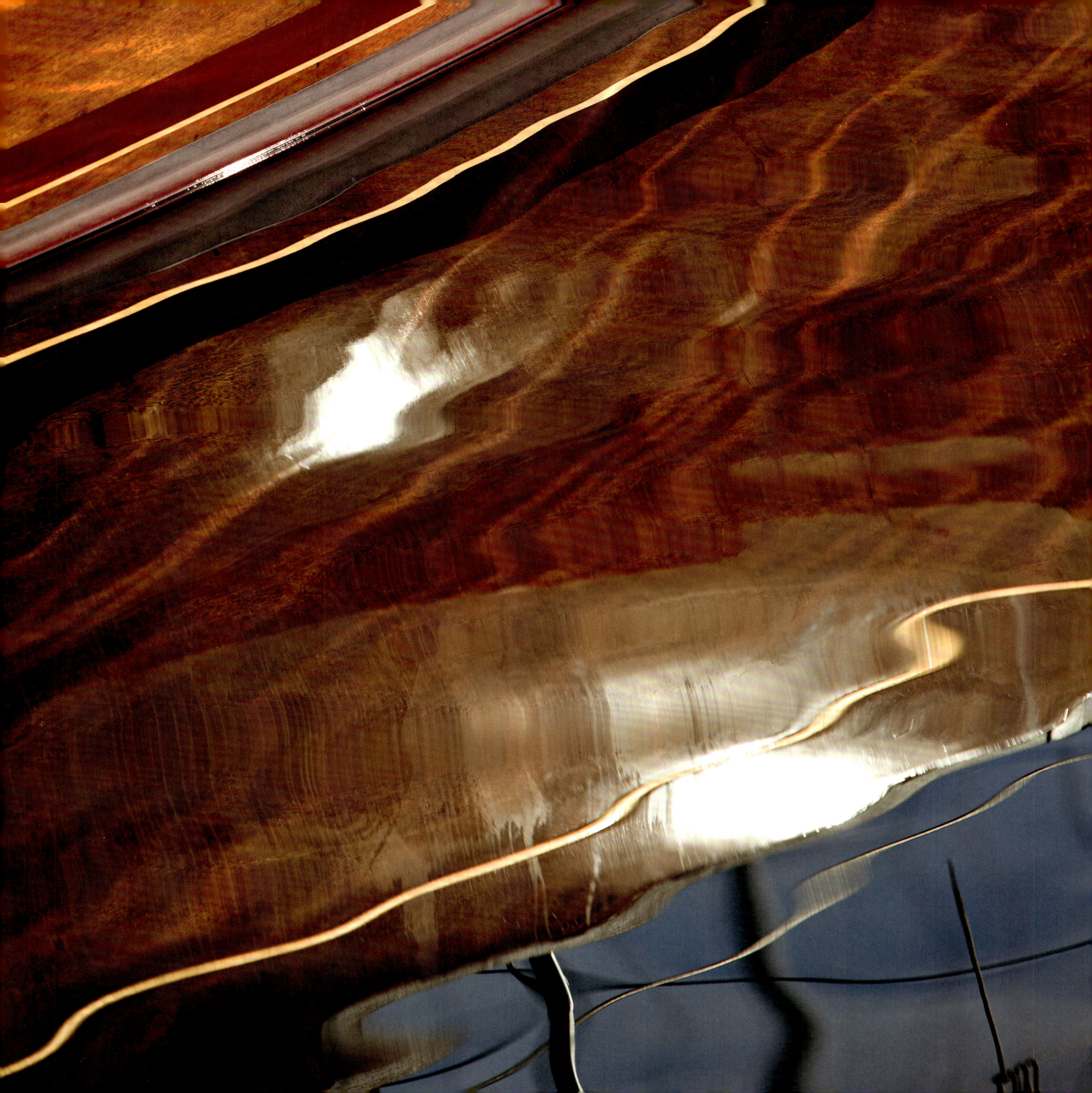

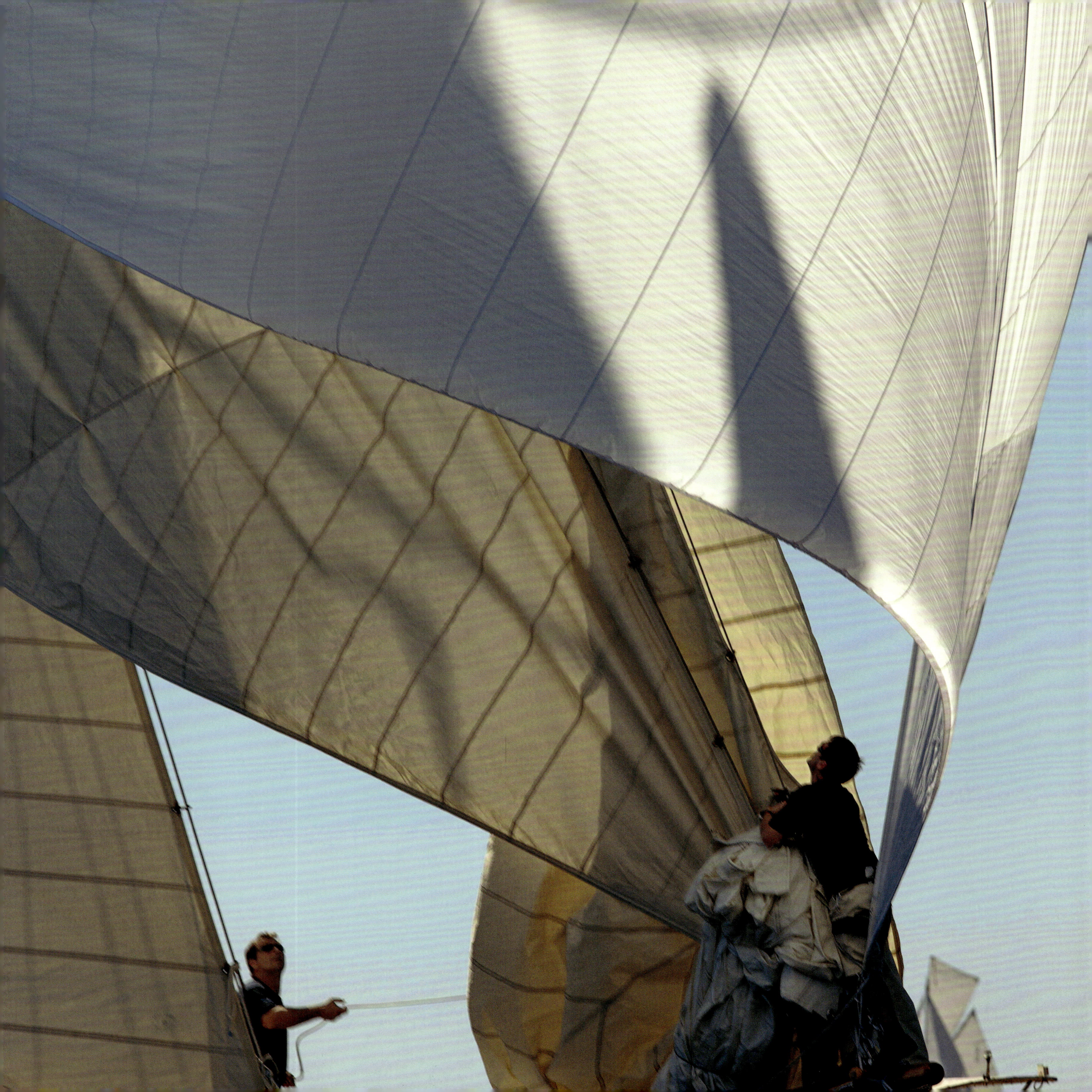

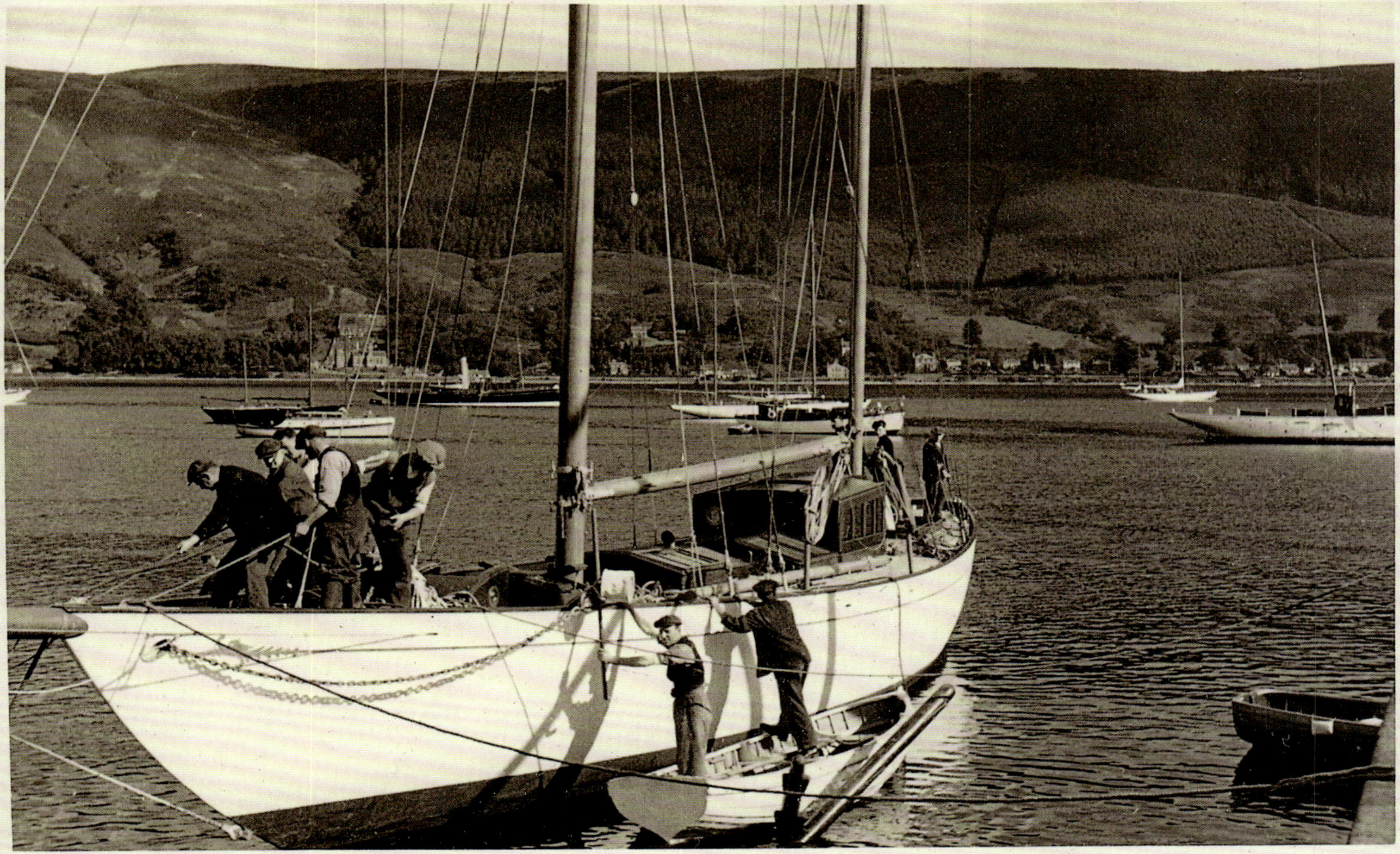

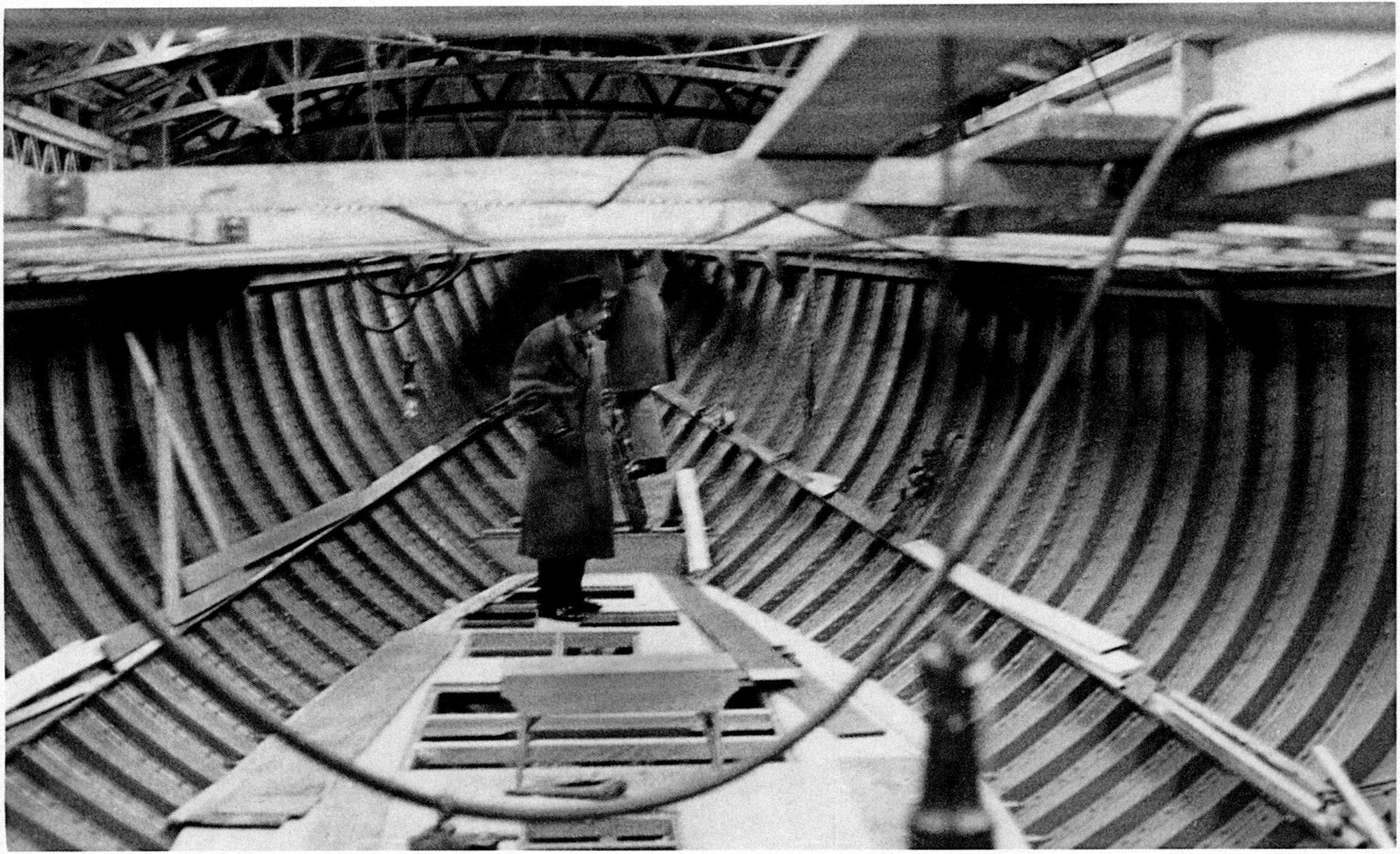

THE HISTORY OF *EILEAN*

The Yard – William Fife & Son

This legendary boat yard, like many famous enterprises, had a humble beginning. It all began when a young William Fyfe, born in 1785 to mill- and cartwright John Fyfe, built a small boat for his own use. It was so well built that it was sold almost immediately and William decided to build boats rather than become a millwright like his father. William worked with an older brother John but he, unlike William, did not have that streak of genius like his brother and so remained a builder of fishing boats that according to contemporary reports were 'rough and leaky'.

Young William began by building fishing boats and gabbarts, the local form of trading vessel on the Clyde. They gained a reputation for good design and sturdiness of construction. His first yacht *Lamlash* (1812) sailed as far as the Mediterranean. At this time, all boats were driven by wind power. However in 1812 Henry Bell installed the newly invented steam engine of William Watt in a small paddle-boat called the *Comet*. The success of this means of propulsion resulted in a demand for steam-driven paddle vessels and William Fyfe was asked to build one. He built *Industry* that plied the Clyde for fifty years and was a prediction of what was to come as Fife-built vessels came to have a reputation for longevity. So successful was *Industry* that he was asked to build more steamers. He refused, saying he wanted to build sailing boats that were 'fast and bonnie'.

The second William Fife, born in 1821, was apprenticed to his father in the yard. The first William's dream of designing beautiful sailing boats had to take second place to providing for a large family and money was to be made building fishing boats and commercial traders. He abandoned his dream to his son who had to wait for several years before the chance came to design a pleasure yacht.

At this stage it is interesting to wonder how the Fife yard prospered and became famous. It was based on the shores of the Firth of Clyde in a small fishing village called Fairlie. The topography of the coast was not favourable for launching boats, especially later, when yachts had deep keels. At low tide Fairlie Bay was a vast expanse of sand. There was no deep water close to the shore to facilitate launching. It was essential to carry out a launch at high tide even if it was at midnight. Over the years the Fifes developed a strategy for this, using old boat hulls to float out the new vessels and eventually they built a floating dock that made launching much easier.

The reputation of Fife boats grew, not only because of the designing genius of the Fifes, but also because of the superbly skilled craftsmen employed in the yard. It was a true family

'The reputation of Fife boats grew, not only because of the designing genius of the Fifes, but also because of the superbly skilled craftsmen employed in the yard.'

ABOVE William Fife II. William Fife III.

FACING PAGE The brothers James and Robert Fulton pay a visit to the William Fife and Son shipyard to see the hull being built. The frames and the planking are in place, as well as the bilge stringer halfway along the frames and the clamp strake at the top. The hull is still totally open with just a few temporary beams for strength.

business. According to old Scots law, the eldest son inherited everything when his father died and so with each generation the eldest son William became the owner of the yard. However in the first two generations several of their brothers also worked there.

The second William Fife not only designed yachts, he also worked at the tools alongside his brothers and local craftsmen. This family relationship was not only restricted to the Fifes, most of the able-bodied men of the village worked in the yard. Whole families were involved, brothers, sons, uncles and grandparents. Skills were passed on from one generation to the other. Overseeing all this was the second William Fife who was a perfectionist about every small detail. He would often take down a frame that did not satisfy him and replace it with one which met with his approval. On one occasion a workman dropped a plane on the deck and dented a plank slightly and the plank had to be replaced.

The success of the Fife yard was closely linked to the Industrial Revolution which saw huge fortunes made by enterprising men in iron, steel, coal mining, mills, manufacturing and railways. It was a desire to escape the smoke and pollution of industry that spurred the 'nouveaux riches' to build houses on the shores of the Firth of Clyde and what was more natural than to want to sail on its waters?

The newly formed Clyde Model Yacht Club (1854) provided many clients for the yard and the second William was a member. This was a time of great activity and many magnificent yachts were built. It was also the beginning of the age of the Corinthian yachtsman, people who sailed their own boat instead of having a paid skipper and crew.

In 1865 the second William produced *Fiona*, the yacht that was to begin the golden era for the yard. She was known as 'The Fawn o'Fairlie' or 'The Terrible Fiona' because she was so successful in all her races. One faithful client was the Marquis of Ailsa with his *Bloodhound*, *Sleuthound*, *Foxhound* and *Beagle*. It is obvious his other hobby was hunting! *Bloodhound* had a long and successful career till 1907 when her current owner Sir Thomas Dunlop asked William Fife to break her up. The Marquis of Ailsa immediately bought her back and had her refitted. Regretfully the following year she was sunk due to a collision in the Solent.

Another success was *Annasonna* who won forty-four flags, forty-one of them firsts in her maiden year of racing. The yard became so busy that William ended up designing some yachts to be built by other yards. He also built two yachts for himself, *Clio* and *Cyprus*. Although now established as a yacht designer, William still built the occasional fishing boat and trading vessel. The second William was a believer in well-based and well-founded principles but he did

TOP Most of the deck beams are now in place; their shape will determine the deck camber. There are cutouts reinforced by carlings for the hatches and at the level of the cockpit and the doghouse.

BOTTOM *Eilean* is a composite construction: frames and beams are made of steel, but the keelson, the planking and the deck are made of wood. This was a common building method for sailing yachts of her size.

experiment successfully within the old tonnage rule and the Thames Measurement Rule just as his father had experimented with the lengthening of bows.

The third William Fife was certainly born 'with a silver spoon in his mouth'. Not only had he inherited the designing talent of his father and grandfather, he also inherited a busy well-established yard with a worldwide reputation and a workforce of dedicated craftsmen. His earlier life was easier than the previous generations'. An apprenticeship at Fairlie was followed by a spell at Fullarton's yard in Paisley where iron ships were built. After that came the management of the Marquis of Ailsa's boatyard at Maidens in Ayrshire. During that period he designed several yachts, one of which was the 'plank on edge' *Vagrant* built in 1884. She is still in existence at the Scottish Maritime Museum in Irvine. She requires some restoration work to which Panerai has contributed.

Over the years the one question everyone asks is 'What makes a Fife design so special?' The answer is that it has magical qualities. This non-technical answer is all that can be offered. Fife designs cast their spell on all who admire them. It is not because Fife was the only successful designer of his era. Watson, Mylne, Herreschof, and Anker were all equally good designers but a Fife design has something that makes it special. Even Fife when asked about his designs could only come up with the enigmatic 'if it looks right it is right'. The fact that Fife designs were so renowned over two generations says something about the talent of the designers who produced beautiful and fast yachts in spite of having to adjust to all the requirements of the changing measurement rules. It is no coincidence that the second William Fife was called 'the grand old wizard of the North'. His son took his place as the sorcerer's apprentice and became a wizard in his own right.

The third William Fife was also a crack helmsman. Normally reticent, canny and revealing little about himself or his business to the press, he became a different person when at the helm of a yacht. The crew were kept on their toes as he was prone to employ short tacks. Once, when trying out a boat he had designed, he found the tiller did not give him enough room in the cockpit. He had to lift it over his head when tacking and on one occasion lost his cap and was knocked on the head. The owner assured him it would be shortened when they went ashore. William asked if there was a saw on board and the offending tiller was shortened with a hacksaw while he continued to race.

His genius was recognised by other contemporary designers as shown by this quotation from Mr C. E. Nicholson in 1932 when referring to the 6 Metre class: 'The class and its chief

ABOVE In 1936, *Eilean* begins to take shape in the William Fife and Son shipyard; the 16-ton lead ballast keel has been cast and fitted in place. The assembly of these two major parts using long bronze keel bolts is a tricky operation; the stress on the keel bolts must be perfectly vertical.

ABOVE Robertson's yard in Sandbank after a winter refit.

designer Mr Fife should be given all credit due to them. In Great Britain the class is properly called the Fife Class, which has produced nearly all that count over here. To those who can appreciate beauty of form, perfect modelling and workmanship, they fill the eye as the most beautiful little real yachts of small size and heavy displacement ever produced.'

Although he made his mark in the metre classes arising from the 1906 International Measurement Rule, William was already a respected designer. His first designs date from 1876 when at nineteen years of age he designed the 5-tonner *Camelia* in conjunction with his father. Around 1883 he moved to Maidens to become manager and shareholder in the Marquis of Ailsa's yard. While at Maidens he designed *Clara*, a 'plank on edge' design. After two years *Clara* went to America with a crew from the Clyde and won all her races. Fife was beginning to have a reputation in America.

William returned to Fairlie in about 1886. His father was sixty-five years of age but still actively designing, although most of the designs from this time onwards were by the third William. The second William, who died in 1902, lived to see the reputation of the yard spread far and wide by his son's designs. He knew the business was in safe hands.

The third William's designs for the three 'Dragons' built for Mr F. C. Hill with their superb racing records may have been responsible for the original adoption of the carved dragon on the bow of Fife yachts built in the yard in Fairlie. The dragon appeared from that period onwards. It is to his credit that he could design successful and good-looking yachts no matter what measurement restrictions were imposed. His designs span the 1730 Rule (that gave rise to the 'plank on edge' designs), the Linear Rating Rule (giving rise to 'raters'), the 1906 International Rule (metre classes) and the 1919 Revised International Rule which he had a hand in formulating.

Many local racing classes owe their design to the third William Fife. They include the Clyde restricted thirty-foot class to which *Mikado* and *Corrie* belong and which are both still afloat. The Clyde 17/19 class represented by *Hatasoo* and *Katydid*, the 19/24 class by *Ulidia*. In Ireland there is the Belfast Lough one design 'The Birds', such as *Whimbrel* and *Tern*, the Dublin Bay 25s, and the Cork Harbour One Design represented by *Jap*. The Conway Fife Class still races today including new glass-fibre boats that do not always win when racing against the wooden hulls!

In 1898 Sir Thomas Lipton issued his first challenge for the America's Cup and chose William Fife junior as his designer. Colonel Duncan Neill, his sailing advisor, was the uncle

INTRODUCTION 36

of the wife of James Fulton, one of the first owners of *Eilean*. Although *Shamrock* was designed by Fife, she was built by Thorneycroft on the Thames. Sir Thomas was to ask William to design another challenger in 1903. Denny Brothers Dumbarton built *Shamrock III*, and on this occasion G. L. Watson, designer of *Shamrock II*, offered to help with tank tests and gave William his opinion on why his own design had failed to win the cup. Although neither of his designs was successful, the prestige of being chosen as designer did no harm to William's reputation.

The new 1906 Rule introduced the metre classes and saw William again distinguish himself in the 6 Metre designs, contributing also to 15 Metre, 19 Metre and 23 Metre designs. The most famous 23 Metres were *Shamrock* (Sir T. Lipton) and *White Heather II* (Myles Kennedy). These two boats raced against each other over several years and the honours were shared equally. Neither of them beat the other by very much in any race. Today some of his 15 and 19 Metre designs are still sailing, for example *Tuiga*, *The Lady Anne*, *Mariquita*, and the 23 Metre *Cambria*.

In 1914 pleasure yachting came to an abrupt end with the outbreak of World War I. Those yachts and steam yachts not taken over by the Admiralty for war duties were laid up. This did not mean that the Fife yard ceased working. On the contrary it was busier than ever building boats for the Admiralty. The range was considerable, from sailing gigs, motor launches, whalers, steam pinnaces, water boats, and even a mining launch. The shipwrights had a reserved occupation and would not be called to enlist in the armed forces. The yard also built the wooden hulls for seaplanes and the riggers were employed making portable aeroplane hangars from canvas and wire for use in Mesopotamia (present-day Iraq). After the war, William was awarded an OBE for his yard's contribution to the war effort.

William was not only a designer of racing yachts. He designed many beautiful and substantial cruising boats, many of which are still afloat today. To name a few, *Ailsa* (1895), *Cicely* (1902), *Sumurun* (1914), *Moonbeam* (1903), *Moonbeam IV* (1915), *Kentra* (1923), *Belle Aventure* (ex-*Eileen* 1928), *Merry Dancer* (1935), *Latifa* (1935), *Eilean* (1936), *Evenload* (1936), and *Madrigal* (1938). Right up till 1938, at eighty-one years of age William was still designing yachts. In 1939 at the outbreak of World War II the yard was requisitioned by the Admiralty to be used as a torpedo research station. William died in 1944 aged eighty-seven years and the Fife dynasty ended. We are fortunate today that so many of his designs have survived and still grace the sailing scene all over the world.

'William was not only a designer of racing yachts. He designed many beautiful and substantial cruising boats....'

ABOVE *Eilean* heels only slightly while sailing close hauled with jib and staysail. Her high freeboard gives a good protection to the crew seated on deck forward of the main mast.

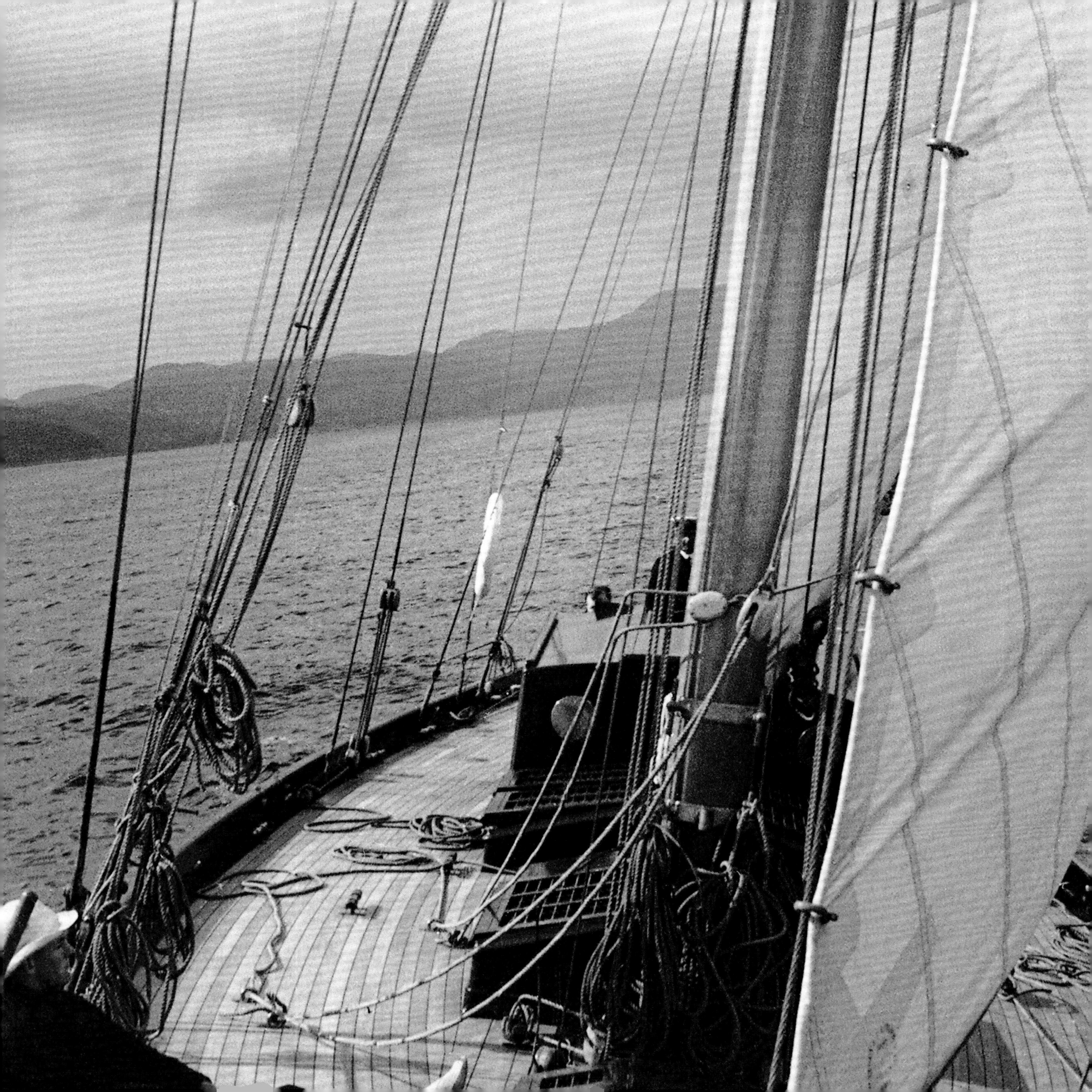

Eilean

1936 was a year of great change in Britain. George V died and was succeeded by his son Edward VIII. The 'uncrowned king' had a short reign of eleven months before he abdicated in order to marry an American divorcee Mrs Simpson. His younger brother George became king and was to reign over an even greater period of upheaval.

This is the story of *Eilean*, an auxiliary ketch designed by the third William Fife, built to the order of the brothers James Vandalle Fulton and Robert Waterston Fulton. She was launched on 24 April 1937 at Fairlie. Aged twenty-six and twenty-four respectively, these young men were both on the board of directors of P. McCallum and Son, iron and steel merchants.

The firm P. McCallum and Son had always been connected with shipbuilding. It started in 1781 with the manufacture of iron and copper nails for wooden sailing ships. As wood was slowly replaced by iron and eventually steel, the firm diversified into the supply of iron and steel plate to the shipping industry. As time went by a separate company Laing and Fulton was formed to manage and own coasters that transported the steel from the Talbot works in Wales and from abroad to the Clyde. Throughout the turbulent years of two world wars, nationalisation of the steel industry and the decline in shipbuilding, the firm had continued as a family concern, diversifying to cope with new situations. Like *Eilean* it is a survivor.

The Fulton family were keen yachtsmen. In fact, the brothers had already owned *Eileen*, launched from the same yard in 1935 although designed in 1929. Their father Louis Vandalle Fulton owned the auxiliary ketch *Eileen* again designed and built by Fife in 1929 and now known as *Belle Aventure*.

James Fulton Laing, whose father had married an aunt of the Fulton brothers, had owned the cruising yacht *Gometra*. In 1941 she was discovered in Canada where she had been brought as deck cargo on a small Norwegian steamer. When Germany occupied Norway during World War II, part of the Norwegian gold reserve was shipped to Canada. Half the gold was evacuated by a British cruiser and the rest loaded onto *Gometra* and another Clyde yacht, *Sinbad*. They travelled as deck cargo on a freighter. If the freighter was sunk, it was assumed the yachts would float off and continue the journey.

The first *Eileen* owned by the brothers Fulton in 1935 had a long and varied career and was rescued in Hawaii by Jean-Claude Joffre, who transported her to Antwerp for restoration. Unfortunately he died rather suddenly. After lying for several years in the yard, she was apparently at last about to be restored.

TOP The Firth of Clyde offers a huge variety of picturesque landscapes; the lochs, like fjords in Scandinavia, cut deeply into rocky or wooded hills. The breathtaking scenery of Loch Long and Loch Goil stretches a long way north.

BOTTOM The owner poses for posterity with the captain and two crew members, enough hands to manage a split rig such as *Eilean*'s while cruising.

FACING PAGE *Eilean* close-hauled during one of the first seatrials; all sails have been hoisted but not yet perfectly trimmed; some tackles are yet to be made fast, sheets and halyards to be coiled and hung. Before the war, the first version of *Eilean*'s deck gear used tackles instead of winches.

There is a letter in the Scottish Maritime Museum in which Fife agrees to build an auxiliary cruising ketch of fifty-six tons for James and Robert Fulton, 7 Octavia Terrace, Greenock. The yard number was 822 and she would be ready by May 1937 at the cost of £8,000 and would be named *Eilean*. The letter was signed by the chief cashier Archibald Boyd. At twenty-two metres she was three and half metres longer than their first *Eileen*. There is no evidence today of why the second yacht was named *Eileen* when their first one and their father's yacht were both named *Eilean*. Perhaps it was to avoid confusion with names. The name was perpetuated in the family as James Fulton named his eldest child Eilean after the boat. Her son James Gilmour continues the family yachting tradition as skipper of a modern yacht.

Eilean was intended for cruising and was used extensively by the brothers to sail on the Clyde and the West Coast of Scotland. Although they lived and worked in Greenock, *Eilean* was moored off Robertson's yard at Sandbank on the other side of the Firth of Clyde from the Fulton's home in Greenock. When required, the skipper and three or four crew would cross the Firth to pick up the family. During the winter months she would be laid up in Robertson's yard.

The brothers would not enjoy sailing *Eilean* for long. The clouds of war had gathered and on September 3, 1939 Britain was at war with Germany. Both brothers were then called to serve in the armed forces. Robert Fulton was a major serving with the 7th Field Regiment of the Royal Artillery and was killed in action in Tunisia on 14 August 1943. His elder brother James was Lt. Commander in the Royal Naval Volunteer Reserve. He was in charge of HMS. Goodall, a frigate escorting an Arctic convoy to Russia. A German U-boat sank his boat when its torpedo hit the ship's munitions magazine and she blew up. This was April 29, 1945, only a week before the end of the war. He was only thirty-five years of age, had been married for six years, and left a wife and three small children.

Eilean was laid up during the war years in Robertson's yard at Sandbank. In 1948 Mr P. H. N. Ulander, a Swede who worked with James Howden, a Glasgow engineering firm, became the owner. Unlike the Fulton brothers, Mr Ulander raced *Eilean*. He was a member of the Royal Ocean Racing Club and so took part in passage races and raced on the Clyde. Her sail number for the R.O.R.C. was 449. At Clyde Fortnight in 1948, racing in heavy weather against *Mariella*, another Fife design, and *Fiona*, *Eilean* lost a man overboard and in recovering him *Eilean* was out of the race. In another race against *Mariella* she came second.

TOP *Eilean* at anchor off Greenock, her homeport. The Firth of Clyde is ideal for family cruising. The variety of coastlines and the proximity of sheltered anchorages at any time make it the perfect waters for sailing for pleasure and relaxation.

BOTTOM Mrs Brenda Fulton, wife of James, always practiced her sports, whether sailing, golf or shooting, wearing an informal dress and white, laced low-heeled shoes. The starboard runner tackle is not there, it is tightened or loosened by one of the two crewmembers when tacking or gybing.

In 1952 *Eilean* was sold to Jack Salem who kept her for ten years. He also owned *Flicka II* built by Fife but designed by Laurent Giles. Jack Salem was a member of the Little Ship Club and the Uruguayan Yacht club. The next recorded owner was a Colonel Louis Franck who registered her as 'The Yacht Eilean Ltd'. This suggests she was used commercially for charter work over the next eight years.

The colourful Labour politician Sir Hartley Shawcross and his friend French yachtsman Antonin Besse became her proprietors in 1964. A leading barrister and youngest man to be made King's Council, he was lead prosecutor at the Nuremberg trials. He was a keen sailor and owned a number of yachts, among them Fife designs, and it is no surprise that he purchased another one. In 1961 he joined the Royal Yacht Squadron, three years before he purchased *Eilean*. He was also a member of the New York Yacht Club and the Royal Cornwall Yacht Club. During his ownership, *Eilean* did not race in the Solent but was used extensively for cruising across the Channel and in the Mediterranean.

Eilean was based in Falmouth. Her skipper, William Paull, was a Falmouth man who had sailed Sir Hartley's yachts for many years. He was also a Fife devotee. One summer the skipper and professional crew sailed *Eilean* to the Balearic Islands where the family cruised.

After four years, *Eilean* changed hands yet again and was bought by Ernest and Richard Cuckson. This is the beginning of her association with Antigua. Two Antiguan residents conceived the idea of an Antiguan Sailing Week and *Eilean* was one of the first fourteen boats to participate in the event.

Richard Cuckson had previously crewed on the schooner *Lord Jim* that was involved in charter work in the Caribbean and owned by Captain Jol Brierly. After two years Richard became a professional skipper and returned to Britain. Along with his brother Ernest he purchased *Eilean*. She spent her time between the Mediterranean and the Caribbean for the next two years.

In 1974 *Eilean* is listed in Lloyds Register as 'Ketch Eilean Ltd', now in the ownership of John Shearer. The new owner, an architect, lived on board and operated her as a charter vessel. *Eilean* became known worldwide in 1982 when the pop group Duran Duran chartered her to film a video for their record album *Rio*. She was sailed by Simon le Bon who was later to be rescued from his capsized yacht *Drum* in the Fastnet Race of 1985. Locations for the film were chosen for them by Jol Brierly who knew *Eilean* from previous years. Simon le Bon made another attempt at the Fastnet race in 2005. Again he sailed with the same

ABOVE James Louis Vandalle Fulton at the helm of *Eilean* swaps his jacket for a woolly jumper but keeps his tie on. The cockpit with its cushions, steering wheel, compass and binnacle: everything has been restored to its original state on the new yacht.

ABOVE *Eilean* turns her back to two symbolic places in the world of British yachting, the famous Royal Northern Yacht Club in Rothesay and Hunter's Quay.

FACING PAGE Before the war, James F. Lang, cousin of the brothers James and Robert, owned this 1925 sloop, *Geometra*, designed by Alfred Mylne. Later, he had another sloop, *Nereide*, a 51-footer, built in 1937 to plans by Johan Anker, which he kept until 1972.

FOLLOWING PAGES Before 1873, the Ponte alle Grazie in Florence was taken up with shops. Later, the 'Giovanni Panerai watchmaker's shop' had to move into town on the via Cavour. This photo taken around 1900 shows the dome of Santa Maria del Fiore and the Palazzo Vecchio in the background.

crew in *Drum* now owned by Sir Arnold Clark. This time they were completely becalmed and had to abandon the race as the band was due to play in Tokyo before they could finish. In her role as a charter yacht *Eilean* crossed the Atlantic several times. Unfortunately, on a return journey to the Caribbean she collided with a ferry off the coast of Portugal and broke her mizzen mast.

Eilean returned to English Harbour in Antigua where John Shearer converted an old tug into a workshop and began the mammoth task of repairing her single-handed. He recycled the tug's fuel tanks to fabricate new ribs. It was a seemingly endless task not helped by the fact that *Eilean* sank at her mooring. After she was refloated, it was discovered that termites had eaten through the masts and bowsprit. After twenty years of hard work and a vision of restoring *Eilean*, John had to accept that he was not going to realise his dream.

Happily for *Eilean*, in 2006 the elegant lines of the dilapidated Fife design caught the eye of Angelo Bonati. Her teak hull had resisted rotting and termites and she was deemed worthy of restoration. In her fragile state she could not make the Atlantic crossing and so she made the passage on a ship specialising in the transport of boats.

In February 2007, *Eilean* arrived at the boatyard of Francesco Del Carlo at Viareggio. Here she would be consigned to the magical hands of Guido Del Carlo and his workforce, with Enrico Zaccagni, project manager. *Eilean* would re-emerge as the elegant yacht launched from Fife's yard on 24 April 1937 and the rest is history.

May Fife Kohn

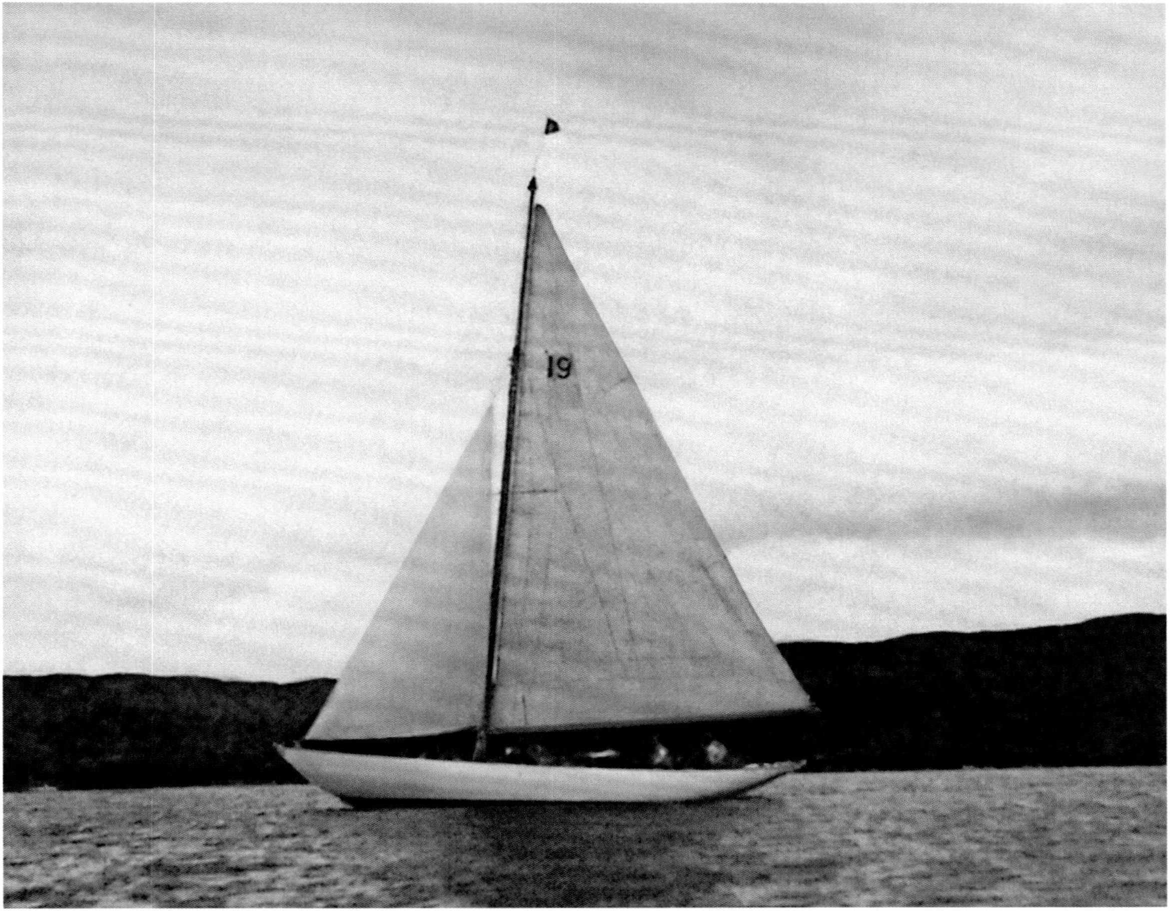
19

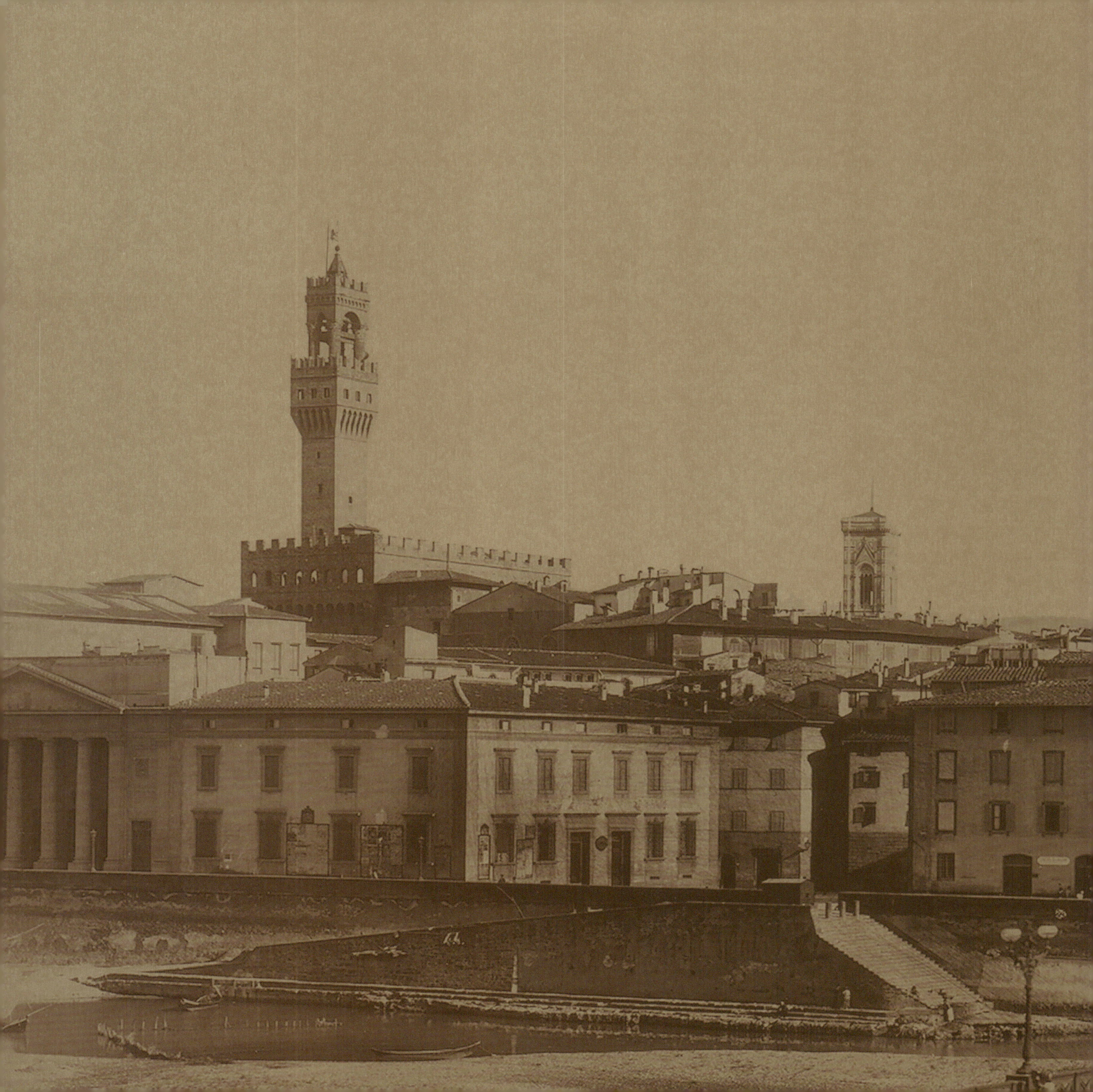

THE BIRTH OF A LEGEND

1

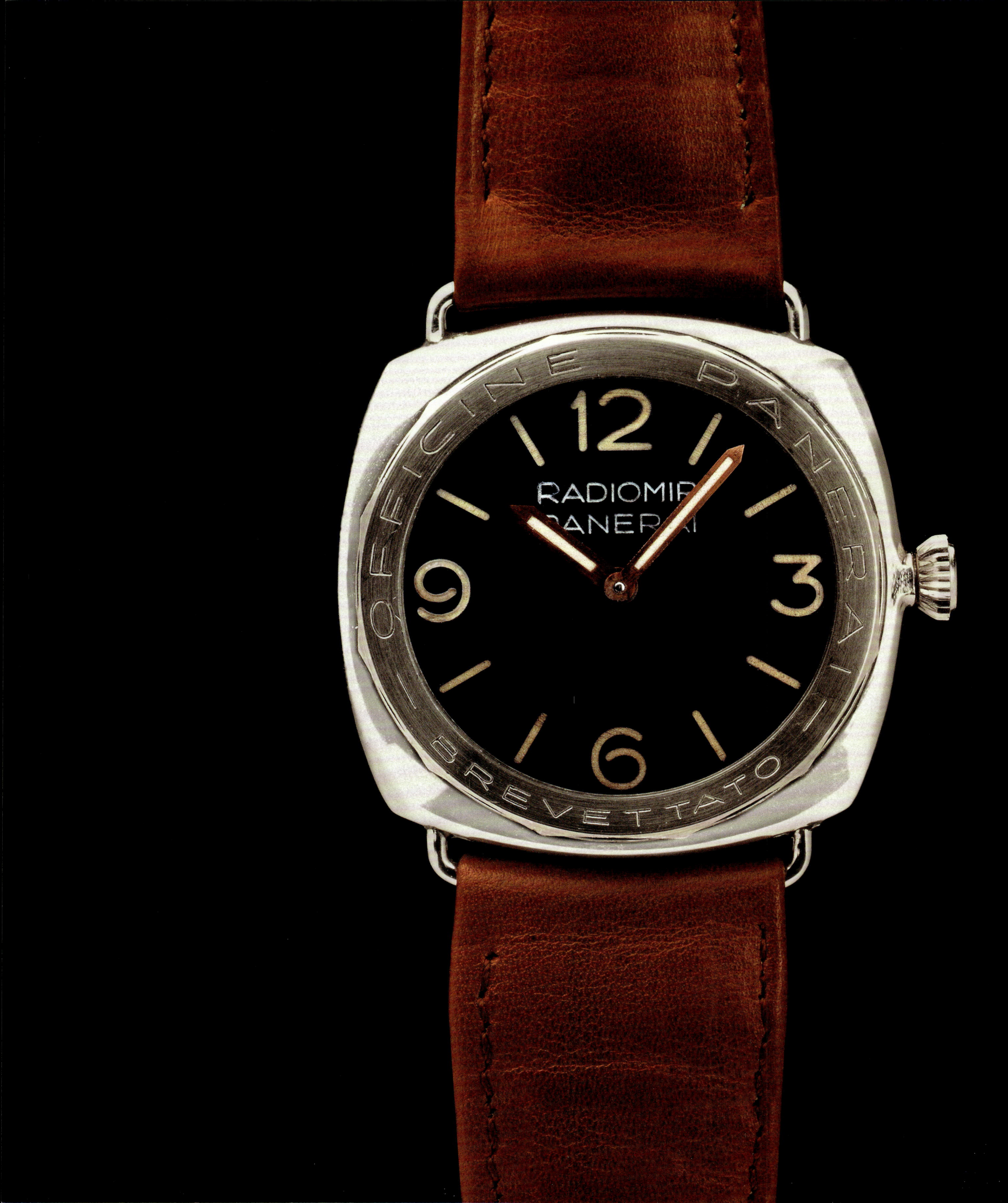
OFFICINE PANERAI
BREVETTATO
RADIOMIR
PANERAI
12
3
6
9

HORA ITALICA, PANERAI AND THE SEA

Clocks have a venerable history in Italy. Indeed several historians believe it is probably where these new "time machines" first saw the light of day. They were already in existence between 1200 and 1300 and one of the masterpieces of the era in relation to the art of time measurement was the Astrarium of Giovanni de' Dondi: astronomer, philosopher and doctor originally from Chioggia, who also taught in Florence. The Astrarium, completed in 1364 operated with weight movement, had seven dials and displayed, in addition to the time and minutes (which may have been the first time that these appeared on a clock), the month, day and the movement of the Sun, the Moon, Venus, Saturn, Mars, Mercury and Jupiter. This was completed by a perpetual religious calendar.

After Dondi, Renaissance Florence became the European centre of mechanical watch-making and of advanced technical skill in virtually every field. In 1443, in Florence, the artist Paolo Uccello – famous pupil of Tommaso Masaccio – completed the frescoes of the clock face, immediately above the main entrance to Santa Maria del Fiore. Only a few years later, in 1476, this church would also have the highest gnomonic meridian in Italy, and one of the highest in existence: 90.109 metres, from the perforation in the lantern of the Brunelleschian cupola all the way to the floor, where the solar image was projected. The original movement of the mechanical clock has been lost, but the dial has survived. It is one of the greatest testaments to the *hora italica*.

Lorenzo della Volpaia, the founder of a Florentine family of clockmakers completed his masterpiece in 1510: the 'Planetary Clock', which has recently been restored. It stood 235 cm high and had a quadrant 73.67 cm in diameter. It displayed the time, the calendar, and both average planetary motion and true planetary motion. This had never been done before. The clock was a technical wonder, purchased by the Guelph civic leaders in order to prevent such an extraordinary object from being purchased by nobles from other cities, who would then remove it from Florence.

The construction of the first pendulum clock is almost universally attributed to Christian Huygens, the Dutch scientist who invented it in 1656; but the law of isochronism governing the small oscillations of the pendulum, along with its application in clockmaking, came from Galileo Galilei. It was for this reason that Leopoldo de' Medici, the Prince of Tuscany, was already in possession of a clock with pendulum motion in 1658. One must remember that communications were very different centuries ago, so even if Huygens' creation in Holland was known in Florence, it had probably not been fully analysed or described, and the chances of its having been copied in its totality are very slim.

ABOVE Window of the Orologeria Svizzera, Piazza San Giovanni, which opened around 1920 when the nephew of Giovanni Panerai, Guido, became the head of the firm. Panerai has kept the same inscription on the shop window to this day.

FACING PAGE An example created in 1938 for demonstration purposes and probably greatly altered at a later date. The dial is already extremely different from that of the first models, both in terms of construction and in terms of the numbering. It carries the wording Radiomir Panerai, and the engravings on the bezel and the caseback probably refer to the 1935 patent.

FACING PAGE This torch, manufactured by Panerai in 1970 for the Italian Navy, is not very different from the models used by the commandos during the last World War. Totally waterproof and entirely made of metal, it includes a safety switch and bears the mark Officine Panerai Brevettato on the crown.

Just a few hundred feet from the clock dial painted by Paolo Uccello, behind the Baptistery and the cathedral, stands the most famous and exclusive shop dedicated to the Italian wristwatch: the Officine Panerai. The genesis of this new way of keeping time begins some four centuries later.

The watchmaker Giovanni Panerai – the first in Florence – first operated from the Ponte alle Grazie. He was the founder of the dynasty and the company which, in a sense, brought the ancient art of time measurement and instrument construction back to the City of Flowers: which, following its brief infancy in Italy, had developed in Germany, France and England, to settle finally in Switzerland. It seems probable that the shop was already open in the decade between 1850 and 1860, and that it would have been similar, at least in size and structure, to the shops still operational on the Ponte Vecchio today.

In either 1873 or 1876, depending on the source, the Ponte alle Grazie underwent major restoration, which involved the demolition of the houses along its parapets and the forced eviction of the shops. A period of transfer thus began for the Giovanni Panerai watchmaker's shop, which in any case was continuing to grow. This led to its eventual establishment at its current location, the Archbishop's Palace in Piazza San Giovanni, around 1920. In the meantime, Giovanni Panerai (1825–1897) was succeeded by his son, Leon Francesco (1873–1934). He had four children: Guido, Emma, Dario and Pilade. Guido, the firstborn (1873–1934), gave a new boost to the family business: he expanded the firm in part because of his relations with Antonio Fracei, his father-in-law and owner of a mechanical workshop, which, amongst other things, produced mess tins for the military. It may well be that the Panerai family's first relations with the armed forces date back to the time of Guido's marriage to Guglielmina Fracei, around 1900; but it was not his work for the Army that would make the Panerai Company famous, but his collaboration with the Navy: the Regia Marina.

The work with the Italian Navy almost certainly began before the transfer to Piazza San Giovanni. Those first relations had involved the supply of pocket precision chronographs – watches whose movements were often adjusted to meet the technical needs of the military – but shortly thereafter the collaboration became a good deal closer by virtue of an invention fundamental to the company's growth: radio-luminous sights. Thanks to micro-mechanics and the experience he had gained in the watchmaking sector, Guido Panerai was also able to develop a business based on the construction of high-precision instruments such as tools and lathes (which in turn would become

THE BIRTH OF A LEGEND 48

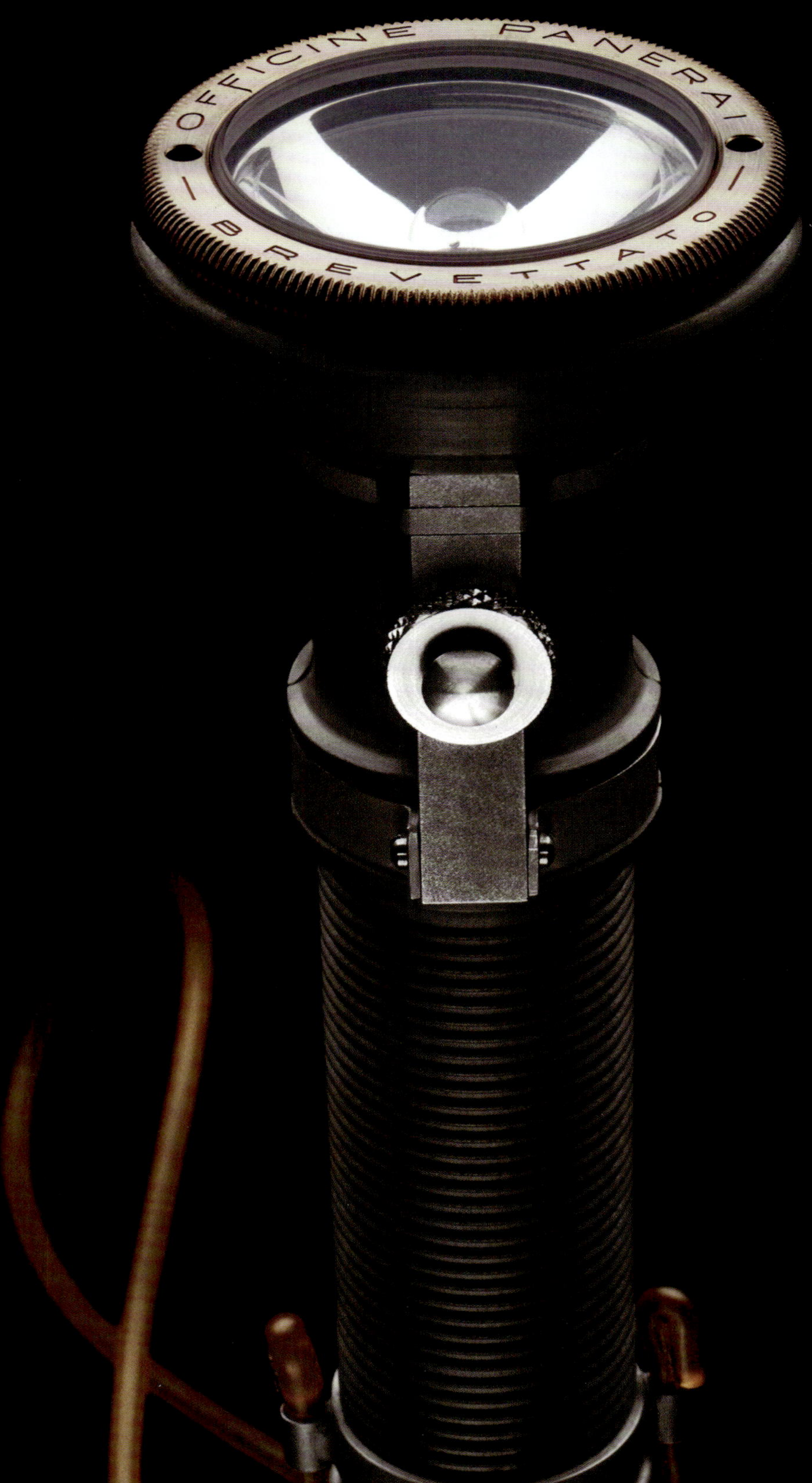
OFFICINE PANERAI
BREVETTATO

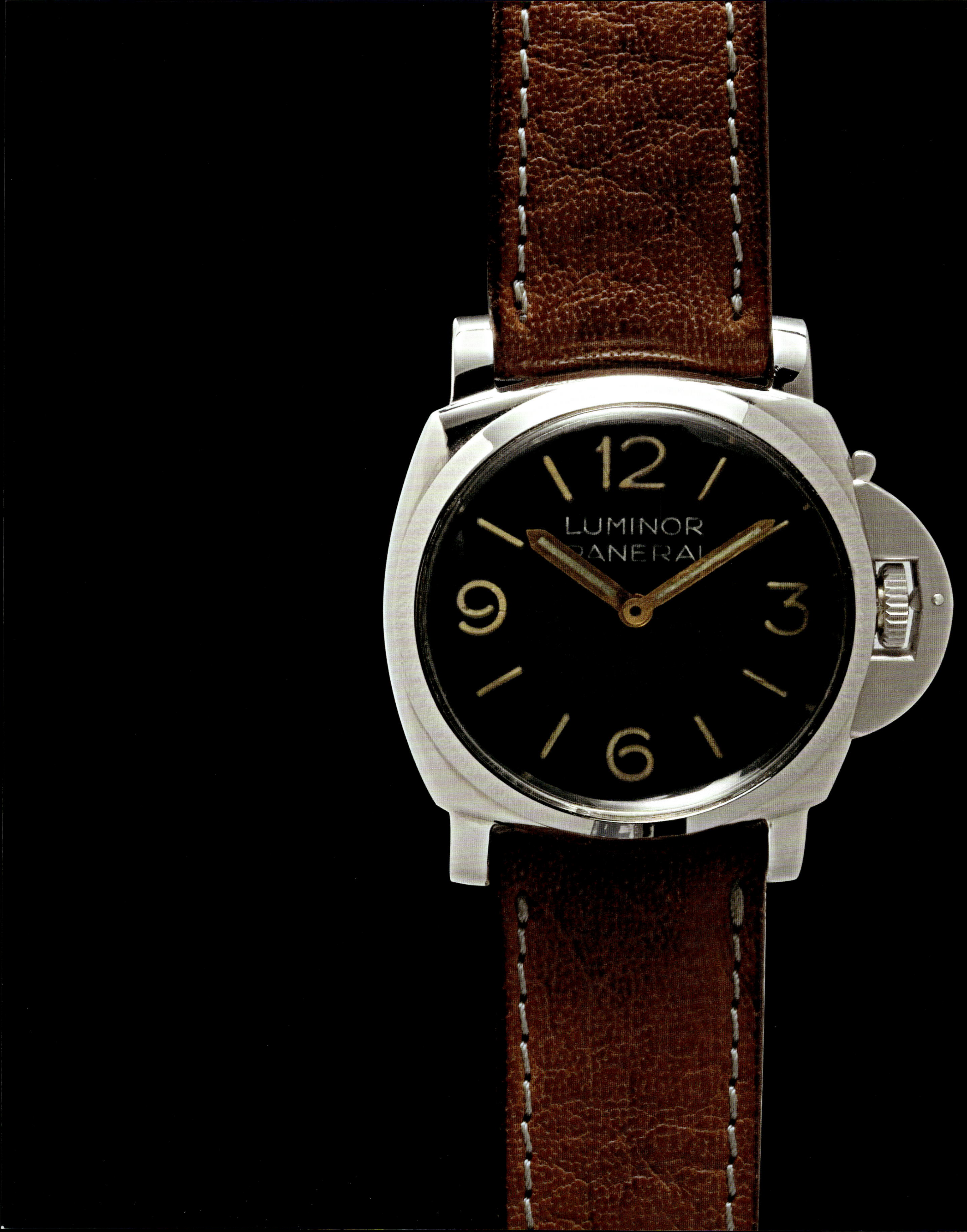
LUMINOR
PANERAI

acclaimed); and, subsequently, on the design and production of special lenses, under consultation with the Arcetri Observatory.

The radio-luminous sights, also known as 'Ronconi Sights' or 'Panerai Sights', caused a small revolution in the arms sector: they allowed targeting in total darkness and rendered the 'dials and grids of sighting devices and binoculars self-illuminating', all thanks to the high luminosity achieved by a radium–based powder or paste. The innovation's secret lies not only in the self-illuminating characteristics of the compound but also, indeed primarily, in its methodology: instead of being applied directly onto the metal parts as a varnish, the powder or paste mix was placed into small air-tight glass or methyl methacrylate tubes, which were in turn inserted into the small metal cavities created in the sight-and-targeting device or in the various types of dials and grids.

In the meantime, Guido Panerai had registered a series of patents for his innovation: two in Great Britain in 1915, three in France in 1915 and 1916. The Marina Militare (Italian Navy) was not the only beneficiary: the company also crafted devices for use by the Air Force and the Army. The term 'Radiomir', a type of acronym that condensed the original definition of radio-luminous sights, first appears in a supplement to patent number 491014, registered in France at 2.30 pm on 23 March 1916.

During the First World War, the collaboration between Guido Panerai and the Italian Navy intensified. The Radiomir sights greatly increased the company's prestige in the eyes of the Admiralty; and Guido's absorption with Panerai, the luminosity of sights and dials, and his obsession with improving the existing inventions of the time, are attested by his unflagging search for both Italian and foreign achievements in such matters.

Panerai's strength was an extreme specialisation which developed on several levels: time control (a series of instruments capable of measuring hours, minutes and seconds as accurately and reliably as possible); high-precision optical and machine-finish control; the perfect water tightness of diving devices; and, thanks to the 'Radiomir' technology, extraordinary visibility under all conditions of use for instruments requiring a dial or a graduated scale with reference numbers or indices. It was in the period between the two World Wars that the Officina Meccanica di Precisione G. Panerai moved from a small factory to a medium-sized one with approximately 100 workers, and fully developed its concept of manufacture. On 3 October 1935, Italian armed forces attacked Ethiopia; but the conflict – which was resolved in seven months – ran the risk of triggering an even greater one with Great Britain, which firmly

FACING PAGE This Luminor Panerai watch was manufactured in the late 1940s–early 1950s. This model uses the new tritium-based luminescent product, Luminor.

opposed Italian expansionist policy in Eastern Africa. The tension between the two countries was extreme. A month earlier, Great Britain had already sent the Home Fleet into the Mediterranean Sea to strengthen the Mediterranean Fleet and prove that it was not bluffing. Britain, had it desired to, could have deployed approximately 800,000 tons of warships, of which fifteen were battleships, each with over 29,000 tons of displacement. In the face of this imposing deployment, Italy found itself almost defenceless: it could deploy only two antiquated battleships and seven heavy cruisers. Because the aerial situation was no better, the Italian Navy had to think of alternative methods to counteract the superior British fleet; so on the same day in which the Home Fleet entered the Mediterranean, the Commander of the 1st Submarine Group of La Spezia gathered together all the commanders on the base to set out the new strategy. This was based upon stealth methods: surprise attacks against enemy units and bases that could be carried out with unusual methods and material: submarines and midget submarines; high-speed explosive craft and motorboats armed with torpedoes; specialised military frogmen and deep-sea divers (assault swimmers and scuba divers, both strapped with explosives); and self-propelled or piloted torpedoes – which became the most efficient weapons of all. Italy, which had been developing naval assault methods since the First World War, had significant experience in this area.

Almost twenty years later, these assault craft were further developed. One, designed by Teseo Tesei and Elio Toschi, two captains of the Genio Navale (Naval Engineers), was informally known as either a 'self-propelled torpedo' or a 'self-propelled Tesei', although its technical designation was SLC: *siluro a lenta corsa* (slow-running torpedo). It could navigate both on the surface and underwater and was propelled by an electric engine rather than by compressed air. The SLC was piloted by two crewmen who sat astride the craft and were protected by a small wavebreaker, a type of metal windscreen that also contained the control panel and the steering instruments. The prow consisted of the warhead, which contained one or two charges, activated by time fuses. The SLC, in essence, was a midget 'spider' submarine: 6.7 m to 8 m in length; approximately 53 cm in diameter; and weighing from 1,300 to 1,800 kg, depending on the type.

The initial training programmes commenced in early September 1935, when the go-ahead was also given for the creation of instruments to equip the assault-craft: compasses, depth gauges, torches, respirators and so on. One request made by the Commander of the 1st Submarine Group to the Commissione Permanente of the Ministry of the Navy related to 'a special luminous watch for deep-sea divers.... In March 1936, the Standing Committee delivered a Radiomir wrist watch to the Command of the 1st Submarine Group, which when tested at sea, both during the day and at night, proved excellent in every respect. It was therefore decided that ten examples of said watch should be ordered and these were thus utilised during all exercises with highly satisfactory results'.

No information is available on the pressure-resistance of the first 'Radiomir' watches, which in any case were not yet diving watches as they are currently known, though they were 'water-resistant' or '*étanche*' models. But because commandos and scuba divers operated at a depth of between ten and eighteen metres during drills, we can reasonably assume that the water-resistance was guaranteed during long diving exercises to a depth of at least forty to fifty metres. Perspex glass protected a dial of unusual design: an alternation of Roman numerals, Arabic numerals and baton indices with a triangle highlighting 12:00; medium-sized baton hands; and motion work around the hour circle. The watches had a 5513 or 618 calibre movement (almost identical), 16 lignes, 17 jewels (rubies) and manual winding on Cortebert *ébauche*, a simple and reliable movement. It was manufactured in Staybrite steel, the corrosion-resistant metal of its time, with two fine lugs welded to the case, to which a loose leather strap was attached. The strap in turn had been pre-cut and treated for waterproofing; was long enough to be secured over the sleeve of a diving suit; and was fastened with a large steel trapezoidal buckle. Italian commandos and assault divers carried out their initial training with these watches.

Demand for diving watches picked up quickly in autumn 1938. The 'Radiomir' model went into production, and from the experience gained during the drills, it gradually underwent a series of modifications. The first related to the dial, where 'mixed' numbering was replaced, over time, by four large, Arabic numbers at the cardinal points, a series of baton indices and no Roman numerals. This, however, was essentially cosmetic; the true revolution lay in the construction of the new dial. This was no longer created from a single base but from two overlapping plates (the upper plate having perforated numbers and indices), which produced a 'sandwich' effect. The 'Radiomir' paste was then placed in-between. The plates were sealed, and the larger quantities of 'Radiomir' paste that could now be used achieved an unsurpassed luminosity: so much so that during the course of certain night exercises, commandos were forced to smear the dials with mud or seaweed so they would not be spotted by sentries.

ABOVE One of the first prototypes designed for supply to the crew of Italian Royal Navy assault craft. The dial is still a traditional Rolex dial, its numbers and indices covered in Radiomir paste.

ABOVE Photo of a human torpedo prototype (slow-running torpedo), during an exercise. Based on the torpedo equipped with an electric motor, its speed underwater did not exceed 3 knots, about the speed of a swimmer. It measured 6.80 metres in length for a displacement of 1.3 tons.

FACING PAGE The cover of this magazine, *7 Anni di Guerra* published at the end of the 1950s, shows the attack of an enemy ship in Gibraltar by an Italian commando during the war.

The third significant modification (which, together with the structure of the dial, is still the distinguishing feature of Panerai watches today), dates back to the early 1940s and relates to winding-crown water-resistance. This had proven to be the watch's weak point during diving: in the long run, the winding and unwinding of the crown mechanism could ruin the threading and thus compromise the water-resistant properties of the crown itself. At this point, Panerai researched a radically new device based on a compression system using a small bridge with a lever attached by screws to the side of the case. Upon lifting the lever, the crown could turn freely and thus wind the spring or adjust the hands; upon lowering, the lever would coaxially compress the crown against the case, creating a seal that would prevent any infiltrations. With the bridge-lever movement in place, the watch was completely waterproof even at the more demanding depths the commandos often reached during military exercises and operations. In the 250 training dives conducted by the end of 1939 alone, thirty to forty metres had been attained. The watch therefore, in theory, could be utilised at even deeper reaches. Indeed, there was talk of 200 metres, but even at far less than this, the absolute record of the time had been broken with the creation of the first true specialised 'diving model'. Panerai had made watch-making history.

With the outbreak of the Second World War, Panerai was also producing and supplying other specific instruments to equip commandos and their self-propelled torpedoes. These included compasses and inclinometers (all with "Radiomir" dials), which were attached to certain slow-running torpedoes; depth gauges; and the compasses that commandos and assault swimmers attached to their wrists. Between 1940 and 1943, Italian assault-craft crewmen sank five battleships and and twenty-three merchant ships. The reliability of the Panerai equipment was of course, of utmost importance. The most spectacular of these operations was carried out in the Egyptian port of Alexandria, where a mission led by Durand de La Penne exploded the British warships *Queen Elizabeth, Valiant* and the oil tanker *Sagona*. This exploit even inspired a film: *I sette dell'Orsa Maggiore* (*Hell Raiders from the Deep*), filmed in the 1950s using original Panerai materials and equipment and in consultation with Durand de La Penne himself.

After the war, the commandos' watches, compasses, depth gauges and other equipment continued to be employed for many years: scuba divers and other operators in charge of the removal of mines from ports and canals, or the restoration of conduits and other underwater systems destroyed during the war, found them invaluable. Moreover, the Italian Navy underwent reorganisation after 1945; Panerai continued to supply it with watches and

7 ANNI di GUERRA

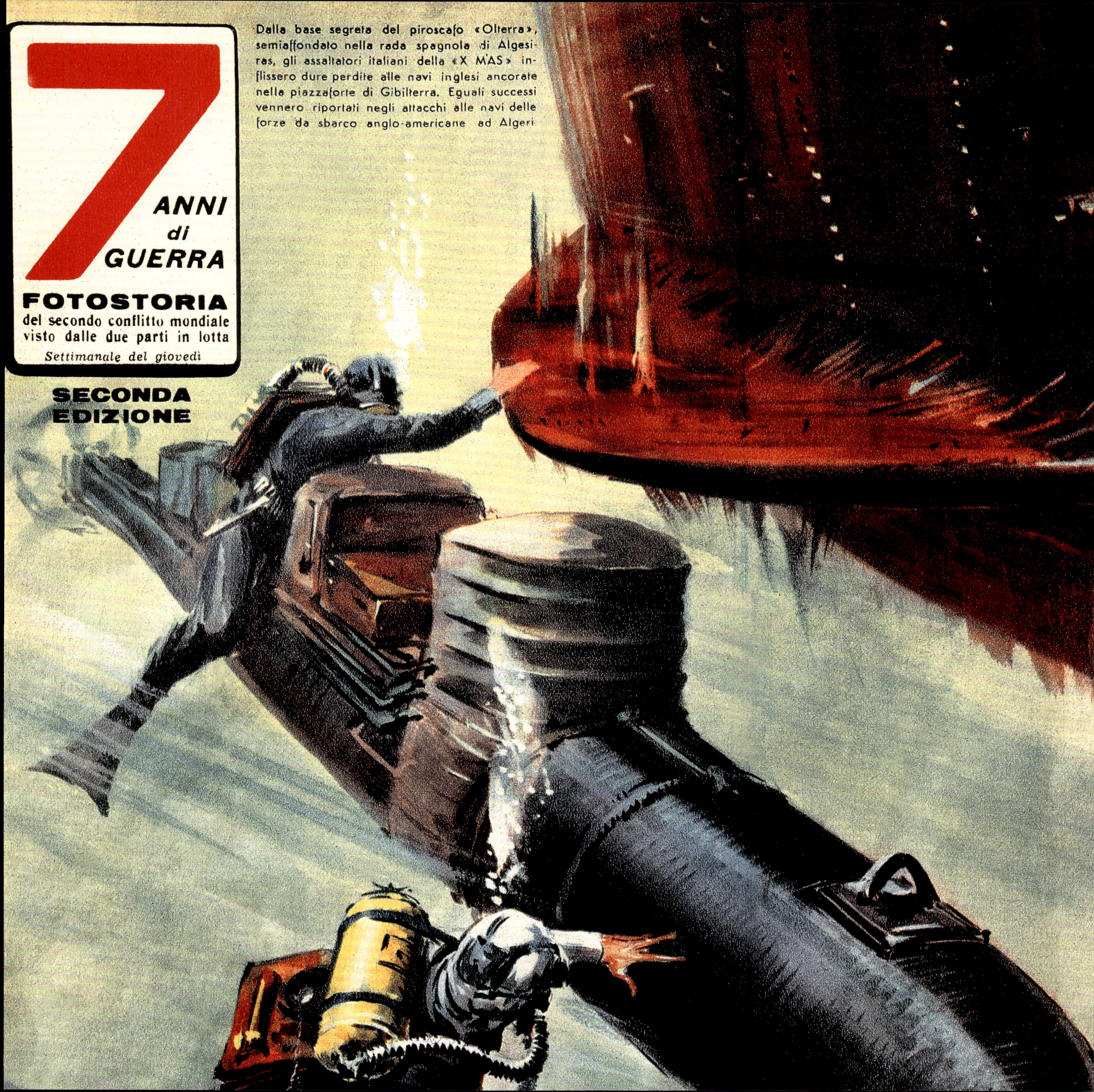

FOTOSTORIA
del secondo conflitto mondiale
visto dalle due parti in lotta
Settimanale del giovedì

SECONDA EDIZIONE

Dalla base segreta del piroscafo «Olterra», semiaffondato nella rada spagnola di Algesiras, gli assaltatori italiani della «X MAS» inflissero dure perdite alle navi inglesi ancorate nella piazzaforte di Gibilterra. Eguali successi vennero riportati negli attacchi alle navi delle forze da sbarco anglo-americane ad Algeri

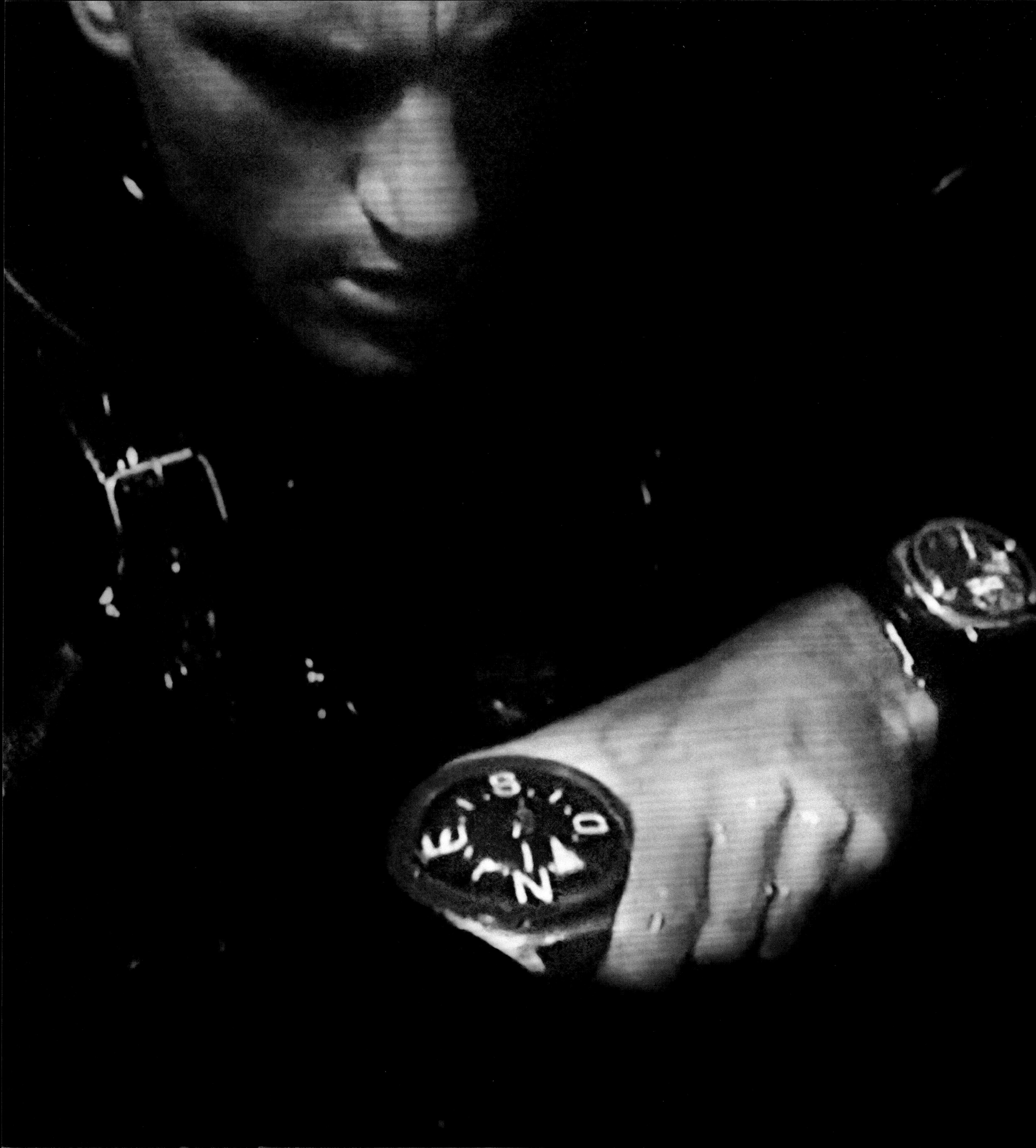

other instruments, using cases, dials and movements from its warehouse inventories. It is for this reason that various models were created or outfitted as prototypes during this period. The Luminor Panerai prototype, with its Marina Militare brand, is one such example, introduced at the end of the 1940s or the beginning of the 1950s – possibly for the Italian Navy's Second Officer, as the 'Mare Nostrum' model had been.

The most significant innovation in the immediate postwar period was the production of Luminor models, with bridge lever, Angelus movement and a new self-illuminating substance. The substance was no longer radium-based; and its primary element, tritium (a hydrogen isotope), was far less radioactive. Panerai took the decision to replace the former, self-illuminating substance with the new one, called Luminor. The replacement was gradual, however: 'Radiomir' dials continued to be used for some time.

At the beginning of the 1950s, along with the Luminor and Italian Navy supplies, the Florentine company also developed several prototypes, identified under reference 6154, that led to the creation of a series of special watches for the Egyptian Navy. Two of these had a cylindrical, screw-locking crown, Rolex movement and a dial marked 'Radiomir'. The Italian Navy contract ran until the end of the 1950s. Panerai continued to supply on-board clocks, wall clocks and Luminor and Italian Navy bridge-lever watches, despite the fact that technical characteristics and the precision of man-made production entailed much higher costs, especially for a state order.

In the 1960s, the Florentine company significantly decreased both its personnel and its business activity, primarily because Giuseppe Panerai was growing ill. His intention was to transfer the company to the Italian Navy, retaining only Orologeria Svizzera for the family. Before this could happen, however, he died, in February 1972; so a few months later the company – under pressure by the Navy itself, given the importance of the supply orders covered by military secret – was taken over by Dino Zei, an officer in the Italian Navy with a degree in industrial engineering, who had maintained a working relationship with the owner of Panerai for some time. 'G. Panerai & Figlio' thus changed both hands and name, becoming 'Officine Panerai S.r.L.'.

It was in 1992 that Zei decided to relaunch the watches created for the Second World War commandos; but as he himself recounts, only a few designs, some photographs and a small number of Radiomir examples remained. The Luminor and Mare Nostrum models were selected for production (now with tachymeter scale engraved on the bezel), and all the planning designs were processed *ex novo*, starting with the reduction of the Luminor case from

FACING PAGE This photo was taken from the 1953 film *I Sette dell'Orsa Maggiore* (*Hell Raiders from the Deep*), which tells the story of Italian commandos during the sabotage of an enemy ship in 1941 in the port of Alexandria. To ensure the authenticity of the scenes, the actors were equipped with Panerai watches, compasses, and altimeters.

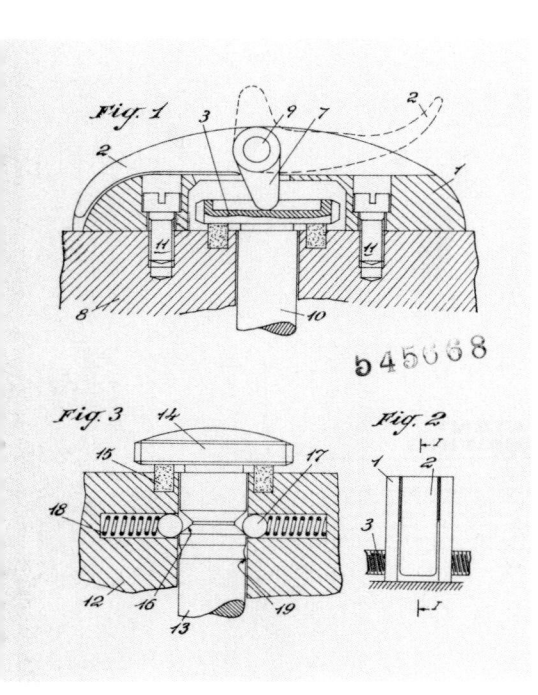

ABOVE The design accompanying the patent issued in Italy (in July of 1956) to Maria and Giuseppe Panerai and relatives to 'Tight-seal device for the control knob of instruments, particularly for the setting and winding knob of watches'.

FACING PAGE Extremely rare model of Marina Militare watch for left-handers, made at the end of the 1950s for the Italian Navy. It includes a 47-millimeter case and a Rolex mechanism with Luminor digits.

47 to 44 mm, and 14 mm thick, to promote normal usage of the watch. Studies were subsequently undertaken to perfect the bridge lever and other details relative to the rotating ring, which culminated in three patented innovations on the part of Bruno Latini, Engineer and Senior Director of Officine Panerai. The launch of the new watches took place in La Spezia on 10 September 1993, on board the destroyer named after Luigi Durand de La Penne; and the collection covered three models: Luminor (reference 5218-201/A; 889 examples produced); Mare Nostrum (reference 5218-301/A; 990 produced); and Luminor Marina Militare (reference 5218-202/A; 90 models, with a darkened antiglare and scratchproof case for exclusive use by the Italian Navy).

Despite a reduced sales network, the new models were extremely successful, although it was a Hollywood star, Sylvester Stallone (known to his friends as 'Sly'), who would bring international acclaim to Panerai watches and open new horizons. Having purchased a Panerai during a trip to Italy, the star requested a special Luminor series watch for use during the underwater filming of his new film, *Daylight*; he then asked for a further special series to be created in his own name. Hence the title 'Slytech'. The watches (originally 300 pieces, although the supply was interrupted before completion, plus a dozen prototypes) bear the actor's engraved signature on the base plate.

Financial and distribution issues, unfortunately, caused that production to be restricted to twelve Luminor and two Luminor Marina models, which placed Officine Panerai in serious financial difficulty. In that same year the company launched a few Luminor Sub prototypes with rotating ring, and Slytech Luminor Black Seal models with antiglare case. These should have been produced in 1997, but the small series was never completed.

The financial, distributional and other difficulties that were plaguing the company ultimately led Officine Panerai to its decision to transfer the watch-making sector. The search for a partner or sponsor had been ongoing since 1995, but it was only the following year that the Vendôme Group came forward. This giant in the luxury sector (and parent company of Cartier) is today known as the Richemont Group. The agreement was ratified in March 1997. In addition to the assignment of the 'Officine Panerai' trademark to the Vendôme Group, the agreement provided for the transfer of technical documentation, patents, watch sector warehouse inventories (loose parts and movements included), along with everything relating to the production and inventories of wrist compasses, depth gauges and underwater torches. At this juncture, the Tuscan firm became 'Panerai Sistemi S.p.A.'; but under any name, this was the beginning of a further and glorious new lease on life, and the beginning of a worldwide launch of the historic 'Panerai' brand.

THE BIRTH OF A LEGEND

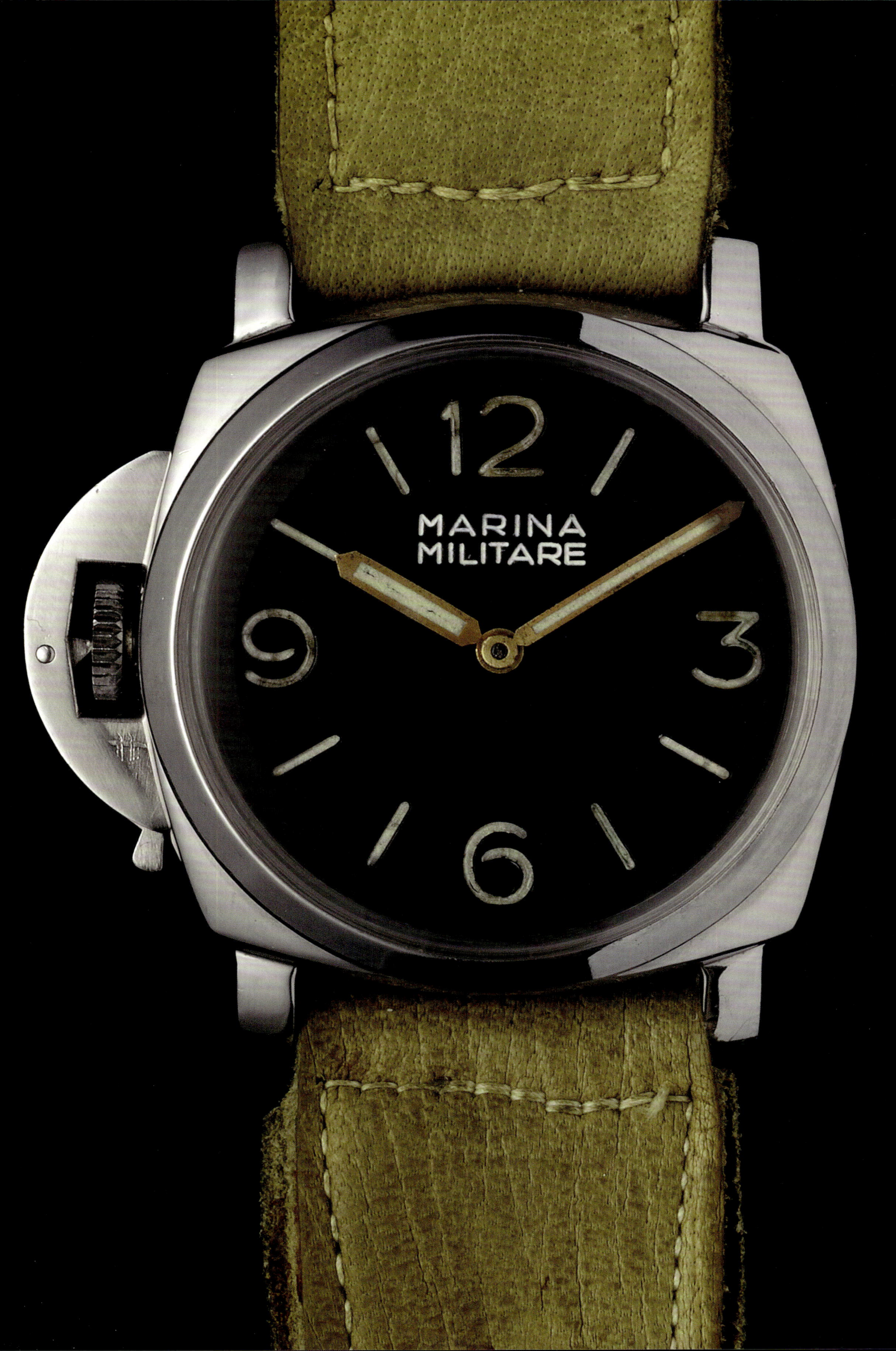
12
MARINA
MILITARE
9
3
6

LUMINOR
SUBMERSIBLE
28
PANERAI
Regatta
SWISS MADE
45
15
30
REG
T.M.

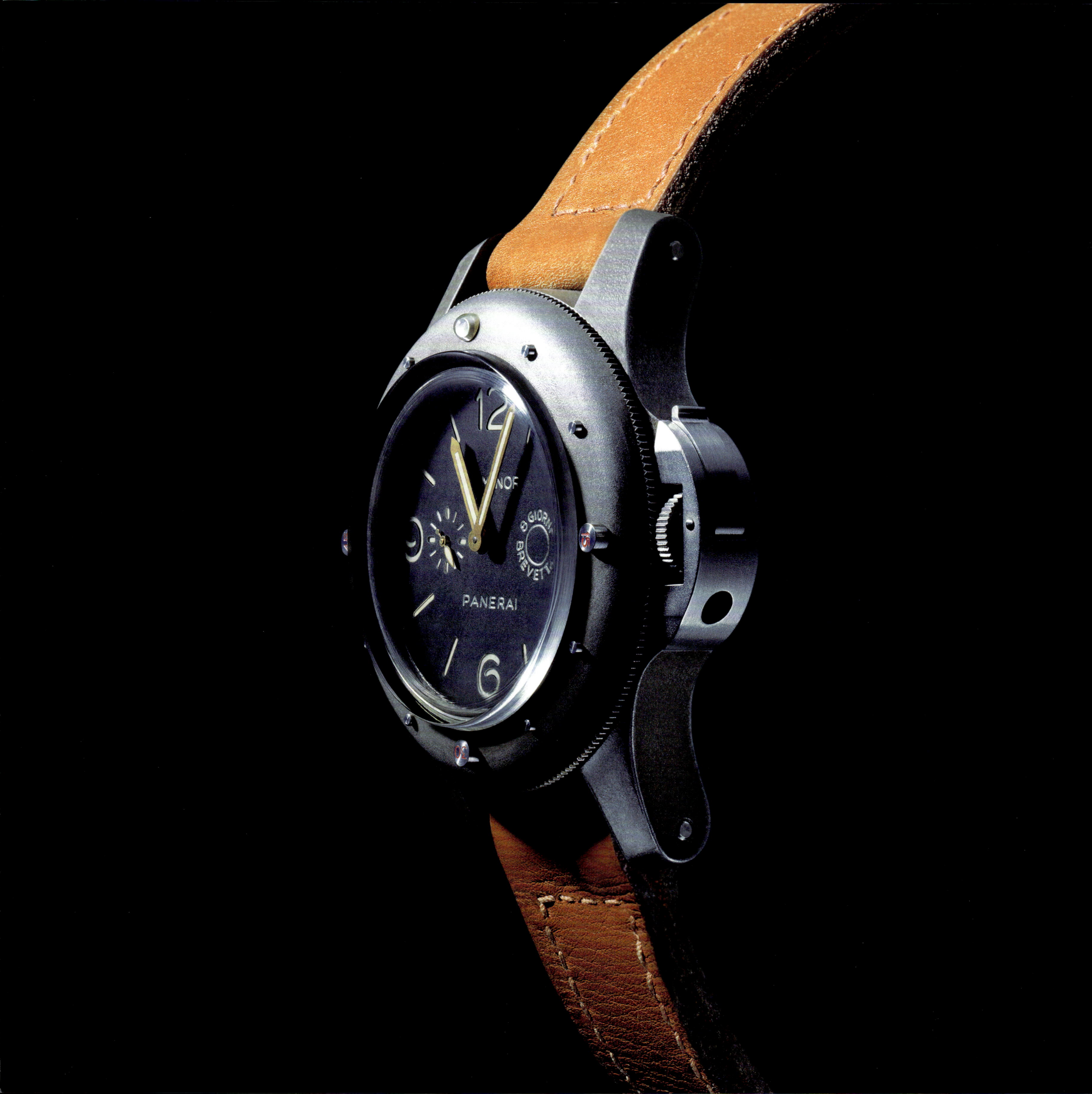
8 GIORNI
PANERAI

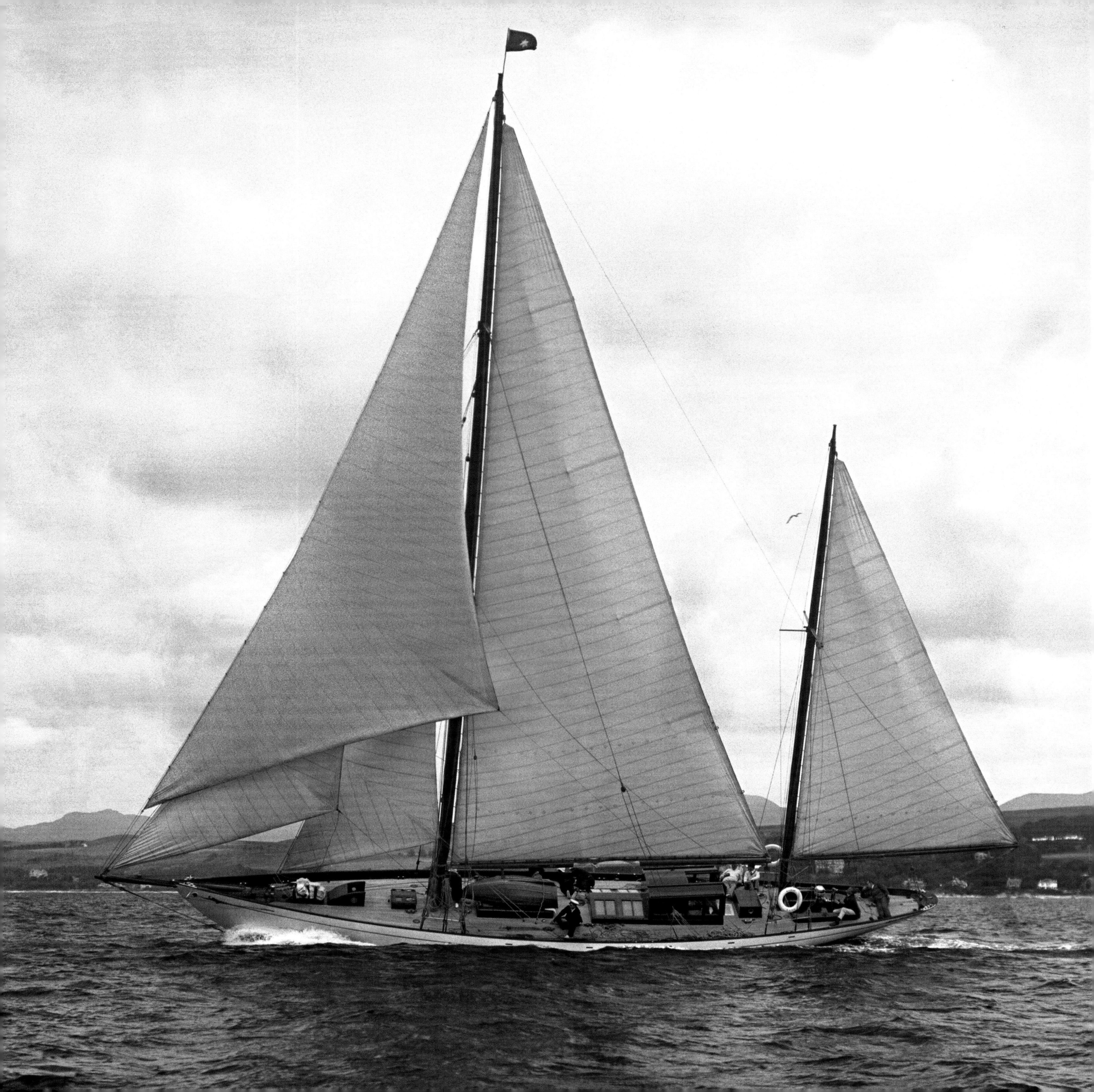

EILEAN,
FIRST RACES

As May Fife Kohn has explained in the Introduction, the Fulton family's passion for the sea goes back several generations, to the time of their association with the McCallum enterprise. The Fulton brothers, James and Robert, masters of *Eilean* in 1936, were not fierce competitors but genuine yachtsmen, members of the great clubs that organised races on the Clyde: the Royal Clyde Yacht Club, Royal Western Yacht Club, Royal Gourock Yacht Club and Royal Largs Yacht Club. From their home near that of their parents on Octavia Terrace in Greenock, the elegant area of lovely estates facing the water, they could follow all the races and, weather permitting, see all the way to the Royal Clyde Yacht Club. Accomplished sportsmen, they were adept at water sports and hunting, as well as golf, which they enjoyed on the course just off Octavia Terrace.

The 1938 season of regattas on the Clyde was dominated by an architect who specialised in high performance and seaworthy cruisers, the Scotsman Alfred Mylne. With three ketches over 35 metres long, including *Thendara* (1937), two 24-metre sisterships, *Fiumara* and *Albyn* (1934), and a yawl *Fiona* (1931), slightly longer than *Eilean*, the architect was the most successful racer and won seven of the nine regattas during the first two weeks of July. At just 59 tons, *Eilean* found herself close to the 60-ton limit of the large class and struggled to get among the top three boats.

The Scottish Handicaps regattas began on 1 July 1938 on a sunny day with a gusty westerly, the perfect weather conditions to create action-packed races. There was just enough wind for the first big boats race, *Thendara* – then owned by Sir Arthur S. L. Young, a Member of Parliament and renowned yachtsman – made the best of the rare opportunities to win the race ahead of *Albyn* (now *Eileen II*) and *Eilean*. The lack of wind in the afternoons of the following two days forced the organisers to shorten the circuit. On the fourth day, in front of Gourock, the race was again won by *Thendara* in very little wind accompanied by drizzle. *Eilean* came back for the Royal Yacht Club Regatta from 9 to 11 July. On the first day, the fresh wind favoured the schooners and forced the 12 Metre to stay home. After the rain in the morning, the next race took place on the most beautiful day of the year for sailing, when the wind and the sun were in complete harmony. The ketch *Albyn* took line honours ahead of *Thelma*, followed by *Eilean*.

The following year, the regattas were overshadowed by the dreadful threat hanging over the country and the rest of Europe. The Dragons and the 6 Metres were to the fore on the Clyde, in particular *Circé*, the champion of the architect David Boyd. After a few family cruises, *Eilean* was brought ashore where she stayed until the end of the war.

PAGE 60 The Luminor Submersible 1950Regatta 3 Days GMT Automatic Titanio watch, comprising an automatic mechanism and a 47-millimetre case, was made totally of titanium by Officine Panerai. With a three-day mechanism and resistance down to 300 metres (30 bars), it also indicates the duration of the immersion.

PAGE 61 This watch, dating from 1956, is the Luminor Panerai Prototype. It was one of the prototypes made for the Egyptian Navy submarine commandos. At the time, they were provided with about a hundred Radiomir and Luminor watches, which included an eight-day mechanism and a 60-millimetre steel case.

FACING PAGE In this photo taken by Beken in 1938, *Eilean* is sailing close-hauled on the starboard tack, under yankee, jib and staysail. The crew consists of the captain, seen here wearing a white cap, and two of his deckhands. James, in a grey suit, is lying across the afterdeck admiring the power of the sails on the weather side of his majestic yacht. *Eilean*'s pennant at the masthead is a rectangle with a six-point silver star, on a background of half-gules on the leading edge side and azure on the other.

FACING PAGE For his second book about the year 1947, *The Yachting Year, Volume II, 1947–8*, Eric C. Hiscock asked David Cobb and Jan Main to create a two-colour cover illustration in the stencil style of the time. The front cover shows a ketch reaching, typical of that period and quite similar to *Eilean*.

PAGE 66 On Saturday, 26 June 1948, during one of the Northern Royal Yacht Club Clyde Fortnight regattas, *Eilean* was carrying P. H. N. Ulander's pennant. When a crew member fell overboard, the event was captured by the Rolleiflex of the photographer Ian George Gilchrist, who was on his own boat just behind and under the lee of *Eilean*, and recovered the victim.

PAGE 67 Since the beginning of the sport, the yachting press has been a place where ideas and information about new boating equipment and products have been exchanged. In 1948, a new synthetic material, Araldite, arrived in Great Britain and revolutionised the bonding processes.

PAGE 68 The British magazines, *The Yachtsman*, *Yachting World* and *Yachting Monthly*, always covered the Northern Royal Yacht Club Clyde Fortnight Regattas, which start at the end of June on the Firth of Clyde. The names of the cutter *Eileen* and the ketch *Eilean*, the two sailing yachts commissioned by the Fulton brothers from William Fife and Son, appeared regularly in the records of classes 'over 20 tons' or 'over 60 tons'.

As May Fife Kohn reminded us, the two Fulton brothers were killed during the war. In spite of the general sadness on the Clyde, the sailing festivities – like the *Clyde Fortnight*, which started in the last week of June or at the beginning of July – went ahead after the victory. In 1948, the replacement of the Dragon and Scottish One-Design classes was achieved with the help of fifteen universities and twenty-two colleges. The yachtsman P.H.N Ulander had just acquired *Eilean*. He had made his name before the war on his 30 square-metre Skerry Cruiser Tarpoon, designed by the architect Knud H. Reimers and built in 1936. The series, which originated in Scandinavia and was introduced to Britain by Uffa Fox, was very successful in Scotland, where a small fleet remained very active in the 1930s.

Ulander entered *Eilean* in the two *Royal Northern Yacht Club Fortnight* regattas on Saturday 26 and Monday 28 June 1948. In the over-20-tons class, it was remarkable to see the famous yachtsman Alexander William Steven, who, at 82 years of age, had just bought the 12 Metre *Jenetta*. May Fife Kohn has described the misadventures of *Eilean* during these races against *Mariella*, Ronald Teacher's yawl designed in 1938 by Alfred Mylne (his last sailing yacht built at the William Fife & Son shipyard) and the yawl *Fiona*. On the Saturday, a crew member on *Eilean* fell overboard. He was quickly rescued by photographer Ian C. Gilchrist's yacht, which was following, but the ketch was disqualified. *Mariella* won both races. A little later, in July, *Eilean* was entered for the Clyde-Kingstown race but did not start. *Mariella* was the winner once again.

The following year, in 1949, the Royal Western's cruise circuit had to be shortened because of the lack of wind for the largest boats in the class, in particular the 109-ton yawl *Vadura*, who struggled to get any speed. *Mariella* and *Eilean* took this opportunity to run ahead in the company of the 12 Metre *Jenetta*, always game for a challenge. This period of calm weather remained exceptional during those two weeks: for the other races, the easterly wind blew frequently in gusts and caused many incidents: man overboard, split sails.... The most exciting duel was between *Mariella* and *Jenetta* where, in a steady strong wind, A. W. Steven did not hesitate to hoist his spinnaker, forcing his rival to do the same.

In 1950 and 1951, the world of regattas turned toward sailing yachts designed specifically for the new ratings rules, which relegated the great pre-war yawls and ketches to the back of the fleet. Some, such as *Latifa* and *Bloodhound*, still managed to glean a few cups. After that, *Eilean* raced only for pleasure and most of her outings were cruises; the ketch was put up for sale at the end of 1951.

THE BIRTH OF A LEGEND 64

The Yachting Year

VOLUME II
1947-8

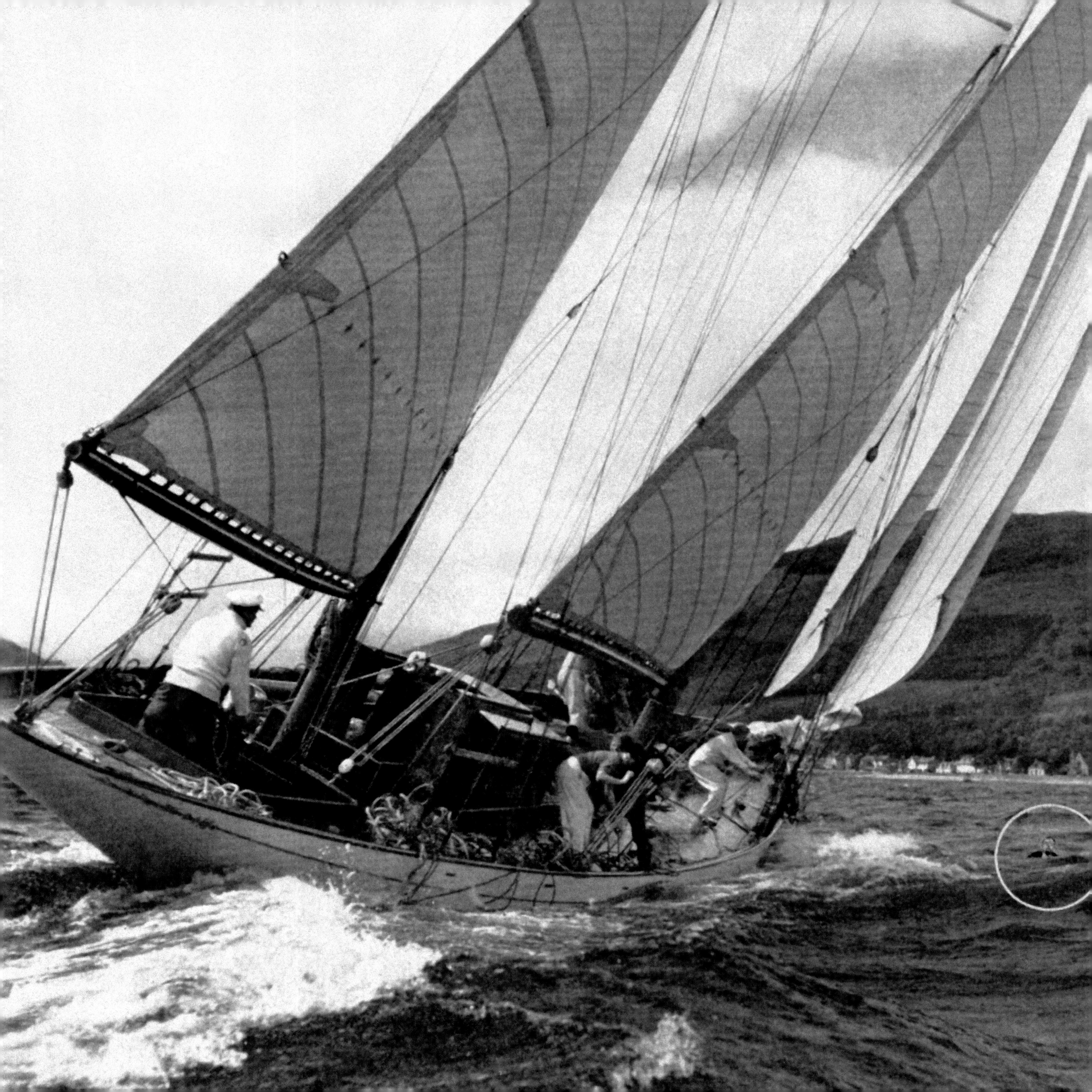

EILEAN AND FULTON BOAT DESIGNS

The first *Eileen* belonging to the Fulton family and *Eilean* are both ketches. This type of vessel, as well as yawls, were very much in favor towards the end of the 1920s and during the 1930s. An overview of some of the work of the greatest naval architects of that era, on both sides of the Atlantic, shows how this preference was based on real technical benefits and excellent racing results. It should be noted that the only difference between a ketch and a yawl is in the position of the mizzenmast in relation to the rudderpost. On a ketch, the mizzenmast —the smaller of the two—is forward of the rudder. It is bigger than on the yawl, where it is called a jigger.

Stormy Weather

BELOW The building of *Stormy Weather* by the Henry B. Nevins shipyard, City Island, New York, took only four and a half months. This 16.43-meter LOA cruising yawl, as she was referred to in the plans of the architect, Olin Stephens (1908–2008), turned out to be a very competitive offshore sailing yacht. Her agent, Philip Le Boutillier, found her name during an evening reception. Attending the naming ceremony, on 14 May 1934, the architect John Alden admitted "In my opinion a better design would be impossible to achieve." As of 1929, Olin was the architect for Sparkman & Stephens, which became the signature of winners for the next fifty years.

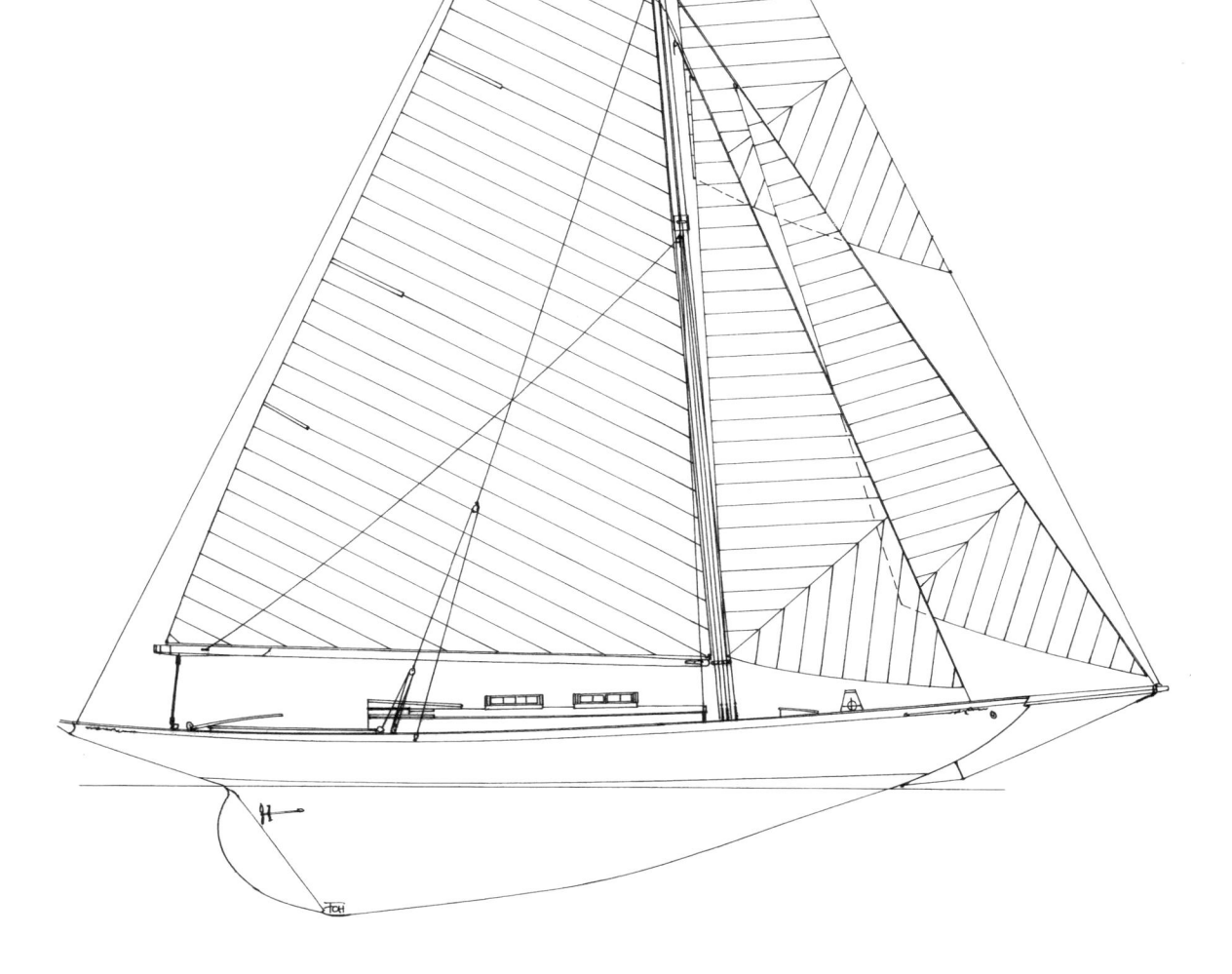

The second *Eileen*

ABOVE After the death of Louis V. Fulton in 1934, his sons, James Louis Vandalle (1909–1945) and Robert Waterson (1912–1943), put the yacht up for sale when they commissioned a more modest cutter from William Fife, *Eileen* (17.90 meters), which was launched in June 1935. In 1936, when the cutter was already on the market, the two brothers approached William Fife III to order the ketch *Eilean*. In 2001, *Eileen* was transported as cargo from Hawaii to the Lowyck Shipyard in Ostende for her restoration where the work was managed by the naval architect François Chevalier.

The first *Eileen, Belle Aventure*

BELOW Launched in Fairlie in June 1929, *Eileen* was a perfect example of her designer's motto, "What looks right is right", and she was certainly his most beautiful ketch. At the time, she carried a large gaff-rigged mainsail and a Marconi mizzen sail. *Eileen* sailed on the Clyde and in the Hebrides Islands for the next five years before being bought by Hugh Mclean who renamed her *My Lady of Aros*. In 1938, her next owner, Sir Alexander MacCornick called her *Alison*. For the last 30 years, under the name of *Belle Aventure*, she has been well maintained by the best shipyards and can be seen in the same impeccable state as in her heyday.

Karenita

ABOVE Designed by John G. Alden (1884–1962) and launched in the autumn of 1929 by the G. Lawley and Sons shipyard, Massachusetts; this 22.80-metre ketch reflected the elegance of her designer, a notable sportsman with great finesse. Her first owner, Lloyd Desmaret kept her for only two seasons. The yacht changed name three times, to *Simoon* in 1931, *Watchett II* in 1934 and *Avenir* in 1935, before being spotted by a young actor called Errol Flynn who bought her in 1936 and called her *Sirocco*. Found as a wreck in the Virgin Islands, she was restored by a Frenchman in 1988 and returned to her original name *Karenita* before joining the fleet of exquisite sailing yachts in the Mediterranean.

ATMOSPHERIC TEMPERATURES

The normal atmospheric temperatures, in degrees Fahrenheit, for the month are shown by isotherms (in dotted *red* lines) on the main body of the chart.

FOG

The dotted *blue* lines show the average percentage of all available ships observations in which fog was reported.

MAGNETIC VARIATION

The lines of equal magnetic variation for the Epoch 1975 are shown by *gray* lines on the main body of the chart. (See inset chart for the rate of annual change.)

EXCEPTIONAL ICE SIGHTINGS
△ Berg (year sighted)
○ Growler (year sighted)

DMAHC OFFICES IN THE PACIFIC OCEAN AREA

San Diego, California, Building 654, U.S. Naval Air Station, North Island.
Honolulu, Hawaii, Building 1710/3300 Hickam Air Force Base
Atsugi, Japan, Building 181, U.S. Naval Air Station.
Cubi Point, Republic of the Philippines, Building 120—6, U.S. Naval Air Station.

DEFENSE MAPPING AGENCY HYDROGRAPHIC CENTER REPRESENTATIVES:
New York, New York, 201 Varick Street, Room 711.
New Orleans, Louisiana, 600 South Street, Room 712

HYDROLANT AREA DESIGNATORS

HYDROLANT area designators "A", "B", "C", and "D" have been replaced by the number or numbers designating the REGION or SUBREGION in which the information in the HYDROLANT is located. Such numbers are in accordance with the N.O. chart numbering system. For example the heading of a HYDROLANT containing information pertaining to Cape Verde Islands which is located in SUBREGION 51 would read as follows: HYDROLANT 0000/71 (51) CAPE VERDE ISLANDS.

HYDROLANTS which contain general information or cover a broad geographic area will be designated GEN (general) and will not carry other designators.

Geographic portrayal of REGIONS and SUBREGIONS will be found on the back of the Pilot Chart for March 1971; page IV-8 of N.O. 1-PCL (Portfolio Chart List) dated 1 March 1971; and on the cover of N.O. Pub. 1-N-B (Catalog of Nautical Charts, 1st Edition 1 April 1971).

OCEAN WEATHER STATION VESSEL H

Ocean Weather Station H will be manned from 1 August to 31 March. It performs weather functions only and provides other very limited services in emergency situations.

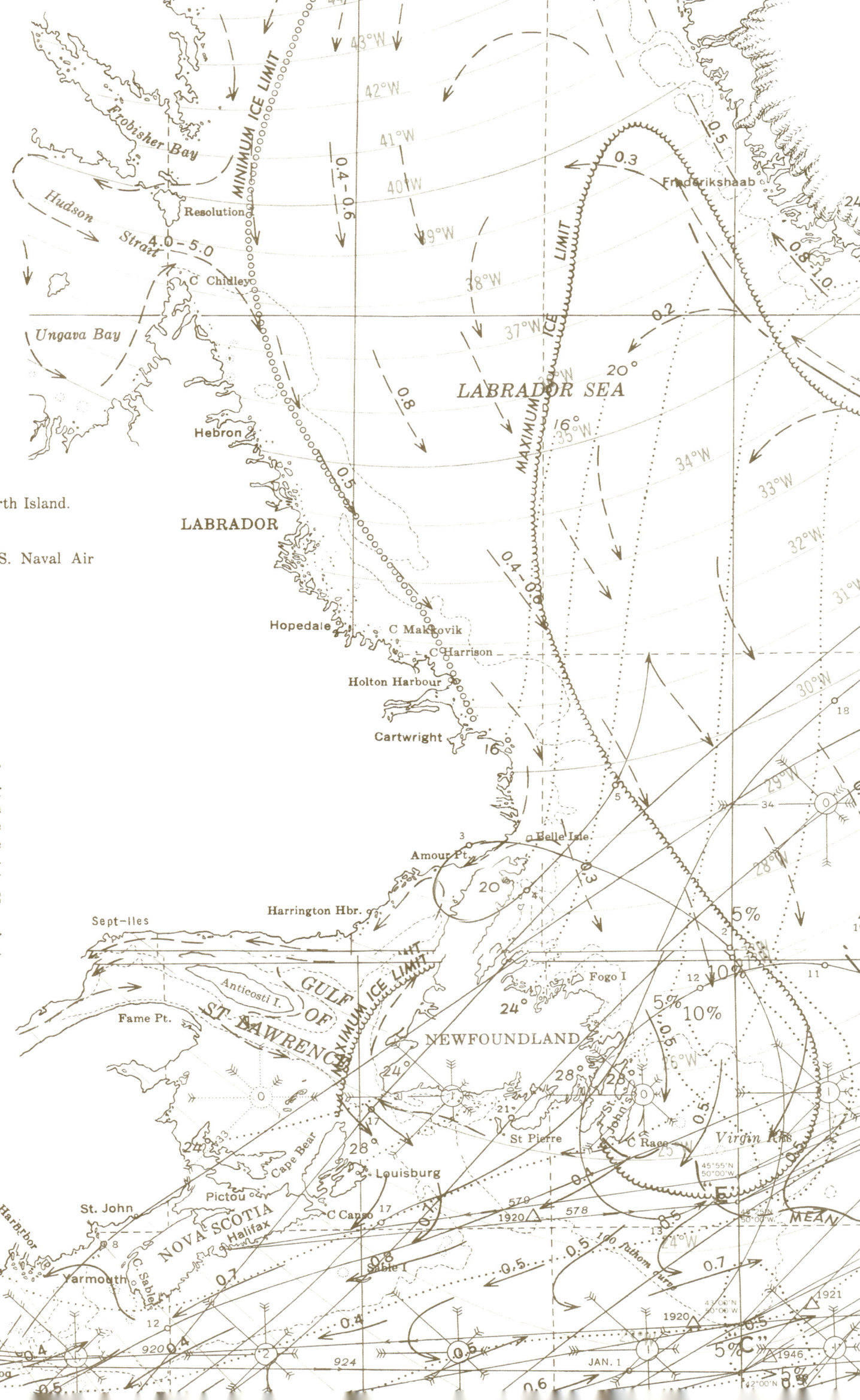

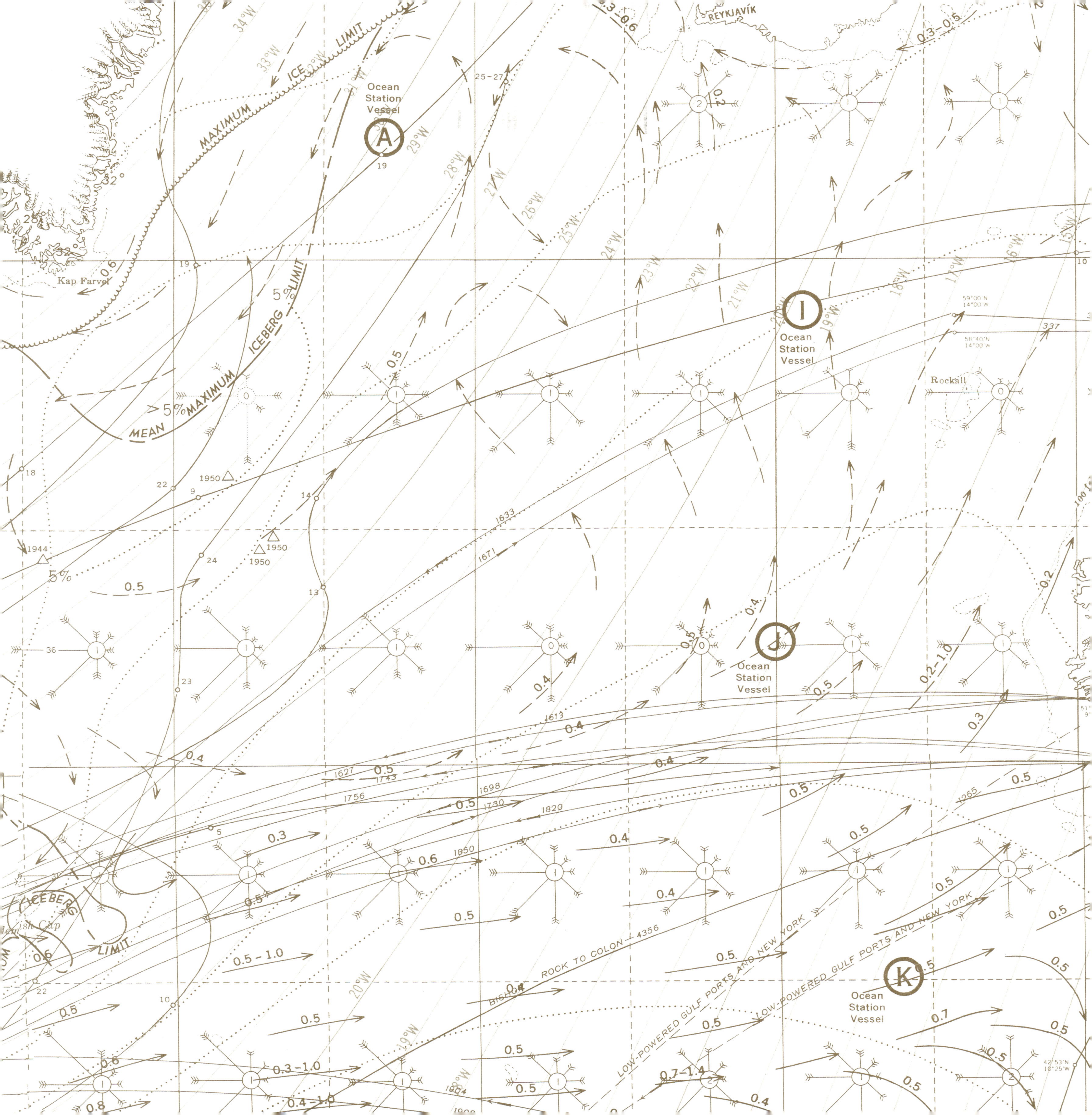

REYKJAVÍK
Kap Farvel
MAXIMUM ICE LIMIT
MEAN MAXIMUM ICEBERG LIMIT
5%
>5%
ICEBERG LIMIT
Ocean Station Vessel
A
Ocean Station Vessel
I
Ocean Station Vessel
J
Ocean Station Vessel
K
Rockall
BISHOP ROCK TO COLON 4356
LOW-POWERED GULF PORTS AND NEW YORK
LOW-POWERED GULF PORTS AND NEW YORK
34°W
33°W
29°W
28°W
27°W
26°W
25°W
24°W
23°W
22°W
21°W
19°W
18°W
17°W
16°W
15°W
20°W
19°W
59°00'N 14°00'W
58°40'N 14°00'W
42°53'N 10°25'W
1950
1944

Escapade

BELOW Rigged as a yawl with bowsprit and outrigger, *Escapade* (22.25 meters) was one of the great yawls that dominated offshore racing from the 1930s. For her owner, Henry G. Forbes, the aim was simple: to gain line honors in the Bermuda Race and to be able to return via the Intercostal Waterways. Designed by Phil L. Rhodes (1895–1974), *Escapade* was launched on 25 May 1938 at the Luders Marine shipyard in Stamford, Connecticut. She is a superb yacht with a large sail plan, a wide beam and a blue hull, which gave rise to her nickname "Blue Max." *Escapade* earned the title "Queen of the Lakes" in 1950 and the following year she won every single race she entered.

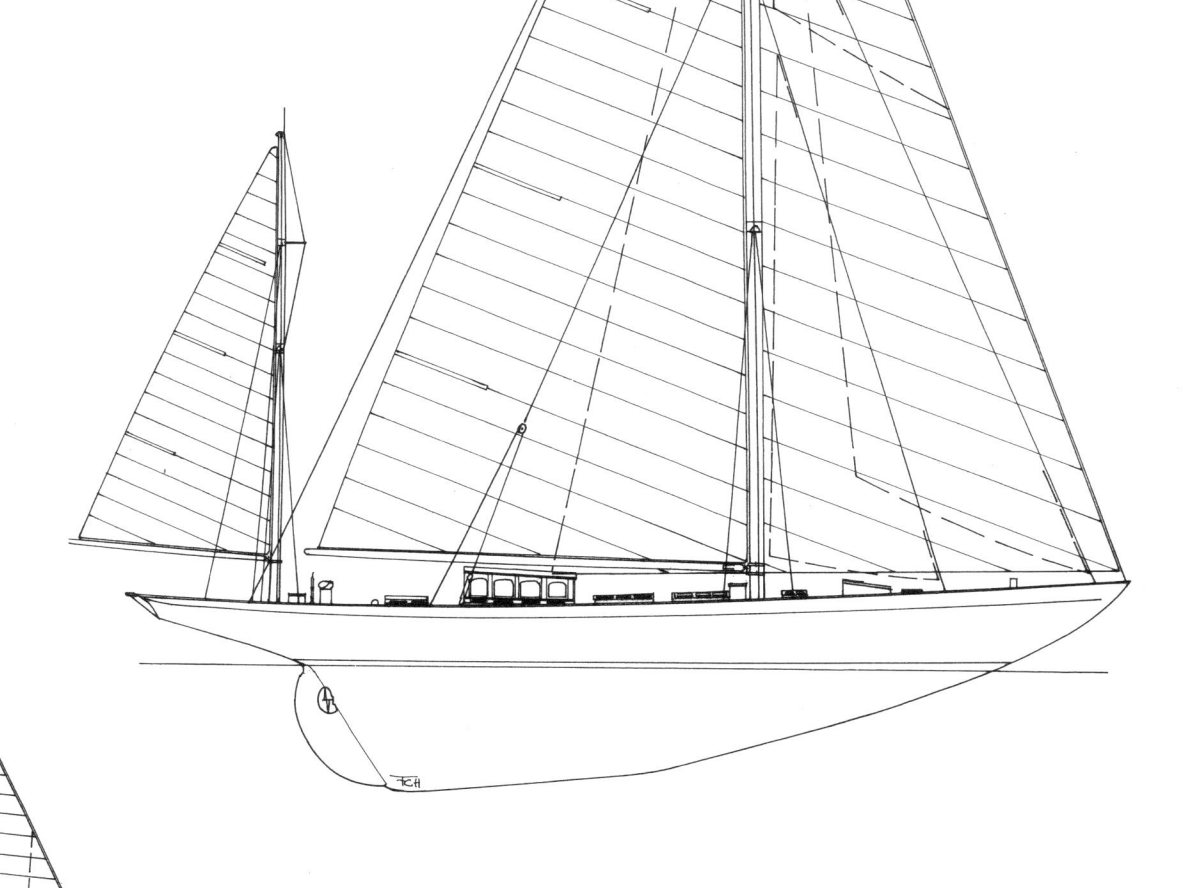

Mariella

ABOVE The yawl *Mariella*, built by the William Fife and Sons shipyard in Fairlie, was designed by Alfred Mylne (1872–1951). Son of an ironsmith in Glasgow, Mylne was 20 years old when he started working for Georges L. Watson and was given the chance to work on the plans of *Britannia* (1893), the famous royal cutter. The 24.07-meter *Mariella* was launched for James D. Paterson at the start of the 1938 season. In 1981, she was acquired by an American couple, Mr and Mrs Donald Glen, who decided to restore her in Porto Cervo in collaboration with Malcolm J. Horsley. The teak accommodation was modernized but the oak saloon remained the same.

Latifa

BELOW The yawl *Latifa* was built at Fairlie and launched in 1936. Constructed for ocean racing, William Fife considered her to be his finest design. It was for this reason that she was given her name, a Hebrew word meaning "most beautiful." Fife's sisters had a copper model of her made for a weather vane for the Fairlie Paris Church when he died in 1944, which till swings to windward on the spire. This beautifully maintained classic boat is still a beauty to behold. Restored at Cantieri Beconcini in La Spezia, all of the deck hardware has been preserved giving her an authentic look and feel.

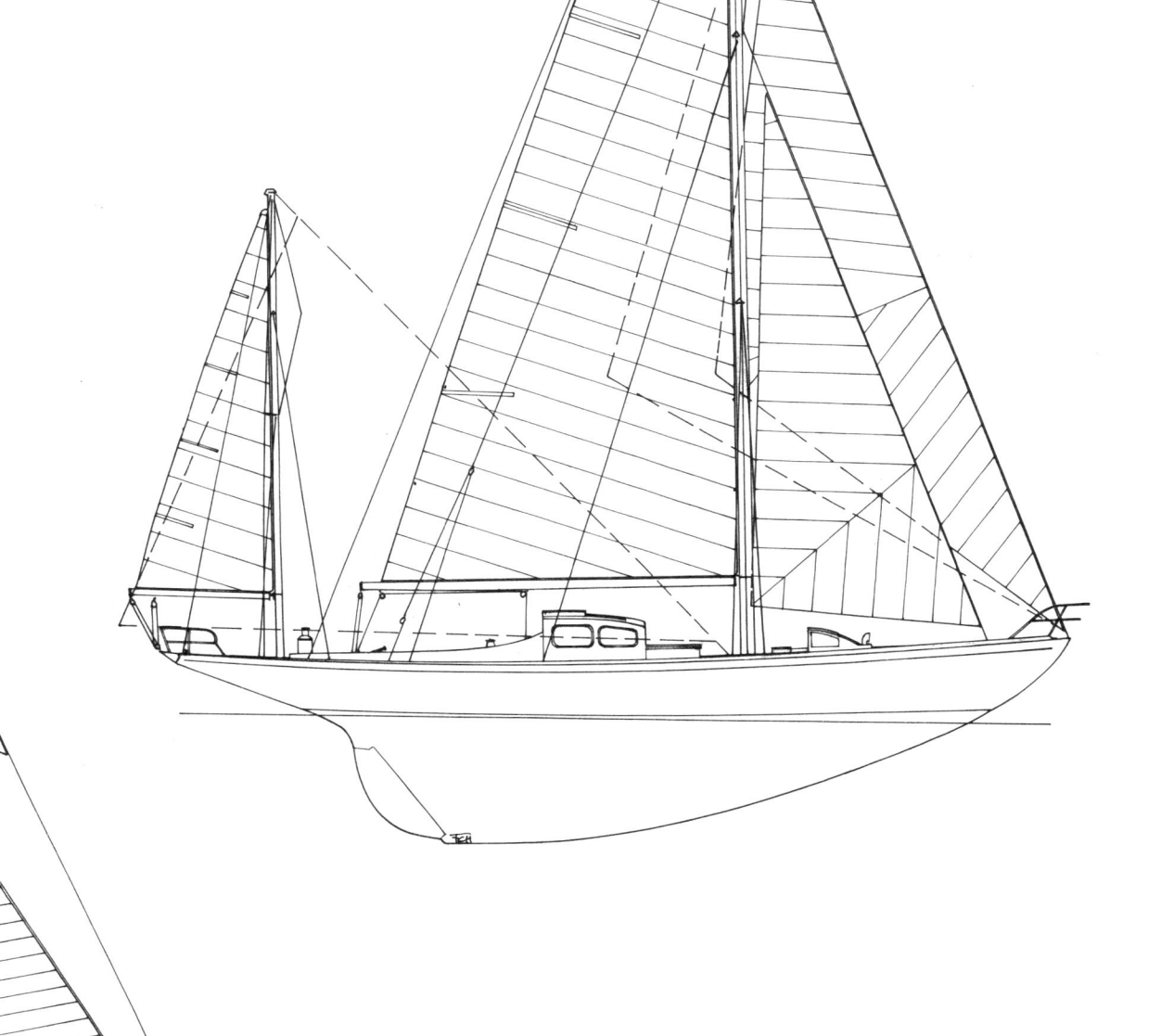

Bloodhound

ABOVE Built at the same time as *Eilean* in June 1936, *Bloodhound* had a remarkable pedigree. Designed by the British naval architect Charles Nicholson (1868–1954), her lines drawing was used for two other famous sailing yachts, *Foxhood* built in 1935, and *Stiarna* in 1937. The three sister-ships were built by the Camper & Nicholsons shipyard in Gosport using the same materials and teak planking. *Bloodhound* had the peculiarity of a yawl rigging and original deck and accommodation plans, designed by Olin Stephens.

MEAN PRESSURE
Isobars of the normal reduced barometric pressure for the month are shown by full and dashed *blue* lines. Any wide departure from the normal pressure reveals some disturbance and may indicate a coming gale.

The United States Government has not ... of Estonia, Latvia and Lithuania

The gale figures for t... *red* numerals within ... These show the averag... able ships observatio... least force 8 were ... given, gales may hav... too infrequently to gi...

On the Wind

BRITISH EXHIBITION—COPENHAGEN, Sept. 18-Oct. 3.—Messrs. Kenneth Long & Co., Ltd., Marine Export Concessionaires, are displaying notable marine products, Precision Marine Radio Receivers, Aquajet Outboard Motors, Afco Engineered Yacht Equipment, Granta Folding Canoes, Danforth Anchors, McGeoch Ships' Electrical Fittings. Large attendance of Scandinavian buyers is anticipated.

"ALONE AT SEA," by J. A. Hampton, reviewed in the August issue of *Yachting World*, is being distributed in the British Isles by Capt. O. M. Watts Ltd.

NEW MONITOR PRESSURE SPRAYER, price 35s, will spray water, oil, paraffin up to 10 ft. It is manufactured by Monitor Engineering & Oil Appliances, Ltd., Birmingham, 9.

ABBEY KAPOK Manufacturing Co., Ltd., have brought out a booklet on the properties of Kapok. Copies can be obtained from them at Selinas Lane, Dagenham, Essex.

EUSTACE WATKINS, LTD., Chelsea Manor Street, London S.W.3, now offer the following E.W. Lightcraft:—

	£	s
9 ft General-purpose Dinghy	46	10
9ft Sailing Dinghy	69	10
12 ft General-purpose Dinghy	65	0
12 ft Sailing Dinghy	97	10
12 ft Inboard Dinghy Launch	195	0

An illustrated catalogue is available.

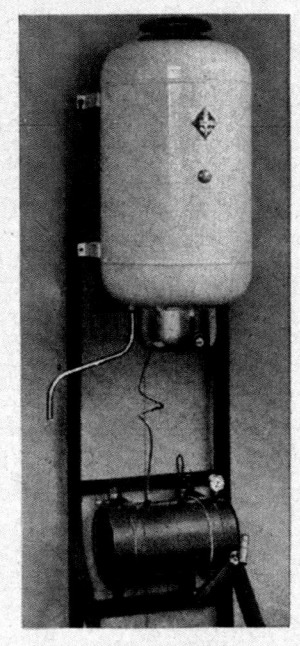

A WAR MEMORIAL to the ex-Cadets and staff of the Royal Naval College, Dartmouth, killed during the 1939-45 war, is contemplated and a fund has been opened. Subscriptions should be made out to the Royal Naval College, Dartmouth, War Memorial Fund and sent to the Commanding Officer of the Royal Naval College.

FELTHAM 8-10 h.p. PETROL/PARAFFIN ENGINE has now been approved by the Ministry of Transport as standard design for installation in auxiliary motor lifeboats of Class B. This engine is manufactured by Bruce & Holroyd, Ltd., 86, High Street, Feltham, Middlesex.

TROUBADOUR, 1,250 tons, owned before the war by Miss Barbara Hutton, has been sold by the Admiralty to a shipping company of Haugesund, Norway, who intend converting her. She was sold to the Admiralty at the outbreak of war for one dollar.

A NEW DINGHY BLOCK has been produced by Viking Marine, Ltd., Cole Road, Twickenham, Middlesex. With Tufnol sheave and cheeks of polished B.B.3 Birmabright, it weighs 1 oz, will take up to 1-inch rope, and can be safely loaded up to 224 lb. (Illustrated below.)

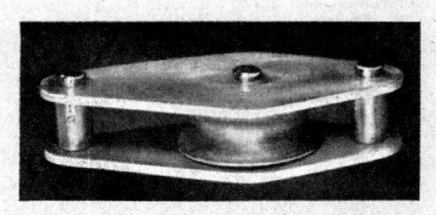

ARALDITE, new synthetic resin adhesive for bonding metals, glass, china and other materials, originally developed by Messrs. Ciba, Ltd., Basle, is being marketed in England by Aero Research, Ltd., Duxford, Cambridge. It is claimed that this adhesive possesses exceptional strength and endurance.

SYDNEY-HOBART RACE: E. A. Wedderspoon and Pat Garvin intend to enter their new yacht *Estrellita* for the next race. Built at Raymond Terrace, Hunter River, near Newcastle, Australia, she is a 90ft auxiliary schooner with a 165 h.p. engine and is claimed to be the largest yacht in the Southern Hemisphere.

NEW MARINA AT NASSAU, BAHAMAS, is nearing completion. Accommodating 100 vessels, this Marina, under the direction of Robert H. Symonette, a young Bahamian yachtsman, will provide first-class facilities for servicing yachts.

NEW ST. MALO - LA BAULE SERVICE: A new 2nd class express railcar service is now running on Tuesdays and Thursdays between St. Malo and Le Croisic in connection with the sailings of the British Railways (Southern Region) Southampton-St. Malo steamer *Falaise*. This railcar serves Pornichet, La Baule, Pouliguen and Barts-sur-mer, and takes less than three hours to do the 148-mile journey between St. Malo and La Baule.

STORAGE WATER HEATERS (BOTTLED GAS AND PARAFFIN) SUITABLE FOR YACHTS, ARE MANUFACTURED BY BARRALETS. LTD., WATER HEATERS, ADDINGTON SQUARE, LONDON, S.E.5.

MOULDED PLYWOOD VIKING CLASS 24FT. W.L. SLOOPS ARE BEING OFFERED BY LUDERS MARINE CONSTRUCTION CO., STAMFORD, CONN., U.S.A. AS COMPLETE BOATS OR AS BARE HULLS

YACHTING WORLD PUBLICATIONS

YACHT RACING: A Textbook of the Sport, by Major Brooke Hekstall-Smith. Revised and enlarged by G. Sambrooke Sturgess. 332 pp. with 149 diagrams. Price 25s. by post 25s. 8d.

THE NEW N.A.Y.R.U. RULES EXPLAINED (Vanderbilt Rules) by G. Sambrooke Sturgess. Price 2/6 or by post 2/8.

SETS OF PLANS:

	£	s	d
Yachting World Cadet (for young people), designed by Jack Holt, no Royalty	1	5	0
"Uffa King" National 12ft Class Dinghy, designed by Uffa Fox	1	2	6
Designer's Royalty	1	1	0
"Uffa Ace" National 18ft Centreboard Class Boat, designed by Uffa Fox	1	5	0
Designer's Royalty	1	1	0
15ft Knockabout Sharpie, designed by R. F. Freeman, no Royalty	1	3	6
14ft Yachting World Merlin Class, designed by Jack Holt	1	7	6
Designer's Royalty	1	1	0
Yachting World Motor Cruiser, Jenny Wren, designed by Arthur C. Robb	1	8	0
Designer's Royalty		5	0

These publications may be obtained from YACHTING WORLD, Dorset House, Stamford Street, London, S.E.1.

NOTE.—ROYALTIES must be paid by builders to YACHTING WORLD on each boat as soon as the keel is laid.

On The Clyde

A NEW race in the cruising category is likely to be on the programme of the Clyde Cruising Club next summer. At the half-yearly general meeting of the Club, at which Mr. Robert J. Dunlop, Vice-Commodore, presided, it was announced that two members had offered to present to the Club a challenge trophy for a race down the Firth of Clyde and return. It has already been suggested by the donors that the event should start at Hunter's Quay and finish at Lamlash, and that the award should be known as "The Arran Trophy."

The C.C.C. has, of course, for the past two years, organized a longish race, beginning at Fairlie, where the Club's headquarters now are, and circumnavigating first Ailsa Craig and then the Isle of Arran, and finishing at Fairlie.

This race, in actual fact, took the place of the real long-distance test which the Club ran before the war—from the Clyde around the Isle of Man, or the Rockabill and back. It is to be hoped that the more modest events of the past two years are not going to take the place permanently of the more ambitious. The Cruising Club is not, of course, out to promote ocean racing as such, but events which encourage skill and good seamanship come, surely, within its province.

But to return to the C.C.C. meeting. The report by Mr. John C. Dobie, honorary secretary, on the financial situation was considered very satisfactory. During the year 79 new members had been admitted, and a new edition of the famous Sailing Directions had been issued. Mr. R. G. Mowat was thanked for his work on this latest edition. A discussion ensued as to the number and nature of the races provided by the Club, and after several different views had been put forward the chairman said that, in considering acceptance of the new trophy, the committee would bear in mind the various opinions expressed.

The annual dance of the Club was held last month in the Grosvenor Restaurant, Glasgow, and attracted 450 members and friends. Among those present were Vice-Commodore Dunlop and Mrs. Dunlop; Mr. R. M. Teacher, Commodore of the Royal Clyde Yacht Club, and Mrs. Teacher; Captain John Illingworth (owner of Myth of Malham) and Mrs. Illingworth; Mr. Nigel Laird, Vice-Commodore of the Royal Scottish Motor Yacht Club, and Mrs. Laird; Dr. J. P. Leckie (owner of Cymbeline) and Mrs. Leckie; Mr. W. P. Findlay (owner of Eileen) and Mrs. Findlay; Mr. Walter Bergius (owner of Chameleon) and Mrs. Bergius. Mr. Dobie was in charge of the arrangements.

The principal event in yachting circles on the Clyde this month is the meeting of the Clyde Yacht Clubs' Conference. I hear that at this meeting a statement on the finances of the International Clyde Fortnight will be made.

There is an old test which used to be given to typists—"Now is the time for all good men to come to the aid of the Party." For the word "Party" read "Yacht Club," and you have the password for this season of the year. Annual meetings seem to be the only form of yachting amusement at present.

Mrs. I. M. Seex presented the cups for the 1947 season to the winners, and the following office-bearers were elected: Commodore, Mr. W. A. Rowat, Fortrose; Vice-Commodore, Mr. R. Fraser-Mackenzie; Rear-Commodore, Mr. R. Duffy, Inverness; secretary, Mr. D. Mackay, Scorguie; treas., Mr. G. C. Forber, Inverness.   A. G. CHRISTIE.

Union of International Motorboating

HELD in Brussels on November 6-8 the meeting of the Permanent Committee of the Union of International Motorboating was attended by delegates of eight nations. Great Britain was represented by Lt. Comdr. Arthur Bray. The delegates were given an official lunch by the Brussels Royal Yacht Club, and a banquet by the president. At the latter function a presentation was made to Mr. Arthur Bray and M. Maurice Pauwaert, the only delegates present at the original meeting in 1922.

It was decided that next year's Pavillon d'Or would take place in Holland, and a tribute was paid to Great Britain for her record entry in the 1947 rally held in Belgium.

Recognition of the A.P.B.A. Runabout and 91 cubic in rules should ensure close liaison between America and Europe.

It was decided as a result of last year's meeting to extend the scope of the Union, and to appoint associate members. Members now consist of four classes: (i) One commodore for each country. (ii) Two vice-commodores (vice and rear) for countries of less than 10 million inhabitants; three vice-commodores for countries of 10-20 million inhabitants. (iii) Patron members at the rate of one per 500,000 inhabitants. (iv) Associate members, numbers unlimited. Flag officers to be elected by national authorities.

Consideration was given to the new European Outboard Championship rules. The number of world record certificates issued is an indication of the Union's activities. These are as follows: Italy 96, U.S.A. 41, Great Britain 28, France 20, Germany 13, Holland 8, Belgium 4, Sweden 2.

In 1948 the following programme was agreed: Championship meetings—June 6, Milan, Outboard X Class and all classes; June 12-13, Paris, Outboards; June 27, Liège, Outboard Class A, Grand Prix of Belgium, all classes; July, Mora, Grand Prix of Sweden, Outboards; July 16-19, Geneva or Lausanne, Outboards, C Class and all classes; August 15, Santander, Outboards. Other meetings: July 24-25, Evian, all classes and Tourism; August 1, Venice, all classes and Tourism; August 8, San Remo, Tourism; August 30-31, Oulton Broad, Outboards and all classes; September 11-12, Como, all classes.

LT. COMDR. ARTHUR BRAY, M. A. BUYSSE AND M. M. PAUWAERT.

OFF-SHORE RACING FIXTURES

R.O.R.C.
PROVISIONAL 1948 PROGRAMME

Date	Race	Classes
May 14	Harwich to Hook	All Classes
June 11	Harwich to Norway	All Classes
June 25	Channel Race	2 and 3
July 12	Clyde to Dunlaoghaire (via South Rock and Isle of Man)	All Classes
July 16	Cowes to Dinard	All Classes
July 17 or July 28	Dunlaoghaire to Brixham	All Classes
July 23	Ostend to Solent	All Classes
July 30	Solent to Brixham (via Le Havre only). For Mr. M. Mason's Cup	All Classes
August 6	Brixham to Santander	1 and 2
August 13	Brixham to Belle Isle	2 and 3
August 17	Santander to Belle Isle	1 and 2
July 2	Island Sailing Club Round the Island Race	

IRISH SEA
PROVISIONAL 1948 PROGRAMME

May 14.—R.A. and R.D.Y.C., Beaumaris to Holyhead.
May 14.—R. Mersea Y.C., Rock Ferry to Holyhead.
May 16.—Holyhead to Kingstown.
June 5.—R.D.Y.C., Beaumaris-Middle Mouse-Beaumaris.
June 12.—T.S.C., Rock Ferry-Morecambe Bay L.V.-Bar L.V.
June 18.—T.S.C., Midnight Race, Rock Ferry-Douglas.
July 17.—R. Mersea Y.C., Rock Ferry-Llandudno.
July 30.—R. Mersea Y.C., Irish Sea Race, Rock Ferry-Rockabill-Bar L.V.
Aug. 14.—R. Mersea Y.C., Rock Ferry-Queens Channel-W. Hoyle Buoy-Rock Ferry.
Sept. 4.—R.A.Y.C., Beaumaris-East Mouse-Wreck Buoy-Beaumaris.

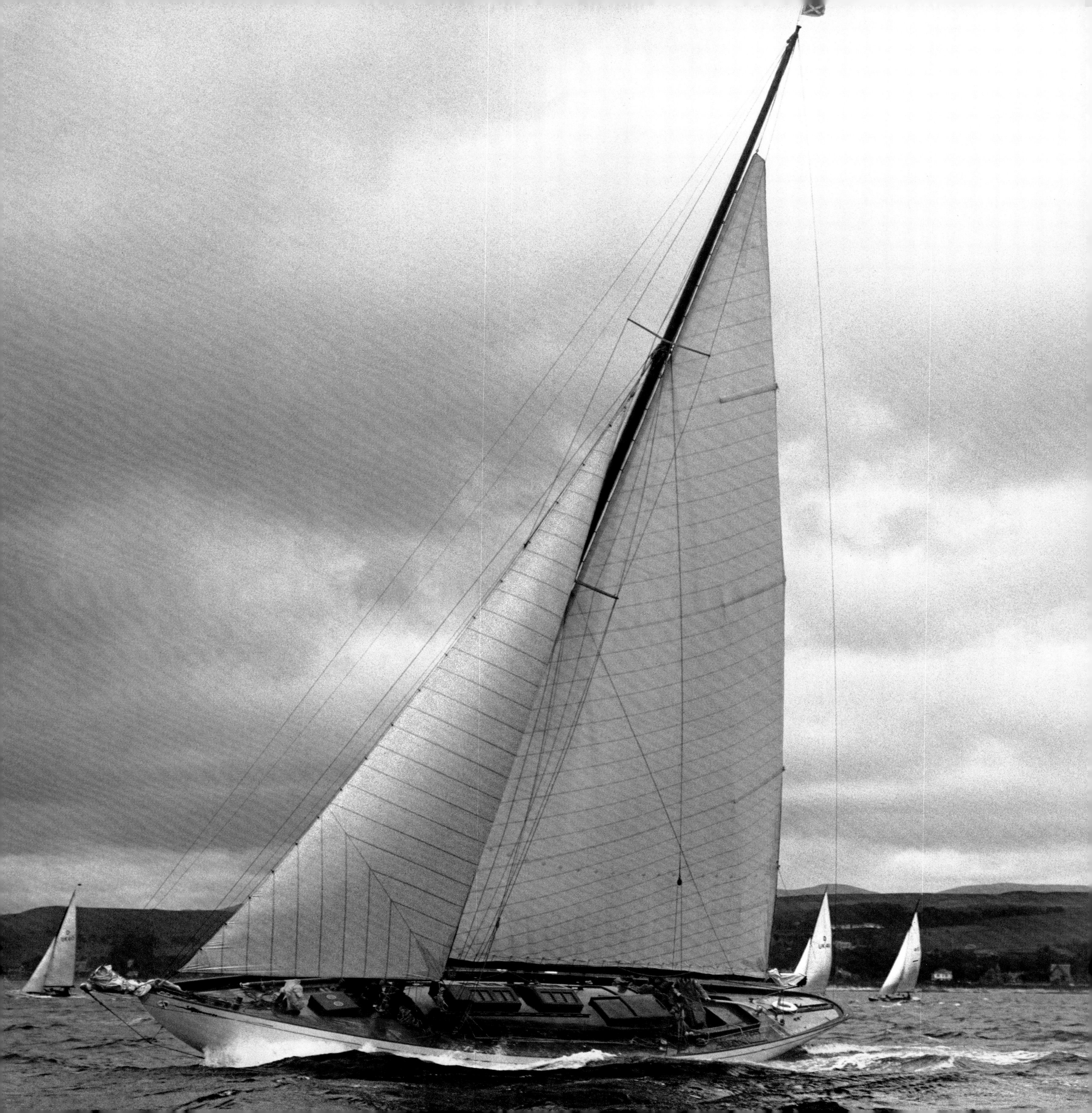

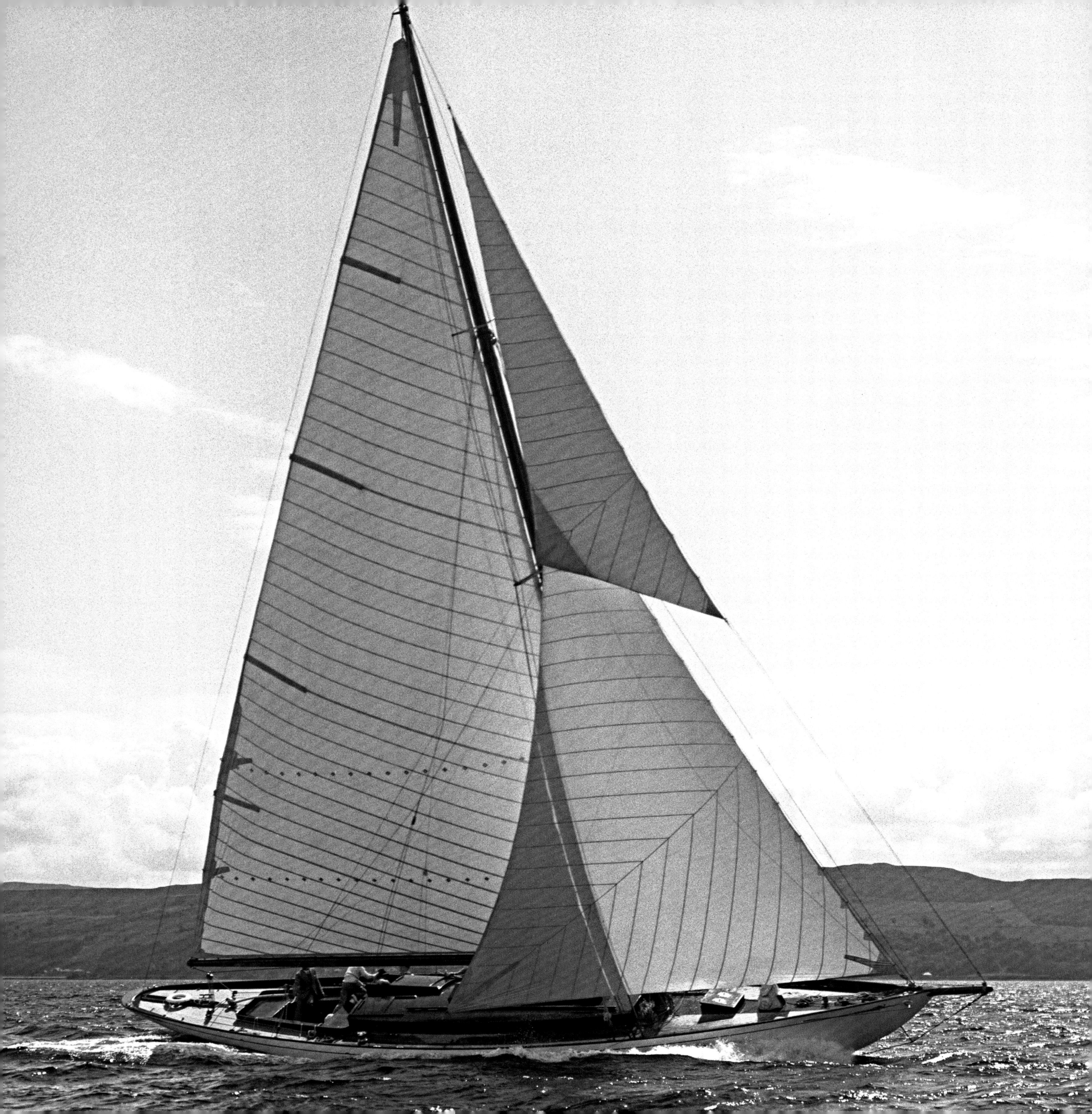

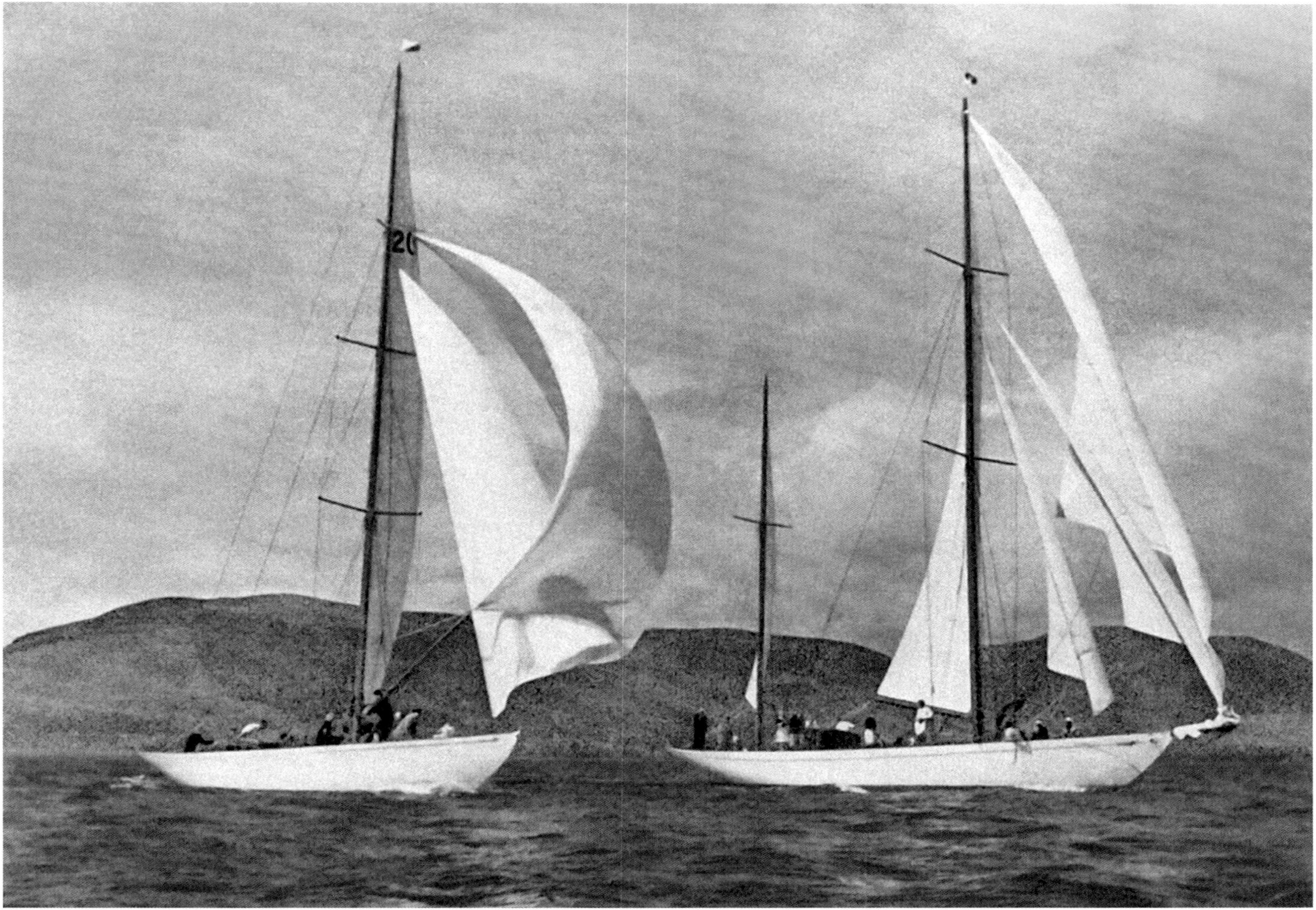

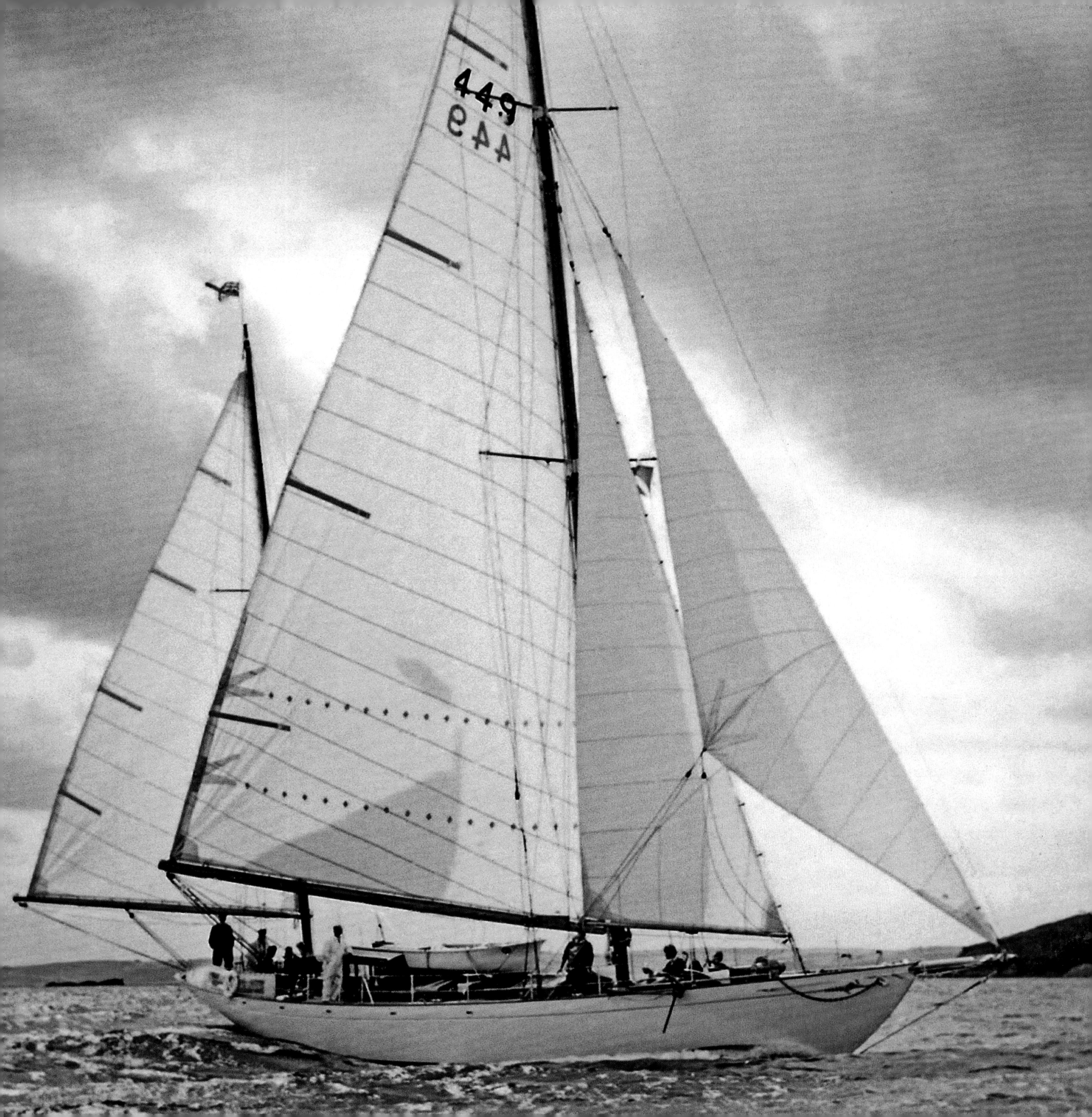
449
449

NEW OWNERS, NEW FITTING-OUT

From 1951, *Eilean* rarely appeared in the regatta records. Not that the ketch was obsolete or badly looked after, but the recent Royal Ocean Racing Club rating rules did not do her any favours. From then on, her owners preferred a second smaller yacht and kept *Eilean* for cruising and chartering. The ketch was modernised, the engine was regularly changed and the sails renewed.

Jack Salem, who bought the sailing yacht from P.H.N Ulander, ordered a new set of sails from Ratsey. At the beginning of 1952, he also had new sails cut for *Eilean* by Kenneth G. Mackenzie, a sailmaker from Sandbanks, and replaced the original petrol engine with a four-cylinder, 30 hp Coventry diesel engine.

At the end of the summer of 1955, Jack Salem put *Eilean* up for sale and acquired *Latifa*, the famous 1936 William Fife sailing yacht which had an impressive record of prizes, from Bermuda to the Fastnet, first as a cutter and then as a yawl. Jack Salem kept *Latifa* until 1970. The public can still admire her taking part in the *Panerai Classic Yachts Challenge*. Having been bought by Colonel Louis Franck, *Eilean* was equipped with yet another set of sails cut by Ratsey and a more powerful engine, a 4-cylinder, 52 hp Parsons. The Colonel, a keen yachtsman, was also the owner of the 6 Metre *Marletta*, which he kept until 1958. *Eilean* received new sails in 1957, this time cut by Gowen. The ketch continued as a cruising yacht, often chartered on both sides of the Atlantic. In 1961, Colonel Franck ordered a 32-metre steel motoryacht fitted with two 320 hp Man engines, from the shipyard De Vries Lentch in Amsterdam. *Bleu Albacore* was launched in June 1962 and the following year joined *Eilean* as a charter boat for the Colonel's company established in Bermuda. *Eilean* was again made more powerful with a 6-cylinder, 80 hp Perkins engine and more new sails ordered from Ratsey before the ketch was put up for sale.

When the new owner, Lord William Shawcross, bought *Eilean*, he had just sold his cutter *Stiarna* – a 32 metre Camper & Nicholsons – to Antony H. David Rowse, a London publisher. *Eilean*'s homeport was now Falmouth. Lord William Shawcross cruised extensively with his family and his friends. The yacht was very well looked after; Ratsey cut a few more sails between 1965 and 1966. To vary his nautical leisure activities, in 1967, Lord Shawcross bought *Faith*, a 20-metre motoryacht designed by Alfred Mylne in 1936. He replaced the two engines with 8-cylinder, 90 hp Perkins. Two years later, Lord Shawcross sold *Eilean* to the brothers Ernest and Richard Cuckson and the ketch returned to her homeport, Falmouth.

PAGE 69 In this photo taken in 1938, *Eileen*, with a cutter rig – although William Fife had originally suggested a yawl rig – powers under mainsail with one reef and staysail, at the hands of a reduced crew despite a fair breeze. Alexander L. W. Stevens is at the helm.

PAGE 70 *Eileen*, under full mainsail, main jib and flying jib. Alexander L. W. Stevens kept this yacht for some ten years before purchasing the 12 Metre *Jenetta*, which was designed by Alfred Mylne in 1939, when he was 92. Rescued by the Belgian Jean-Claude Joffre in Hawaii in 2005 where she was being used as a mobile home, *Eileen* is now undergoing a complete restoration in Ostend.

PAGE 71 During the Clyde International Fortnight, between Hunter's Quay and Kilcreggan, *Eilean* is competing against the cutter *Sonas*, built in 1935 by the William Fife and Son shipyard to a design by Alfred Mylne. The cutter has been called *Irina VII* since 1952 and she was restored in 2002.

FACING PAGE Since 1948, *Eilean* has had the racing sail number 449; this was allocated by the Royal Ocean Racing Club, better known as the RORC. Here, the ketch was photographed in the Solent at the beginning of the 1960s. Already, she has been fitted with halyard drum winches and she is sailing off the wind on port tack with all sails aloft, jib and staysail, main and mizzen.

ABOVE LEFT In the 1960s, three halyard drum winches were fitted on *Eilean*'s main mast and one on the mizzenmast. The spinnaker pole is tied in its supports on the port side of the deck; the stock anchor and the boathook are lashed on starboard.

ABOVE RIGHT *Eilean* swinging in the wind at anchor in the West Indies. Two awnings have been stretched on top of the booms, the swimming ladder is in place and all sails are furled. The tender is in the water and the red ensign flutters on the flagpole.

FACING PAGE Toward the end of 1955, Colonel Louis Franck acquired *Eilean* on behalf of the company Yacht Eilean Ltd. The ketch was given a new set of sails and fitted with a more powerful engine. The Colonel was a keen yachtsman and the owner of the 6 Metre *Marletta*. In August 1959, *Eilean* took part in the Royal Yacht Squadron regattas, including the *Britannia Challenge Cup* and the *New York Yacht Club Challenge Cup*. In 1963 he sold *Eilean* to Lord Shawcross.

The Cucksons only kept her for three years before putting her back on the market. Then in 1973, *Eilean* was acquired by the charter and broker company, McKinney Bancroft & Hughes, under the name of Ketch *Eilean* Ltd., and registered in Nassau, Bahamas. She cruised between the Virgin Islands and the Bahamas, crossing the Atlantic to spend the summer season in the Mediterranean. She was well maintained but the structural work required by her great age was not done. Based at first in Saint Thomas, *Eilean* moved to Antigua, which became her favorite resort island.

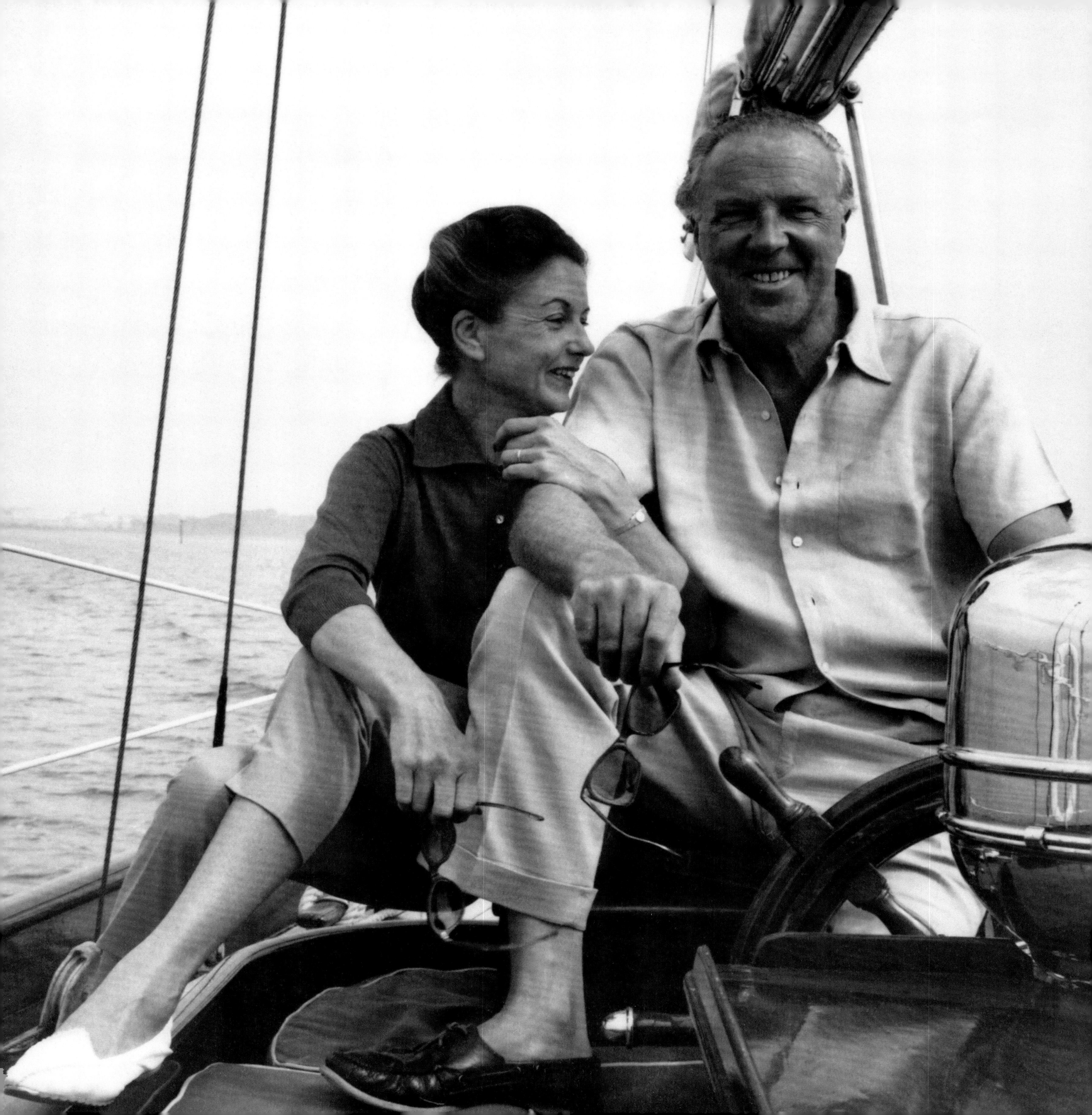

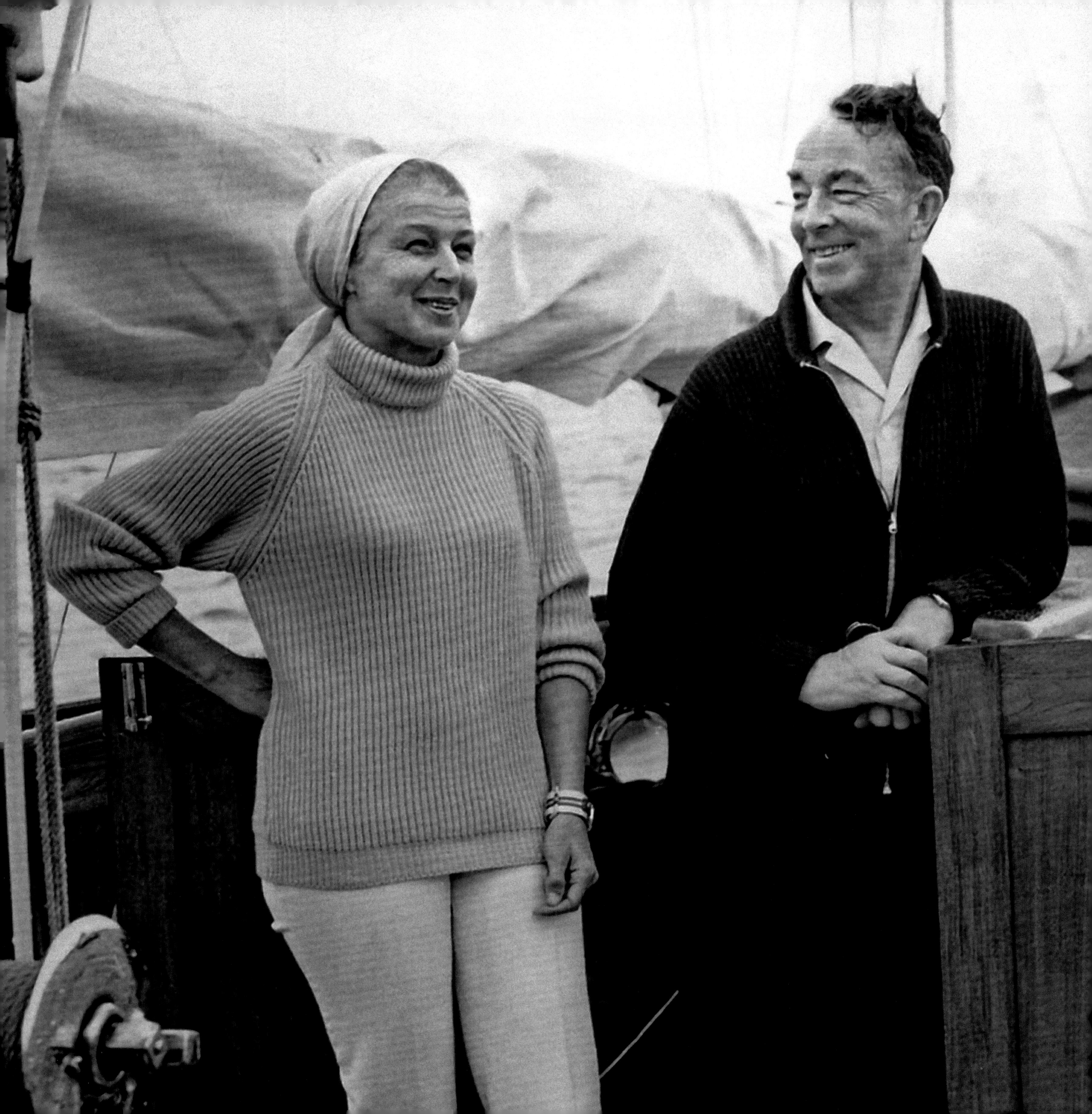

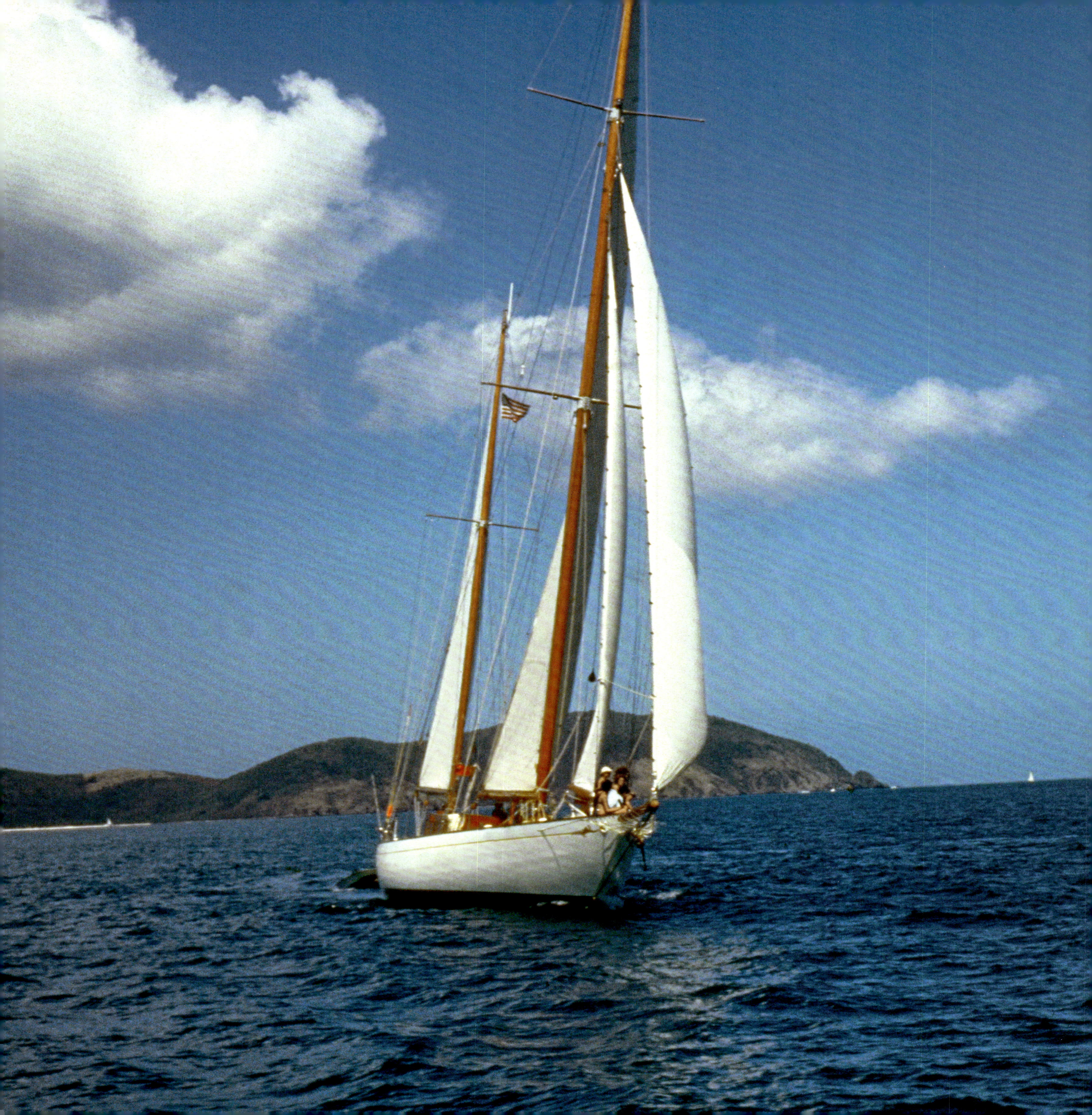

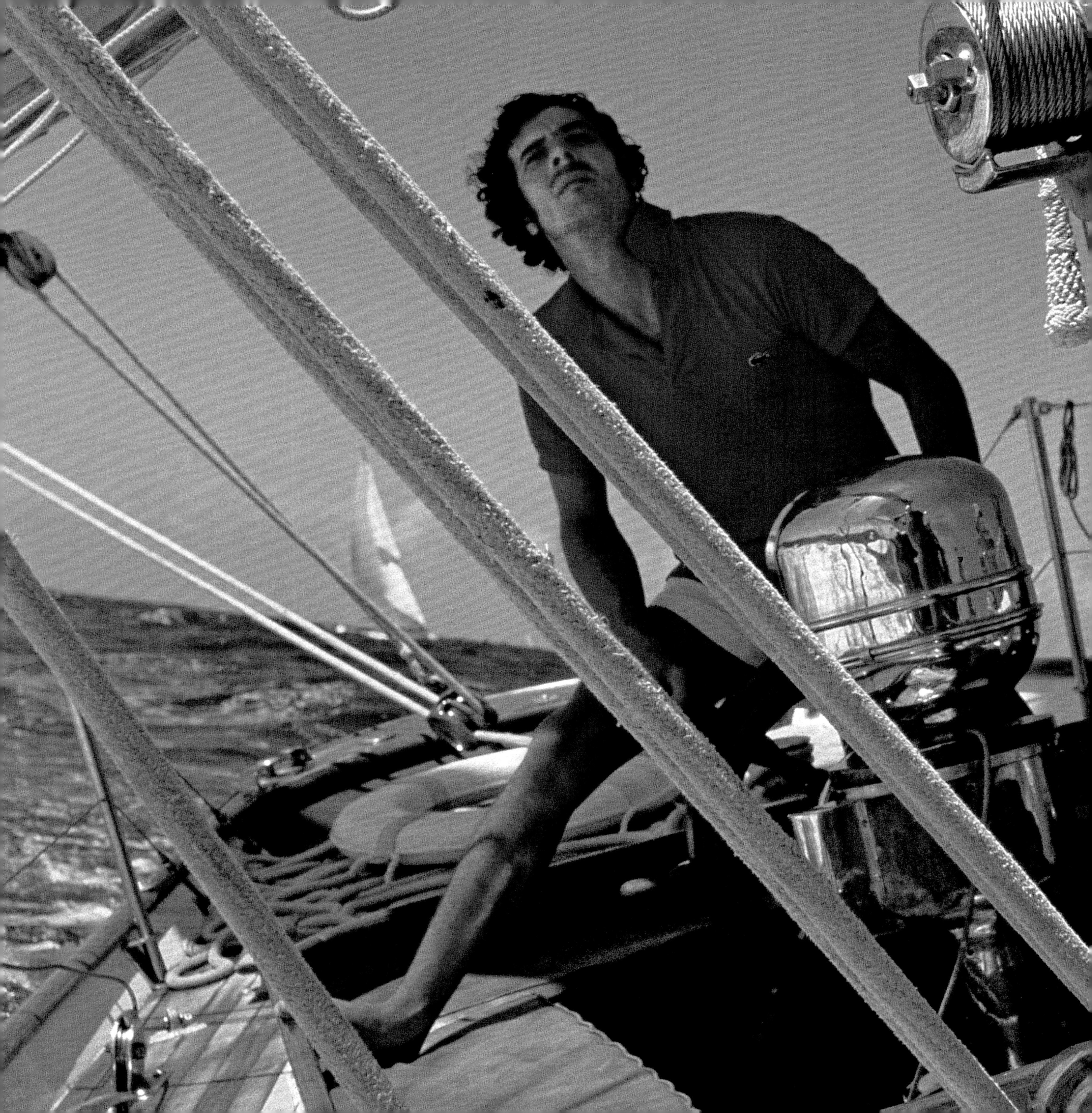

JOHN SHEARER, ARCHITECT AND NAVIGATOR

John Shearer already knew of *Eilean* when he discovered her off Malta in 1974. He was so overwhelmed that he decided there and then that this yacht would become his home, his life. As someone who was already passionate about classic sailing boats, he appreciated that *Eilean* was one of the most elegant ever built by William Fife III and that it would be difficult to find a finer yacht. In good condition, she was also the right size for him to live on board and entertain keen sailors on the high seas or in remote, attractive anchorages when chartered. In high season, whenever *Eilean*'s gangplank was laid on the quay, a queue of rich visitors fascinated by the authenticity of this masterpiece would quickly form. Maintenance was not a problem as far as John was concerned as he was a jack-of-all-trades and determined to reinvest all the profits from his charter work into the ketch.

Shearer acquired what he called 'the most beautiful of the Fifes' in 1974. Over the following years, he took her to the West Indies in winter to cruise with a few passengers. He lived on board *Eilean* all the year round, assisted by two or three crewmembers. In 1982, as May Fife recalled earlier, the pop group Duran Duran chartered the yacht. Simon Le Bon, the group's singer was filmed boarding *Eilean* in a white suit for the filming of the video of their song *Rio*. John stayed on *Eilean* for several years. 'You can do what you like with this sailing boat', he said. 'I crossed the Atlantic about fifteen times, I went to the States and Latin America…'.

But like many boat owners before him, Captain John found it more and more difficult to find the ideal charter family. *Eilean* could be seen a lot of the time tied up in English Harbour on the island of Antigua. When he had no passengers on board, he went as far as crossing the ocean single-handed; he knew he had faithful customers on the Riviera. As May Fife related, it was during one of these crossings in 1984, on her way back from Porto Cervo to Antigua, in the commercial port of Malaga, *Eilean* was struck by a ferry coming from Morocco that had lost two motors. When the ferry entered the port, it struck four boats, among them, *Eilean*. Although her mizzenmast was broken, John managed to reach his island of Antigua where a total refit was required: 'I risked damaging the boat further,' he said, 'therefore, I decided to decommission her and do some major work'.

Although the cost of that project was way over his budget, John Shearer was skilled and determined: he started the repairs himself. He anchored *Eilean* up a creek in Antigua, tied up alongside a decommissioned tugboat he had refloated, and for months on end, he removed worn parts, welded new ones, forged others, and even cannibalised some of the tug to repair his yacht. But most of the steel frames turned out to be damaged by rust, the mahogany

PAGE 76 Lord Shawcross, on board *Eilean*, which he owned from 1963 to 1969, here with his second wife, Joan Winifred.

PAGE 77 *Eilean* during the 1979 Antigua Regatta. The three deckhands are preparing to hoist the flying jib to the top of the mast to cover the whole of the foretriangle.

FACING PAGE Often sailing his superb William Fife ketch single-handed, John Shearer said she was the most beautiful yacht in the world.

FACING PAGE *Eilean* moored in Antigua, sails furled and hatches open to air the cabin. The crew has gone diving to catch a few lobsters to be served for the evening meal with some exotic fruit. Life on board is governed by the periods of charter. The low season is when *Eilean* is used as a pleasure yacht.

FOLLOWING PAGES For more than twelve years, *Eilean*, a great traveller, graced the West Indies and the Caribbean waters with her beauty. Most summers, she crossed the Atlantic to return to the Solent or the Mediterranean, wherever the charters were booked; sometimes, she headed south and cruised along the coasts of South America.

fittings eaten by worms, and the spars by termites. In fact, *Eilean* was held together only by her teak planking, impervious to rot thanks to its oily composition. While he waited to carry on with the restoration of *Eilean*, John worked as skipper on *Mariella*, a 1938 yawl built by Willam Fife & Son to plans by Alfred Mylne. Once again, he had the unparalleled pleasure of steering a proud classic sailing yacht. Unfortunately, during John's absence, *Eilean* sprang a leak and sank. When the ketch was refloated, she was in a pitiful state. John's original motivation had worn out, the project had grown too big, and too complex for him to manage alone. He admitted the best course of action was to sell her, but the price he put on *Eilean* was thought prohibitive. Derigged, with broken gunwales, removed top rails, unusable deck gear, and still tied up to some Caribbean mangrove branches, *Eilean* was left to stagnate. Professionals did not rate the chances of survival of this noble ketch. Baum & König, brokers in Hamburg, received an offer from an Italian client, who eventually gave up because of the price demanded. Her only chance to be saved would be another case of love at first sight.

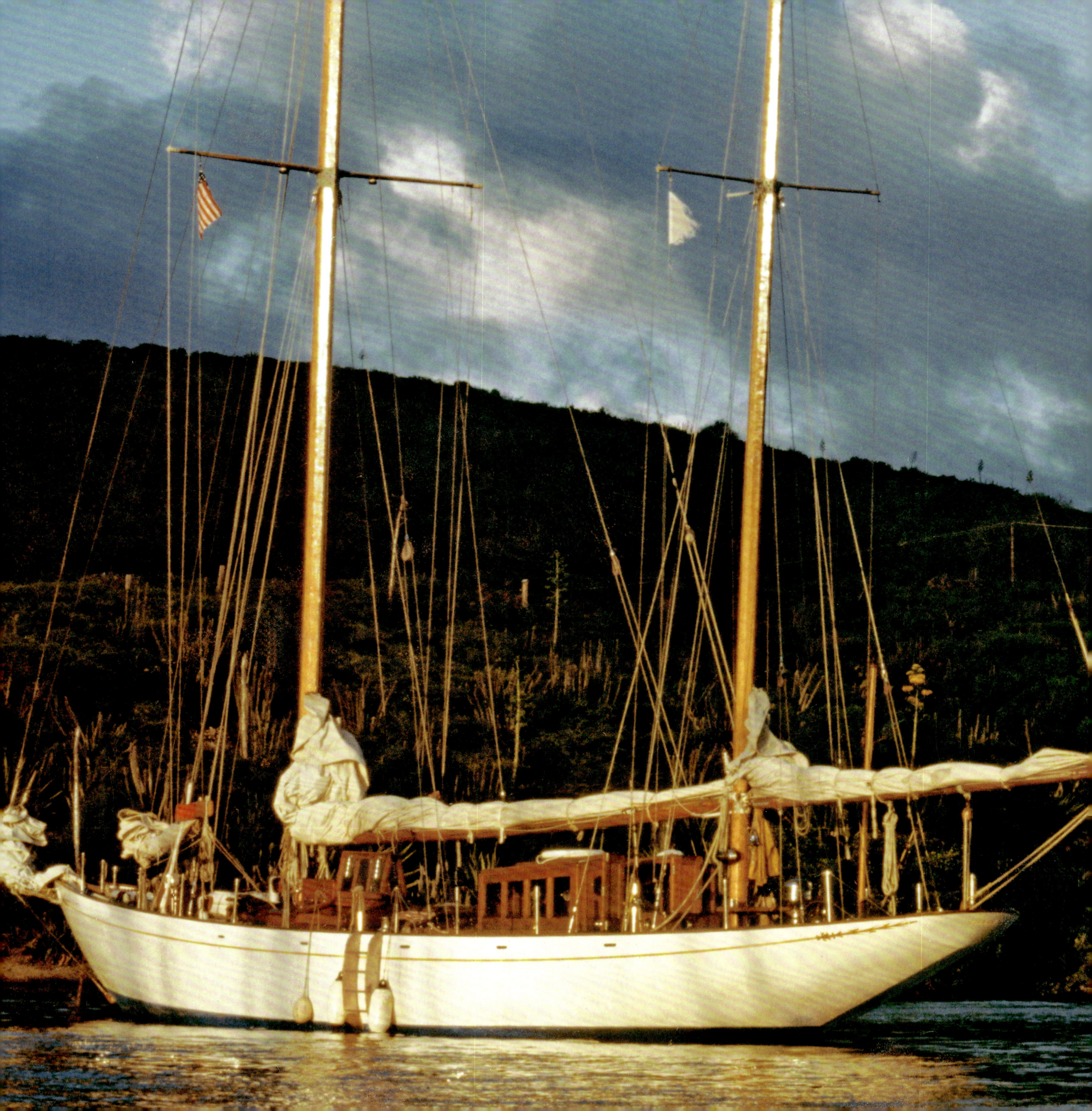

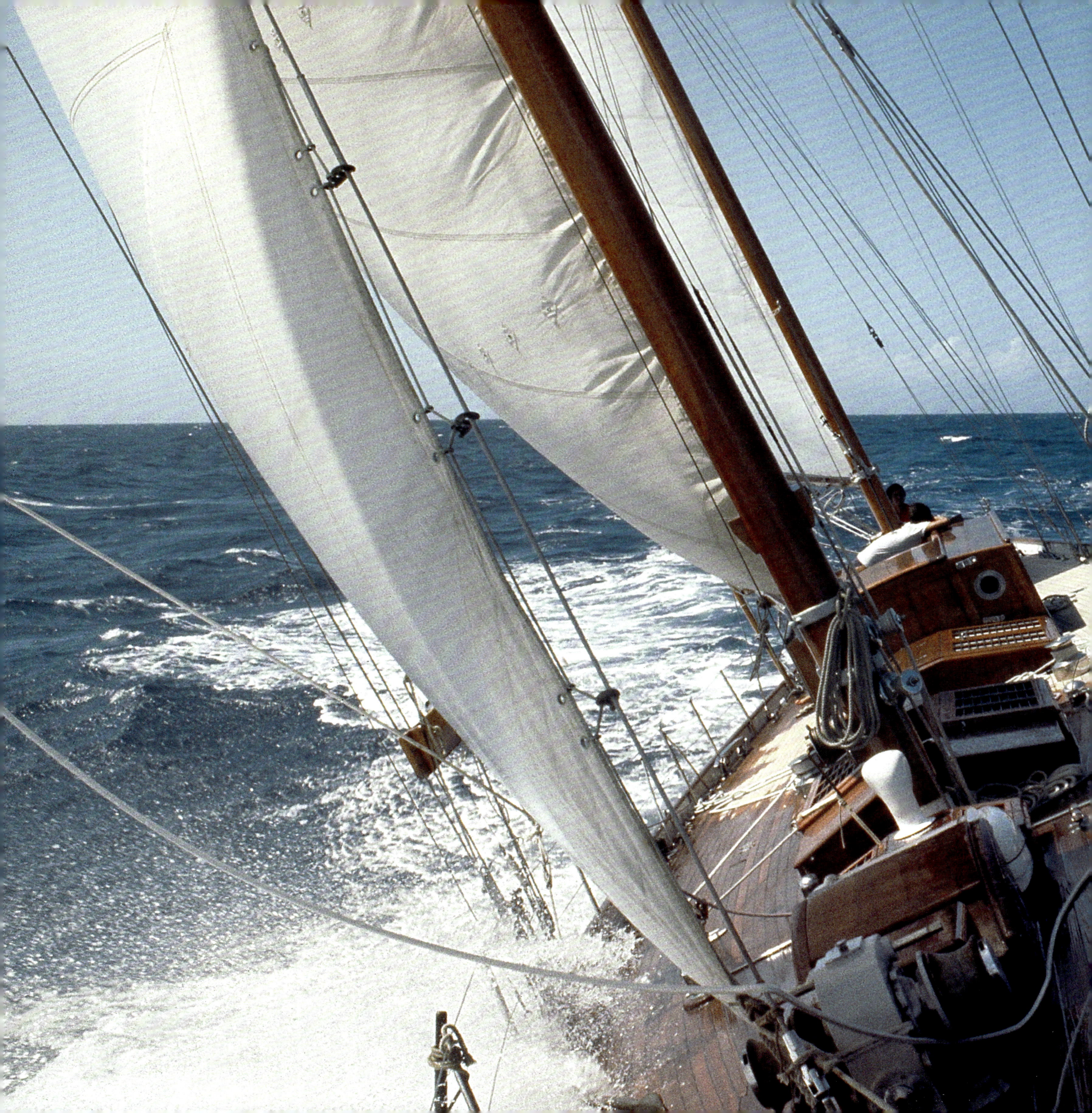

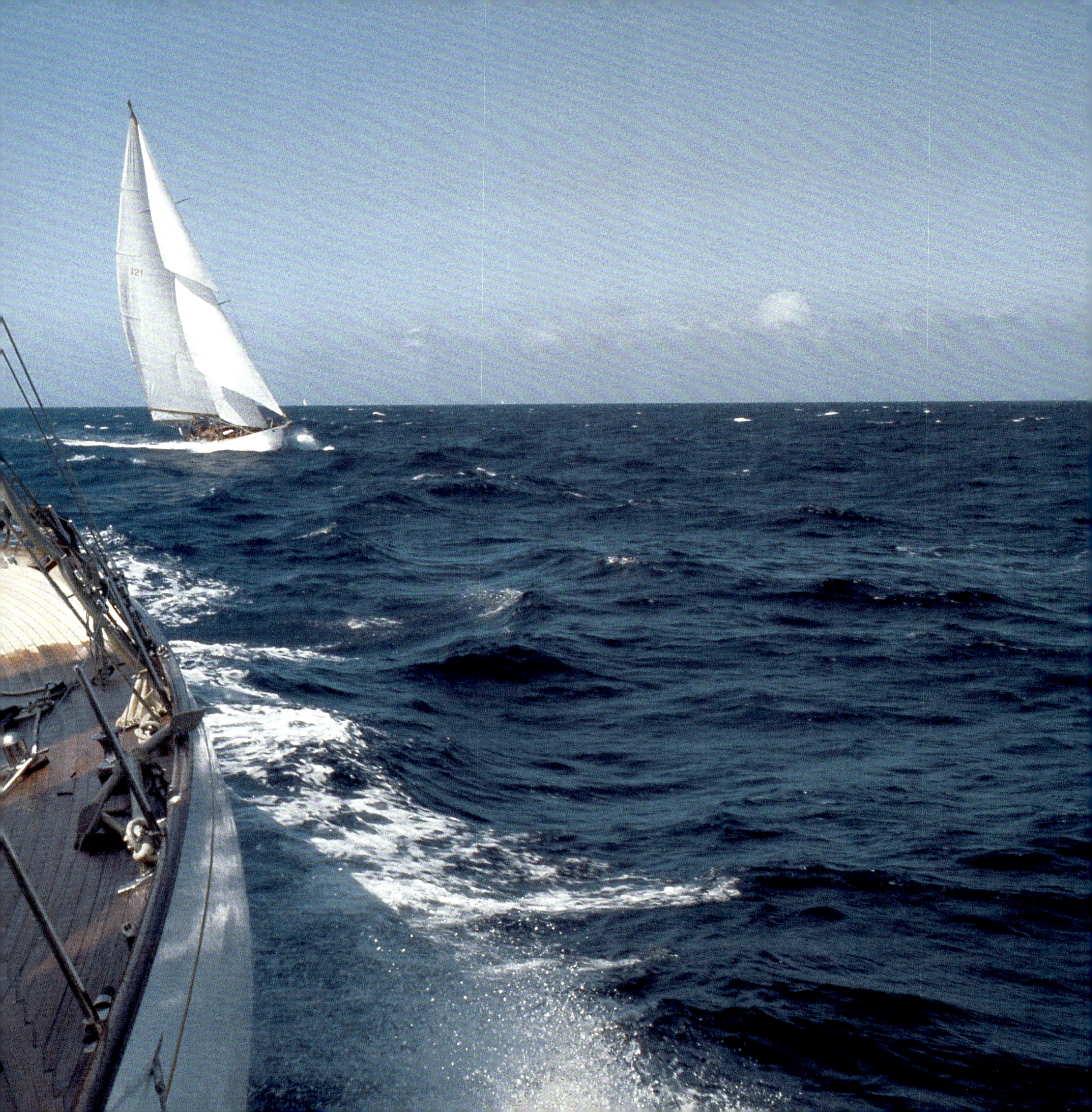
121

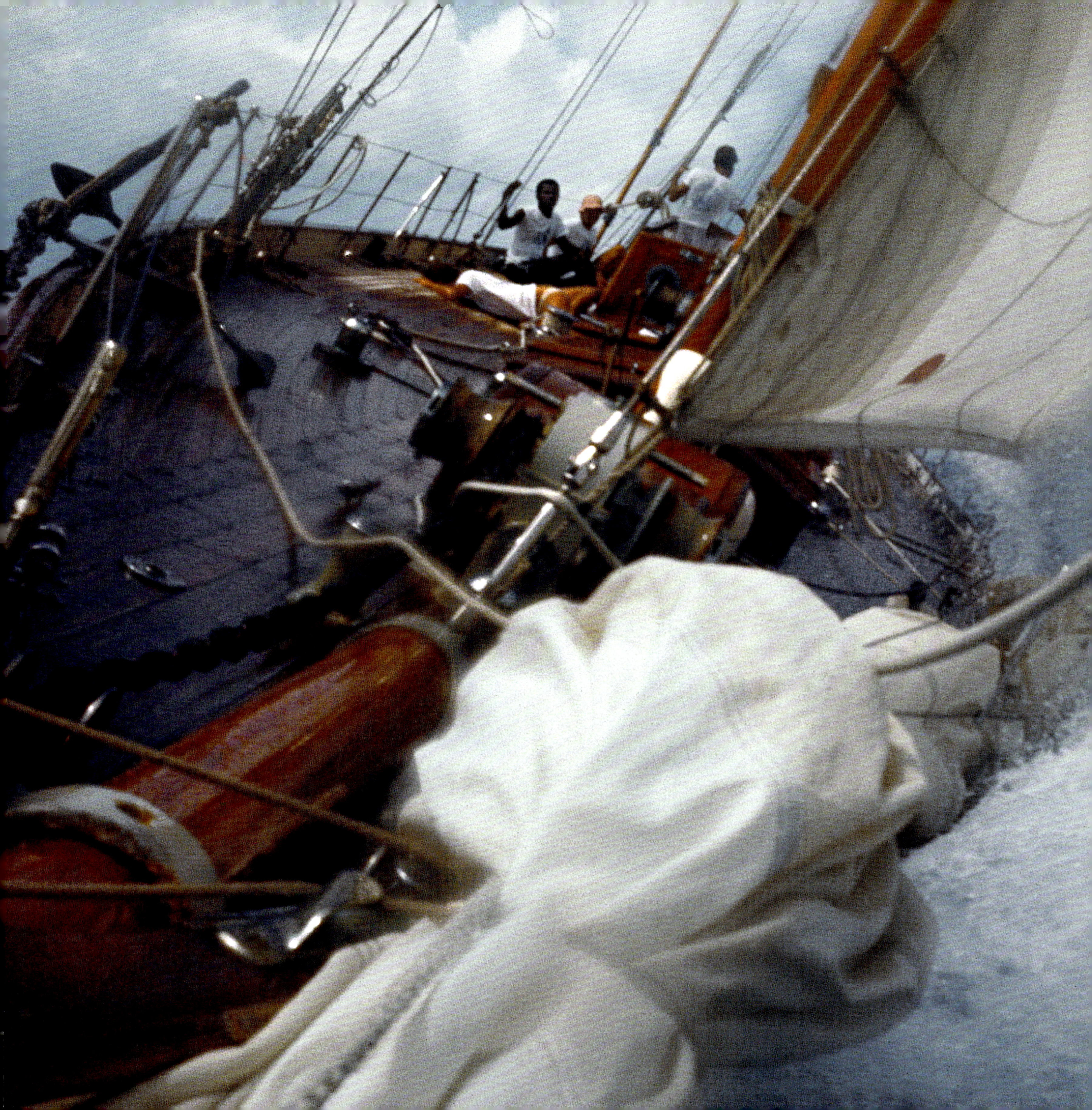

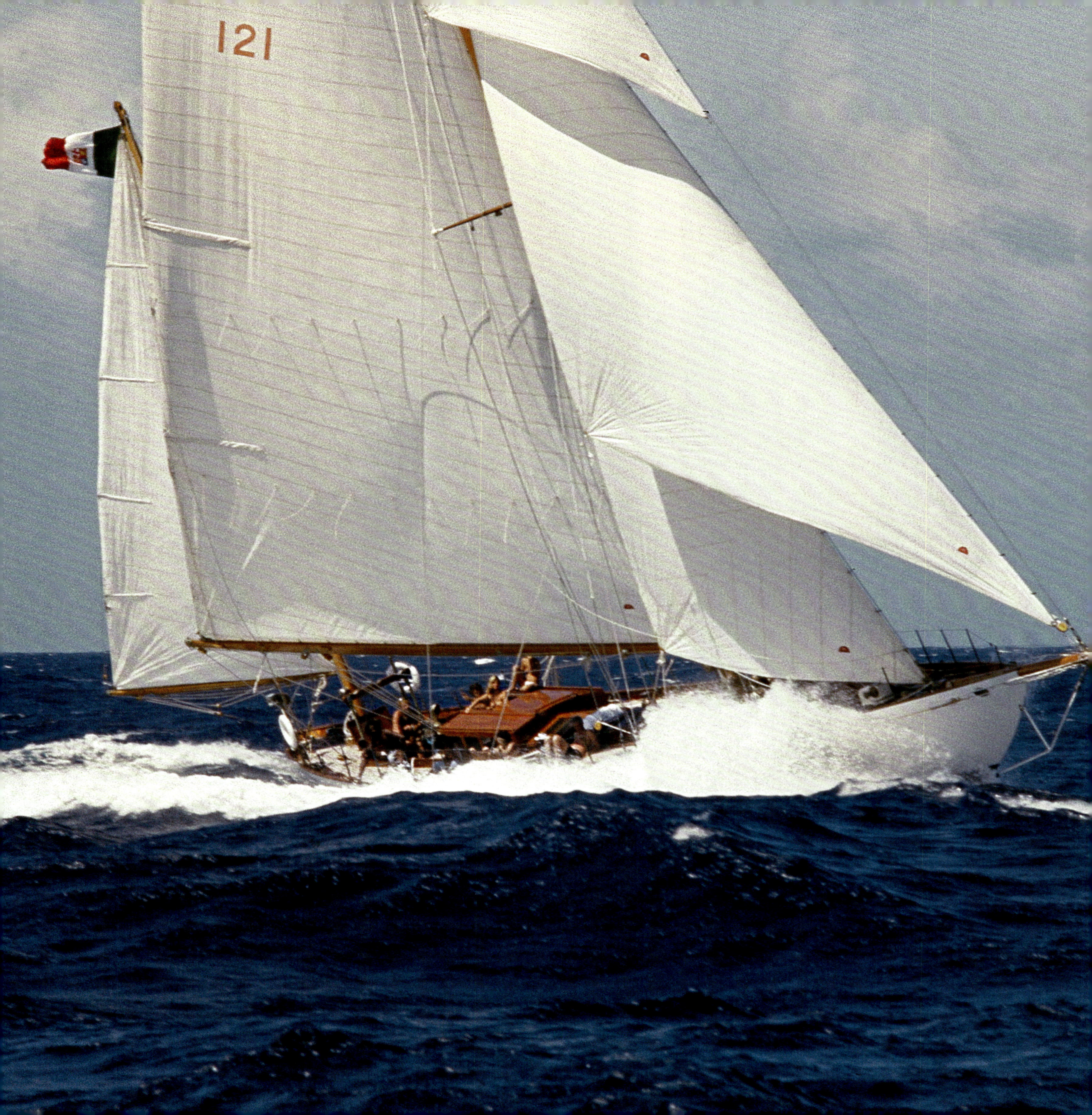
121

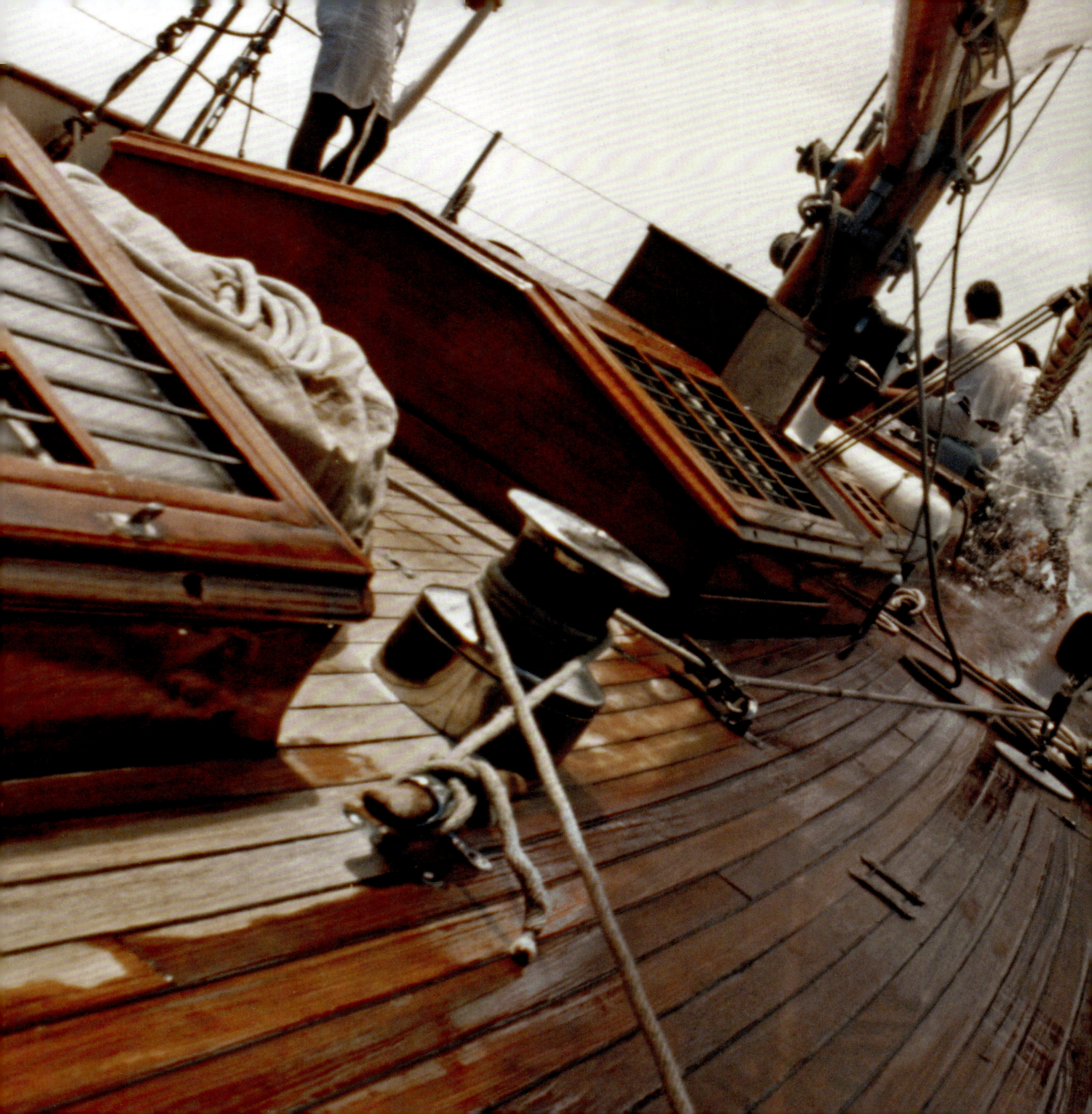

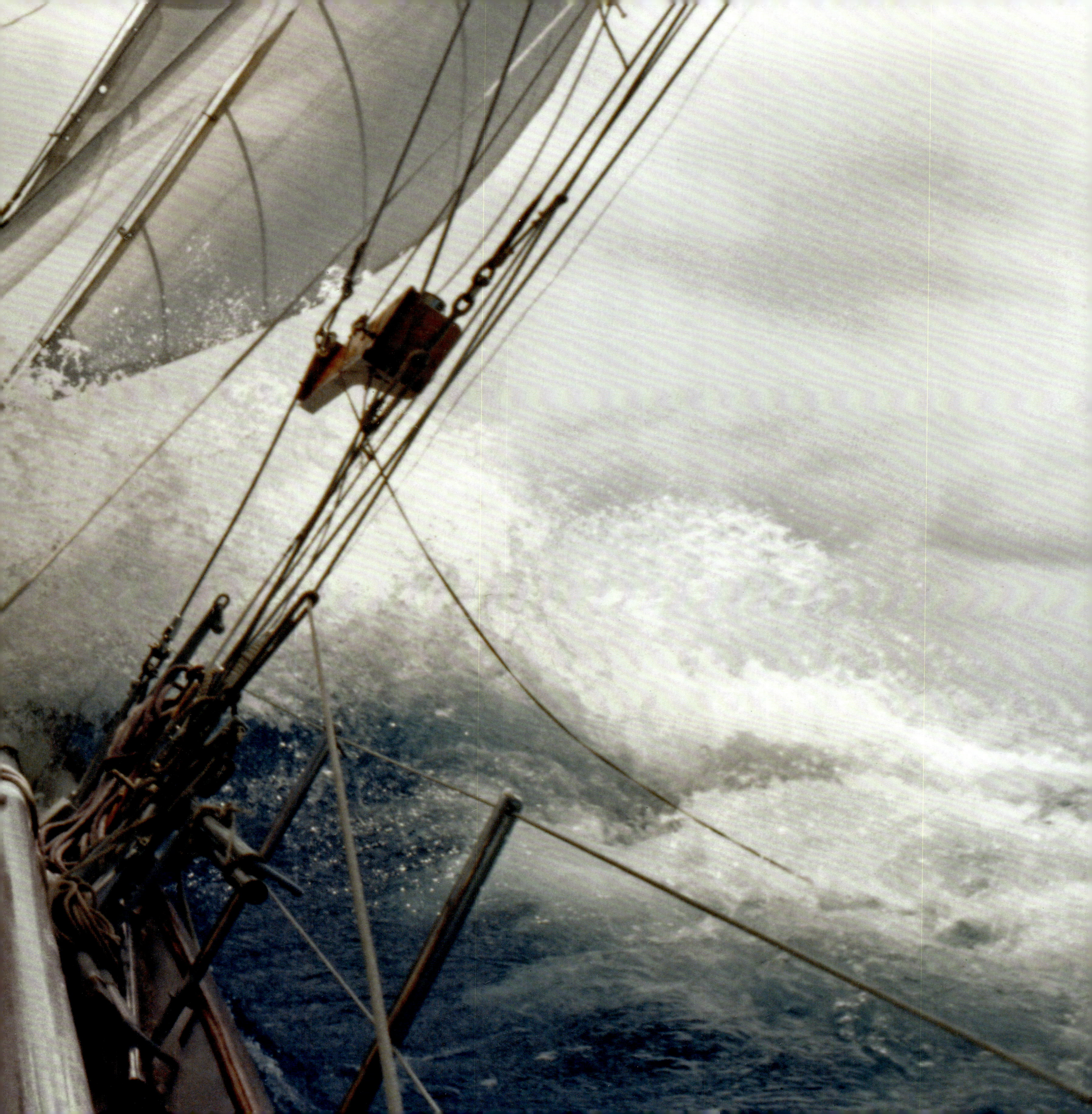

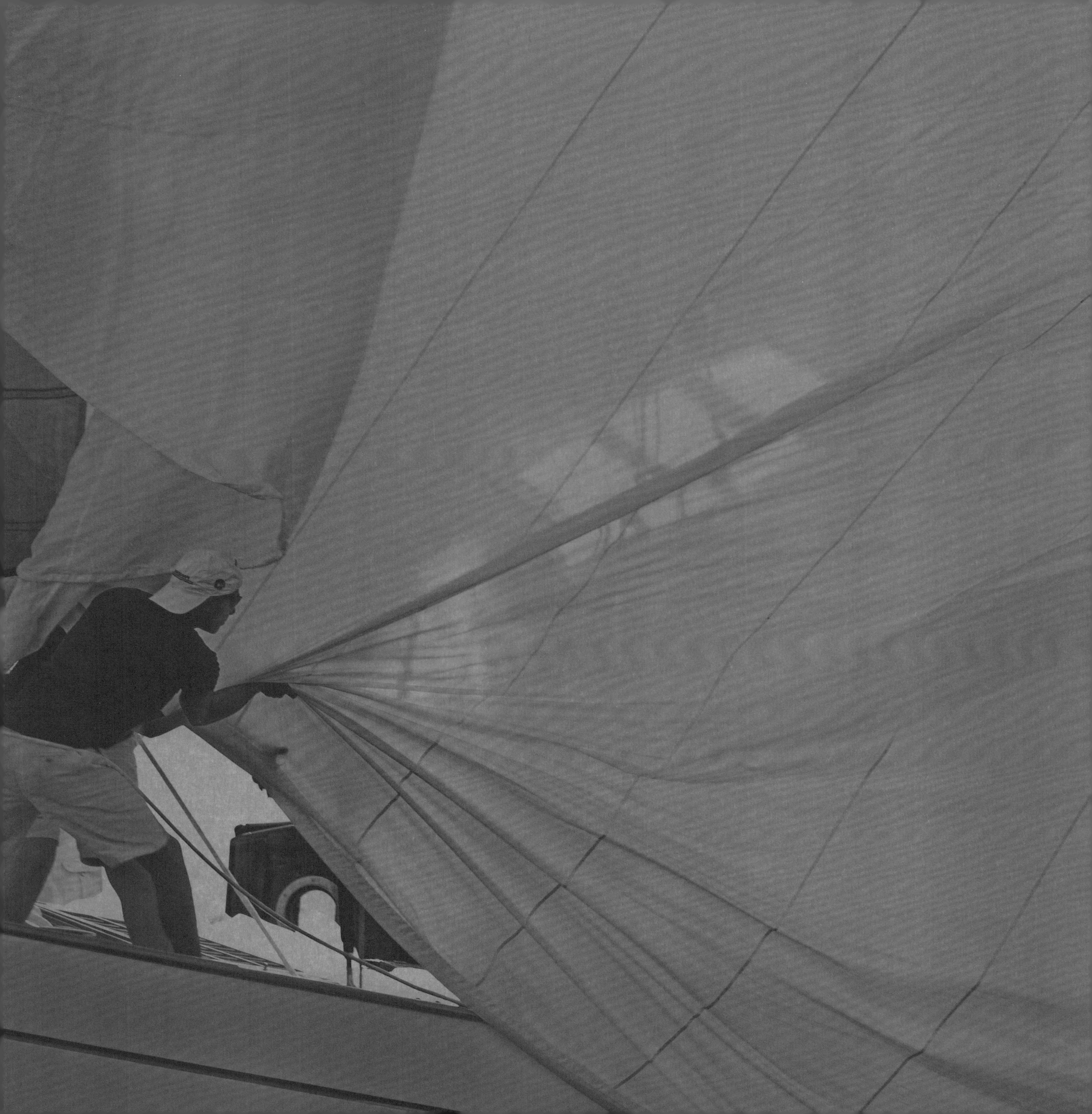

PANERAI AND *EILEAN*

2

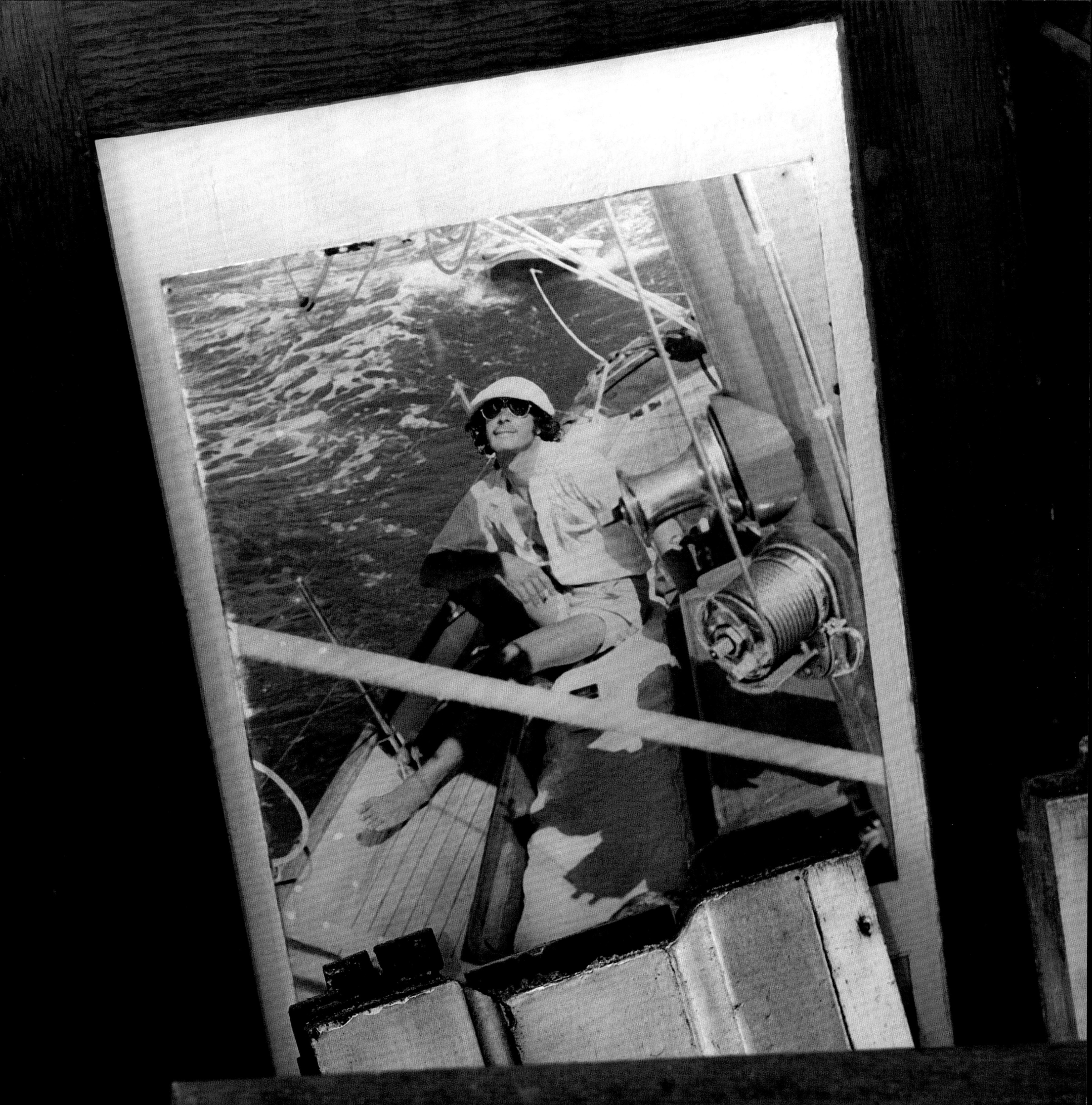

THE DISCOVERY OF *EILEAN*

Since the first Nioulargue – a week of regattas founded by Patrice de Colmont in 1981, when two sailing yachts challenged each other in the bay of Saint-Tropez at the end of the season – many magnificent classic yachts have sailed this famous route. Ten years later, keen agents working for wealthy collectors criss-crossed the world searching for the last few classic yachts from the beginning of the twentieth century designed by the best naval architects. They were particularly eager to find any yacht built by William Fife III, whatever the state of its conservation, but they became increasingly rare. Some restored Fife yachts, such as *Nan* (1896), which had been saved with the help of Philippe Menhinick, the grandson of one of the former owners of the yacht, were discovered without the seller knowing their origin.

Faced with the lack of classic yachts available for restoration, researchers consulted yachting history books hoping to find the ideal sailing yacht and then build a replica; some sort of sister-ship after a time-lapse of several decades. The construction in 2000 of a new *Westward* (Nathanael G. Herreshoff, 1910), the most famous of all the American schooners, which was sunk in July 1947 after the death of her owner, is typical of the lengths to which owners were prepared to go in their quest to possess the most beautiful yacht of all. Carried away by his own enthusiasm, the originator of this replica went on to build the three-masted schooner *Atlantic* (William Gardner, 1903), which held the record for Atlantic crossings for seventy-five years.

When Officine Panerai committed to the organisation of classic yacht races, its management decided to enter a yacht that would fly the firm's pennant. But, being a prime example of all that is authentic with 'state of the art' watches that remain faithful to the design ideals of the models created in 1936, Officine Panerai did not even think of using a mere replica of a period yacht.

Boat stories closely resemble those of precious objects, like Panerai watches. These stories can often be summarised by the words 'love at first sight' and 'passion'. This is what happened when *Eilean* and Officine Panerai met. It was as if *Eilean*, in danger of dilapidation at the time, was waiting for someone.

They met on 13 April 2006. That day was the first day of Antigua Classic Week, which had already been included in the Panerai Classic Yachts Challenge. After a marvellous series of regattas, Carlo Falcone, the Italian honorary consul in Antigua, offered to take Bonati to a inlet where, it is said, one can taste the best *piña colada* in the Windward Islands. While sailing around the coast, they spotted what looked like the wreck of a classic yacht

FACING PAGE This photo of John Shearer in his heyday, which was found stuck inside a door removed from a locker, had survived a sinking and salvage. The woodwork and furniture were badly damaged in the process and should have been treated there and then for mould and worms if any of it was to be saved.

PRECEDING PAGES On classic sailing yachts, it is more and more common to use a code zero, which enables the crew to set a large sail area in light air. Taking the code zero down is always a spectacular manoeuvre but less risky than that of a traditional spinnaker because it is tacked on the bow instead of at the end of a boom.

FACING PAGE When he planned to restore *Eilean* himself, John Shearer labelled every item of furniture before removing it. But this undertaking proved to be beyond his means, mainly because the yacht had been submerged for some time and, the panels having been left untouched for years, Shearer's markings had nearly disappeared.

PAGES 94–97 Referring to the original plans, kept in the Irvine Maritime Museum, the team was able to determine the modifications which had taken place over the years. Looking closely at all the details, it was obvious that *Eilean* had suffered considerable damage during the twenty years she had spent in the mangrove. Nevertheless, the most important thing was that she had kept her shape.

PAGES 98–99 The starboard side of *Eilean* had been exposed to the tropical sun daily, while the portside was shaded by the tugboat alongside which she was moored. In spite of this uneven treatment and the differing condition of both sides of the planking, the symmetry of the hull was in no way affected, proving the quality of her construction.

PAGES 100–101 Even though the boat had been damaged, all her owners kept to the original William Fife III deck plan layout. A few winches were added in the 1950s, but the bronze deck gear and the superstructures remained the same.

alongside a tugboat in the mangrove. They were struck by the elegance of the lines of this seemingly abandoned boat and asked that the launch approach the coast to have a better look. Falcone and Bonati were welcomed by John Shearer who invited them to visit his yacht, *Eilean*. Her pedigree and her size were exactly the image Panerai wanted to promote. Neither too big nor too small, a reasonable asking price, and she just happened to be for sale. The acquisition project was very quickly formalised and the yacht was purchased for Panerai. Bonati immediately thought of having the boat restored in Italy, looked for a yard on the Tuscany coast with the capacity to complete the work, and assembled the best Italian experts. Two years later, *Eilean* was reborn as a fitting image of excellence, elegance and precision for the Florentine brand.

BUNK

JOHN'S CABIN
PANEL ABOVE 3
PIECES

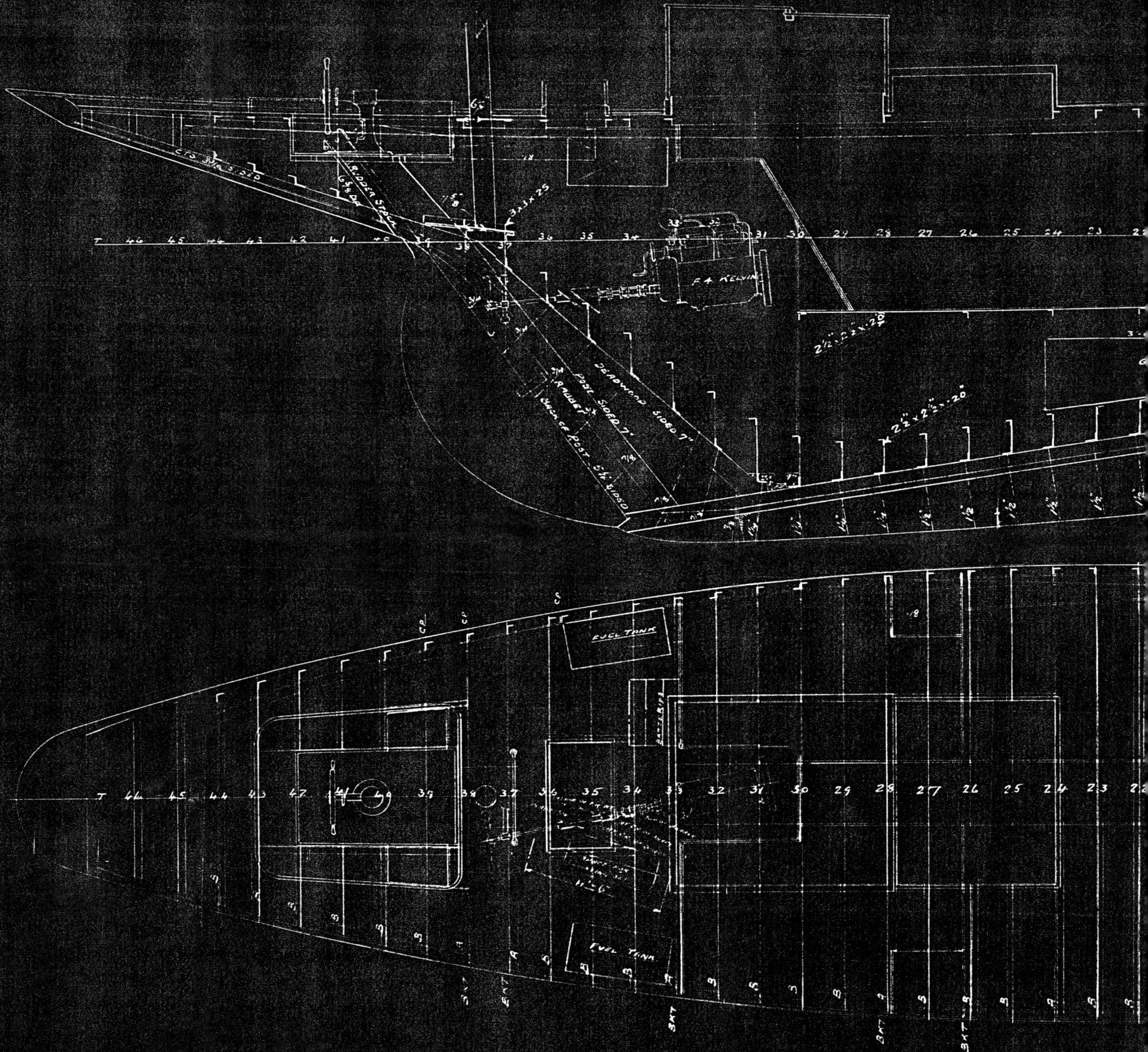
RUDDER STOCK
F.4 KELVIN
DEADWOOD SIDED 7"
POST SIDED 7"
FUEL TANK
FUEL TANK

N⁰ 822

SCALE ½" = 1 FOOT

MAST STEP PLATES 11" × 40"
FLOORPLATES 12·13·14·15 ARE ·30 THICK
ALL OTHERS ·22" THICK

BKT. KNEES OF ANGLE STEEL
4"× 2"× ·25" MARKED BKT ON DK PLAN

FORE & AFTERS & BEAMS MARKED "A"
ON PLAN ARE 3"× 3"× ·25"
CARLINGS & BEAMS MARKED "B" ON PLAN
ARE 3"× 2"× ·20"

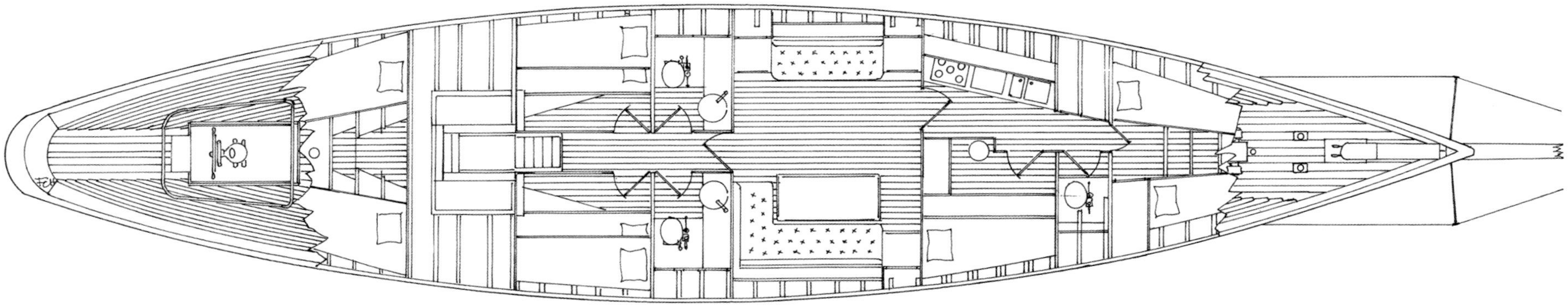

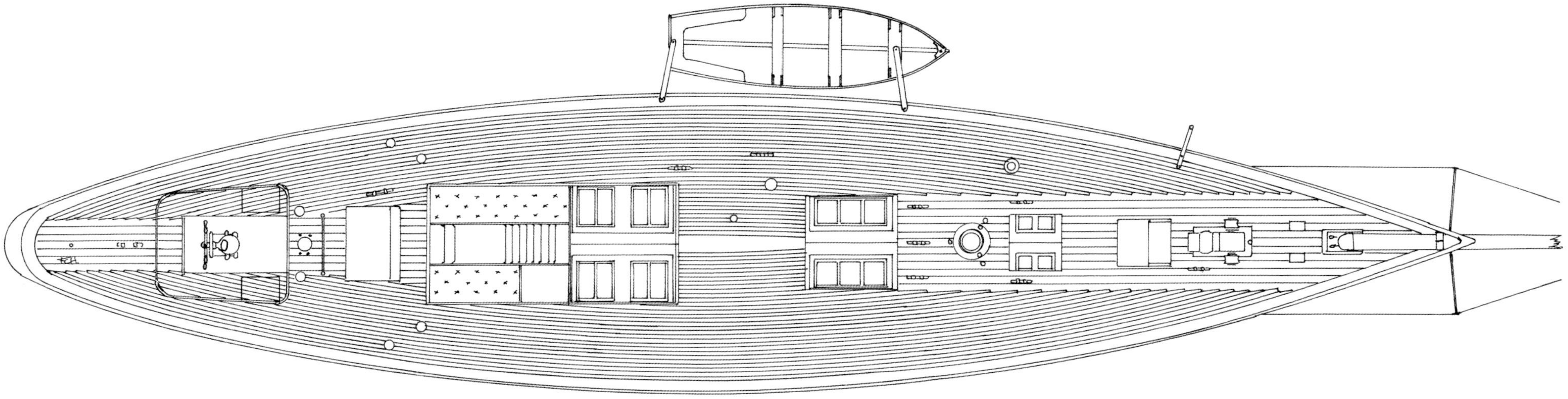

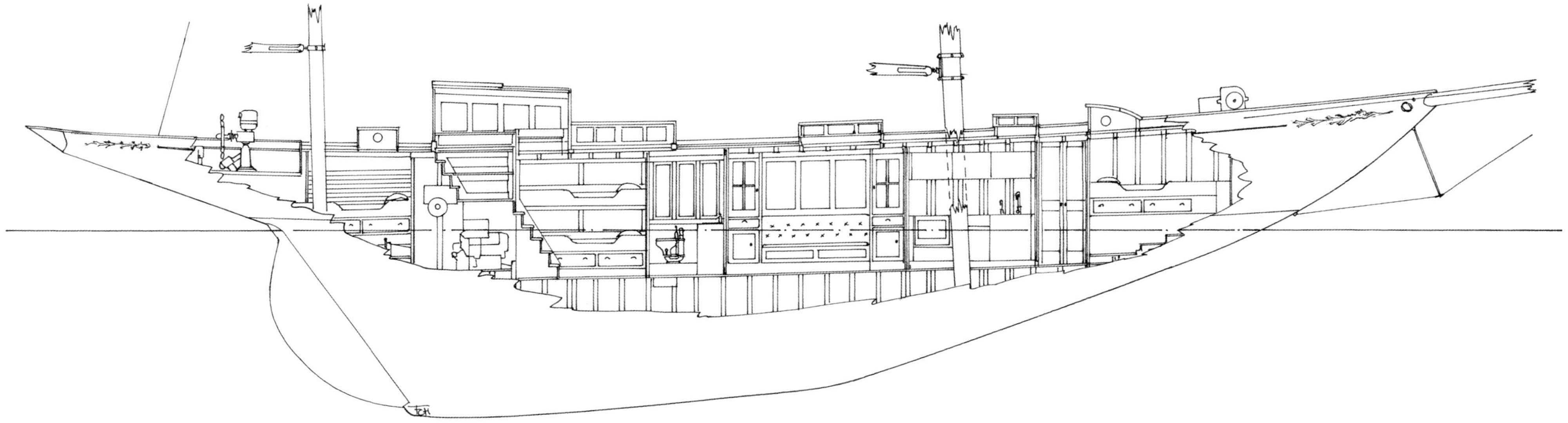

"EILEAN"
WILLIAM FIFE 1907
F. CHEVALIER © 2010

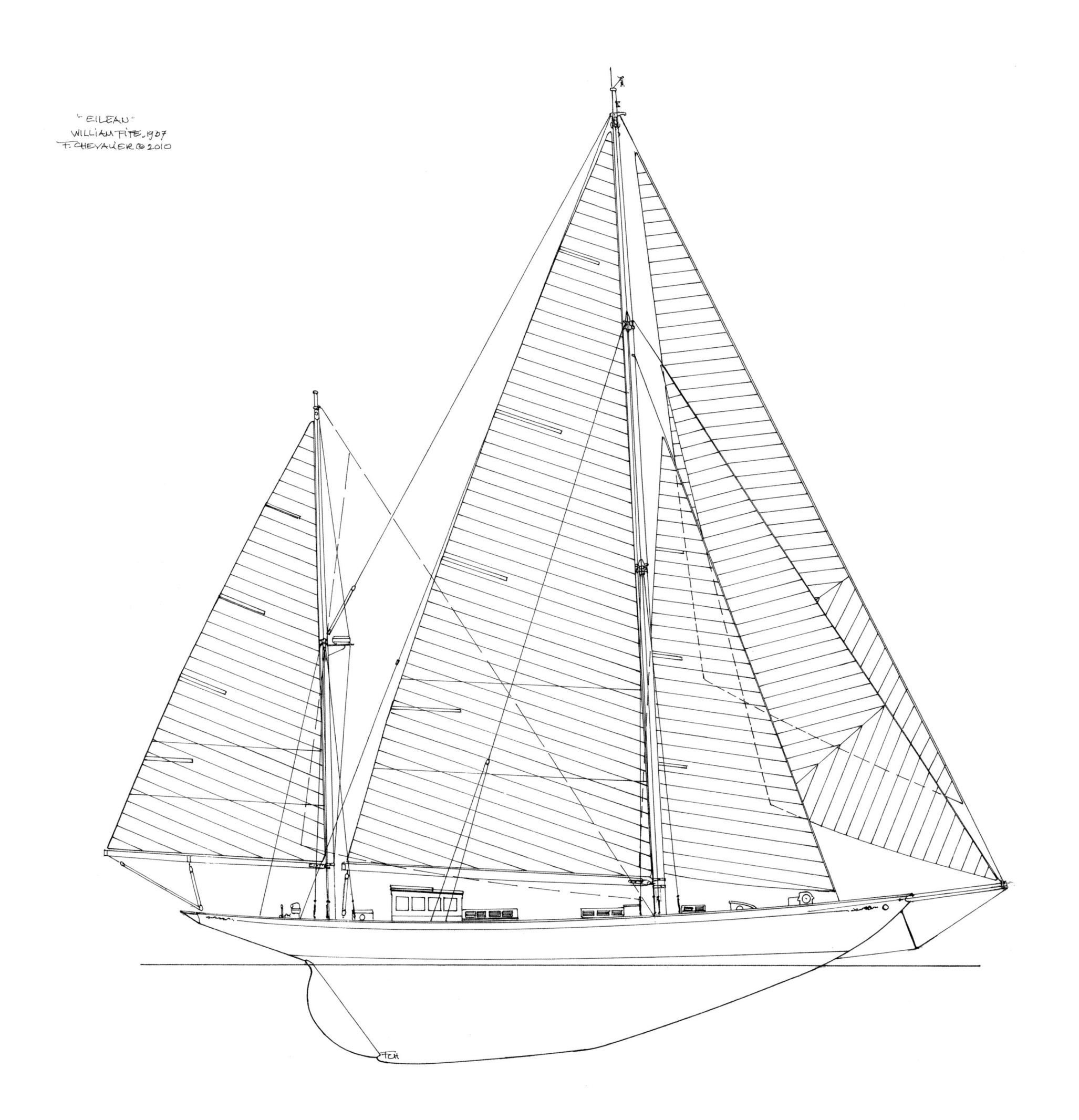

EILEAN

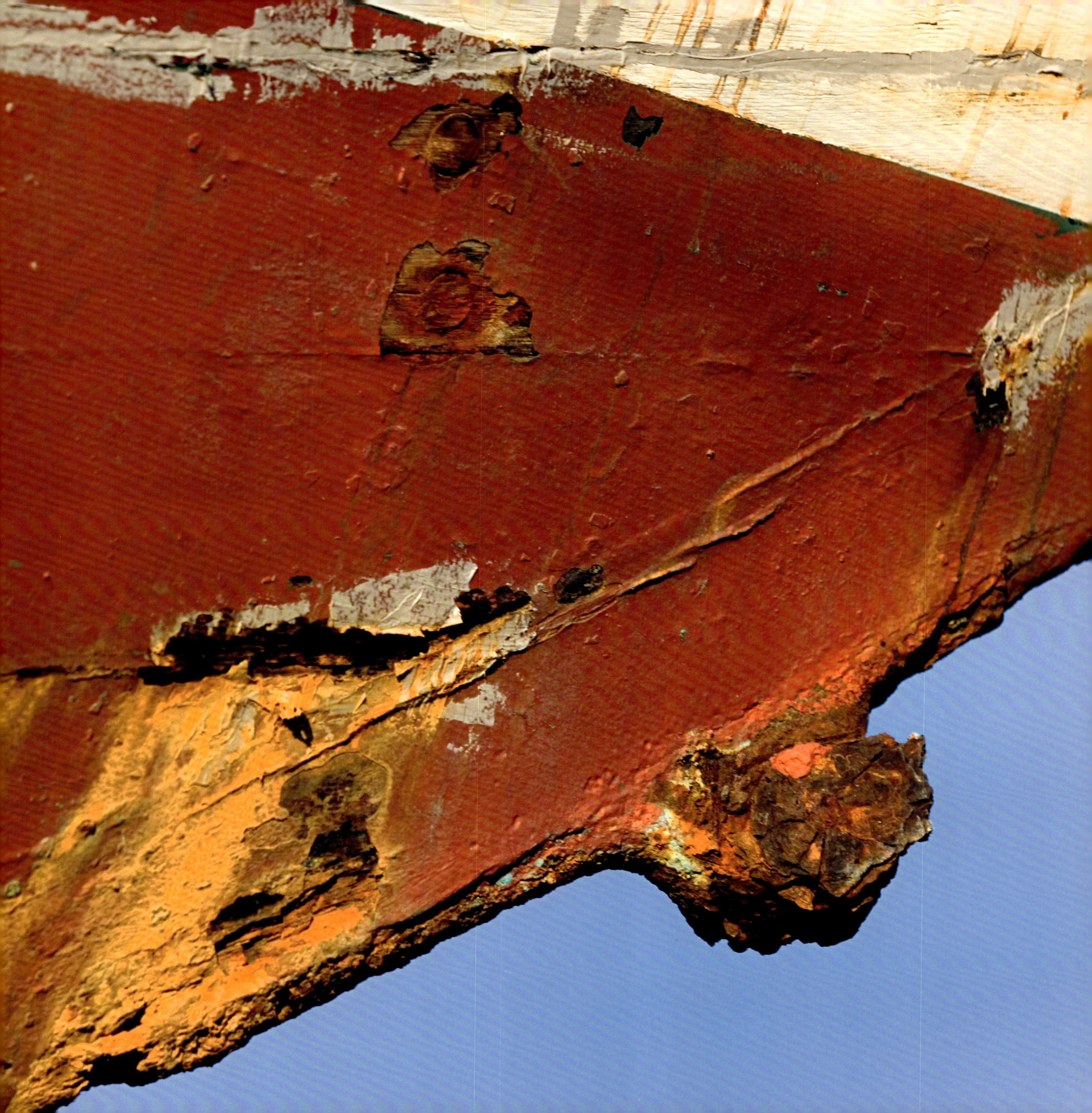

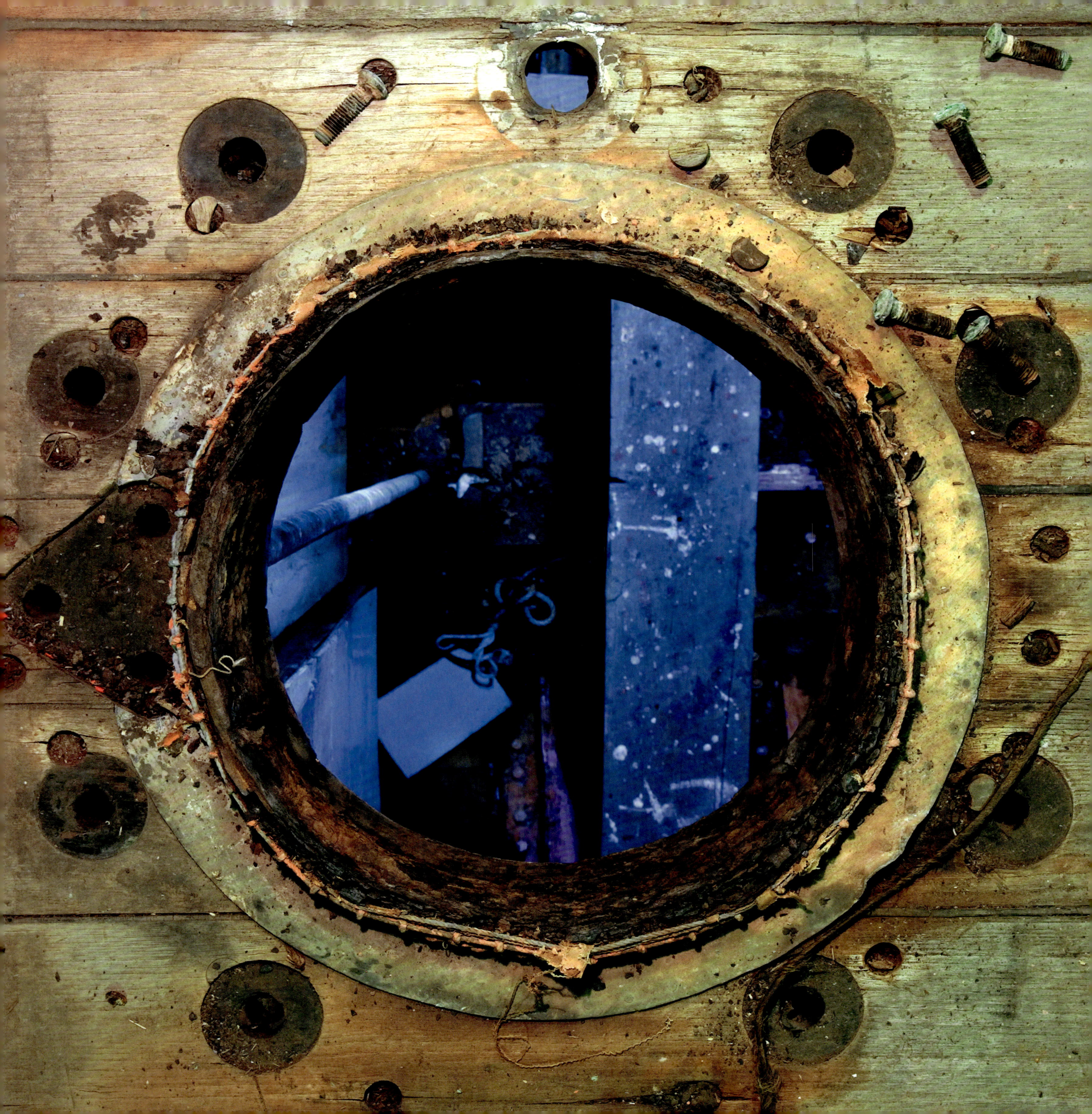

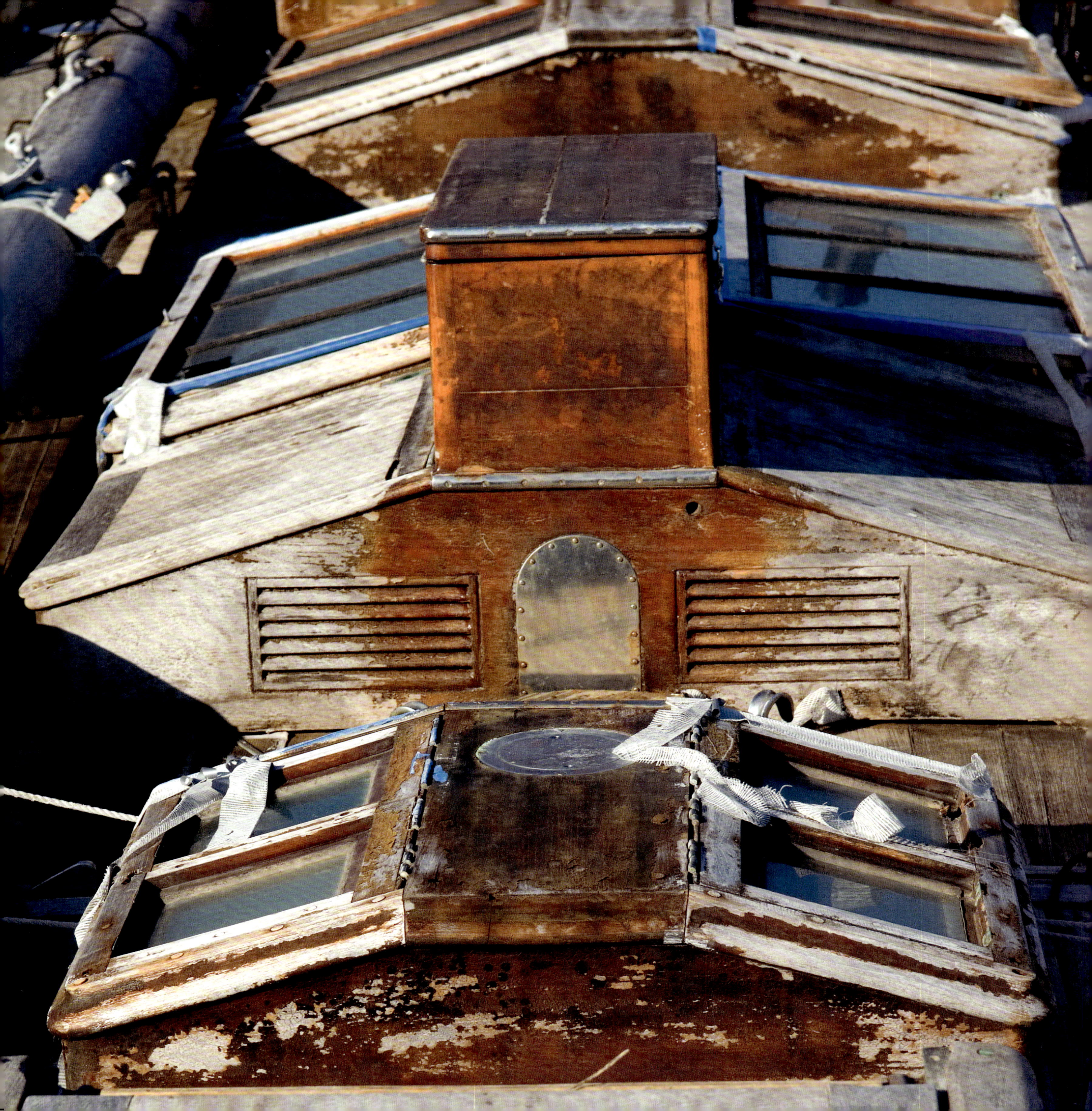

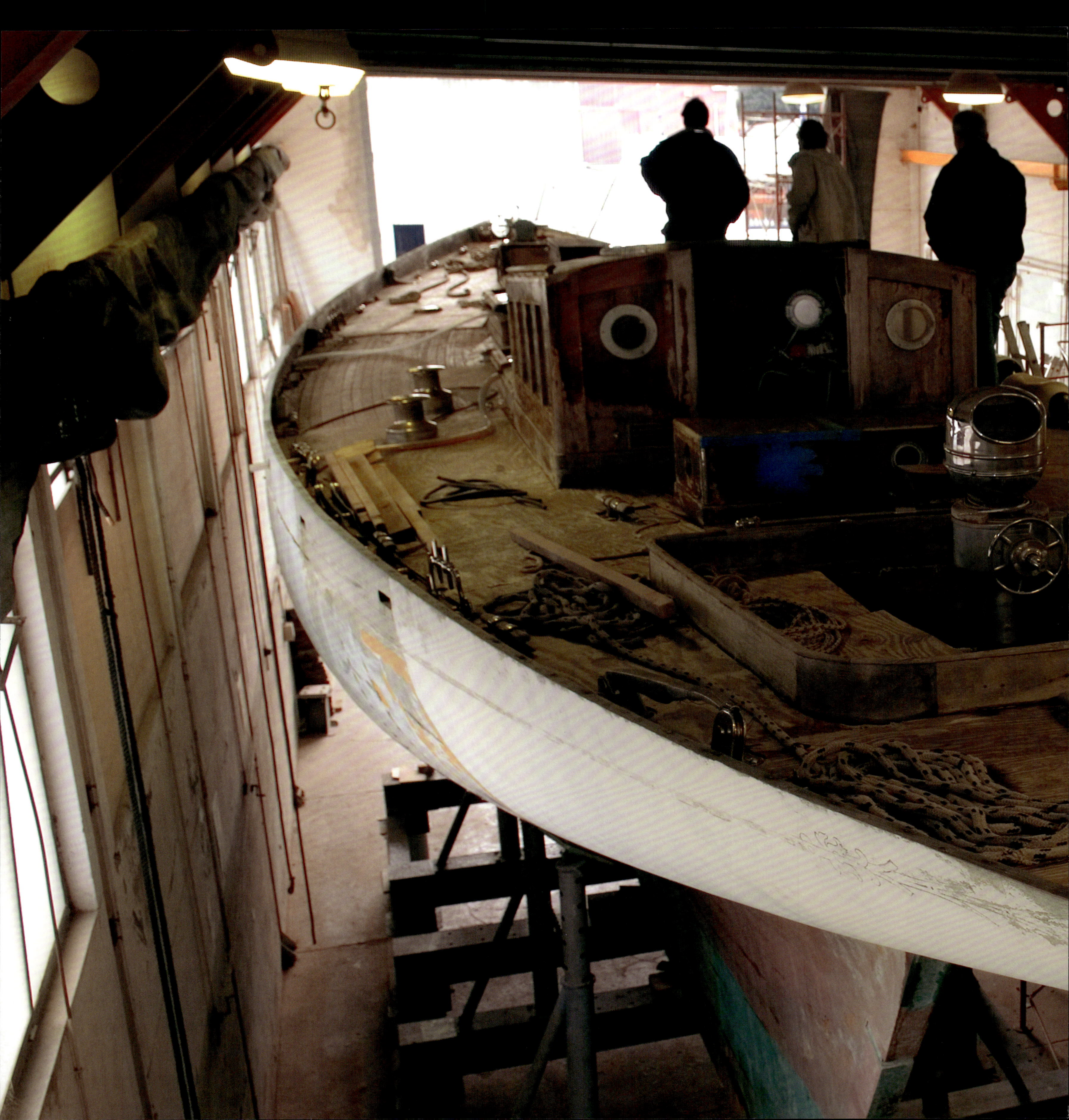

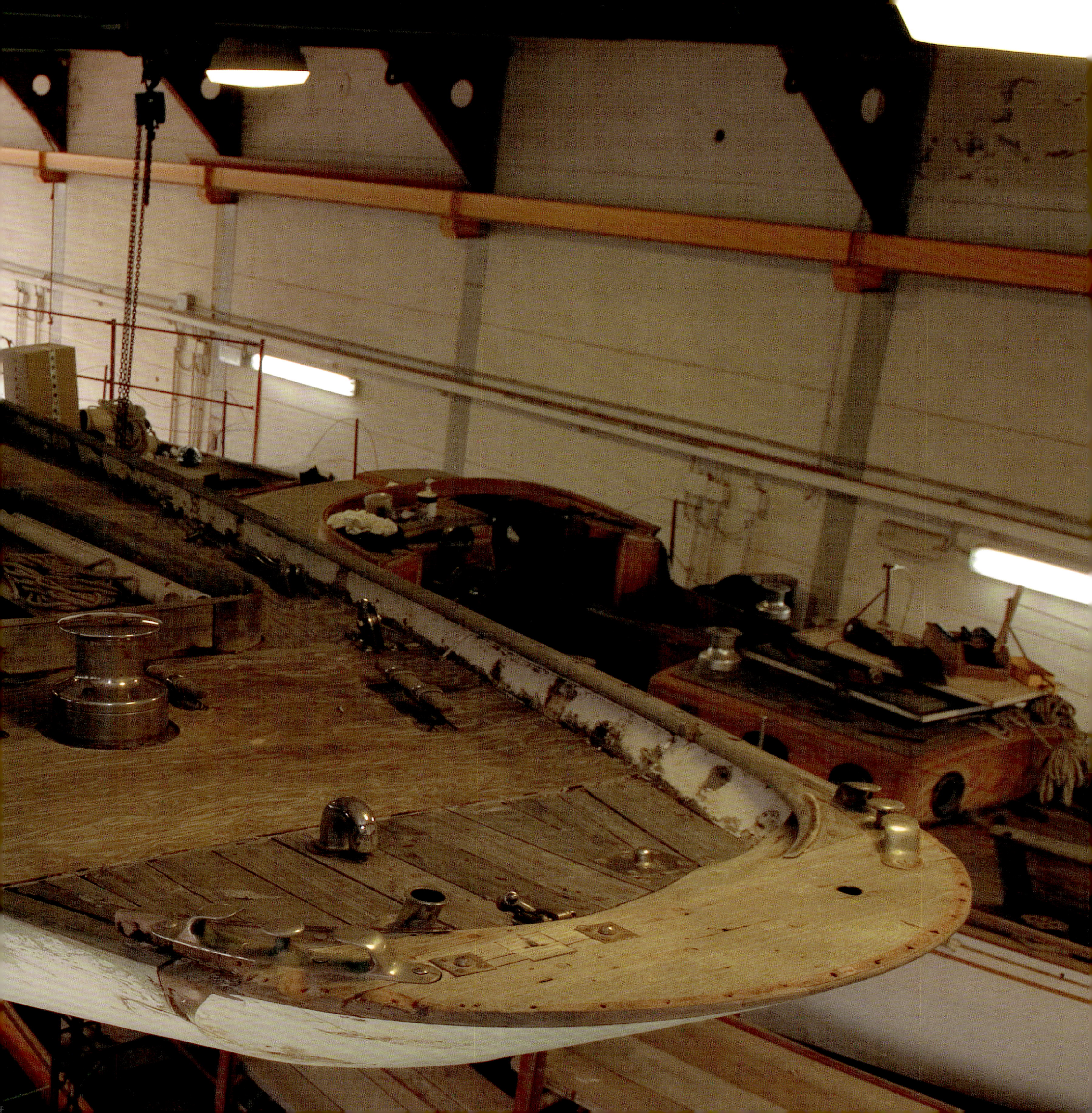

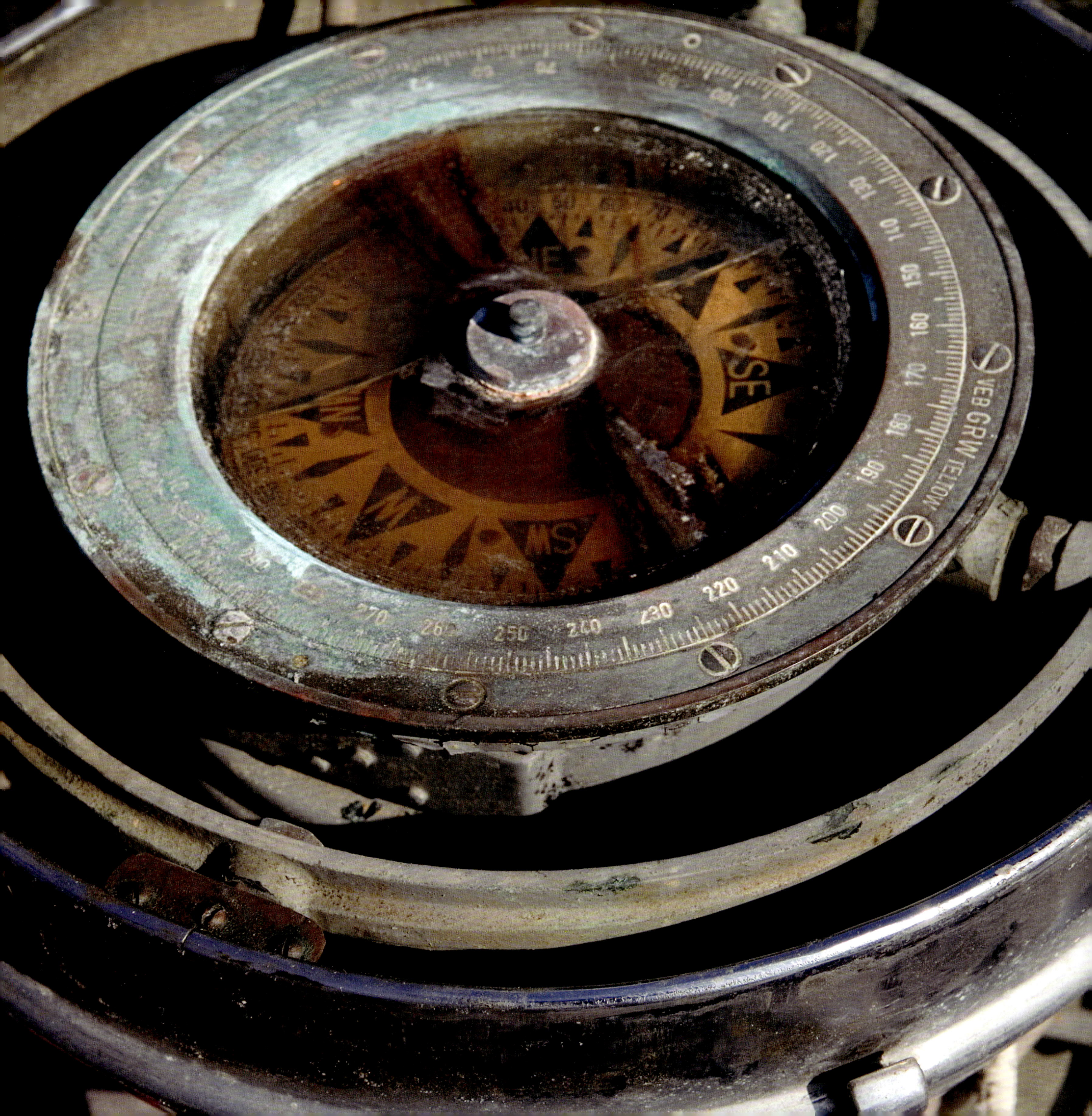
VEB GRW TELTOW
SE
SW

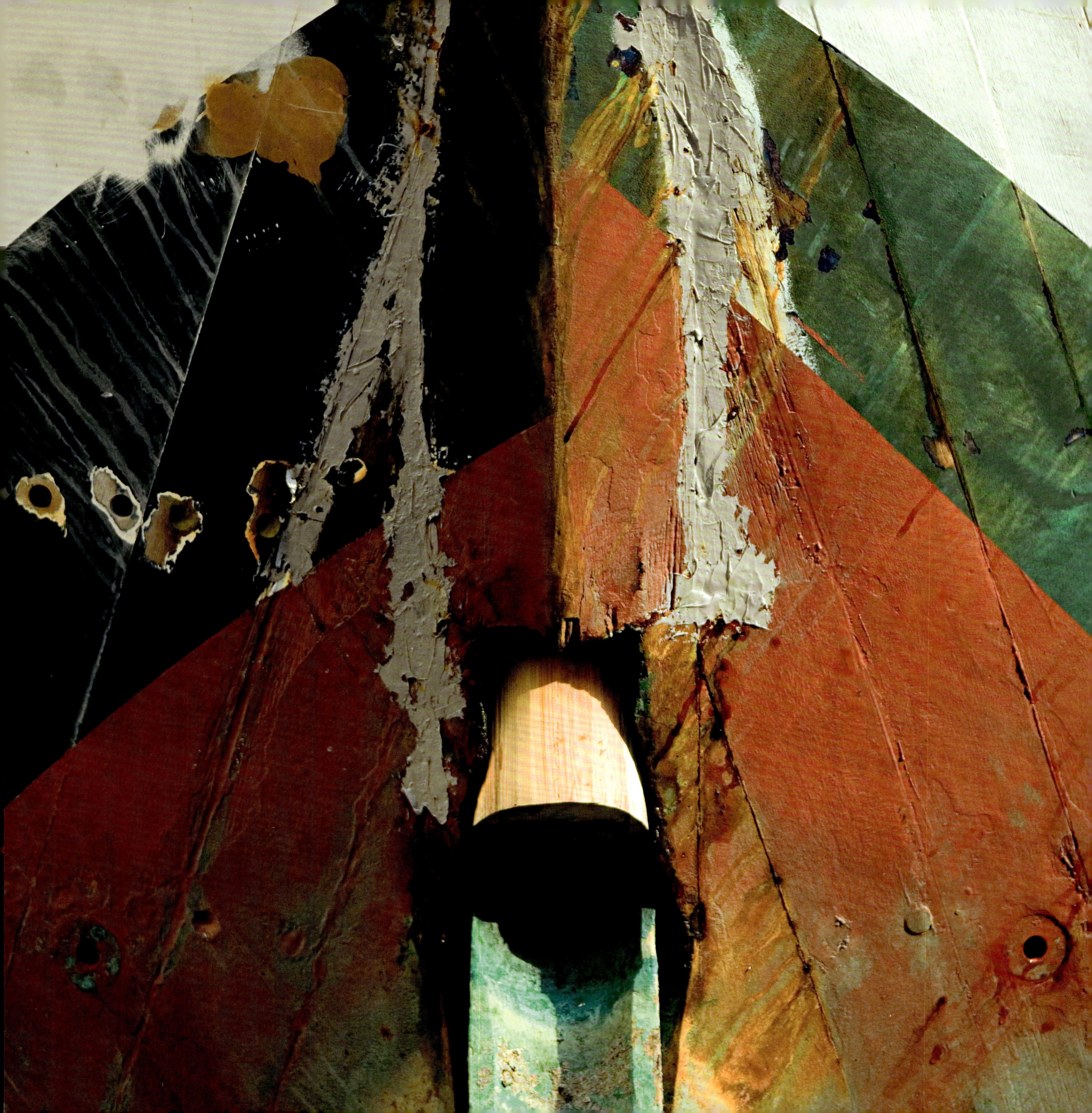

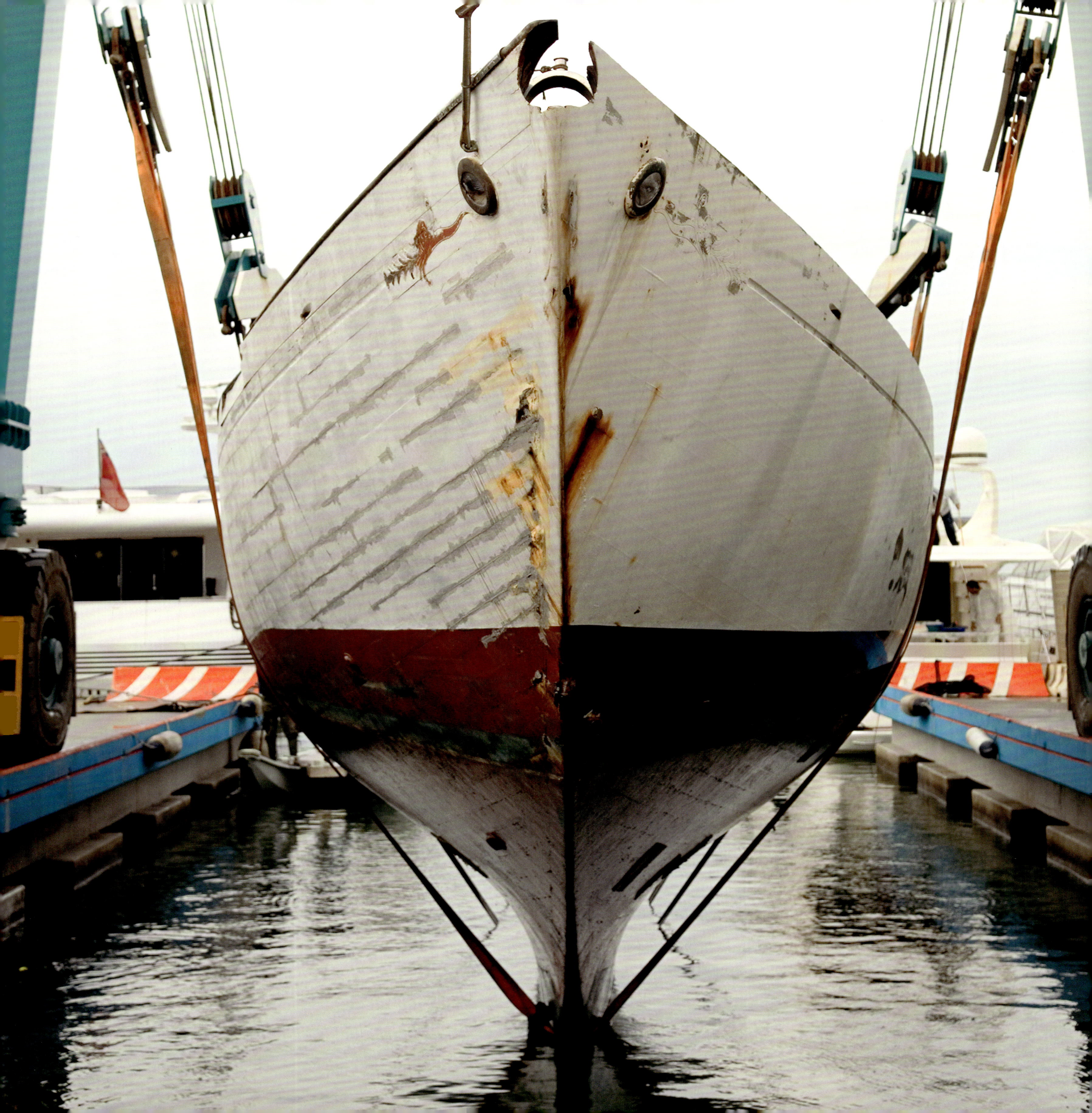

THE RESTORATION OF *EILEAN*: A PASSION FOR AUTHENTICITY

More than two years of work and passion, together with an extraordinary display of traditional skills paired with the most modern technologies, have given life back to one of the most beautiful yachts of all time, *Eilean*. This was not an excessive length of time to achieve the restoration of the ketch to her pristine beauty of 1936. The Fulton brothers, her first owners, had ordered a fine, racy, comfortable, seaworthy and fast sailing yacht. Her construction had been a wonderful example of all aspects of the art of boatbuilding; at the time, she was perfection. More than seventy years later, the restorers wanted the yacht to remain worthy of that heritage. This took more than two years to achieve, which may seem a long time, but when traditional crafts and advanced techniques are both involved, Panerai understood that time is of no consequence.

Angelo Bonati brought together an extraordinary team of knowledgeable people to ensure the success of this restoration. A lover of the sea and boats and an expert in every aspect of nautical craftsmanship, he only wanted the best craftsmen, those who would share his vision of the project as a passionate adventure and a quest for perfection. For this labour of love, and considering the size of the yacht, the Francesco Del Carlo shipyard in Viareggio had reserved a whole hangar for this project and recruited the best team available. Project manager Enrico Zaccagni personally supervised the schedule of the various operations. The architects from Florence, Sergio Landini and Federica Micelli, were appointed to draw the plans that served as a reference for the restructuring of the boat.

Before the work could begin, however, the yacht had to get to the other side of the Atlantic, and she was in no state to sail across on her own. Aside from the absence of a rig in working order, fittings were broken, and she had suffered from being submerged in seawater; the deck was leaking a little everywhere and the only thing holding the hull together was the teak planking, as the metallic structure had been weakened by rust with many points of damage. The side of the yacht permanently exposed to the sun while she was moored in the same place for so long, was most severely damaged. The seams of *Eilean*'s hull were so wide, one could see daylight from inside in many places. In November 2006, Enrico Zaccagni had her towed to Le Marin in Martinique where *Eilean* was hoisted aboard a cargoship bound for Genoa. However, to complete the 180 miles between Antigua and the port, she had to be made watertight. All the seacocks were checked and closed, the gaps in the planking were summarily filled in, the deck and superstructures temporarily covered.

As an additional precaution, inflatable tubes were fitted inside the boat to keep her afloat even if a plank fell off altogether. Each cabin was filled with a buoy. In case of major damage, the height of the topsides would be

PAGES 102–103 Once the deck had been removed, the angle bars of the deck beams showed the same amount of deterioration as the metal frames.

PAGES 104–105 The steering compass in its original binnacle had suffered over the years and it had been submerged in seawater for some time. Each component had to be removed, cleaned, tested and the compass was reassembled in its original state then refitted on the restored *Eilean*. The teak rudderpost had to be cut to extract the rudder. The hull form seen from aft shows the dissymmetry between the waterlines on starboard and portside.

PAGES 106 AND 108–109 *Eilean* stayed in the Francesco Del Carlo shipyard in Viareggio for nearly two years.

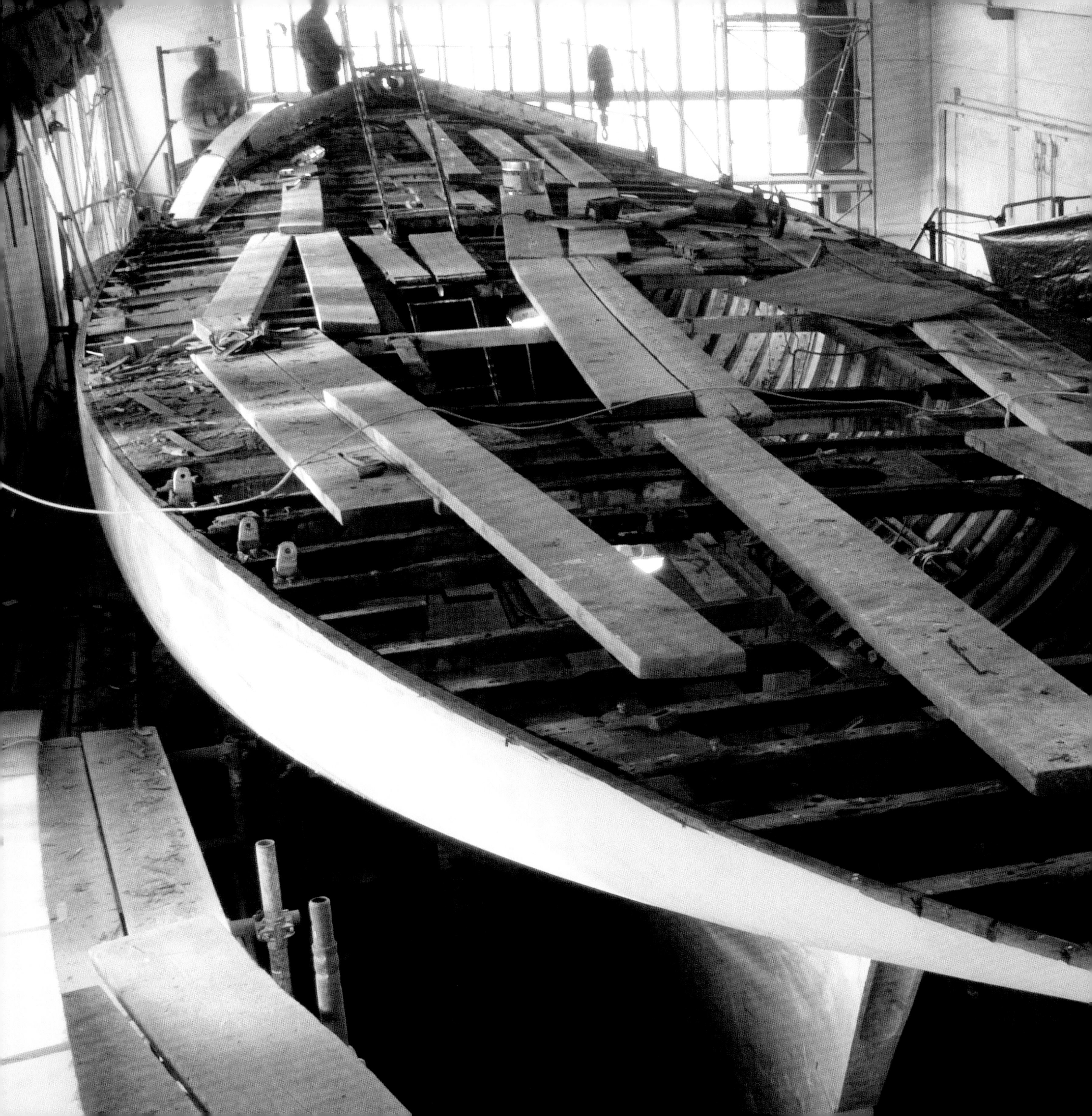

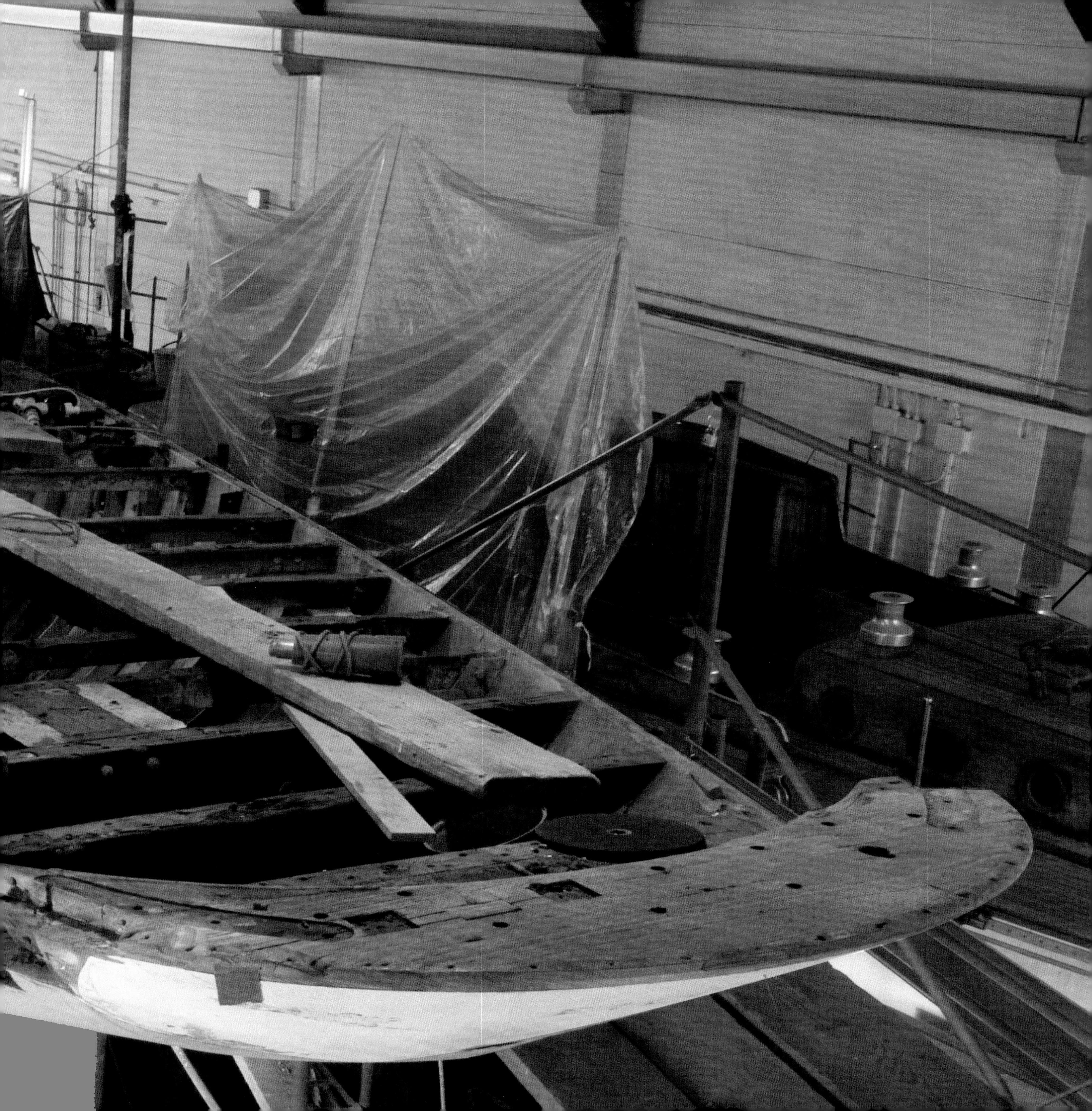

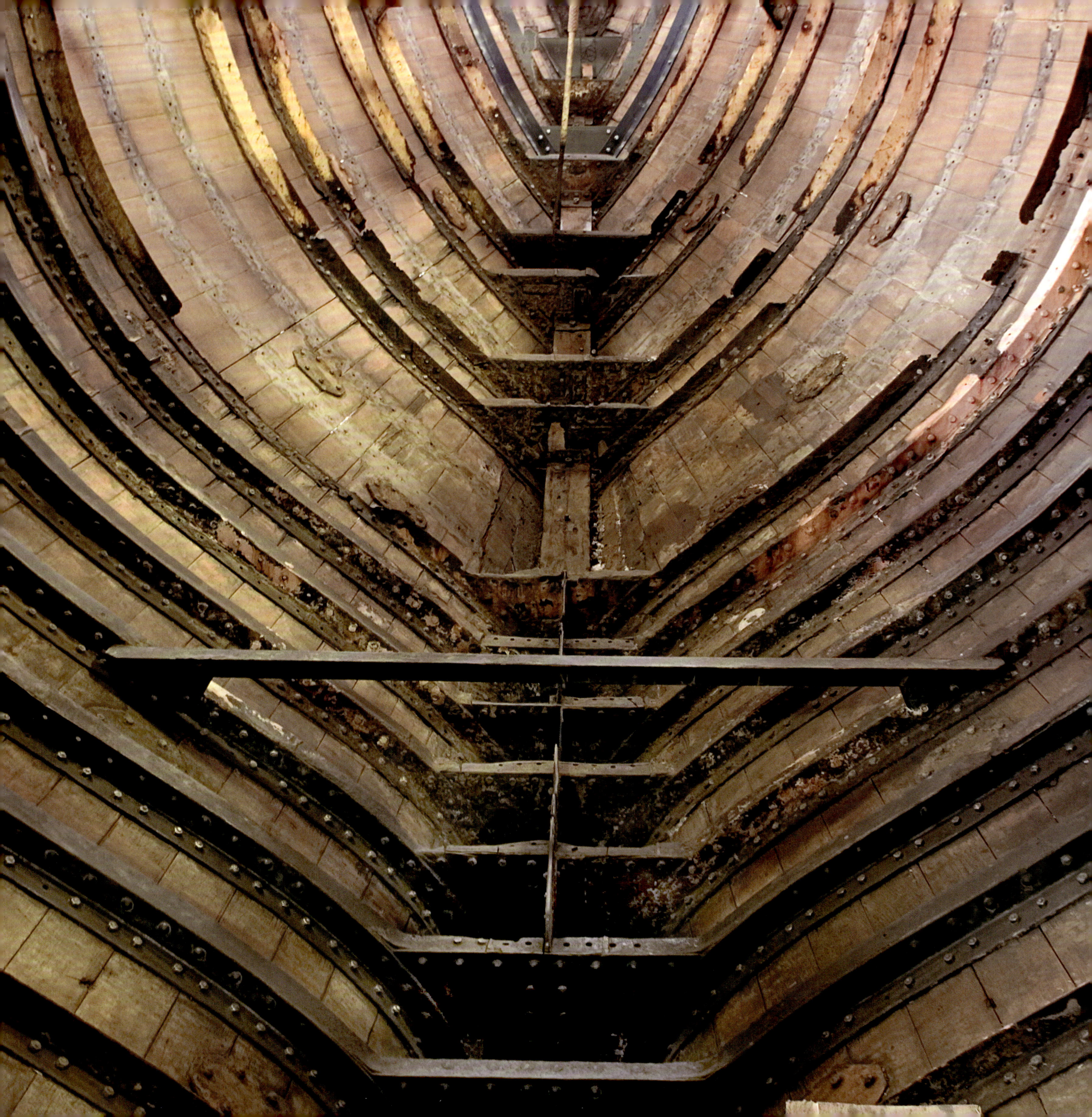

halved but the inflated volume would stop her sinking. Accommodation was provided for the crew on deck because the interior was totally occupied by the inflated tubes. The crew communicated with the tug by radio and the long mooring ropes tied to the stern of *Eilean* absorbed the shocks between the two boats. Finally, after a day entirely taken up by formalities, and in view of the favourable weather forecast, the *Sea Pony* took the ketch in tow on 15 November, at 7 a.m. They left Falmouth and headed for Guadeloupe, Saintes, then sailed through the channels of Dominica and Martinique. The *Sea Pony* and *Eilean* tied up to the quay in Le Marin the following day at half past eleven, having averaged little more than five knots.

For the Atlantic crossing on board the yacht-transporter *Superservant III*, a cradle was built to *Eilean*'s size. The yacht was hoisted on the ship on 3 January 2007 and transported over four thousand miles to the port of Genoa Voltri where she arrived on 2 February. She was put back in the water to be towed along the Italian coast to the Del Carlo shipyard in Viareggio, where she arrived a week later.

Once the restoration team had been assembled in the yard, a detailed inspection was required. Beyond her sad appearance, what was really the state of the boat? What could be kept intact and what needed to be restored, replaced or modified? Instead of pulling the boat apart, it was easier to X-ray her to get the first indications of her condition. So right from the start, the most advanced technologies were used for the restoration. The first appraisal of the state of the boat was made using a laser and a scanner. Every part of the structure and of the deck gear was digitalised and recorded by these instruments, and then all parts were listed according to their assumed condition.

The two sides of the yacht were submitted to the same inspection. Zaccagni and his team were delighted to discover that the hull had not lost any of its symmetry in spite of the age and poor state of the yacht: the reputation of the William Fife & Son shipyard was confirmed. Indeed, the quality of *Eilean*'s construction turned out to be exceptional, particularly if one remembers that the yacht had remained at anchor in the Caribbean in the same spot for some twenty years, with the same side continually exposed to the sun. *Eilean* had been built to the exacting standards required by Lloyd's as far as materials, craftsmanship and finish were concerned, with an eighteen-year guarantee. The longitudinal structural assembly of the boat – from the bow to the keel, transom and rudder – was in teak. The deadwood, between the sternpost aft and the keel, where the floors are bolted, was the only part made of British oak.

FACING PAGE *Eilean*'s lines are as attractive on the inside as on the outside. The restoration work involved replacing the steel frames without affecting the shape of the hull. Old frames were removed a few at a time and used as templates to forge the new ones, which were then galvanised and fitted with temporary bolts.

PAGES 112–113 Guido Del Carlo and his brother Marco took over the running of the yard from their father, Francesco. Guido's son, Adriano, also started a new career in his father's shipyard. Thus, *Eilean* benefitted from the expertise of three generations of shipwrights and knowledgeable advice from Guido Del Carlo, seen standing on the right of Mr Bonati in this photo. The restoration of the windlass is a perfect example of the skills of the Francesco Del Carlo shipyard craftsmen.

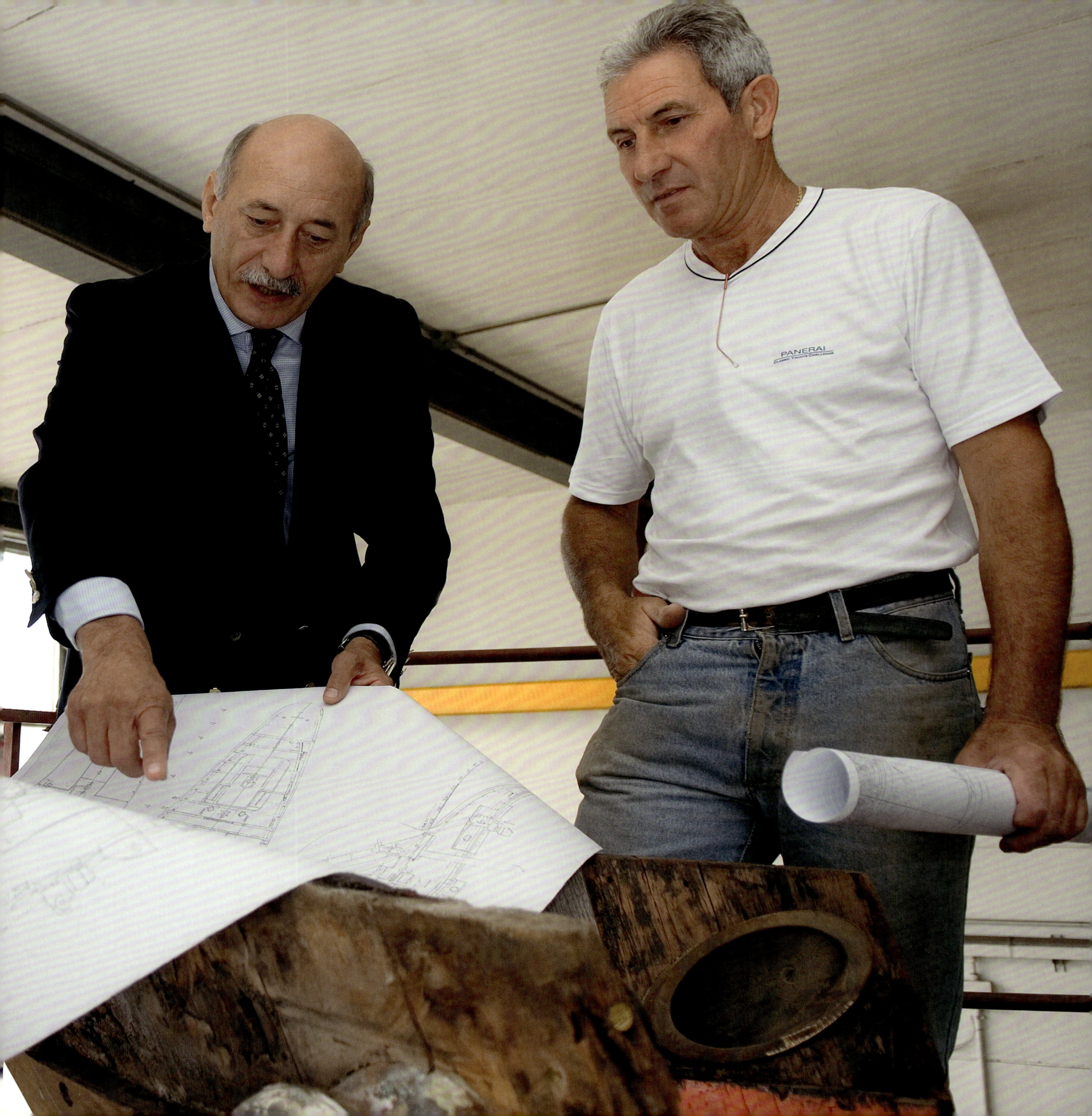
PANERAI

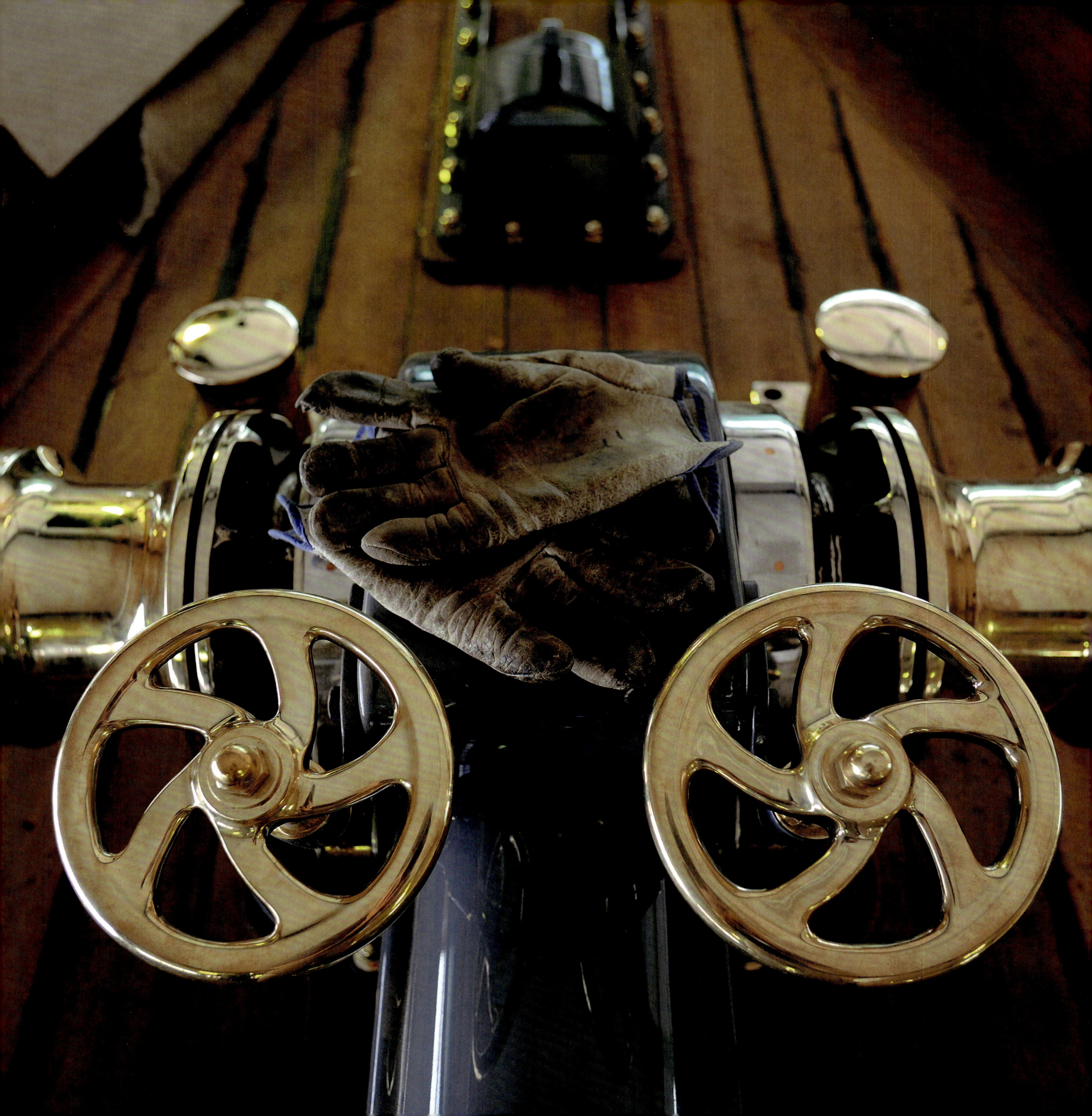

FACING PAGE The bare interior of *Eilean*, without any accommodation, shows the 48 steel frames and the vast size of the hull. With the deck and planking in place, the boat regained the rigidity she had seventy-two years ago.

According to Leonardo da Vinci 'details make perfection', and this could not be more true than in respect of the restoration of a masterpiece of maritime heritage: not a bolt, nor a wooden batten could be out of place in this setting dating from the golden age of yachting. Therefore, to ensure the authenticity and the similitude of each part, the restorers conducted a thorough investigation into the fascinating archives of William Fife III in the Irvine Scottish Maritime Museum and also the Fairlie Restoration. In the former, they found an indispensable original document: the shipyard's specifications dated 22 April 1936, titled *Specification of a proposed auxiliary ketch for James V. Fulton Esq.* and *Robert W. Fulton Esq.* Every part and all materials used were described in detail down to knives, forks, and even the three chamois leathers the crew used for shining the brass! The sail plan, deck plan, accommodation and structural plans were also discovered in Irvine. These enabled the restorers to check the deformations or transformations made to the yacht by her successive owners. The only plan missing was the lines drawing of the ketch so it was necessary to plot the lines and draw the sections before the hydrostatic and stability calculations could be completed.

As the enquiries progressed, the researchers compared the data they had acquired with photographs taken at various times. Throughout her fabulous life, it seemed that *Eilean* had been treated with the respect she deserved: her successive owners had kept her in her original state as far as possible. The propulsion system had been regularly modernised and the power increased. Some minor modifications had been made to the deck, the rig and the accommodation.

The research team was encouraged by these revelations, which provided them with a comprehensive history of the yacht, from her launch until her acquisition by Officine Panerai. The various craftsmen assembled by Angelo Bonati could now get to work. They started by meticulously pulling the ketch apart. The interior accommodation fittings were totally removed, followed by the superstructures, the hatches, skylights, and the doghouse. Once the deck gear, the engine and the piping had gone, all that was left was a bare steel hull lined with Burma teak. Finally, when the deck, which was over four centimetres thick, was removed, the tightly packed angle bars of the deck beams were revealed.

This superb structure was entirely sandblasted inside and outside in order to inspect the condition of the assembled wooden and metal parts as closely as possible. This composite construction method has been in use,

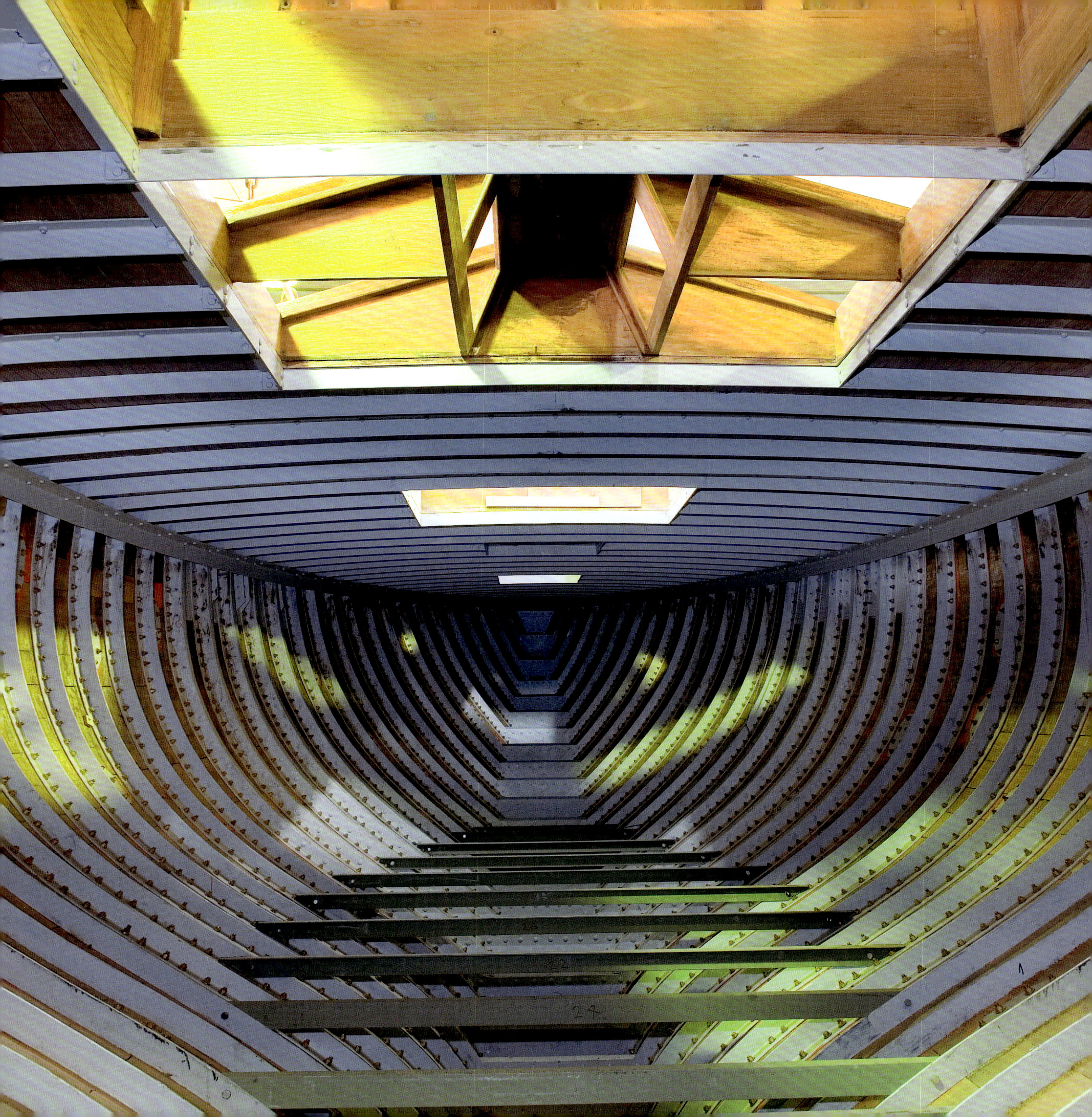

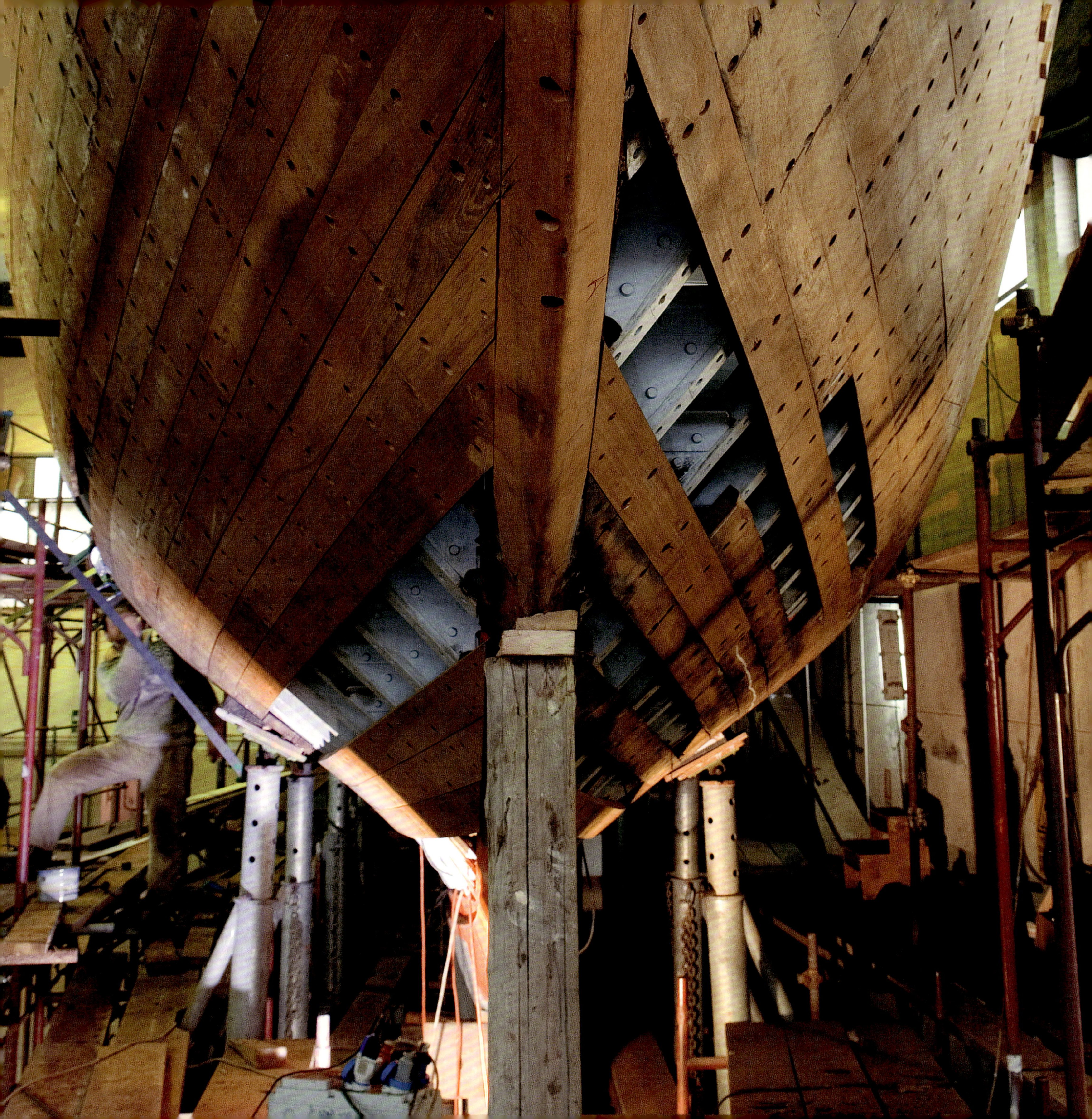

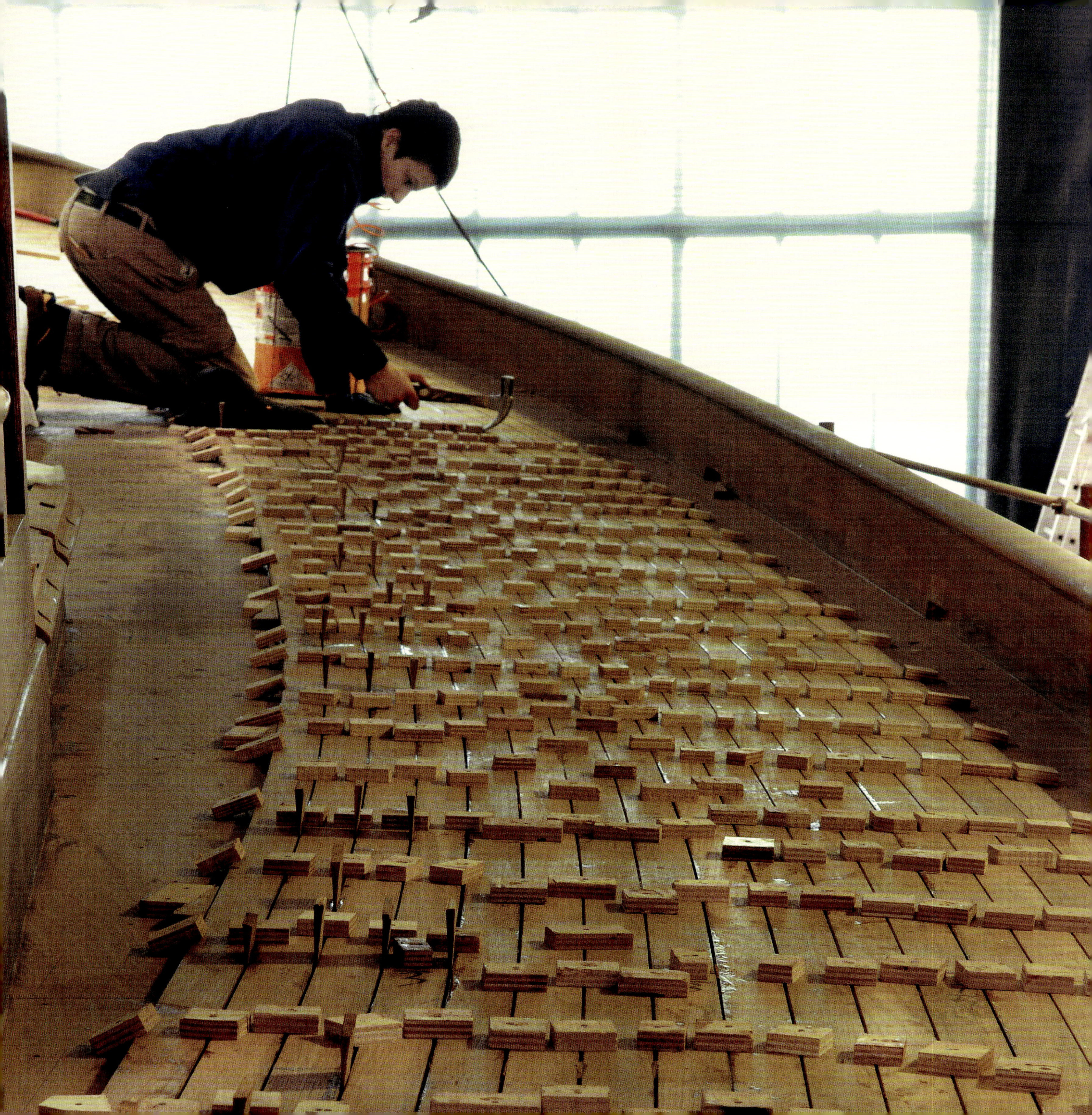

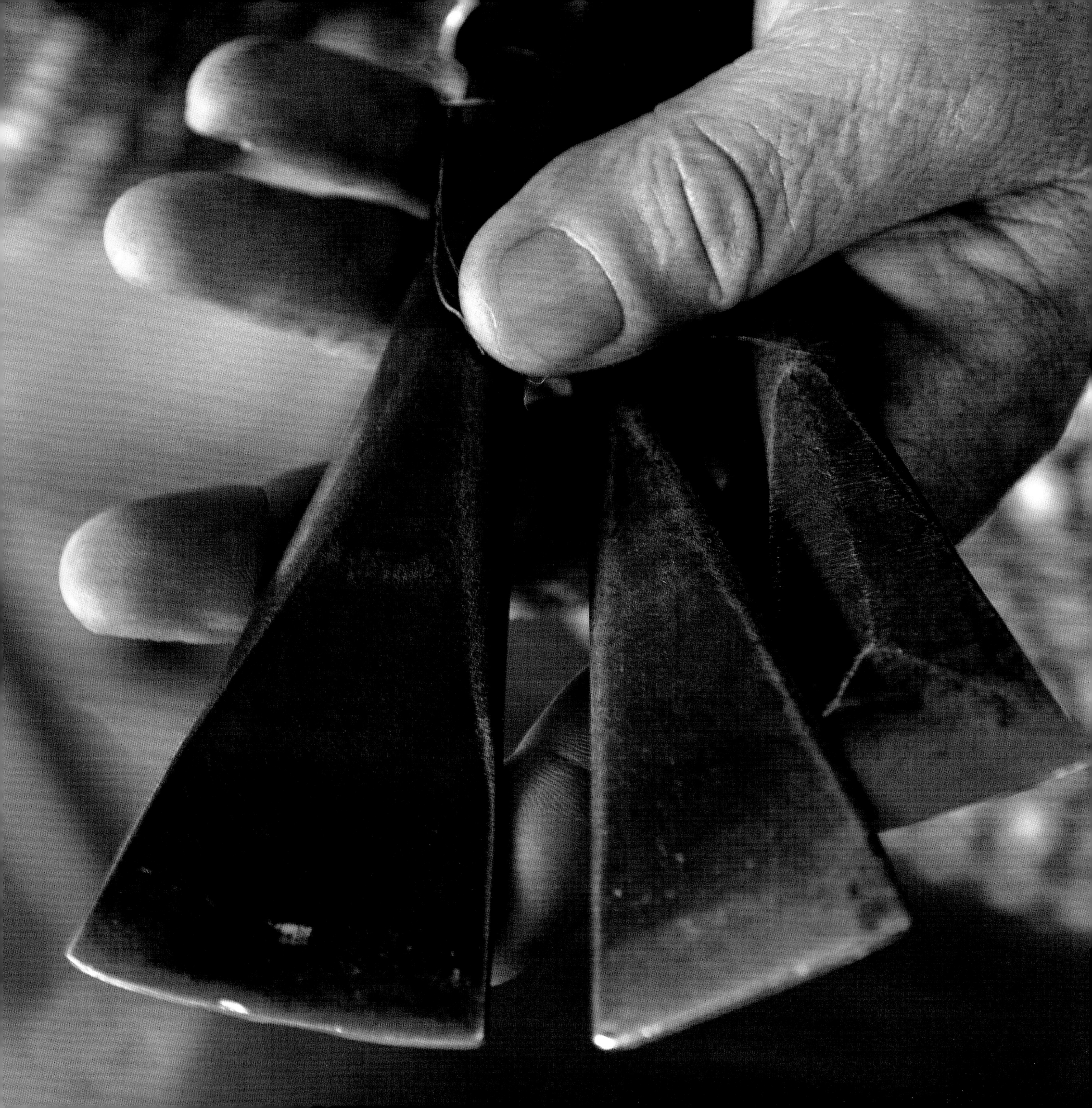

on large ships, since the end of the nineteenth century. There were various applications: alternate wood and metal ribs, all ribs in metal and deck beams in wood or, as is the case on *Eilean*, steel ribs and deck beams. The ribs and deck beams took the shape of angle bars linked by gussets and spread every 40.5 centimetres and doubled at the level of the foremast and chain plates.

This first proper examination of the boat's structure, followed by that of the various equipment, provided a more detailed survey of the ketch's condition. The spars, masts, booms and bowsprit were all beyond repair. They had been shortened by the previous owners, and what was not broken had been eaten by termites. The foremast boom was the only part that could be saved. The whole of the mahogany interior accommodation had been eaten by worms and was irretrievable, except for some of the saloon table items. Some panels fell apart as soon as they were handled. The inspection of the ribs and the floors showed that multiple rainwater infiltrations had ruined the metalwork, which had rusted through in several places. Summary repairs or doubling had been made in time. Pre-war iron differs from today's, and rather than welding the two together, it was decided to completely replace the forty-eight pieces of the yacht's framework with new ones using the same scantlings. The teak planking, of the same thickness as the deck, was damaged on the side that had been permanently exposed to the sun. Luckily, teak is one of the few species of wood into which shipworms cannot burrow, and she did not suffer any harm from these little molluscs. But it was worn or mouldy in several places. Rust had also penetrated the wood, mainly at the foot of the ribs and where the accommodation fittings had created a pocket for rainwater to stagnate. The sternpost was cracked in several places and had to be renewed before the metallic structure could be dealt with. The keel bolts that supported the sixteen-tonne lead ballast were removed and inspected; it turned out they were in a perfect state of conservation.

The shipwrights recruited by Officine Panerai were among the most experienced in the world and used all their skill and imagination to deal with the exceptional requirements of this restoration. They removed the ribs one by one by cutting out the bronze rivet heads, keeping the teak in place and using them as models. Each rib was replaced by a new one, pressed and hammered into an identical shape to that of the original in all three dimensions, taking into account the curvature of the hull and the angle of the planking. Each rib was then galvanised and refitted. The use of bronze bolts rather than rivets made it easier to remove the planks that had to be replaced.

PAGES 116–117 A wooden hull may look spotless when finished but, during assembly, thousands of holes are visible, waiting to receive the rivets fixing the planking onto the steel frames and for the temporary nailing of the teak deck boards onto the marine plywood.

FACING PAGE Caulking consists of filling in the V-shaped seams between the teak strakes with a hemp or cotton cord. The cord is forced into the seams with a caulking iron, the exact thickness of the seam, and a mallet. These are then treated with red lead paint and coated with a mixture of glazing putty rich in linseed oil and more red lead paint.

PAGE 120 On the transom, the name of the yacht, *Eilean*, has been gouged out and coated, ready to be gilded.

PAGE 121 Since 1963, Cantiere Navale Francesco Del Carlo has built a large number of fishing boats and is used to handling large pieces of timber, such as *Eilean*'s solid teak rudder.

EILEAN

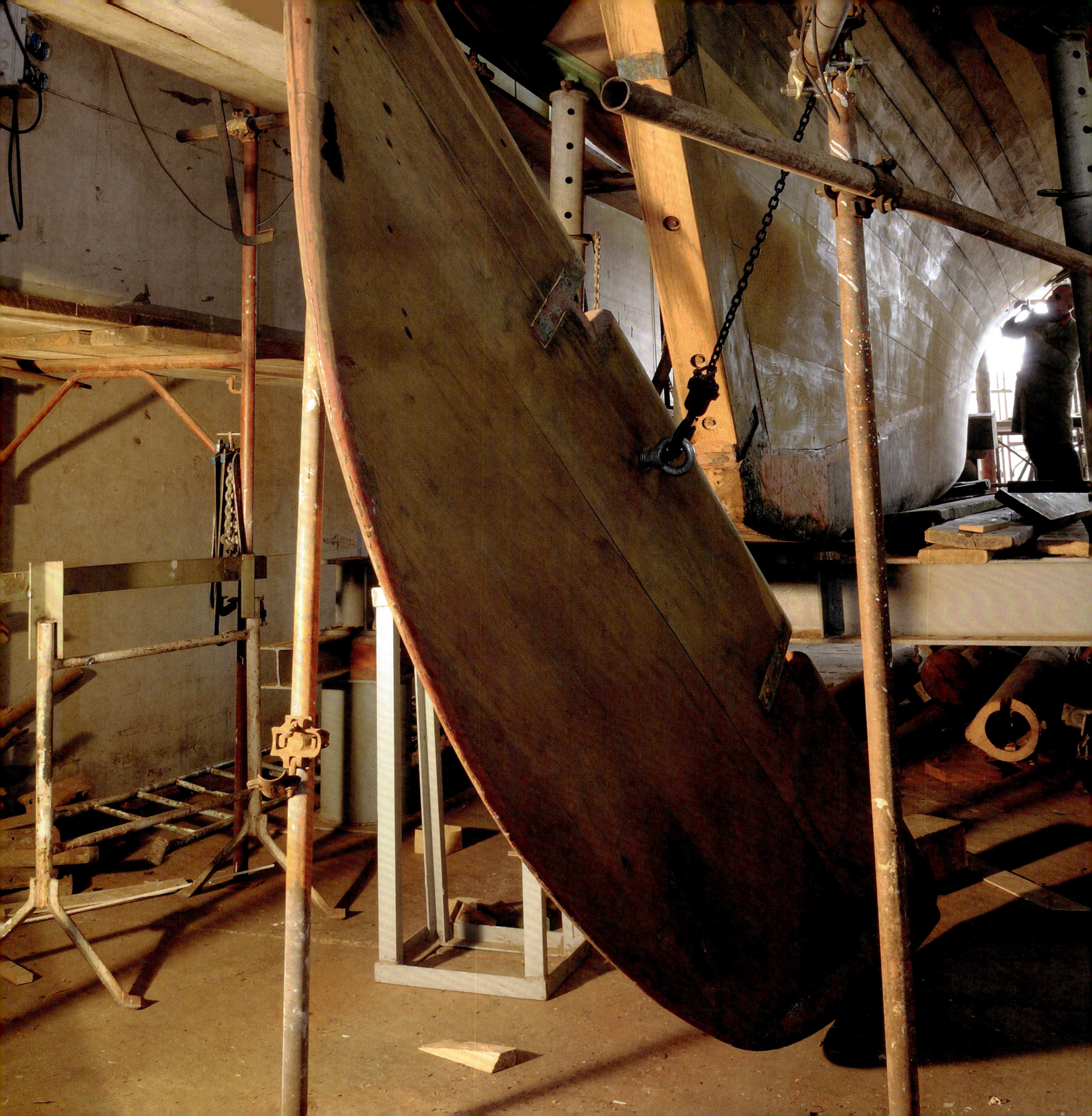

FACING PAGE The gold lettering of the name of the yacht has been carefully masked with tape and the paint spraying operation is in progress. A filler was used after each coat of paint and then meticulously sanded down before spraying the next coat of paint, which would be polished with high-grade sandpaper and burnished.

More than five thousand bolts, specially manufactured in a German foundry, were fitted using plastic gaskets, also newly designed, to insulate the three metals – bronze, zinc, and steel – from each other and against electrolytic corrosion in a saline environment.

Enthused by the grandeur of this work, which revived the best traditions, the artisans took care to employ traditional techniques: thus, the double ribs, the ties between the lower end of the ribs and the floors, as well as the stringers, were riveted on each side of the hull all the way along, just as in the original. Also, each iron rivet, twelve millimetres in diameter, was inserted in its hole then heated with a blowtorch and hot-swaged with a hammer. Well-proven methods, which ensured the greatness of ancient sailing yachts; this maritime heritage continues today among the best builders by being passed on from father to son. Three generations of Del Carlo: Francesco, founder of the shipyard, his son Guido and grandson Adriano, being a prime example of this tradition during the restoration of *Eilean*.

This respect for old skills was not just a bout of nostalgia: in fact, some modern shipbuilding techniques may offer numerous advantages but they do not always take into account future repairs. Obviously, nowadays it is simpler and quicker to glue or weld certain parts together but then, when an eventual repair becomes necessary, it is impossible to separate them and preserve their integrity. Traditional methods do allow for this eventuality.

Finally, all the deck beams were replaced: infiltrations through the deck, underneath the superstructures, had created rust points and weakened the mechanical properties of the angle bars. Therefore, after the restoration, *Eilean*'s metal framework is totally new and the ketch can expect to navigate another seventy years without any major problems.

After the completion of the new framework, to avoid stresses and deformation, the damaged planks were replaced alternately on either side of the boat. Because of the length of the hull, the teak planks constituting the topsides – about thirty on either side – were each made of several planks of about seven metres in length. They were butted and joined together by metal plates on the inside. The technical specifications indicated that each joint must be separated from the next one on the same frame by a minimum of three continuous planks. More than half of the planking was replaced.

The restorers were pleased with the original layout of the deck planks, which they were determined to preserve. Forward, a wide band of straight planks was laid lengthways to reinforce the longitudinal structure, right up to the

EILEAN

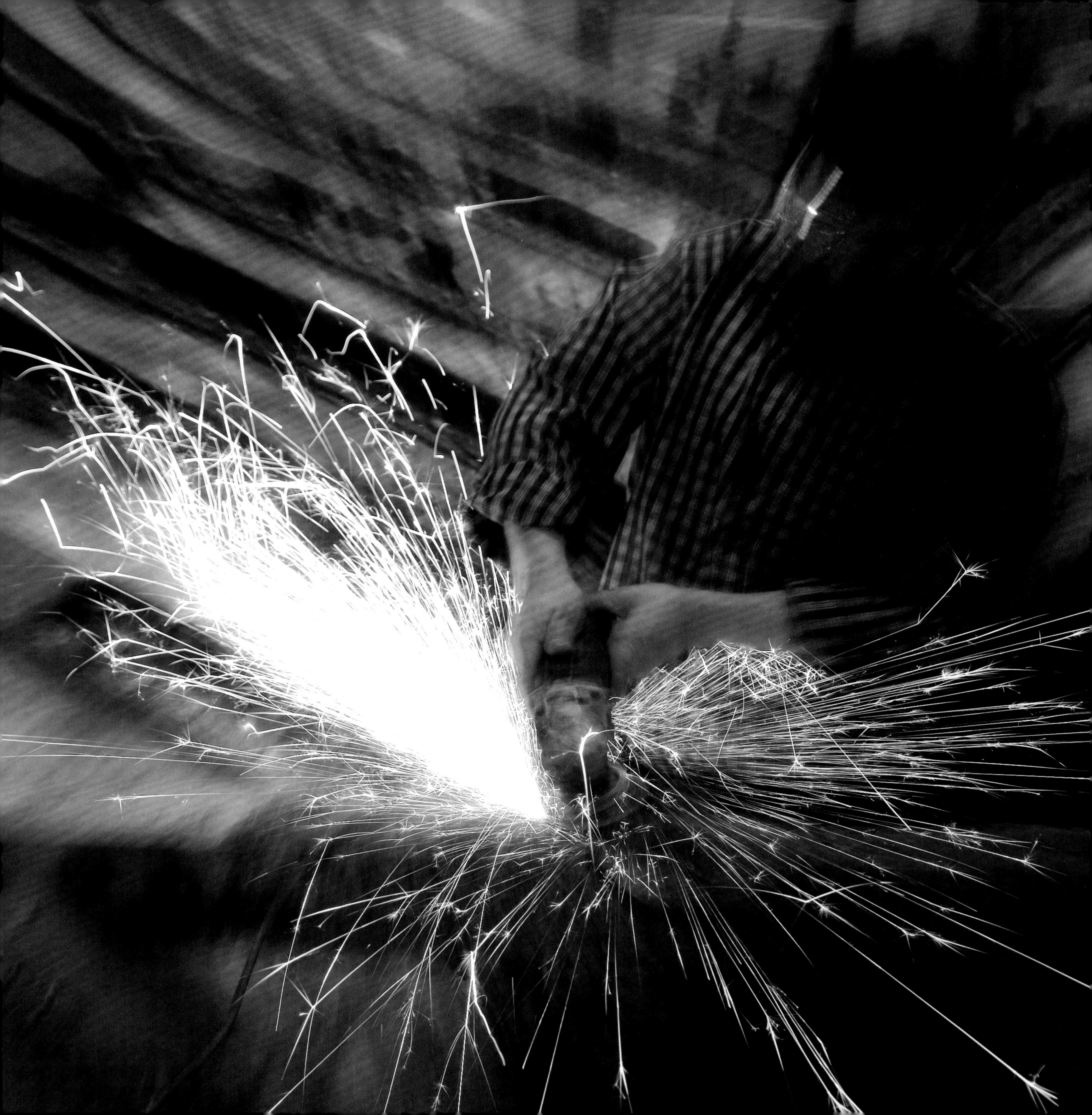

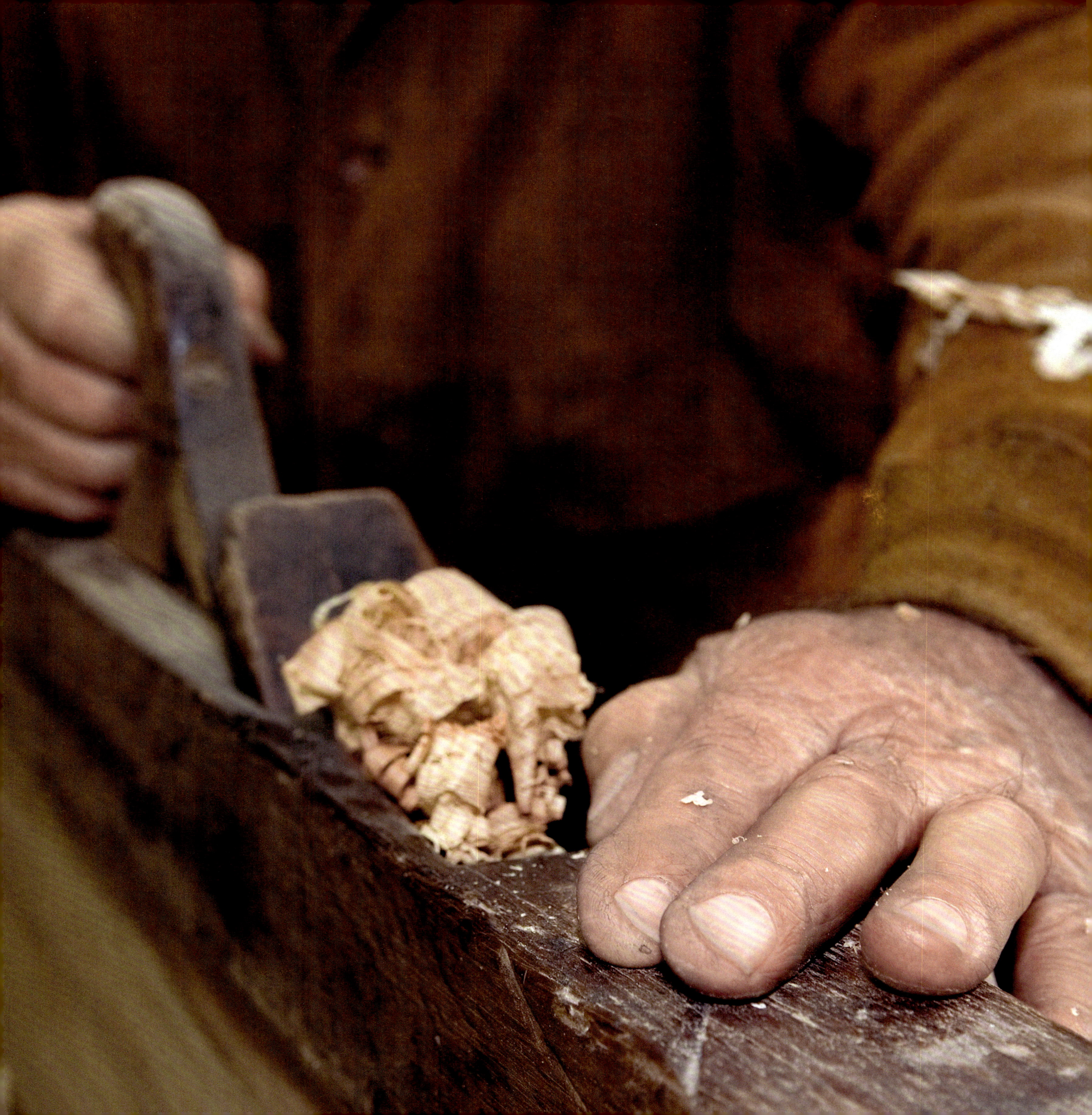

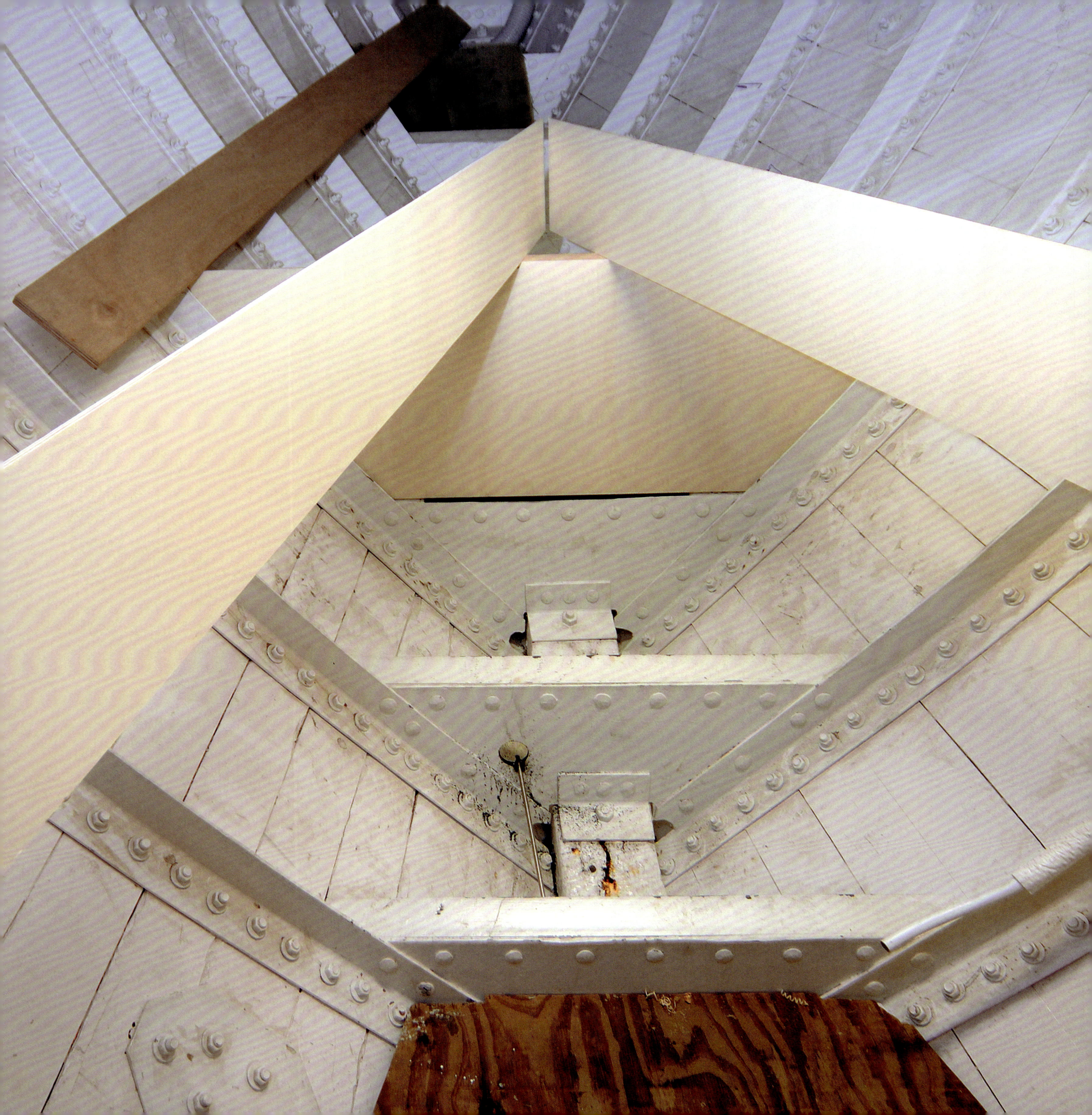

deck hatch just aft of the mast, to strengthen the bowsprit and windlass supports and act as partner. The same layout was reproduced aft of the companionway: the planks were as wide as the forward ones so as to strengthen the structure of the aft overhang, which can weaken over time.

The craftsmen remained faithful to the traditional shipbuilding methods when they offered advantages, but did not hesitate to use modern techniques when those would be beneficial to the ketch. The teak deck planking did not prevent water infiltrations, so a double layer of marine plywood, fifteen- and eight-millimetres thick was used, onto which the teak planks were glued, screwed down, and jointed with black silicone mastic. This 'modern' process offered three advantages: the plywood panels stiffen the hull, the teak planks can move slightly without leaking, and, if necessary, it would be possible to renew some planks without making a hole in the deck. Grooves were cut on the underside of the plywood to give it the authentic appearance of the old deckhead inside the cabin.

The craftsmen proceeded with fitting the waterways – larger planks on the edge on the deck – the bulwark and the toprail above, all in teak. These gave the yacht her definitive profile. Meanwhile, all the teak superstructures had been renovated or identically reproduced and the time had come to fit them on board. The cockpit coaming and the steering wheel bracket were refitted as well as the companionway hatch cover opening onto the engine room, the elegant doghouse, the aft cabins hatch, a deck locker forward of the saloon deck hatch, the hatch to the double forward cabin and the galley before the main mast, and finally, the crew quarter companionway. The renovation and the finish of these fittings, both on deck or down below, are worthy of the reputation of their designer, William Fife III, who had shown an extraordinarily fine eye for detail and harmony in their design. Officine Panerai's team was comfortable with these values of authenticity and modernity, a delicate mixture in a world in perpetual transition. At the same time, the painters had started their lengthy work of finishing the decoration, paying particular attention to the famous dragon drawing at the forward end of the toprail, which was the builder's signature trademark.

The two spruce masts were supplied by the Dutch 8 Metre importer of specialist and rare wood species, John Lammerts van Bueren. They were slightly lengthened to compensate for the extra weight of the modern equipment, but the sail area remained identical to the original. The deck gear included a few bronze drum winches manufactured exactly on the model of those fitted on *Eilean* in the 1950s. The goosenecks and other parts of the rig were all restored or recast in bronze if the radiographic analysis revealed any corrosion. Three bronze winches, matching the

PAGES 124–125 Whether in metal or wood, the construction and restoration of classic sailing yachts in particular, requires comprehensive skill in each operation and an expert knowledge of materials. Whilst working, whether cutting, sawing, planing, squaring, routing, sanding or piercing, the shipwright produces wood and steel shavings.

FACING PAGE Each piece of interior woodwork was made from a template to be sure it would fit in place perfectly. Limber holes at the bottom of the floors let the condensation water run to the lowest point in the bilge, the sump, to be pumped overboard.

PAGES 128–129 During the restoration, the shipwrights and cabinetmakers spent a considerable amount of time taking measurements and transferring them onto their work. Apart from a tape measure, they would also use a protractor, a square, an adjustable back-gauge, or a marking gauge, which allowed them to draw an equidistant line.

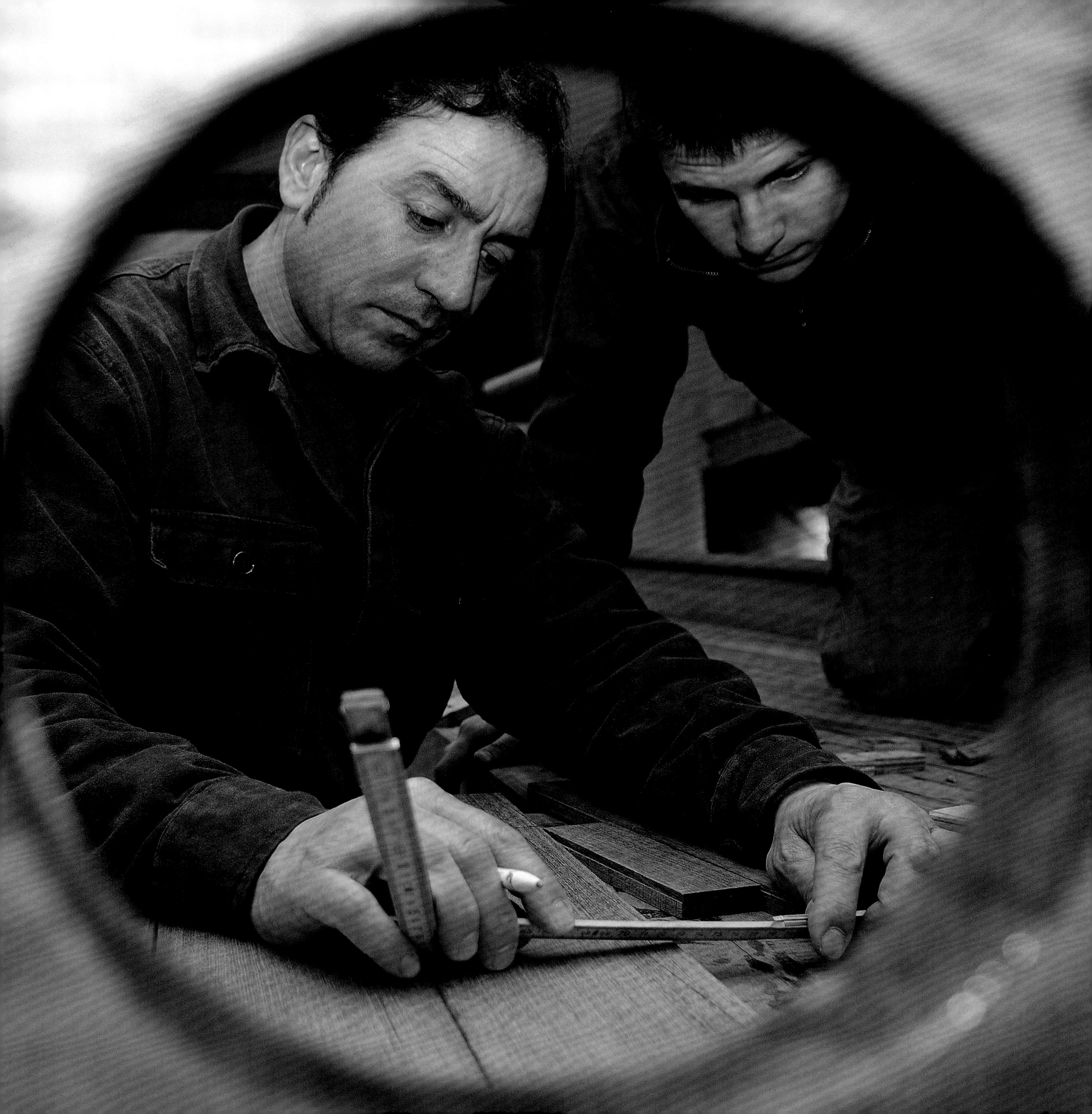

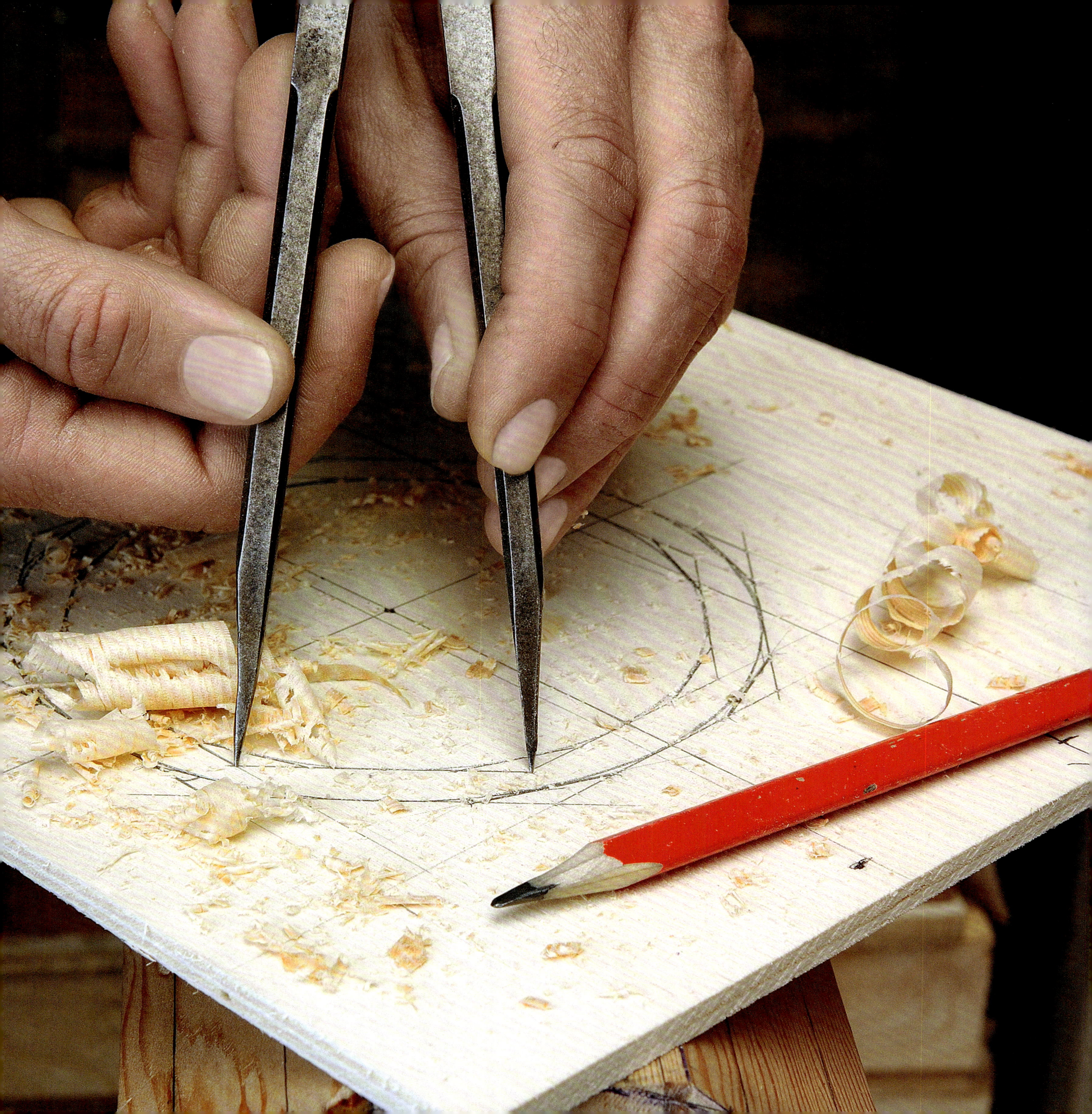

FACING PAGE A restored yacht can be recognised by the fact that all blocks, winches, and particularly the boom end fittings, are stamped with the boat's name. When the yacht is moored stern to, with the gangway in place on the afterdeck, it can be difficult to read the name, which is often lower than the quay.

PAGES 132–133 The manufacture of a steel frame to conform to the shape of the old one by using a template is a task of extreme precision for the blacksmith. Indeed, while the transversal parts of the angle bars are all parallel to each other, the side that fits flat against the planking is at a different angle on each frame, an angle that also varies from the bottom to the top of the frame.

compass binnacle and the other fittings, were put in place on deck. Similarly, four running backstay levers, specially manufactured for the yacht, replaced the traditional blocks and tackles to ease the tacking and gybing manoeuvres. When choosing the deckgear, priority was given to the capacity to manoeuvre the yacht when short-handed, requiring discreet, but efficient modern equipment.

Because it reflected a gracious art of living from a bygone era, particular attention was paid to the accommodation. The layout and decoration, plain, but not austere, were scrupulously respected. The saloon table was restored. The original elegance of the bathroom was reproduced, as well as that of the headlining and the door mouldings. When the ketch was built, the Fulton brothers did not plan to sail with more than a couple of friends, the four crew members having their own quarter in the forepeak. Among the discreet modifications made to allow for a comfortable life on board for more people, the aft bathroom was replaced with a washroom on starboard and a double cabin was added opposite the galley. The afterpeak, which had contained the batteries, the fuel, and paraffin tanks, was converted into the skipper's cabin with two transversal bunks; the engine compartment being accessible from this cabin. An ingenious design allowed the installation of two 110 hp engines, a desalinator, a generator, the automatic fire extinction system, and the heating and ventilation systems.

All those who collaborated with Officine Panerai followed the progress of the restoration of *Eilean* day by day. Particularly in the firm's workshop where clockmakers and engineers played their part by designing and manufacturing four instruments specifically for the yacht: a barometer, a hydrometer, a thermometer, and a clock, each in a 14 x 14 centimetres housing. Each with a black dial on a brushed steel background, they were fixed to the saloon bulkhead. A fifth navigation instrument, a ship's clock in a teak box with a fifty-two-hour runtime, was fitted in the cockpit.

It has taken more than two years of work, passion and enthusiasm, but finally the renaissance of the superb ketch that is *Eilean* has came to fruition. Today, she is defying the passage of time, and having regained her original splendour to the minutest detail, one of the most beautiful sailing yachts in the world is ready to cast off, head out to sea, and enter into maritime legend.

The historical links between Panerai and the Italian Navy have already been described. It was only natural that the firm that designed the Luminor and Mare Nostrum watches chose the La Spezia navy base to bless the restored *Eilean*.

PANERAI AND *EILEAN* 130

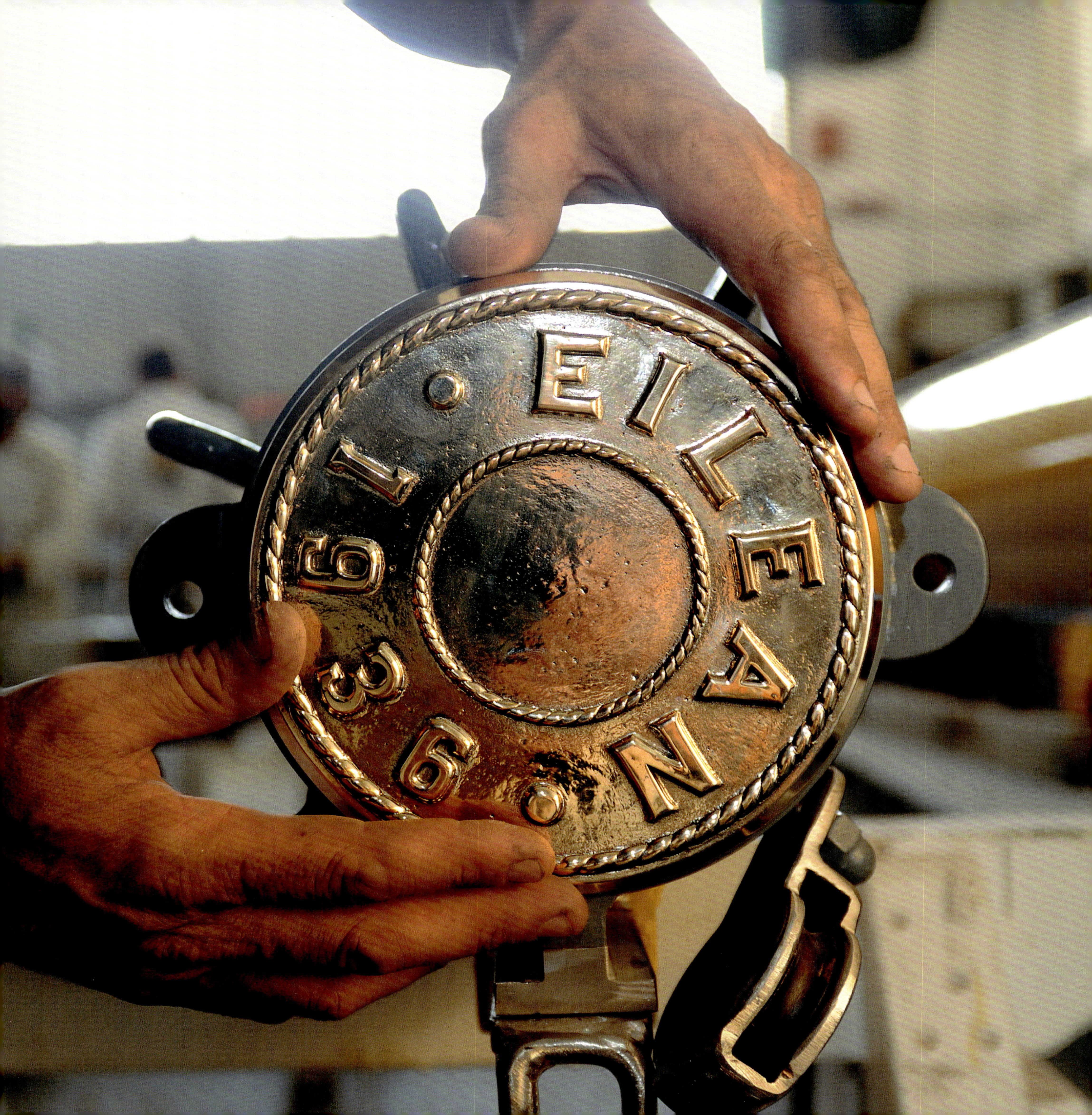
EILEAN
1936

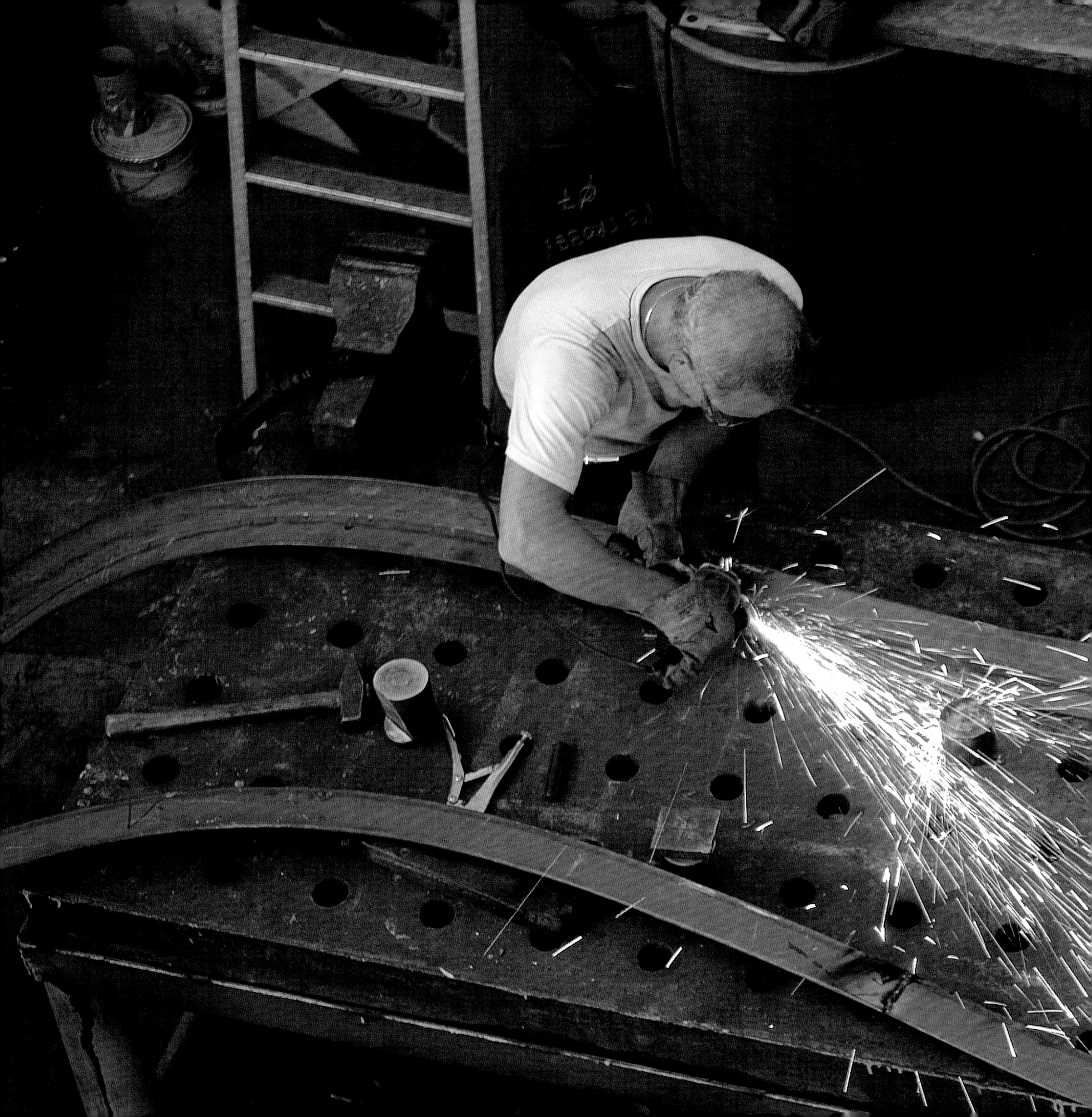

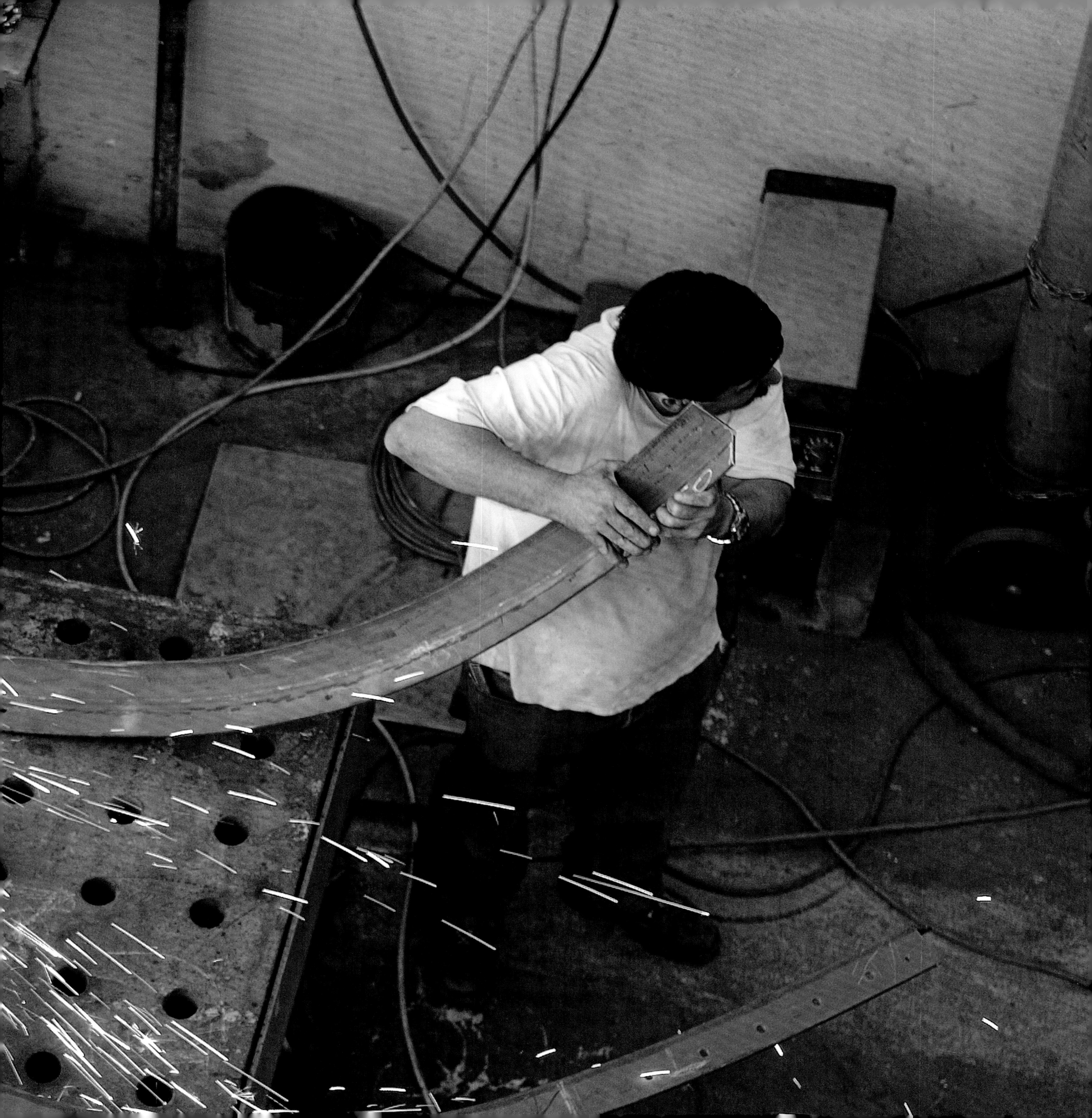

EILEAN

On 22 October 2009 in the pouring rain, in the presence of vice-admiral Franco Paoli, commander of the Tyrrhenian Sea fleet of the Italian Navy, *Eilean* was blessed in front of an assembly of celebrities, journalists from all over the world, and descendants of the former owners as well as May Fife Kohn, grand-niece of the yacht's architect. She came with her husband from Irvine, where the archives of William Fife III are kept; they both work to preserve and promote the achievements of the shipbuilders. May was upset that the vessel used by the Fife shipyard for the blessing of their yachts had been delayed in baggage at the airport. The traditional whisky and kilt were there, but sadly the cup with which she had hoped to surprise the guests was missing. William Shawcross, the son of Lord Hartley, who owned *Eilean* between 1963 and 1969, was very moved as he came down the companionway and instantly recognised the layout and the distinctive light in the aft cabins, produced by the same deck hatch. He felt nothing had changed, even though he had been a mere child and the boat seemed huge to him at the time. He recognised the small oval door handles and was reminded of a thousand other details on board. His emotion was shared by the whole team, which had done so much to preserve the spirit of the yacht. An unexpected guest honoured this simple ceremony with her presence, Mrs Eilean Mary Waterston Gilmour, the eldest daughter of James Fulton who, with his brother Robert, had commissioned *Eilean* in the first place at the Fife shipyard in 1936. 'Seeing *Eilean* restored to her former glory is very moving, and I am sure that all lovers of vintage sailing boats share my emotion', she explained.

    Eilean will resume her life as a great sailing yacht going from one racing venue to another between the spring and autumn on both sides of the Atlantic, but mainly in the Mediterranean, the very *mare nostrum* where she renewed her acquaintance with the sea, rather than being stranded at the bottom of a mangrove. She will well and truly sail for everyone's enjoyment.

FACING PAGE *Eilean* leaving the shipyard in Viareggio and about to be launched. With two propellers, two engines, and two fuel tanks, the ketch is guaranteed to get herself out of any tricky situation and be easy to manoeuvre in port.

PAGES 136–137 To ward off any bad omen, the custom is to place a gold piece under the foot of the main mast. *Eilean*'s is 25 metres high and, like the original, in Douglas pine. The mizzenmast, also in Douglas pine, is only 14 metres high. Of all the original spars, the only one which could be kept and repaired was the mizzen boom.

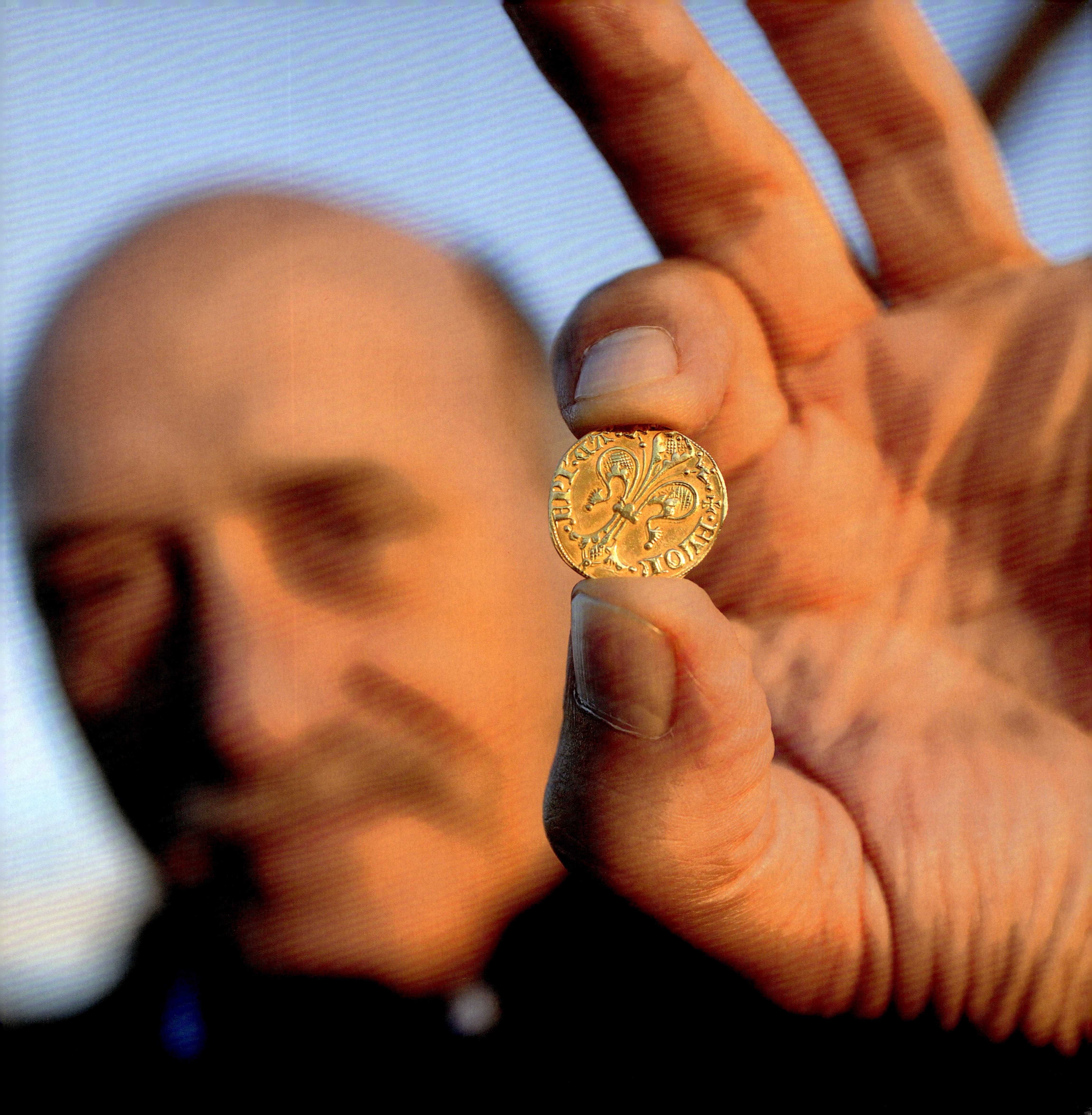

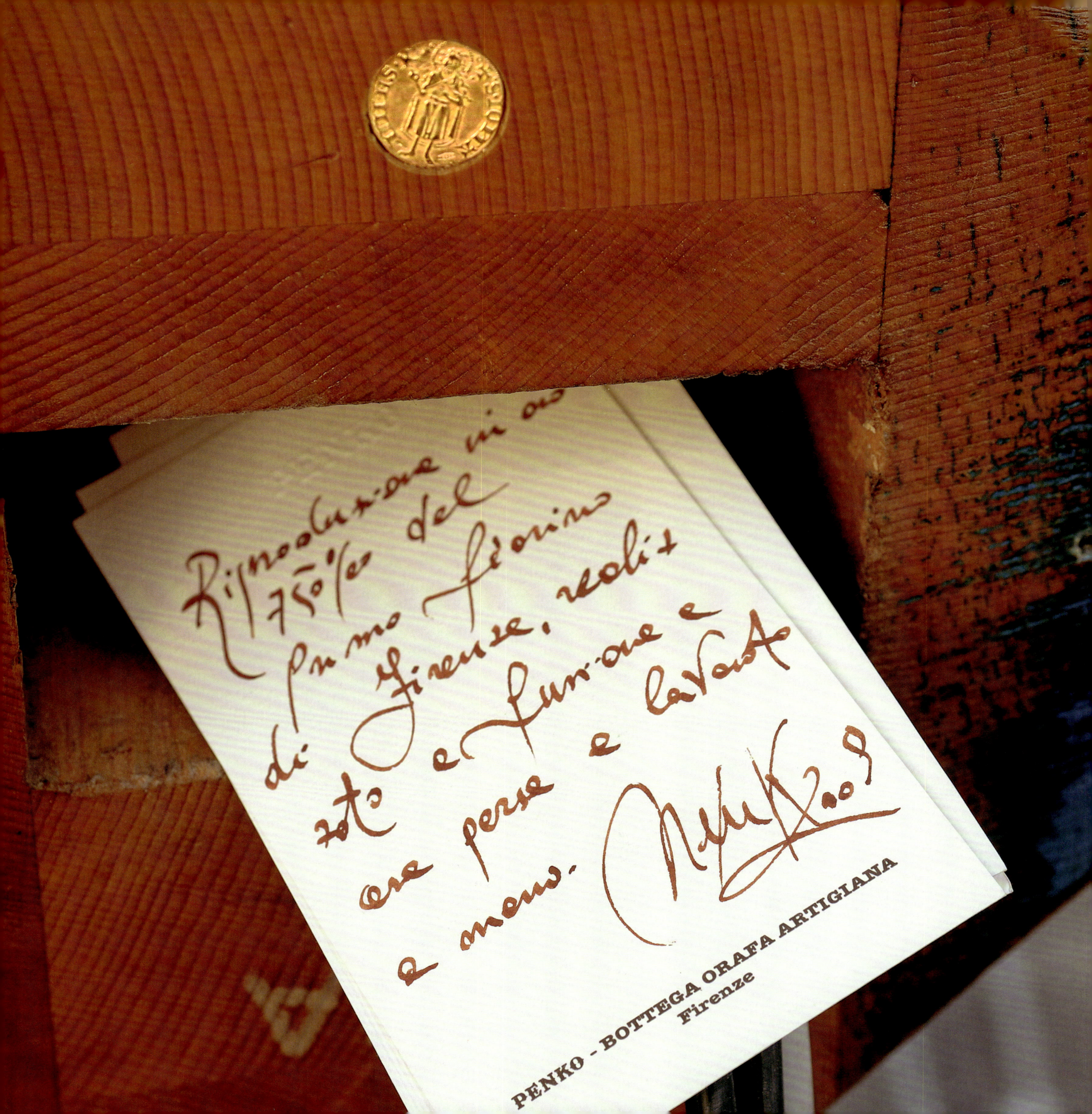

Riproduzione in oro 750‰ del primo fiorino di Firenze, realizzato a furore e lavato ore perse e mew. Paolo Penko 2009

PENKO - BOTTEGA ORAFA ARTIGIANA
Firenze

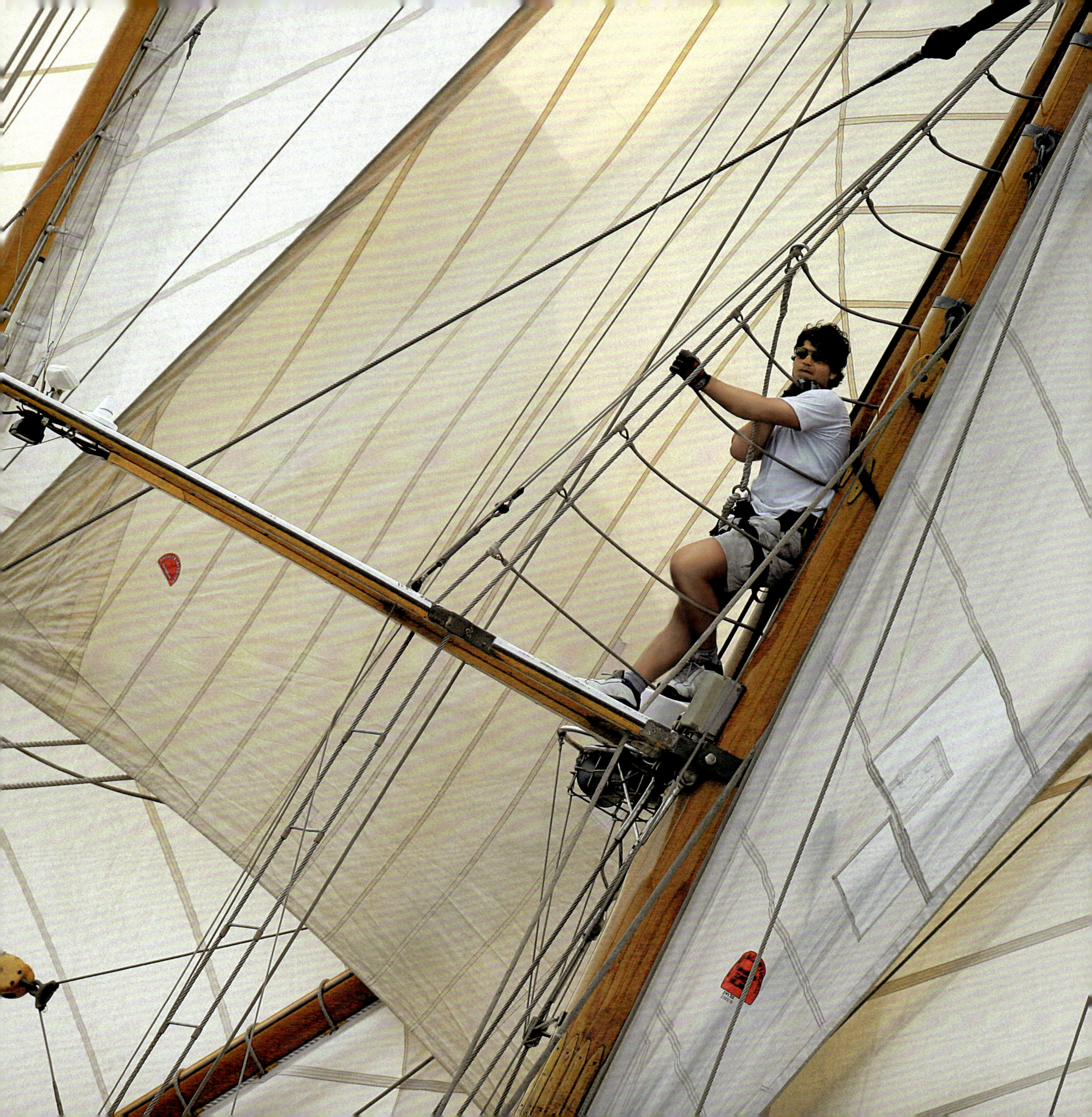

THE PANERAI CLASSIC YACHTS CHALLENGE

The passage of time is inevitable. Indeed, masterpieces can endure, but natural catastrophes, wars or financial crisis remind us that nothing can be taken for granted. The boats that have represented the legacy of the world of yachting since the nineteenth century today benefit from the attention of passionate and often wealthy connoisseurs. The rebirth of these exceptional yachts is almost a social phenomenon, a quest for one's roots and treasures lost or in danger of disappearing. Nothing is more affected by the passage of time than a sailing boat at the mercy of the weather and the seas, which will do anything to engulf her. Fortunately, the sea did not get the better of *Eilean*, one of the last great Fife yachts, in spite of her hundred and fifty thousand miles on the seas.

Just thirty years ago, who would have imagined today's passion for classic yachts? It was unheard of at that time. Then it seemed justified to rebuild Christopher Columbus's *Caravel*, the *Santa María*, to celebrate the 500th anniversary of his first expedition, but the restoration and the refit of sailing yachts, which are now taking part in the *Panerai Classic Yachts Challenge*, was just a dream.

Officine Panerai's CEO is passionate about watches and he is also fascinated by the sea and classic sailing yachts. In 2005, he launched the *Panerai Classic Yachts Challenge*, a series of five great regattas taking place between June and September: the *Argentario Sailing Week*, the *Vela Clásica Menorca Copa del Rey* in Mahón, Balearic Islands, the *Vele d'Epoca a Porto Rotondo*, Sardinia, and the *Régates Royales* de Cannes and *Les Voiles de Saint-Tropez*. The following year, he extended the regattas overseas and added the *Antigua Classic Week*, the *Voiles d'Antibes*, the *Robert H. Tiedemann* 12 Metre Regatta in Newport, the *Opera House Cup* of Nantucket, and the famous *Vele d'Epoca d'Imperia*, abandoning *Les Voiles de Saint-Tropez*, but covering the main meetings of classic yachts all over the world.

The first spring series of classic yacht races take place in Antigua, in the West Indies. Here, sunshine and wind are guaranteed, two conditions essential for the enjoyment of the scenery, clear blue water, and coasts covered with tropical vegetation, from the deck of a Corinthian racing boat. Admiral Nelson was right to choose this island to shelter his fleet from storms. Today, it boasts the lowest suicide rate in the world; this must be due to the gaiety of the people and the warmth of the welcome! In the middle of the 1960s, two new hotels were built: the Inn, in English Harbour run by Peter Deeth, and the Admiral's Inn by Desmond Nicholson, whose daughters often sailed on board the ketch *Eilean* in her heyday. Every Sunday morning, Peter and Desmond organised races between the two hotels

FACING PAGE Up in the schooner *Mariette*'s crosstrees, about which the historian Jacques Tagland has just published a monograph, the deckhand is kept busy. In this prime position, he can communicate to the navigator his observations, such as the areas of flat calm.

FACING PAGE In the middle of September 2006, the *Vele d'Epoca* regattas in Imperia saw the victories of *Bona Fide* and *Moonbeam IV*.

PAGES 142–143 Easily recognisable by her tiny varnished transom, *Outlaw* was designed to the limits of the rating rules by the famous British architects Primrose & Illingworth for the 1963 Admiral's Cup. Restored in 1985 by Mike Horsley, she is seen here taking part in Argentario regattas, which have been included in the *Panerai Classic Yachts Challenge* since 2005.

on board *Sailfish* dinghies, predecessors of the *Sunfish*, in teams of three. The trophy moved from one bar to the other in tune with the victories. In 1967, the two accomplices and a few friends created *Antigua Sailing Week* which raced Classics and Vintage yachts, and founded the English Harbour Yacht Club, which five years later became Antigua Yacht Club. In 1988, the owners gathered aboard the beautiful black schooner *Ashanti of Saba* designed by Henry Gruber in 1954 and created the *Antigua Classic Yacht Regatta*. With the increase of yacht restorations in Europe and in the United States, this sporting week has with time become an event not to be missed. The island's government declared that yachting would be the 'national sport'. Antigua Classic Week in April 2006 marked the debut of Officine Panerai as the first Italian sponsor in the Caribbean home of sailing.

Since 1996, on the other side of the Atlantic, the *Voiles d'Antibes*, organized annually around the first week of June, marks the start of the Mediterranean circuit for the Tradition and J Class yachts. Ten years after its foundation, it has become the first stage of the *Panerai Classic Yachts Challenge* in Europe. Some of the world's most beautiful 'vintage yachts' (built before 1950) always take part in the Panerai Regattas held during the *Voiles d'Antibes*, alongside 'Classic' yachts (built before 1976) and 'Spirit of Tradition', as well as metric class (6 Metre, 8 Metre and 12 Metre) yachts, which shaped the marvellous story of international yachting. Come spring, the boats return to their homeport in the Mediterranean. Some will have been refitted and modernised to optimize their performances, others will have changed owner or crew. Each year the entrants assemble around a hard core of legendary yachts, such as *Ikra*, *Thendara*, *Lelantina*, *Outlaw*, *Adria*, *Cambria*, or *Tuiga*, which have taken part in most races since their inception. Every year, between five and fifteen new boats appear on the circuit, having been recently restored, refitted or even rebuilt. Favoured for the quality of the match races for metric classes and other regattas for classic yachts along the coast between the bays of Antibes and Juan-les-Pins, the Panerai Regattas of the *Voiles d'Antibes*, uphold the purest tradition of yachting – five days of events before the world-renowned jazz festival, which takes place the following month. Around 15 June, the classic yachts based on the Riviera and those from the Ligurian Coast cross the Gulf of Genoa and head for Monte Argentario in Tuscany to take part in the Argentario Week. This fortified town, which stands on a rocky island linked to the mainland by three isthmuses, is a north-facing harbour. Monte Argentario is on the west side of the bay, opposite Porto Santo Stefano. Due to its strategic position in the Tyrrhenian Sea, close to the islands of Giglio and Montecristo, this port has always been involved in shipbuilding,

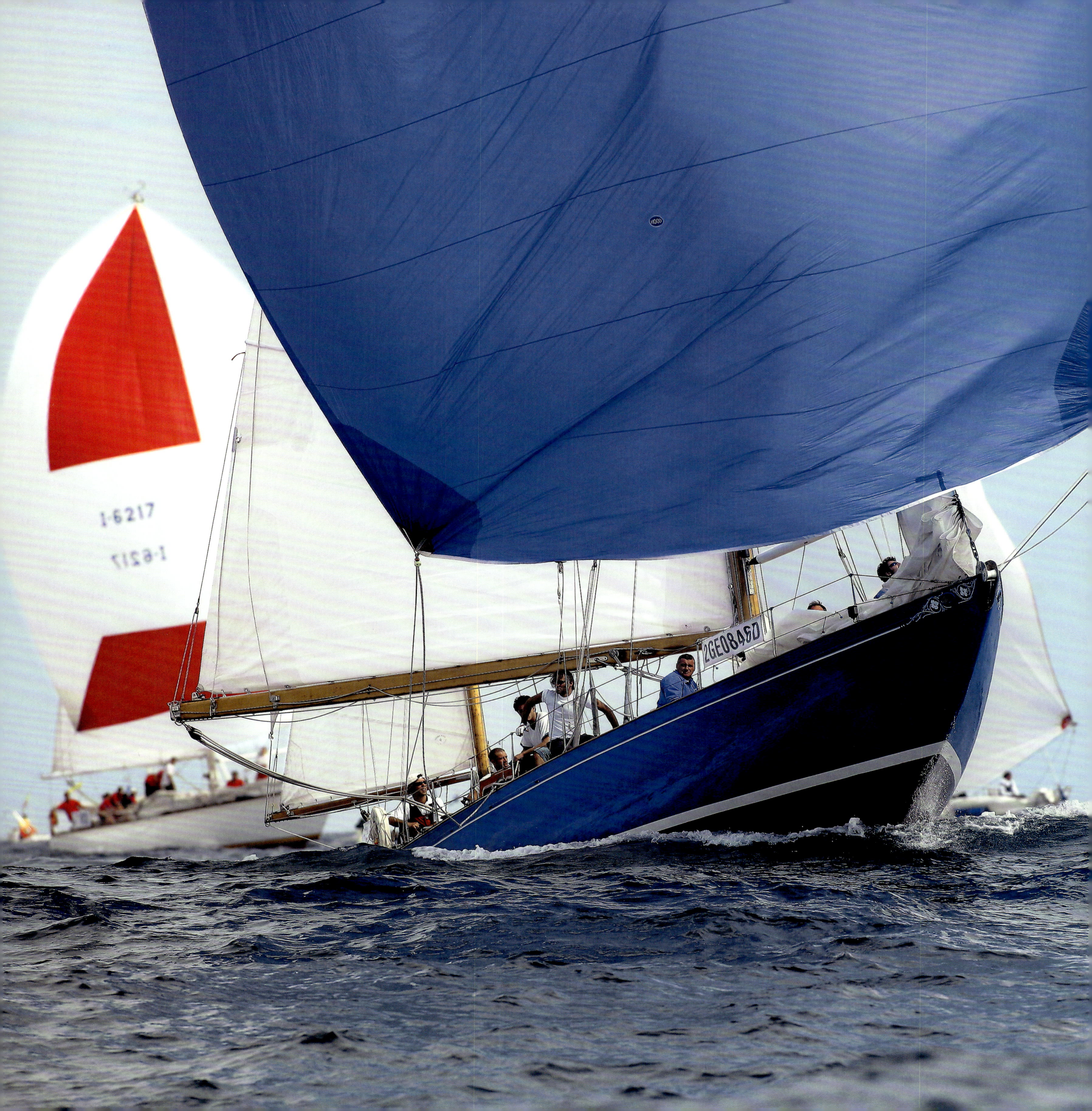
I-6217
2GE0846D

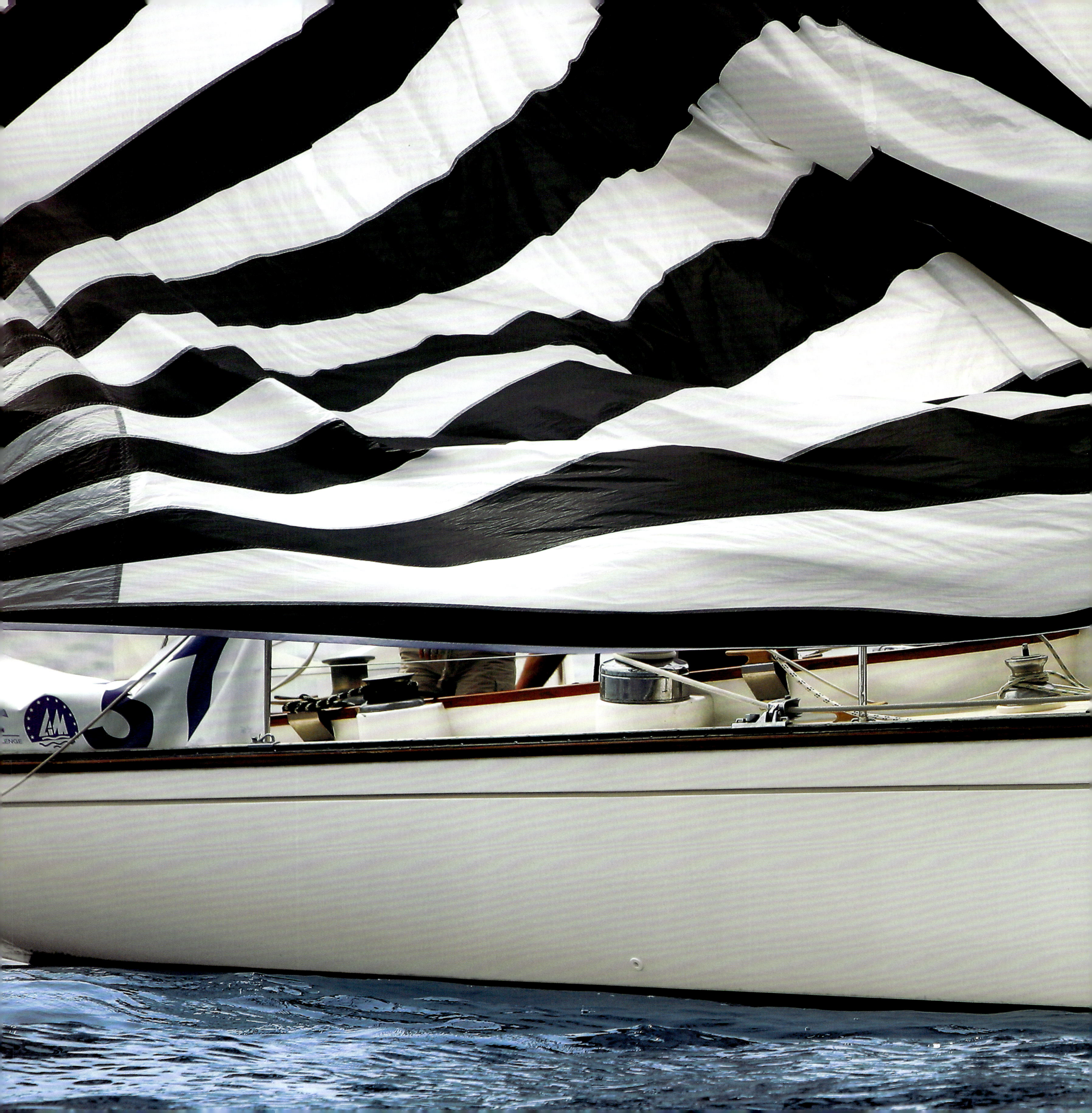

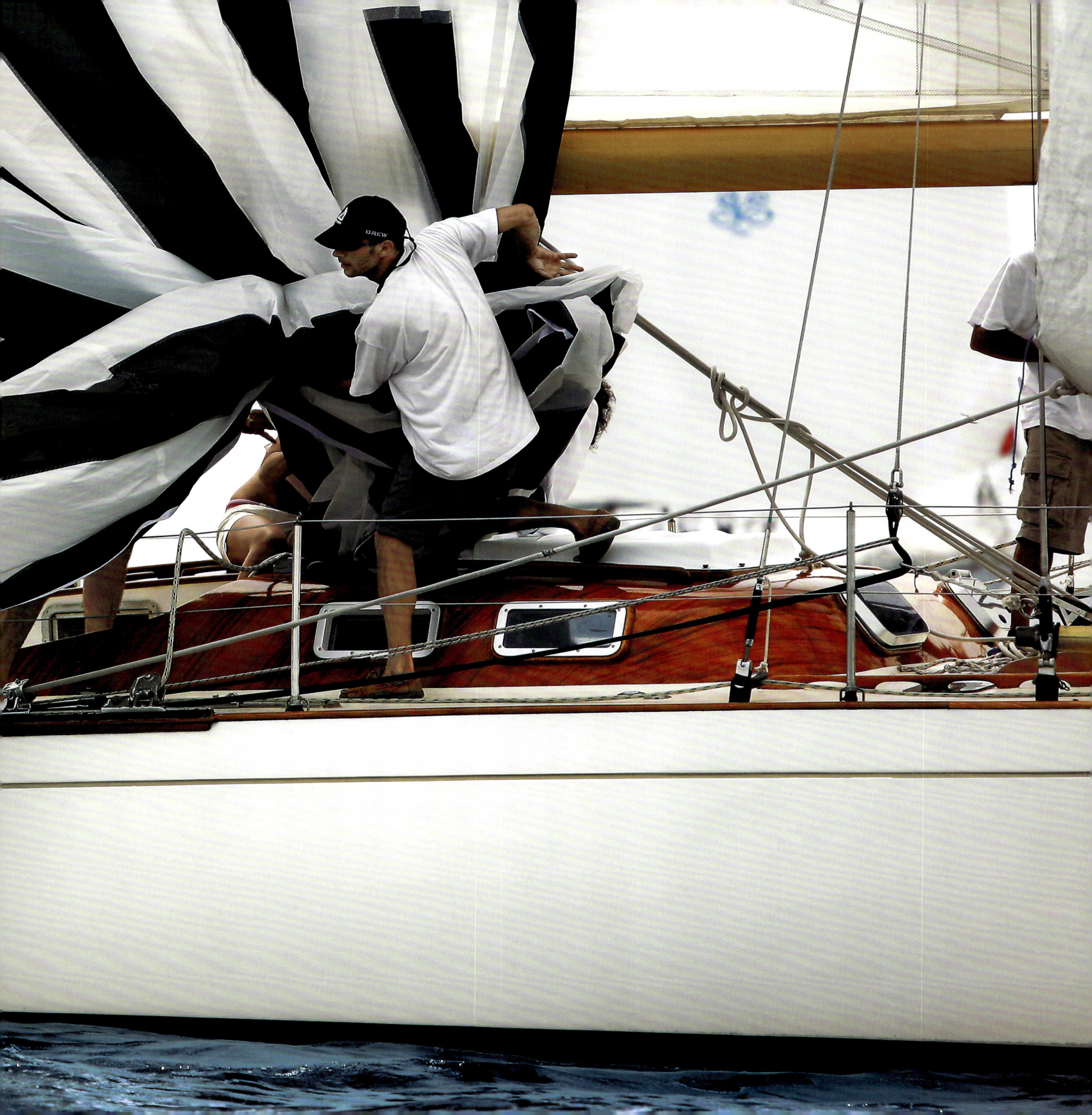

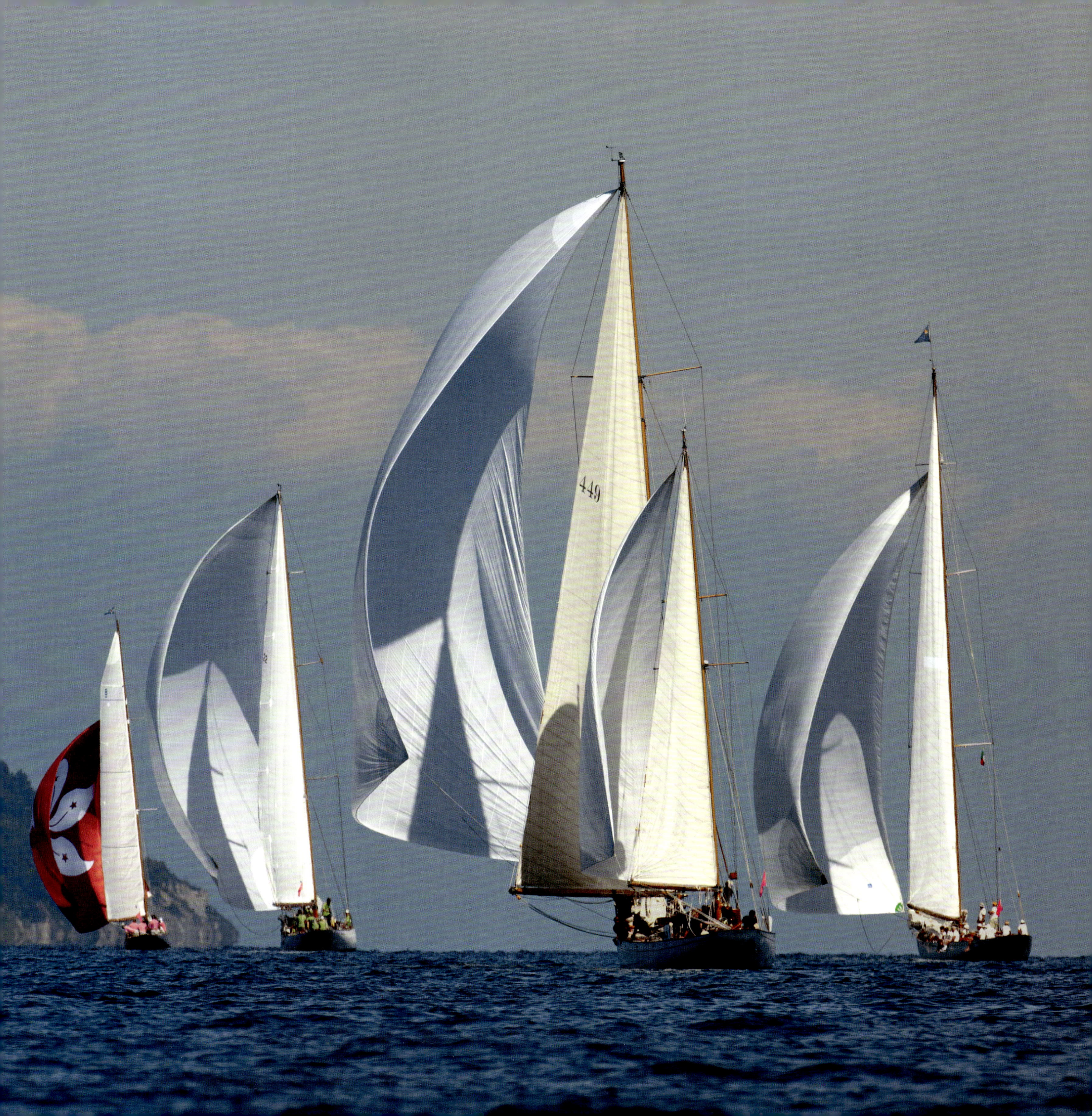
449

and is now focused on the restoration of classic yachts. Three of the most famous Olin Stephens sailing yachts, *Vim*, *Dorade* and *Stormy Weather*, were refitted there during the last few years.

In 2010, the *British Classic Yacht Club Panerai Cowes Regatta*, which takes place in the Solent, joined the regattas of the Panerai Classic Yachts Challenge. July 2002, ten yachts attended the inaugural British Classic Yacht Club Regatta held in Cowes marking the start of an annual regatta which has continued to grow in size and popularity. What started as a long weekend of informal racing has now grown to a week-long regatta of rallying and racing split into many classes. In 2006, forty yachts ranging in size from the International 5 Metre, *Sensa*, to the 95 foot Samuel White bermudan ketch, *Berenice*, attended the regatta, coming from all over the UK and Europe. Aside from the stunning spectacle of gorgeous classic yachts racing in the changeable waters of the Solent, the regatta is known for many things – the varying social calendar, the friendly camaraderie on and off the water and the quality and variety of racing. The highlight of the week is the *Classic Round the Island Race*. Photo opportunities abound as the fleet starts together on the Royal Yacht Squadron line before racing the 60 nautical miles course either east or west about the Isle of Wight. The leader board changes constantly as the tides play their part in the race. This regatta before the *Cowes Classic Week* is now the key classic yacht event of the UK yachting calendar.

Marblehead, cradle of the American Navy and its yachting division, could not miss out on the fun and the new enthusiasm caused by classic yacht racing. The location of the Mystic Seaport Museum, it is the hub of life of wooden boats and other ancient sailing yachts where amateur sport is a religion and passion for the sea a second nature. For the 2010 event, the *Corinthian Classic Yacht Regatta* was included in the North American *Panerai Classic Yachts Challenge* circuit, establishing a link between the different classic yacht challenges in American waters. It takes place on the first weekend of August, followed the next weekend by the regattas on the isle of Nantucket, the Nantucket Opera House Cup Regatta, which has been part of the *Panerai Classic Yachts Challenge* since 2006. Nantucket – 'far away country' in Amerindian language – lies just 70 sea miles from Boston, opposite Cape Cod peninsula.

It was a huge whaling centre until the middle of the nineteenth century, but since the beginning of the last century the island population emigrated. Since the 1960s, the island has become an exclusive resort, like the nearby Martha's Vineyard. On the last weekend of August, the fleet of classic yachts that stayed in the Mediterranean, and those transported as cargo in time, take part in the *Copa del Rey de Barcos de Epoca* in Mahón on the Balearic island of Minorca.

FACING PAGE *Eilean* during her first race after restoration, balloon jib and staysail pulling in the wind, her racing number 449 is visible high up on the mainsail. Even with all these majestic sails well set, the light breeze finds it hard to push these heavy displacement narrow hulls through the choppy seas off Mahón.

PAGES 146–147 The yawl *Agneta* (1952) designed by Knud Reimers and the 23 Metre William Fife *Cambria* (1928) here taking part in the *Régates Royales* in Cannes at the end of September. With her 26-metre varnished hull, *Agneta* stands out and elegance is de rigueur for all on board. The light-coloured spruce masts shine against the sails.

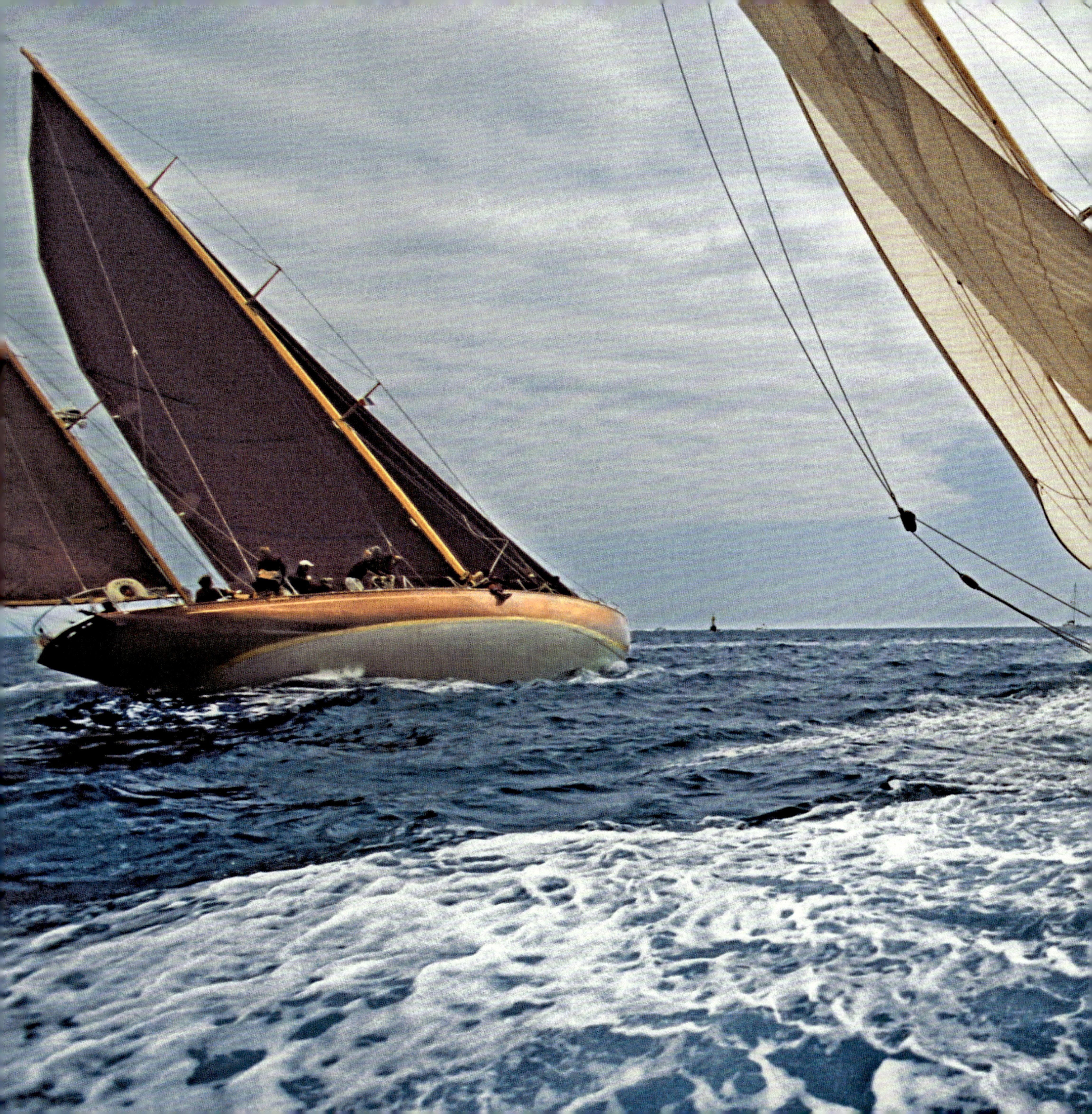

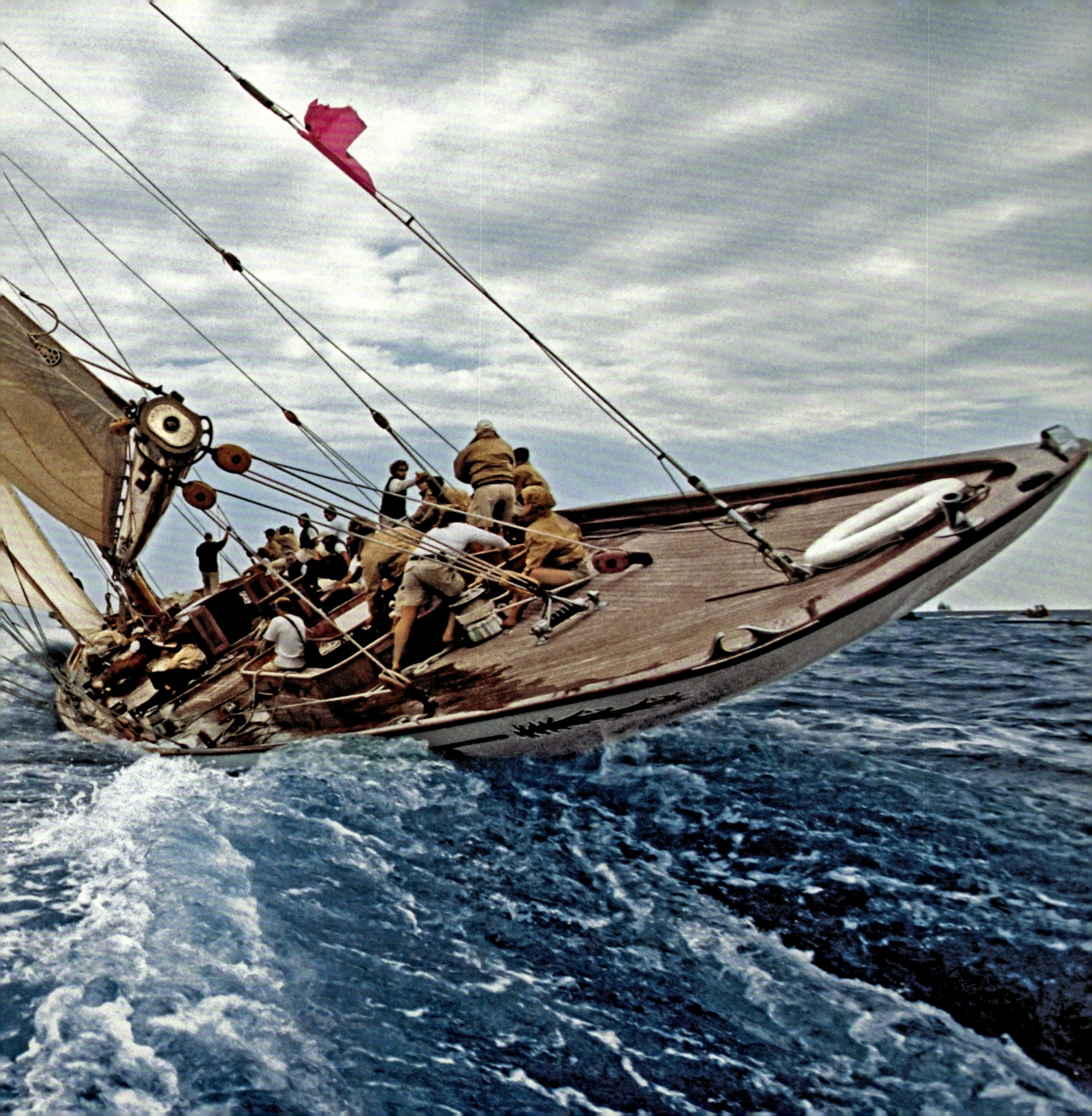

FACING PAGE Changing sails on large classic yachts is always an acrobatic manoeuvre, particularly for the bowman who ends up every time on the bowsprit in a precarious situation.
The flying jib is hanked on the forestay, ready for hoisting to the top of the mast.

In recent years, Spain, and Catalonia in particular (because of Barcelona), has become an ideal refuge for yachts between two periods of charter. Sailing has always been supported by the Spanish Royal family. Historically, the 15 Metre Class owes a lot to them – and it is also heavily promoted by the local government to make of Mahón an international sailing venue. This event has been part of the *Panerai Classic Yachts Challenge* circuit since 2005 (except for 2009), and is co-organised by the Barcelona Real Club Náutico and the Club Marítimo de Mahón.

Back on American soil, on the first weekend of September, in Newport, Rhode Island, the temple of yachting, the *Museum of Yachting Classic Yacht Regatta* takes place; it was here that for fifty-three years – from 1930 until 1983, a fateful year for Newport – all the America's Cup races were organised. The fascinating Museum of Yachting tells of the fantastic J Class epic and the story of the 12 Metre specially designed for this event, as well as that of the major players on the scene at that time, such as Harold Vanderbilt, Sir Thomas Lipton and Ted Turner. After taking part from 2006 in the *Robert H. Tiedemann Regatta*, which is run in Newport for the 12 Metres at the end of July, Officine Panerai entered the annual Classic Yacht Regatta, later in the season. The Twelves race alongside the 6 Metre, the Classic yachts, and Spirit of Tradition classes – much favoured on the coast of New England – and the S-Boat, a class of sailing boats 8.38 metres in length designed by Nat Herreshoff in 1919. Of the ninety-five yachts built, seventy-five are still racing. After this event, which marks the end of the American season, Officine Panerai awards the *North American Panerai Classic Yachts Challenge* circuit, equivalent to the Mediterranean Challenge on this side of the Atlantic. In early September, every two years, part of the fleet of classic yachts meets in one of the most paradisal sites on the planet, Porto Rotondo in northern Sardinia on the Costa Smeralda. Since the 1960s, the Italian jet set settled first on the island of Marinella, and then on the coast where Porto Cervo and Porto Rotondo were created. The meeting place of film stars, political and sport high flyers, this new town acquired a yacht club in 1985, the Yacht Club Porto Rotondo. *The Panerai Classic Yachts Challenge* is a superb event where the most beautiful yachts in the world sail amongst the superb rocky islands of the western Mediterranean Sea.

Founded in 1986, the *Vele d'Epoca di Imperia*, takes place every two years, before the middle of September. It consists of five days of regattas and nautical events. *Imperia* was created because Mussolini wanted to join together the districts of Onille and Port Maurice, separated by the river Impero. The two towns have very different origins,

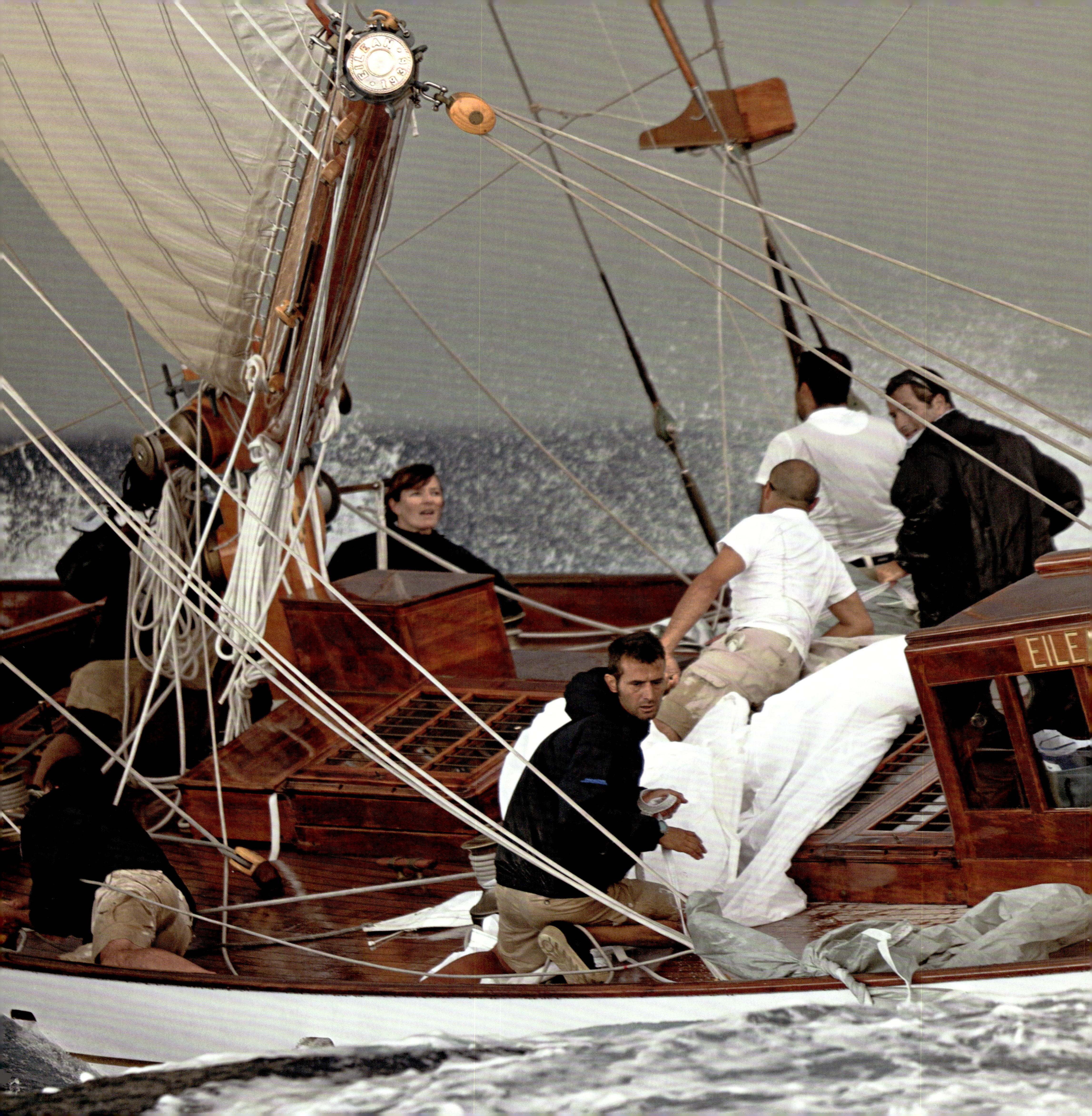
EILE

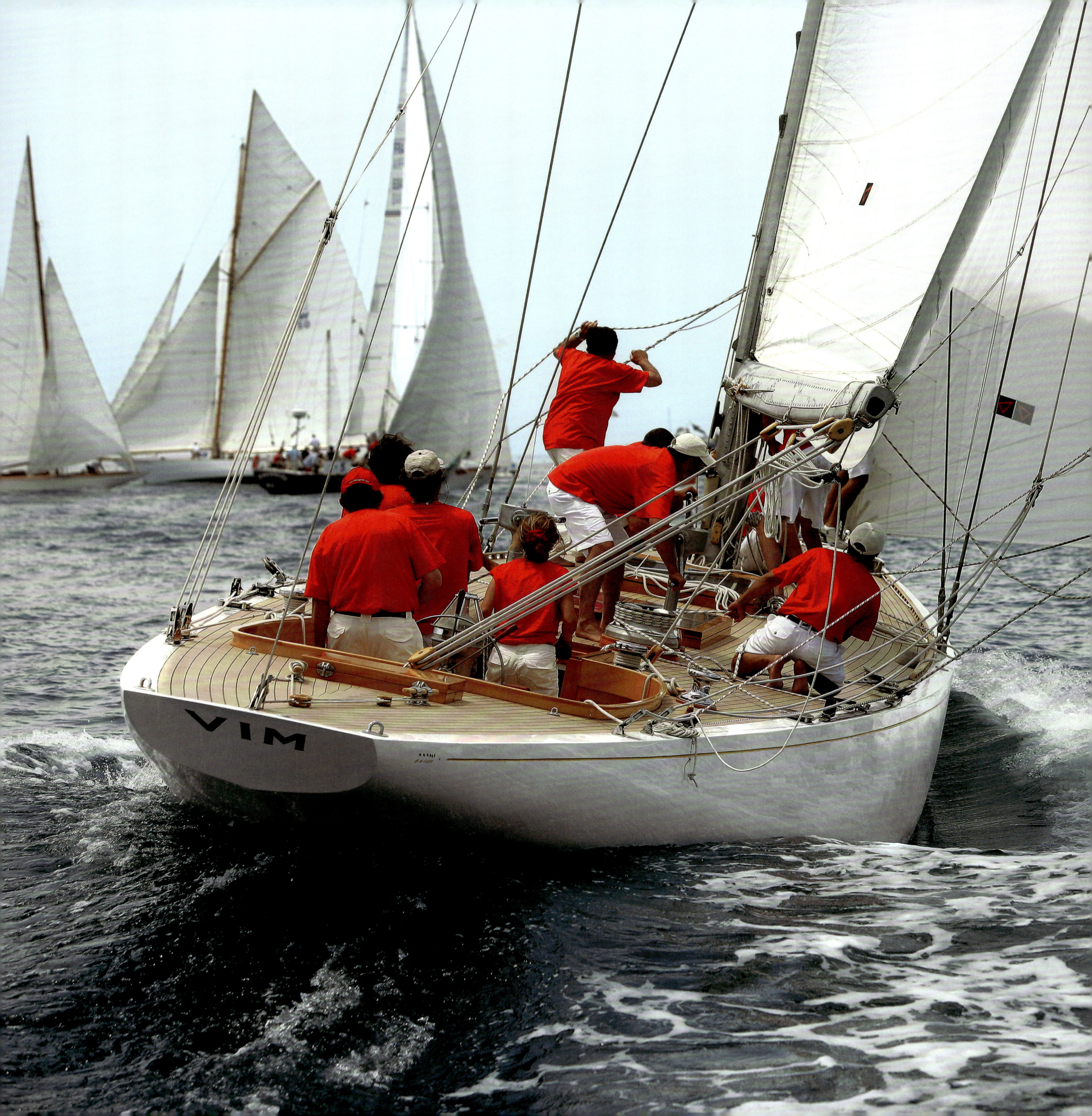
VIM

one belonged to the County of Savoy, domain of the Dorias, and the other was allied to the town of Genoa; today, they are home to a series of classic-yachts regattas, which attract a larger public each year. There were twenty-five competitors for the first *Vele d'Epoca*, but now more than one hundred and fifty sailing yachts parade majestically along the Ligurian coast, to the delight of several hundred thousand spectators. It has become an unmissable occasion for the owners of classic yachts and, being part of the Panerai Classic Yachts Challenge since 2006, this event is widely covered by Italian television.

Out of the forty-plus classic boat gatherings held between January and October, from New Zealand to Italy via the West Indies, the United States, Denmark, and France, the *Régates Royales* in Cannes, has to be the favourite. Most competitors come straight from Imperia, and Cannes always attracts a large number of 6 Metres, 8 Metres, and Twelves at the end of September. Since yachting began, the Cannes Yacht Club, founded in 1860, has always welcomed great yachts at the beginning of the season for memorable regattas. The *Régates Royales* were created in 1929 for the Great Class yachts like *Ailsa* and *Britannia*. Abandoned after the war, they were restarted in 1978 by Jean-Pierre Odero and the navigator Philippe Monnet, firstly with just a few 8 Metres. Supported by the Société Nautique de Genève, Cannes became a major racing venue for J-Class yachts and Dragons. When in 1991, Elizabeth Meyer and her J-Class *Endeavour* chose to come to Cannes, the fame of the *Régates Royales* was made. The following year, a few classic yachts joined the event halfway through the races. In 1994, it became the favourite meeting place for the entire traditional yachting world. Since 2005, the *Régates Royales* have been included in the *Panerai Classic Yachts Challenge* and mark the end of the season.

Conforming to their tradition, Officine Panerai designs limited series watches to be awarded to the winners. Thus, the firm contributes to the preservation of an exceptional maritime heritage, where beauty and knowledge compete with passion and respect for tradition.

FACING PAGE *Vim* (1939), an Olin Stephens design for Harold Vanderbilt, was one of the most famous 12 Metres. She took part in the 1958 America's Cup Challenger selection races, being narrowly beaten by twelve seconds by the last Stephens's design, *Columbia*. With an unlimited budget, she was totally restored in 2003 and now regularly takes part in classic yacht races on the Riviera.

PAGES 152–153 On the start line, the Great Class yachts are vying for position. *Lulworth*, the black schooner *Mariette*, *Cambria*, and *Mariquita* form a pyramid of 3,400 square metres of sails.

PAGES 154–155 To ensure the safety during manoeuvres on schooners, such as *Elena* or *Eleonora*, or even the three-masted schooner *Atlantic*, a crewmember, a minute silhouette against the background of the huge sails, climbs up in the crosstrees to stop any sail snagging when dropped or hoisted.

PAGES 156–157 Scene from the Opera House Cup, which takes place after the 15 August in Nantucket, Massachusetts, a major whaling centre until the middle of the nineteenth century.

PAGES 158–159 Being bowman on *Mariette* involves certain risks when the yacht falls in the trough of the wave.

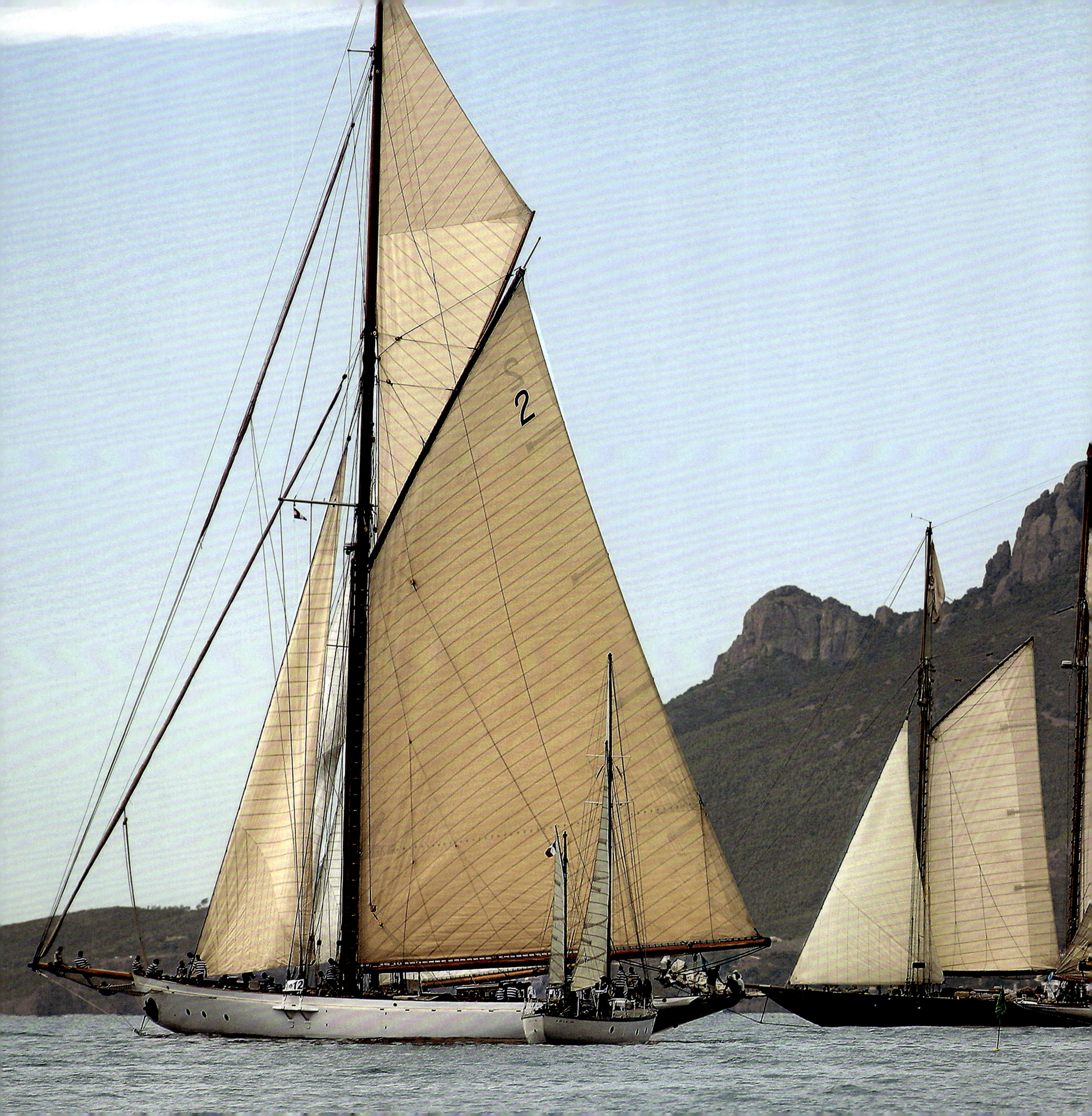
2

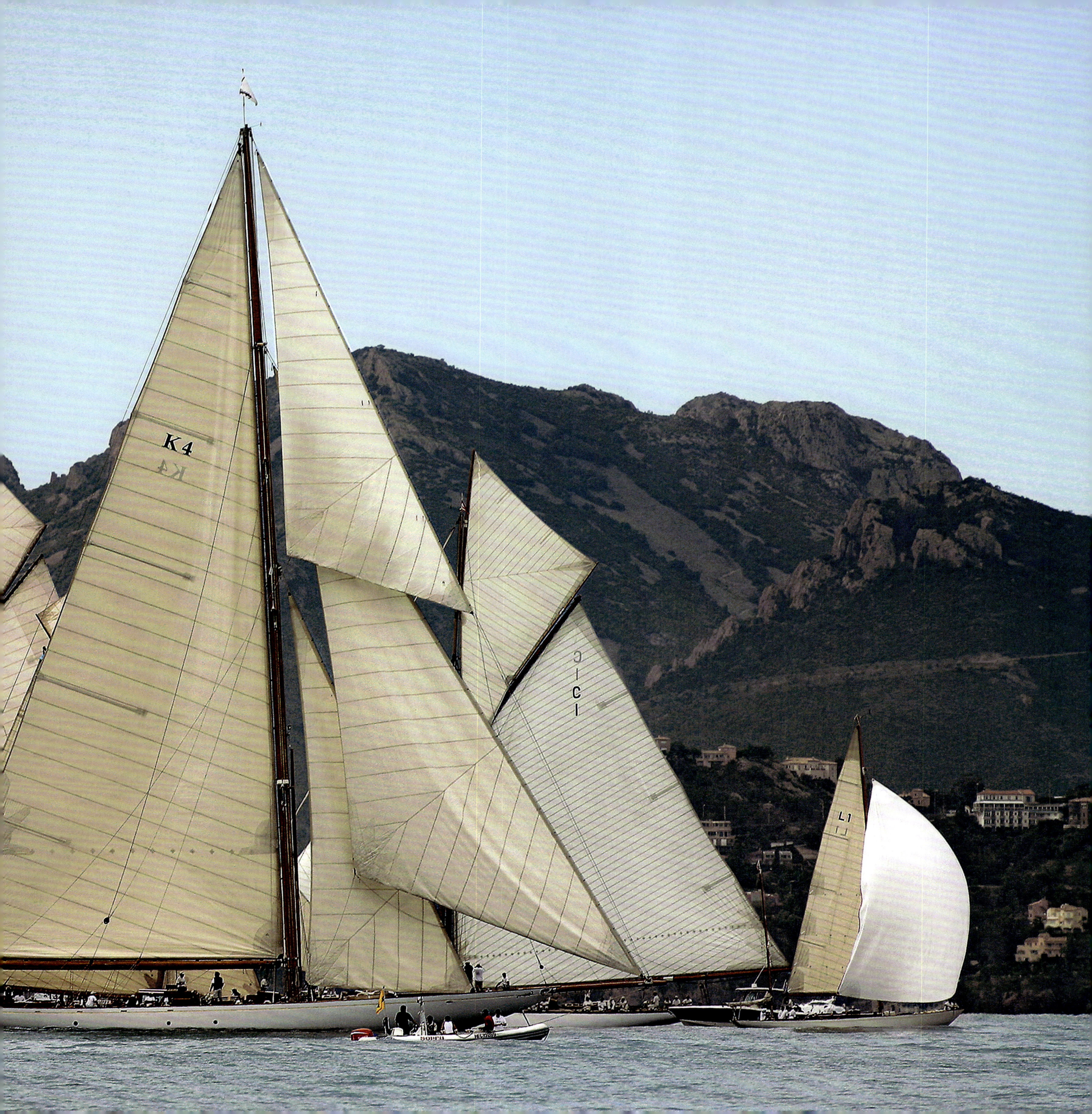
K4
L1

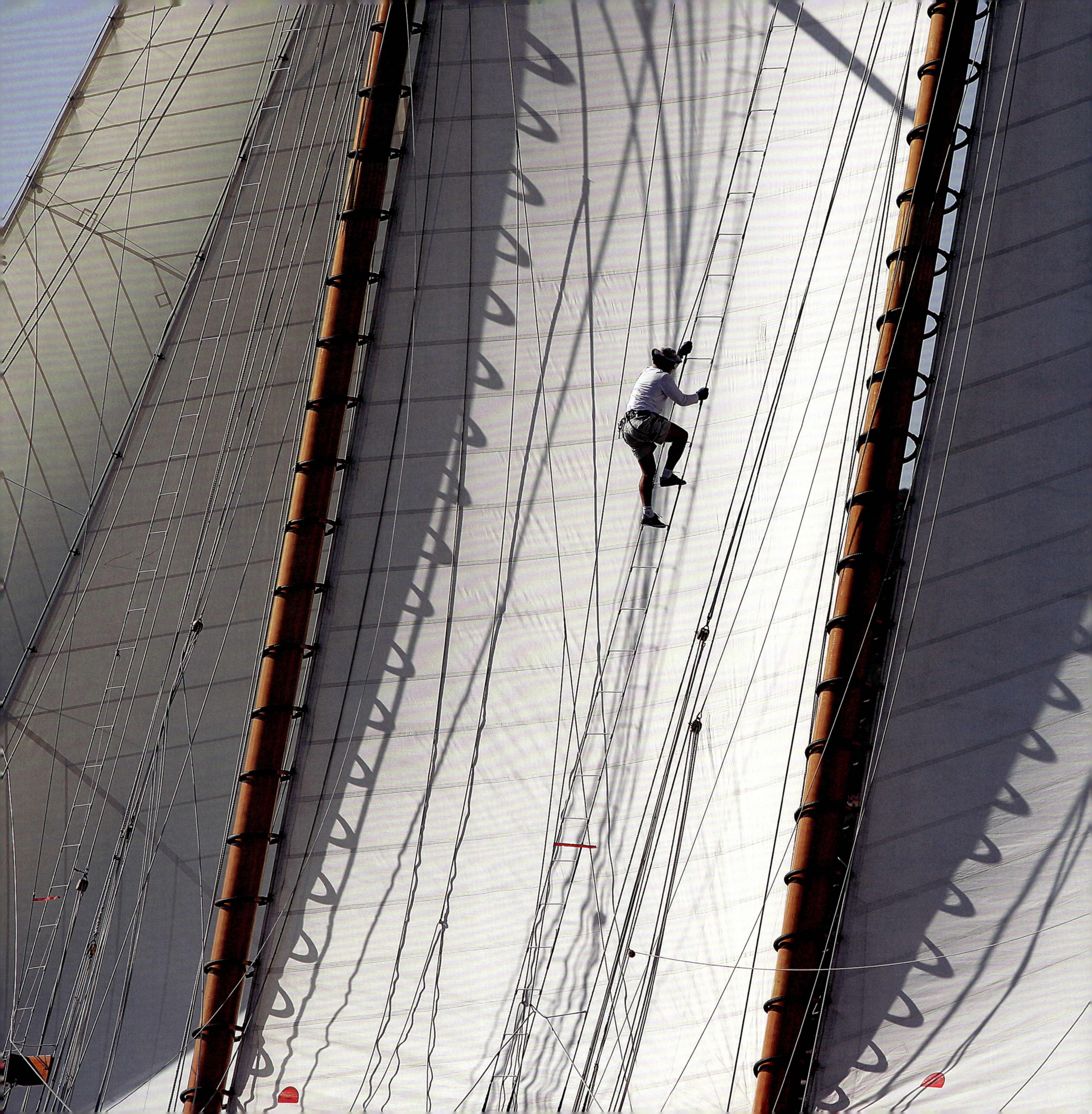

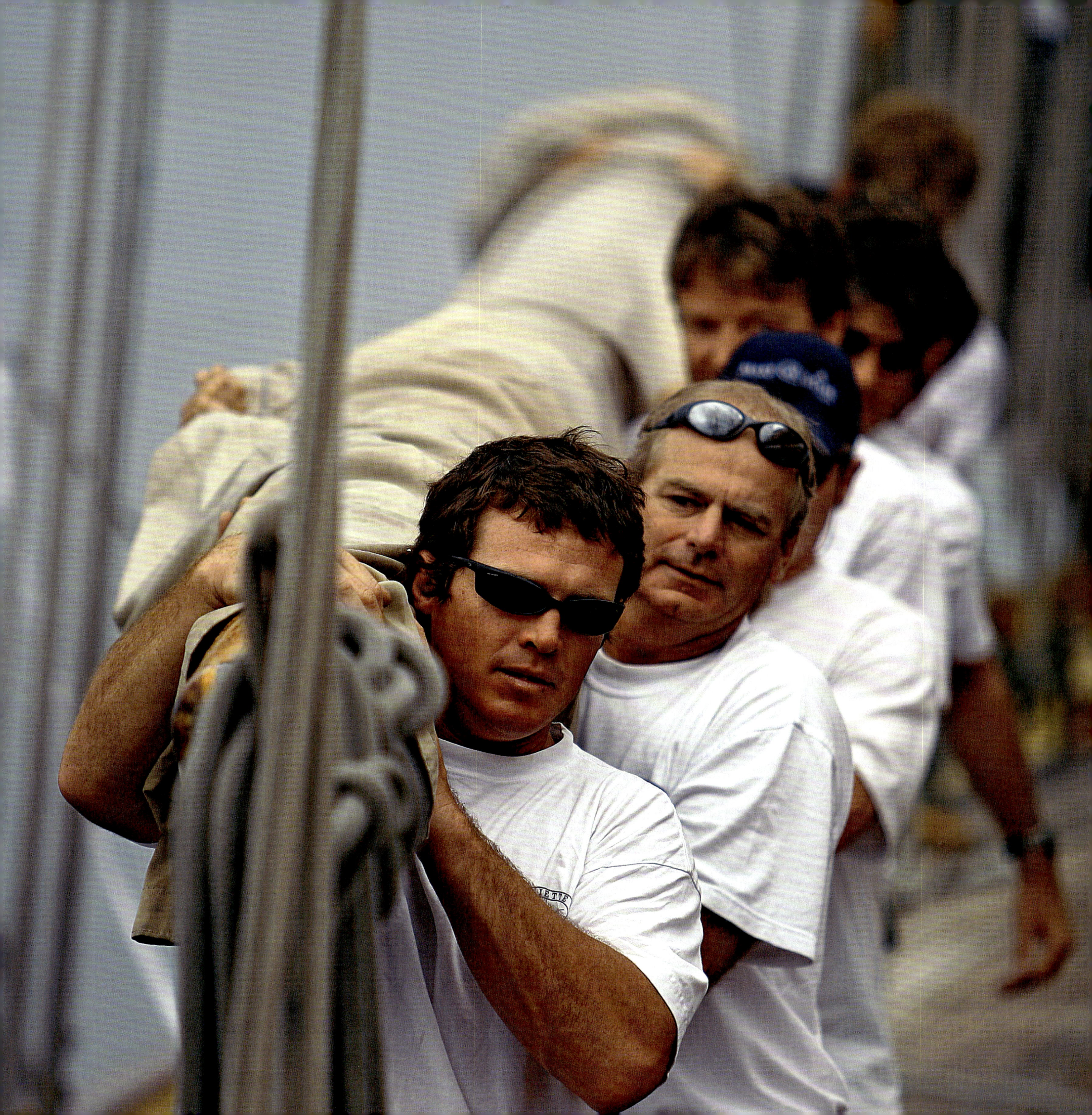

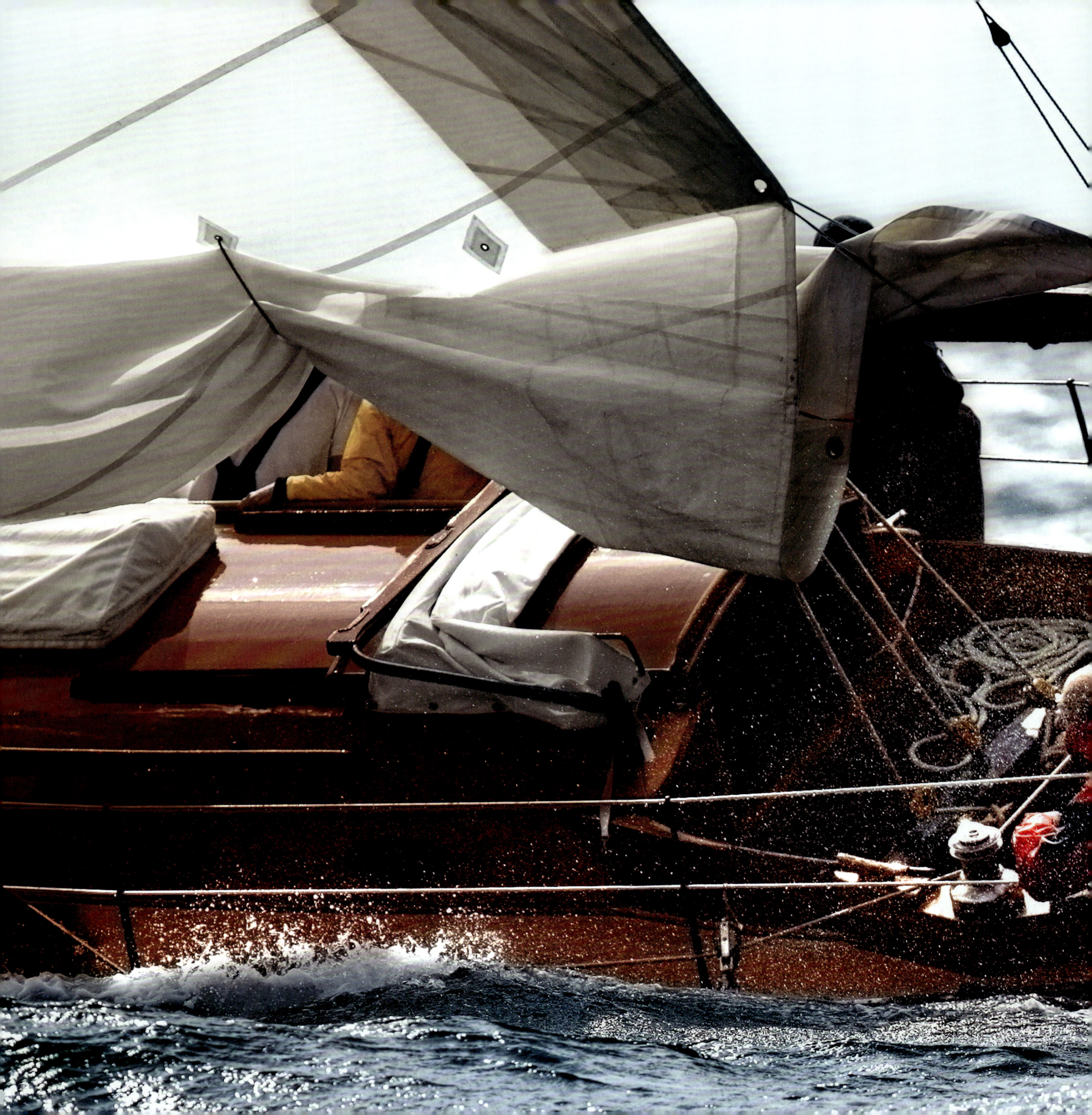

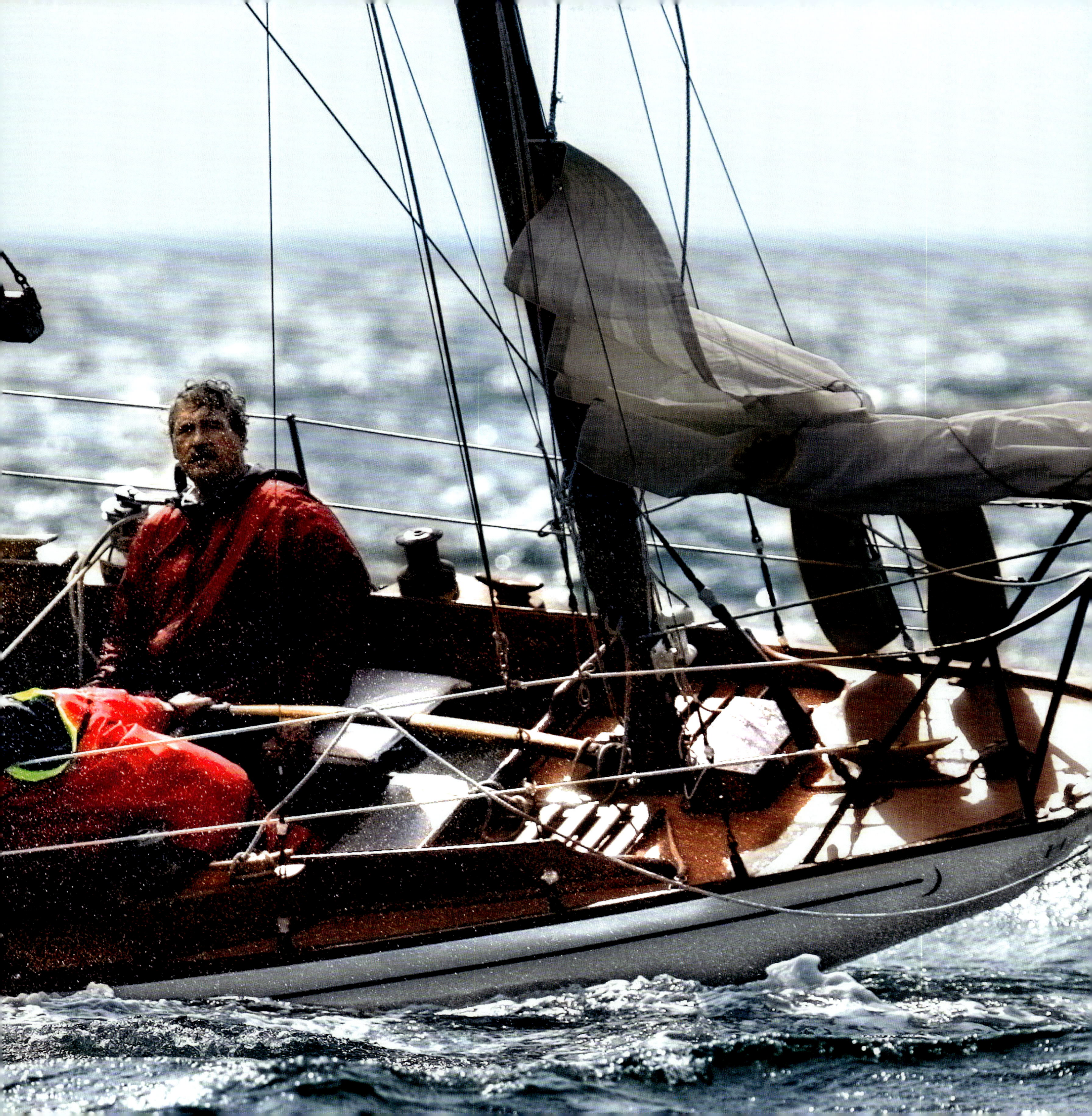

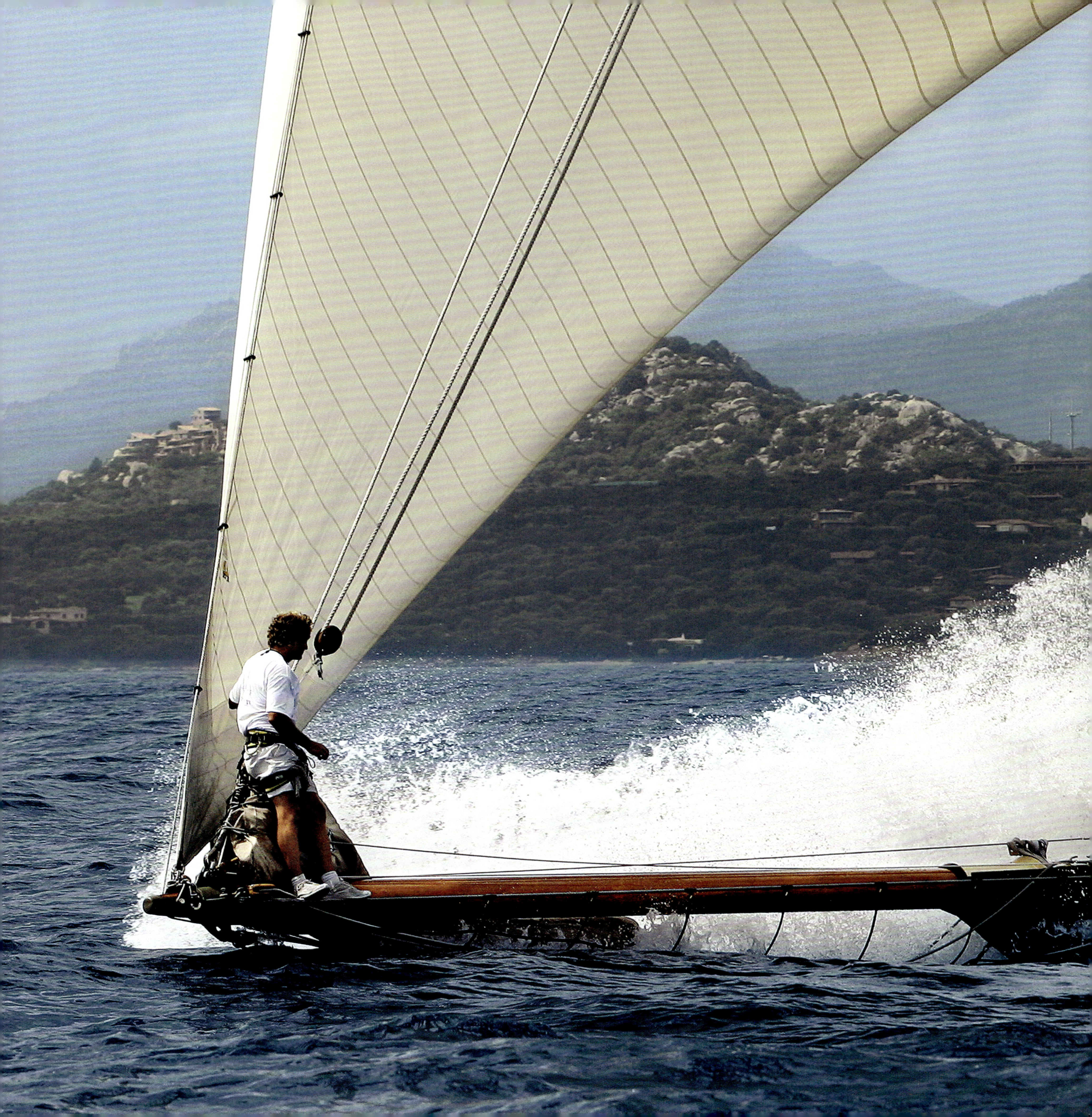

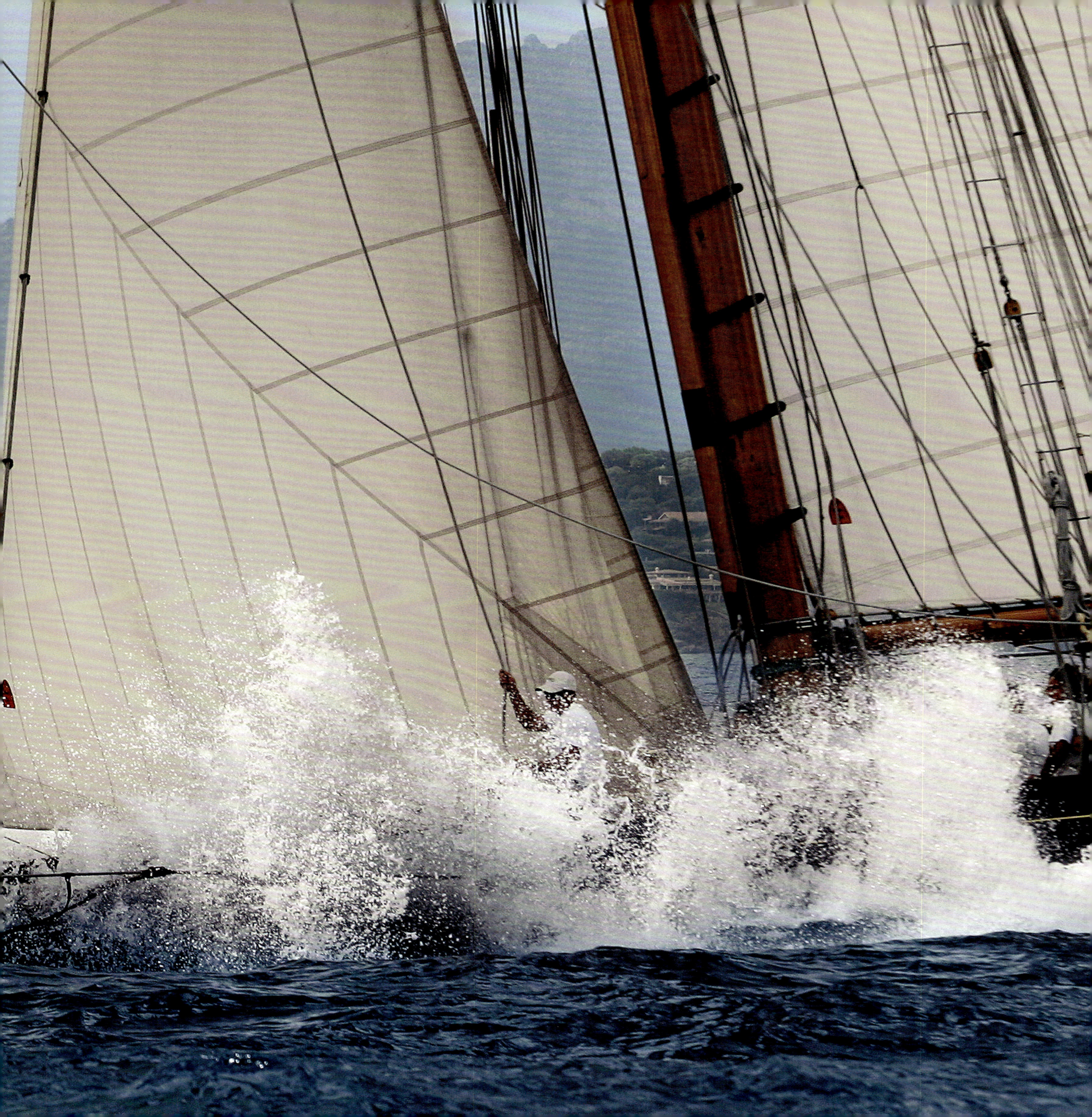

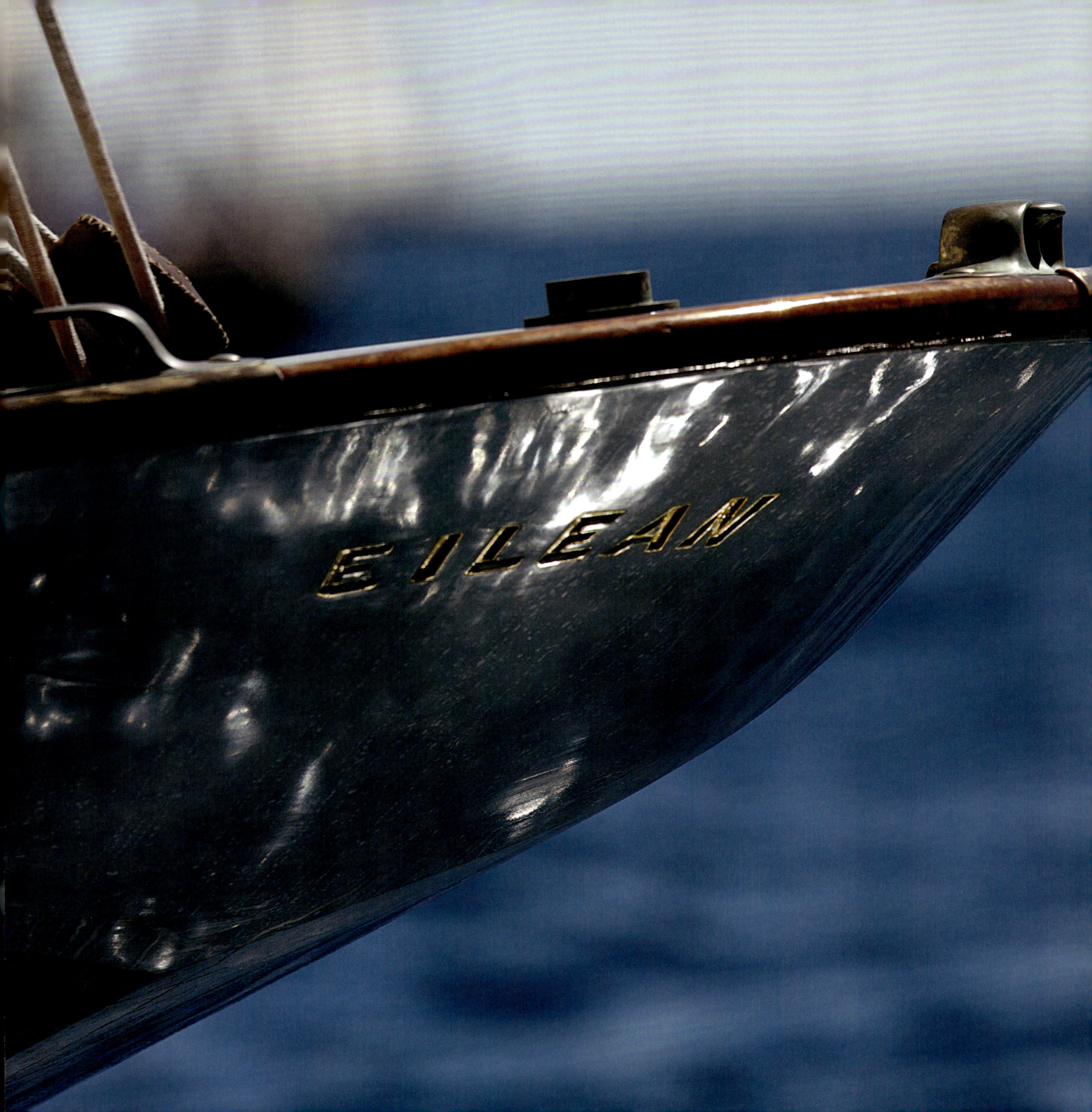
EILEAN

FACTS AND FIGURES

2
Eilean's masts

3
Volume in cubic metres of *Eilean*'s deck-house

4
Thickness in centimetres of the teak planking that forms her hull

6
Cubic metres of mahogany used to make her interiors

18
Height in metres of her mizzenmast

28
Height in metres of her mainmast

36
Number of Atlantic crossings made in the past by *Eilean*

38
Thickness in millimetres of her main deck

50
Square metres of her main deck

50
Weight in tonnes of this boat

60
Percentage of the original planking salvaged

100
Horsepower of each of *Eilean*'s two engines

300
Weight in kilograms of her mizzenmast

301
Square metres of sail area exposed to the wind by *Eilean*

400
Capacity in litres of each of her two diesel tanks

500
Linear metres of teak used to cover her main deck

600
Litre capacity of her water tank

800
Weight in kilograms of her main mast

1,000
Linear metres of the teak planking that forms her hull

5,000
Number of bronze silicon screws holding down her planking

5,000
Wooden screw heads made from the original decking

40,000
Number of hours skilled workmen spent restoring her

150,000
Estimated number of nautical miles *Eilean* has sailed in the past

EILEAN

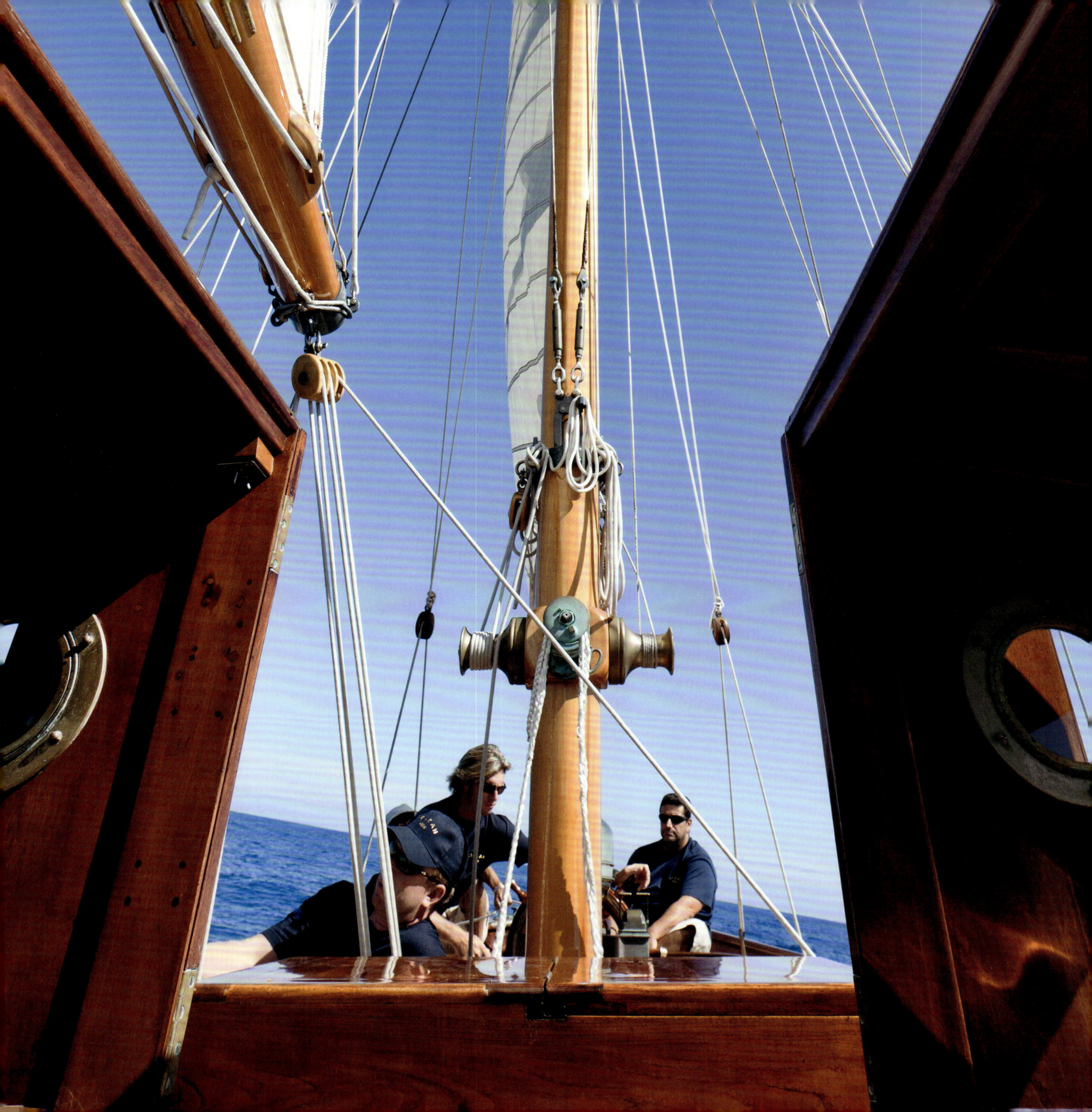

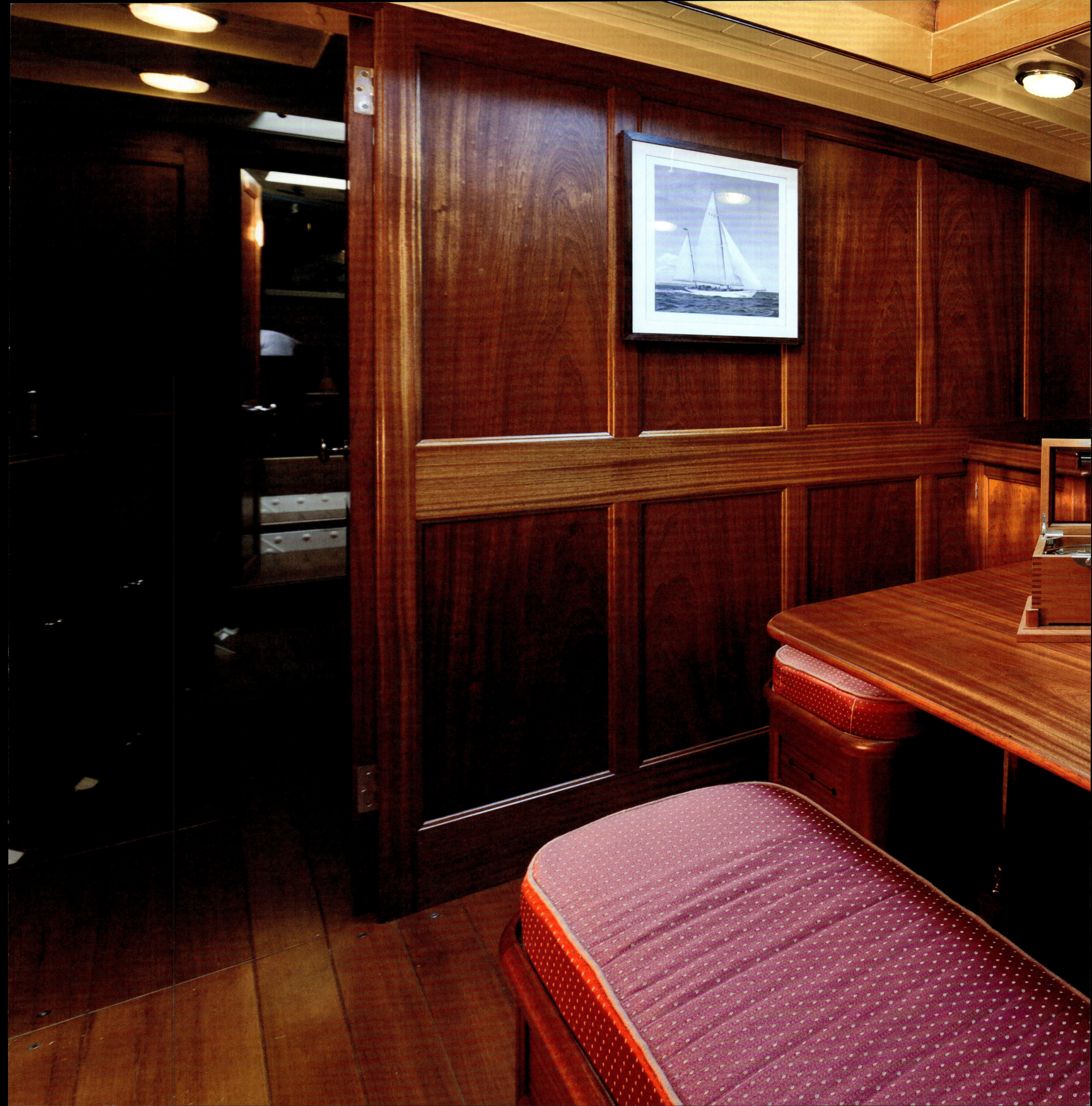

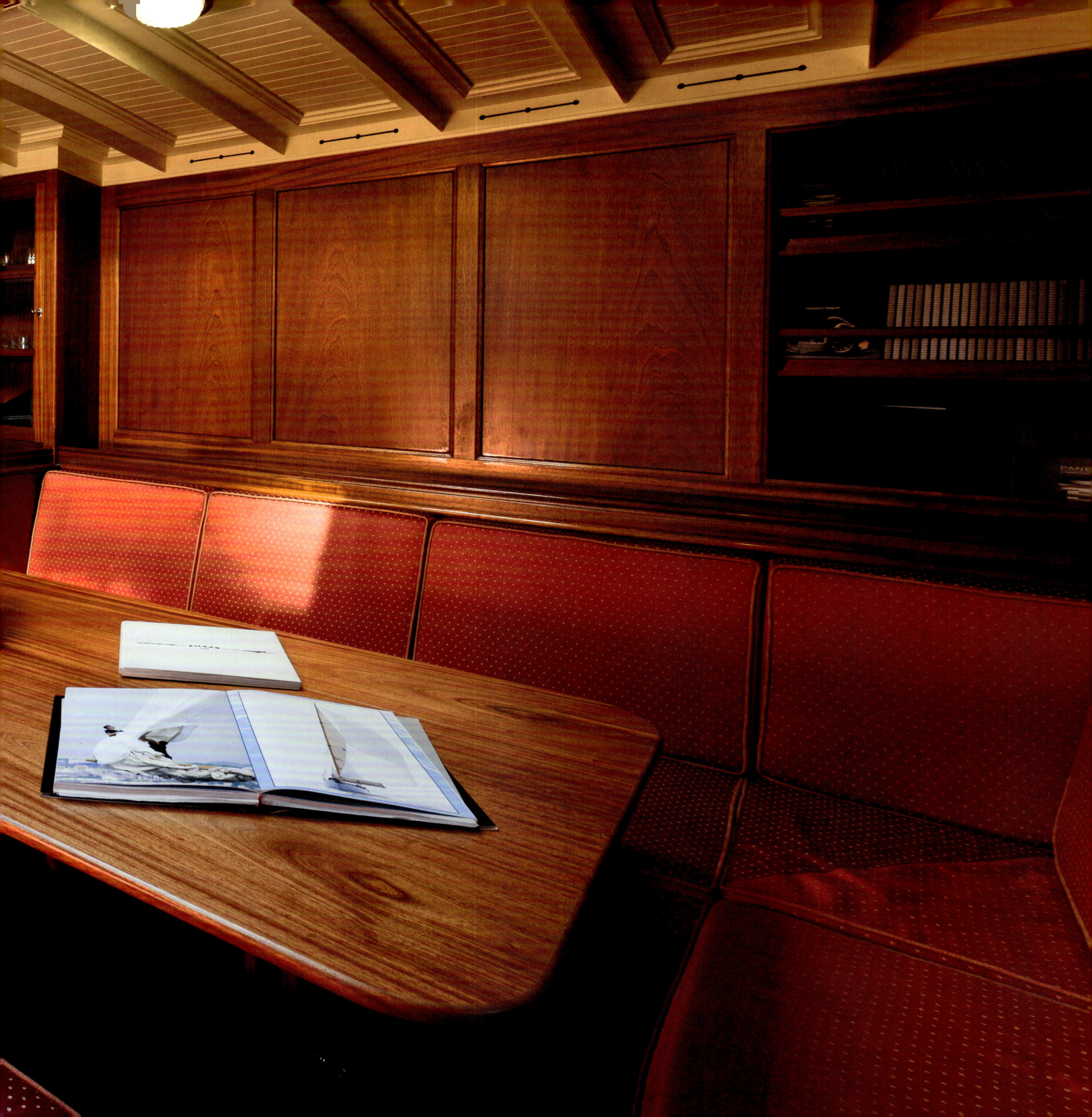

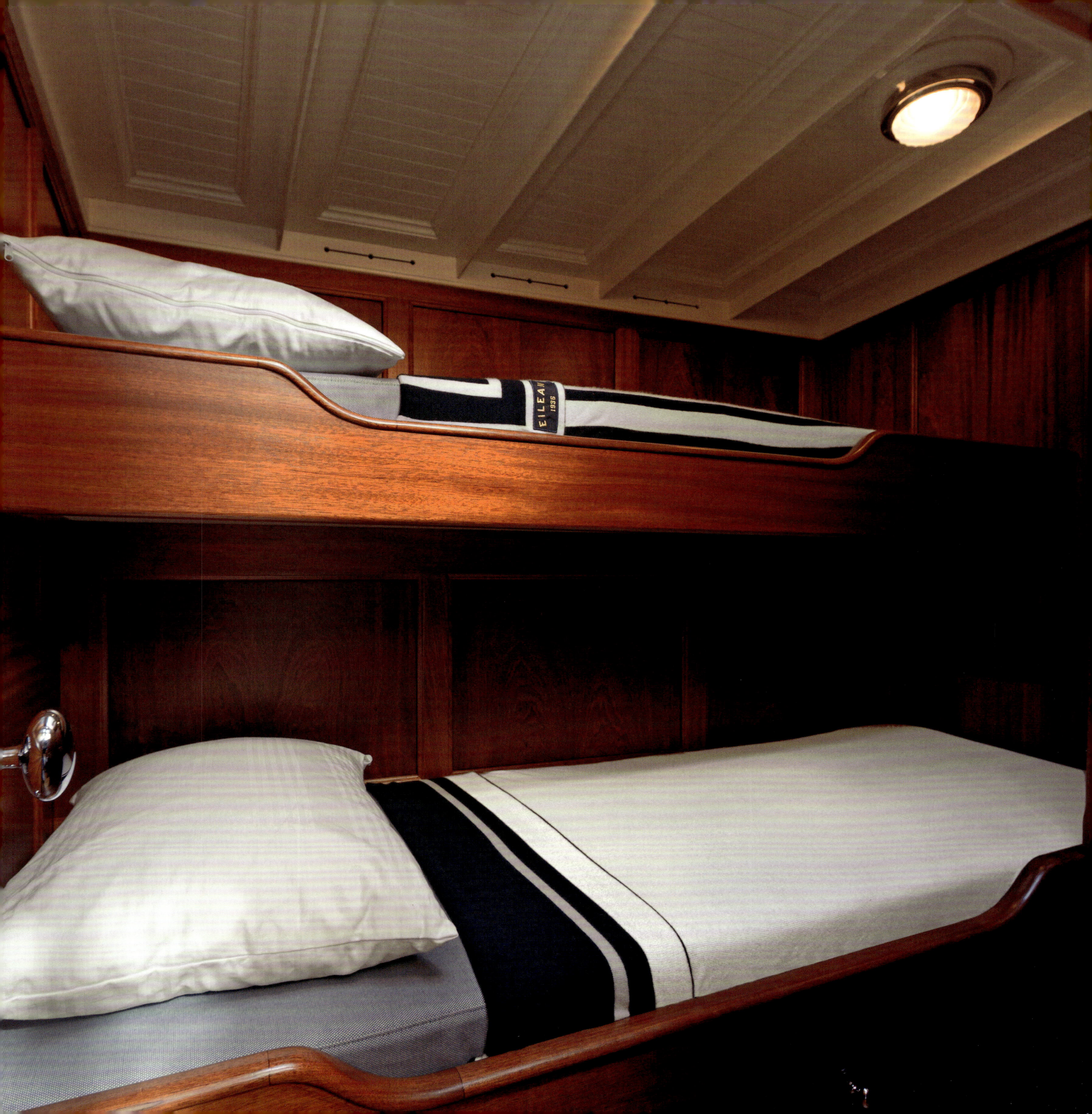
EILEA
1936

EILEAN 1936

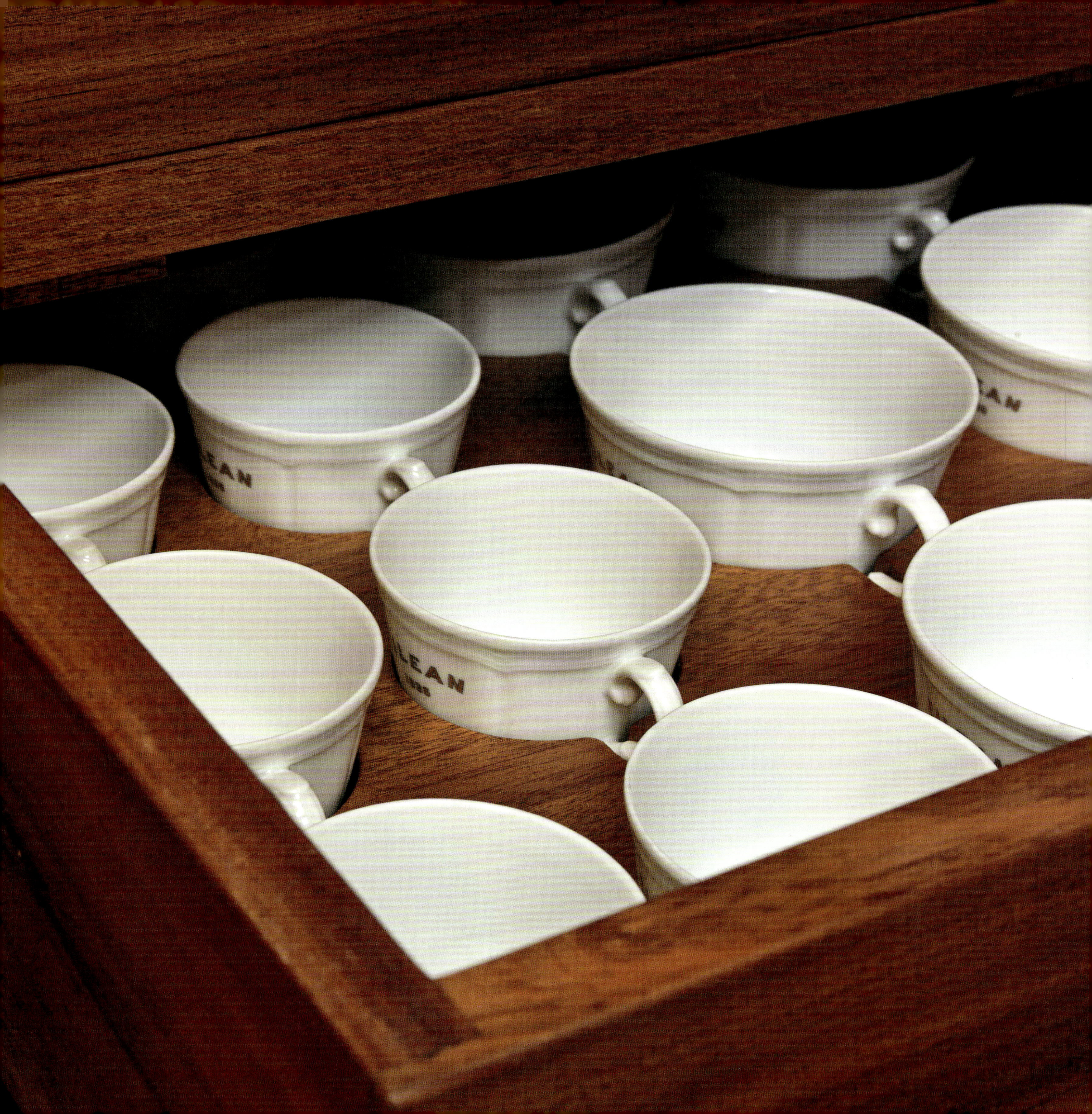
LEAN

EILEAN 1936

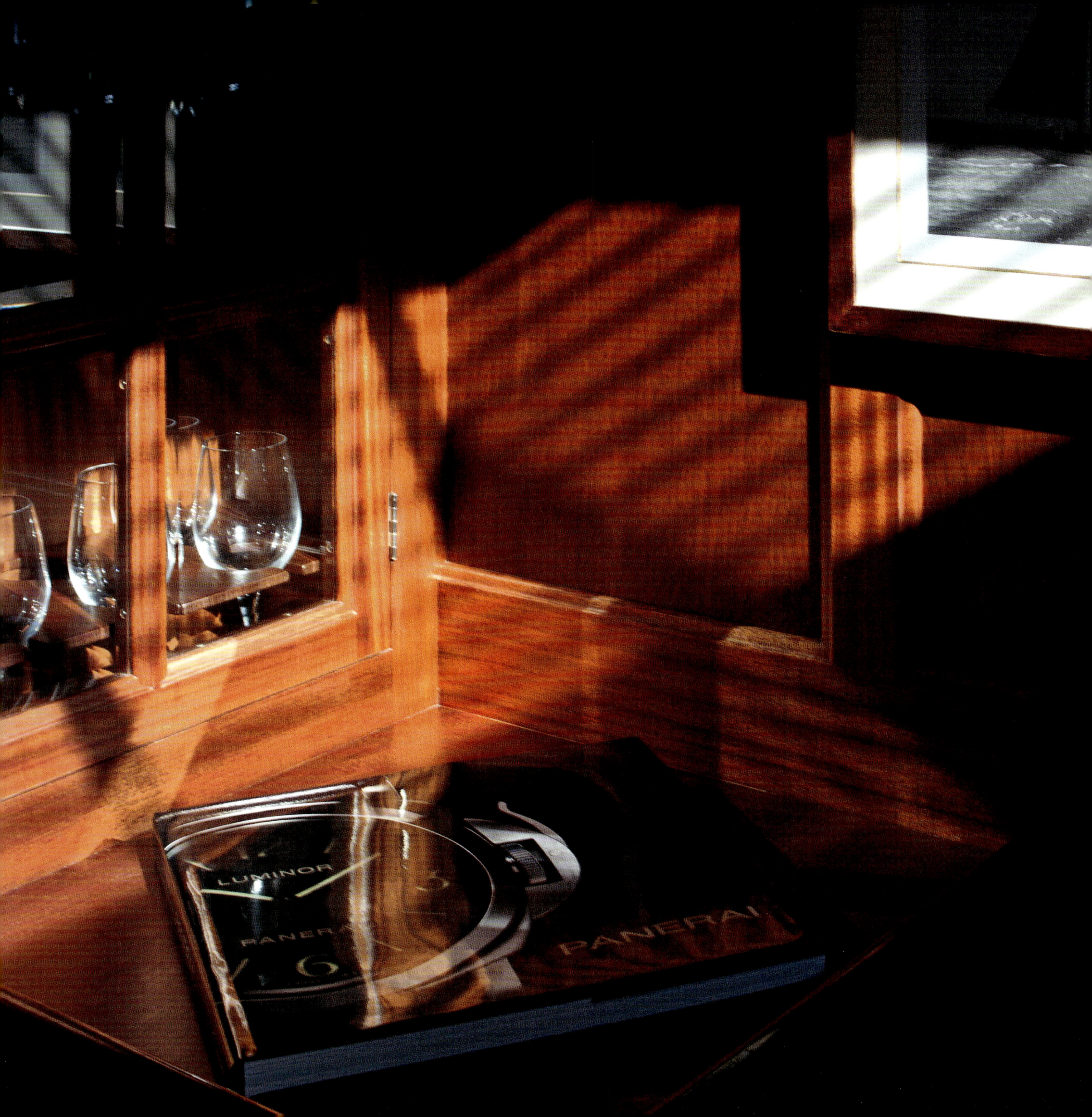
LUMINOR
PANERAI
PANERAI

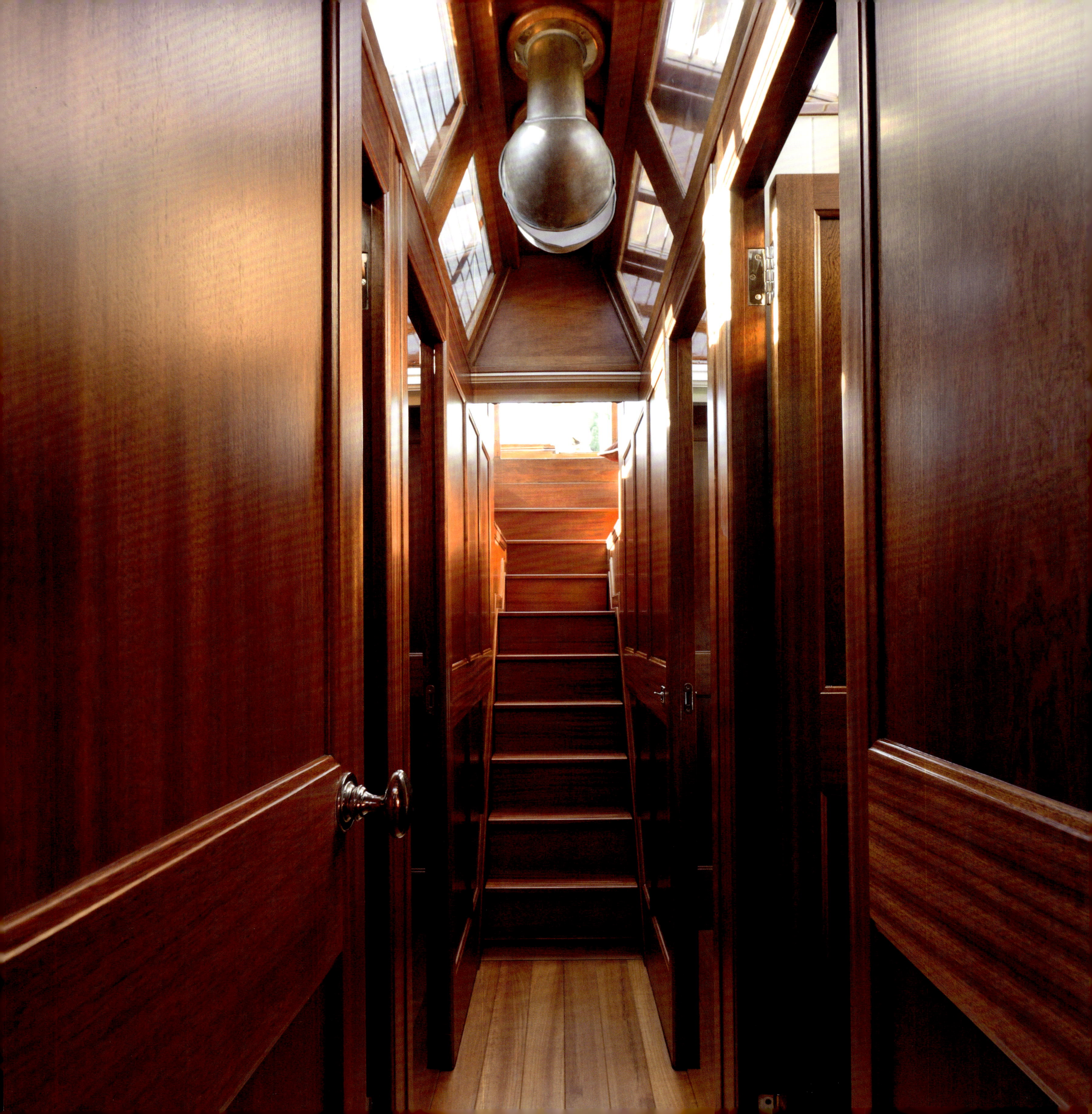

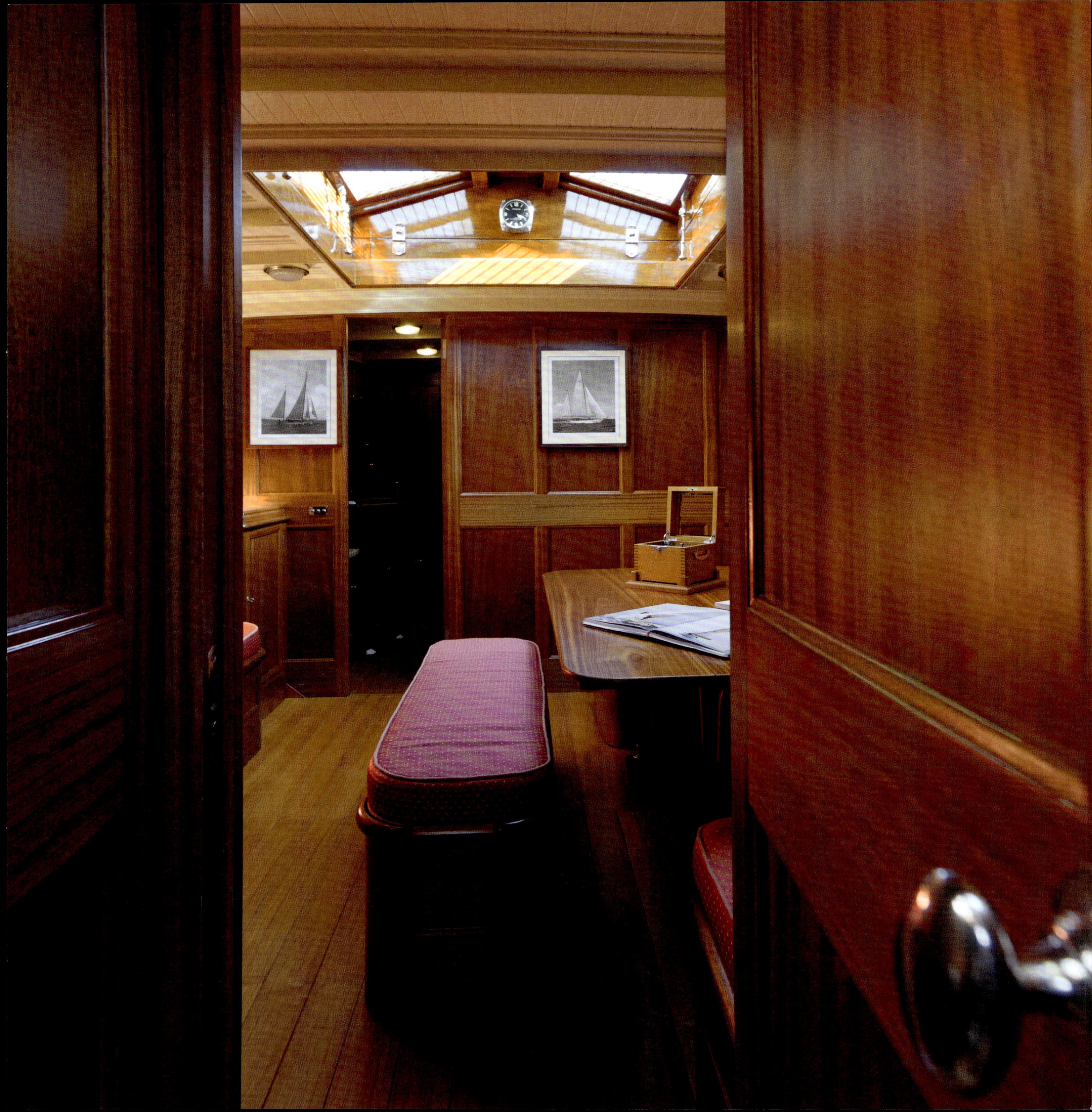

L SWISS MADE L
PANERAI
BAROMETER
hPa
1000
1010
1020
990
1030
980
1040
970
1050
960
1060
EILEAN
1936
L SWISS MADE L
PANERAI
HYGROMETER
%
40
50
60
30
70
20
80
10
90
0
100
EILEAN
1936
L SWISS MADE L

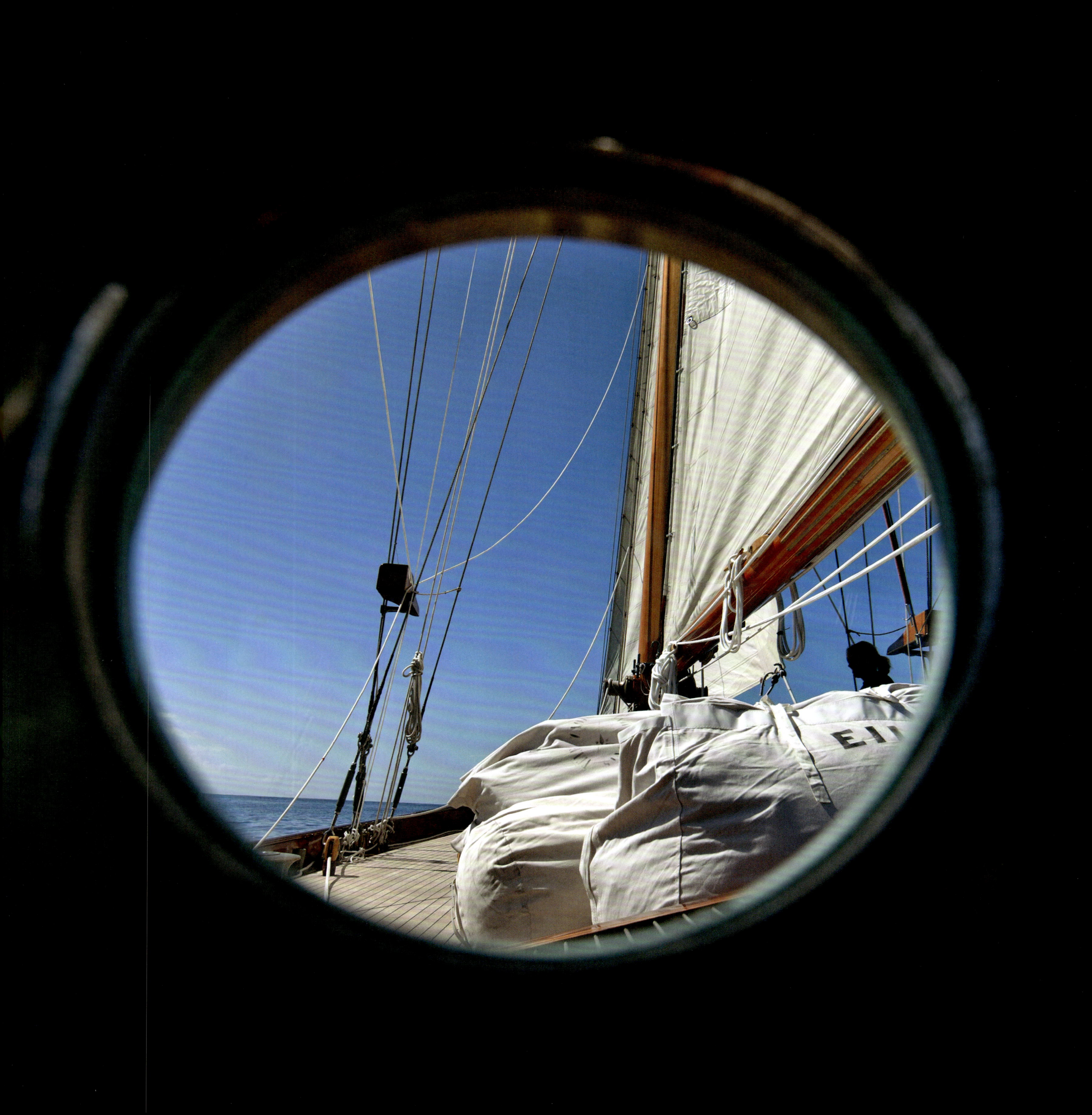
EI

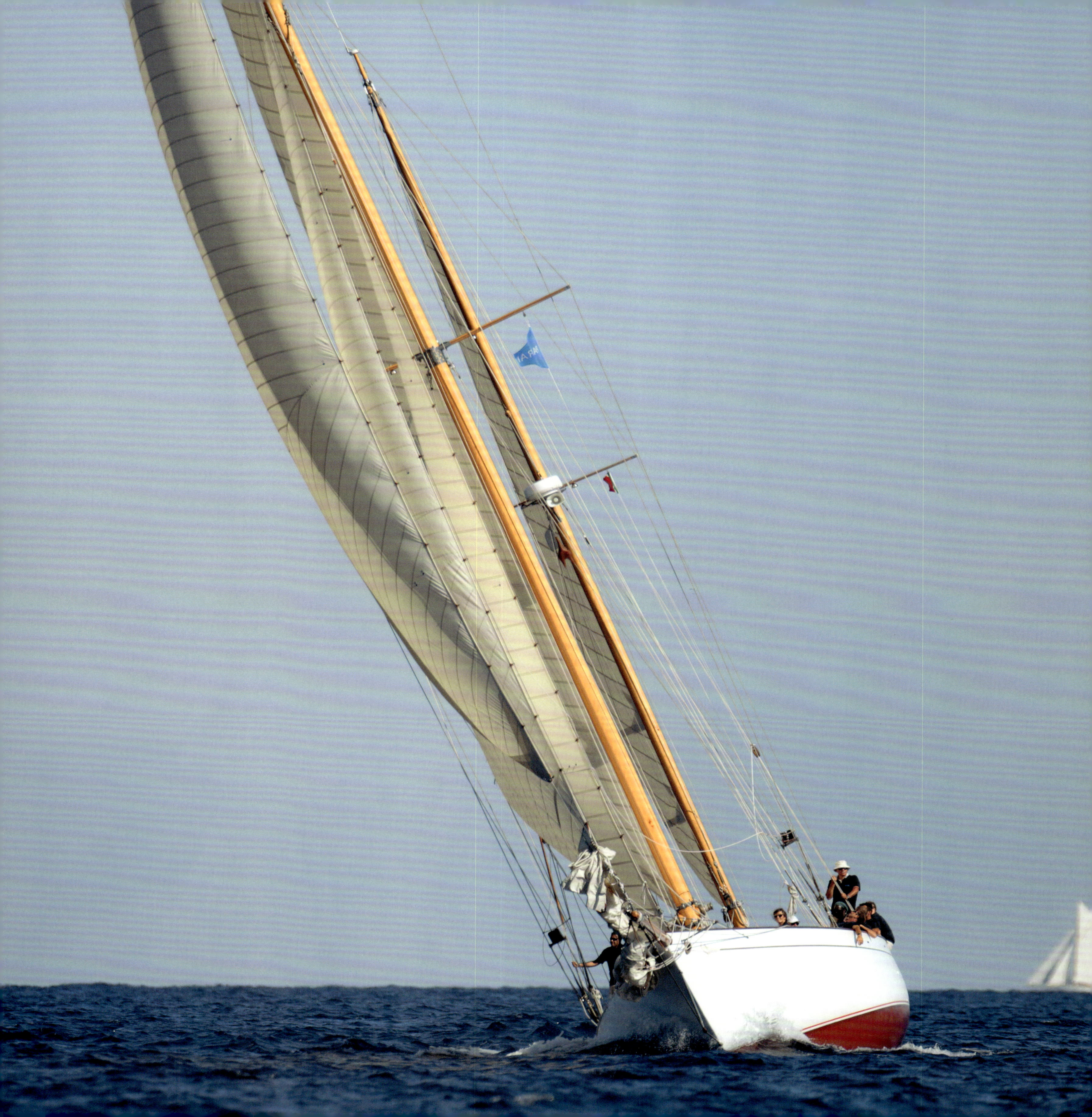

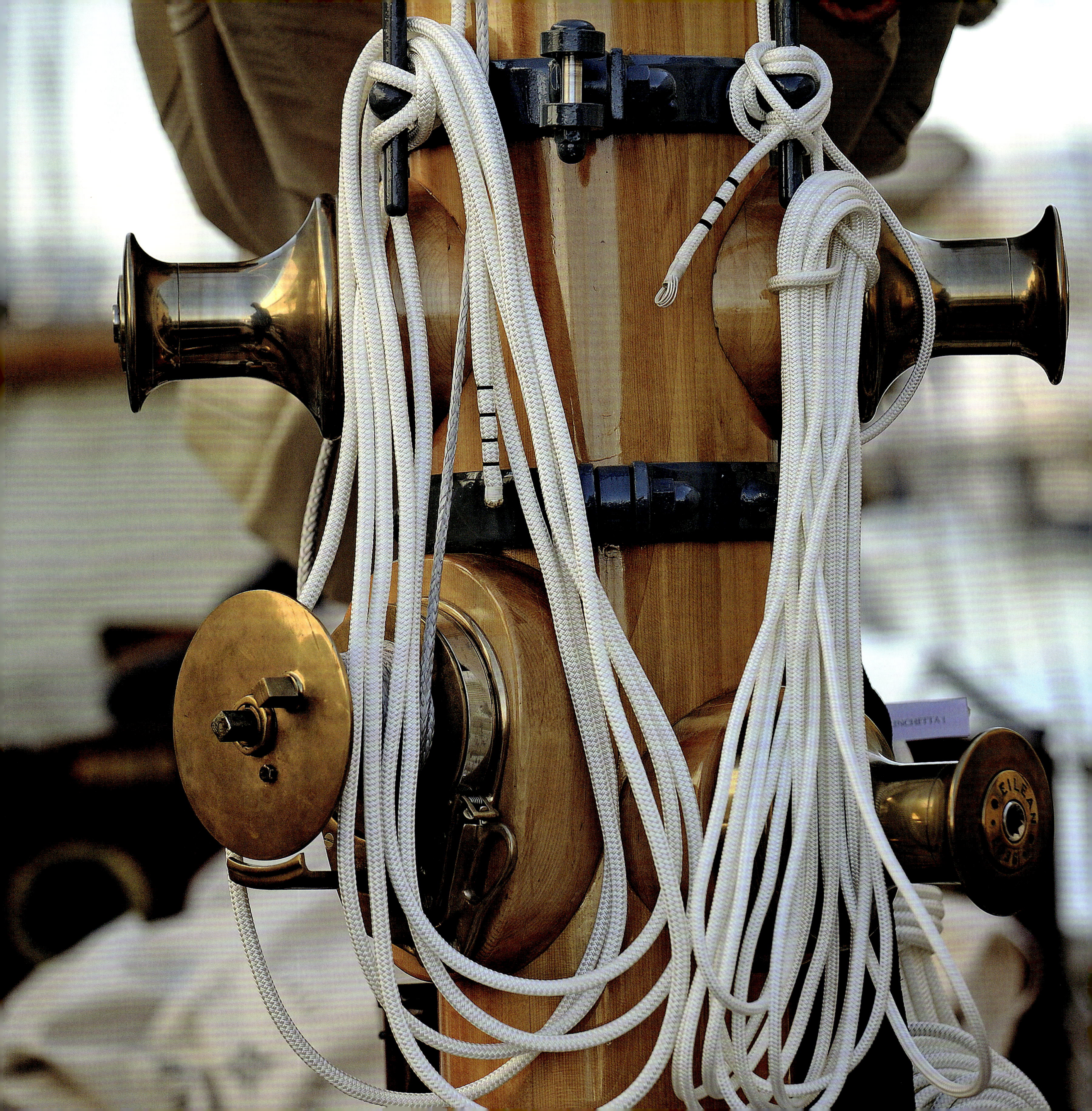

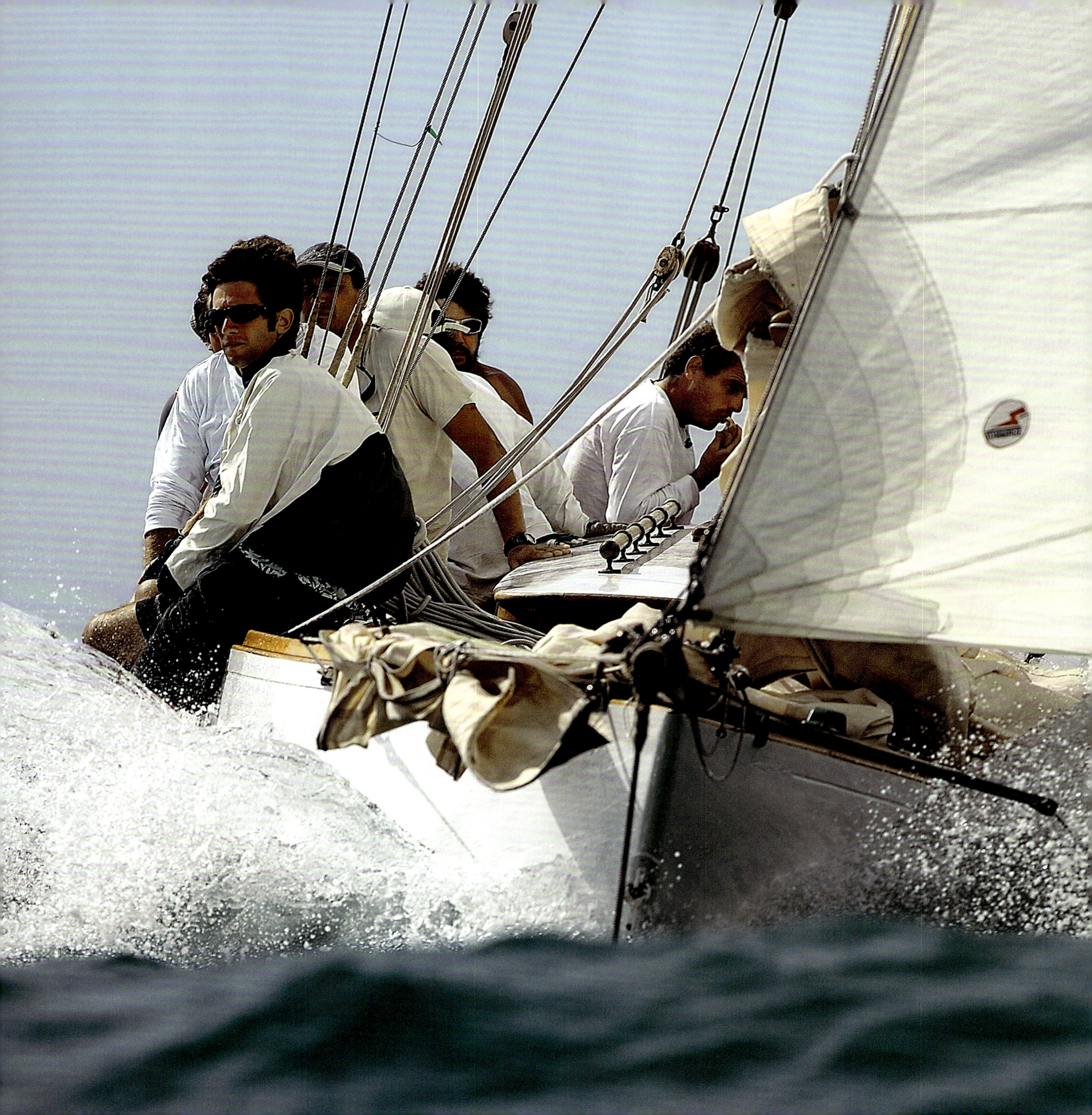

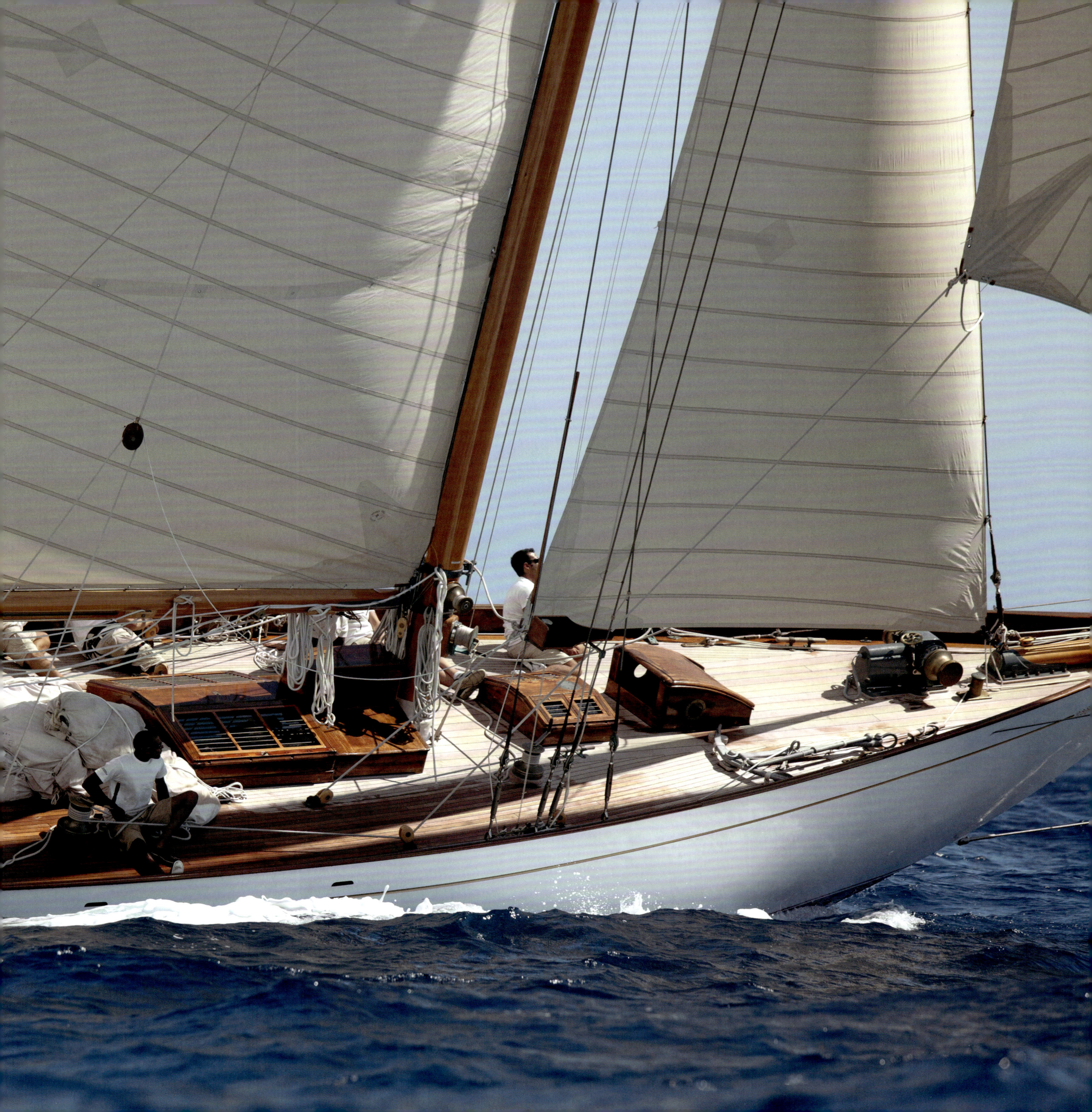

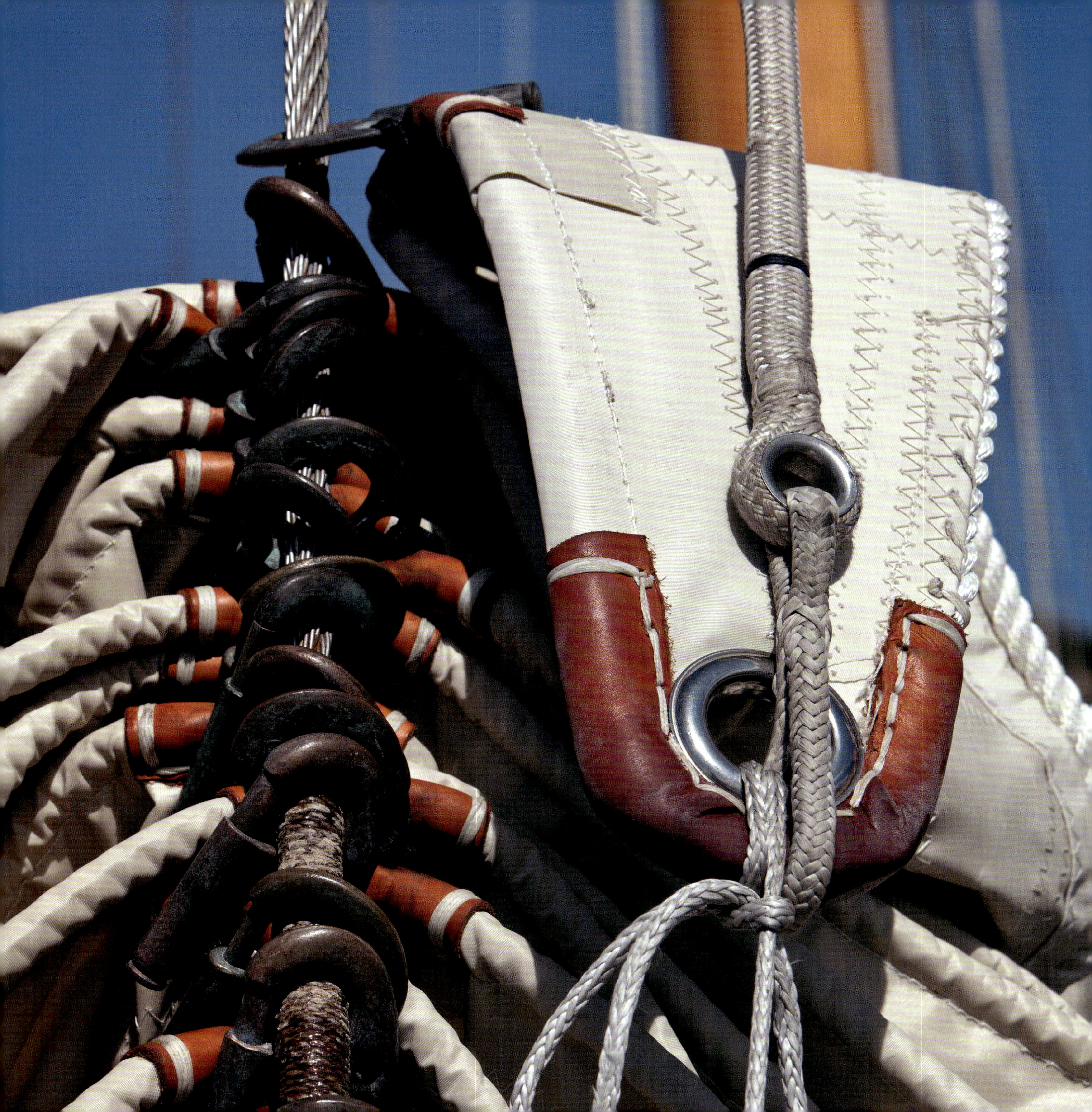

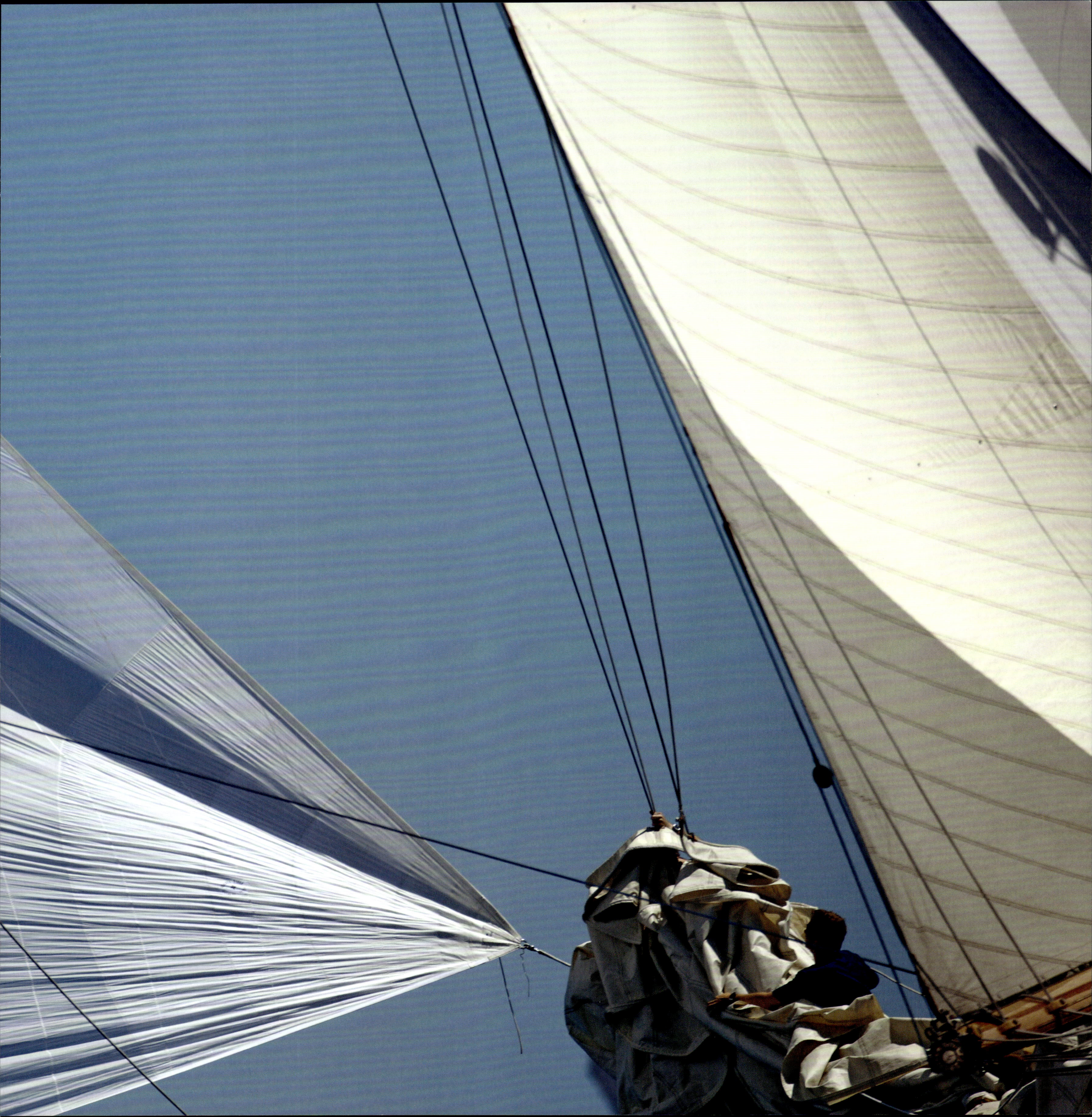

449

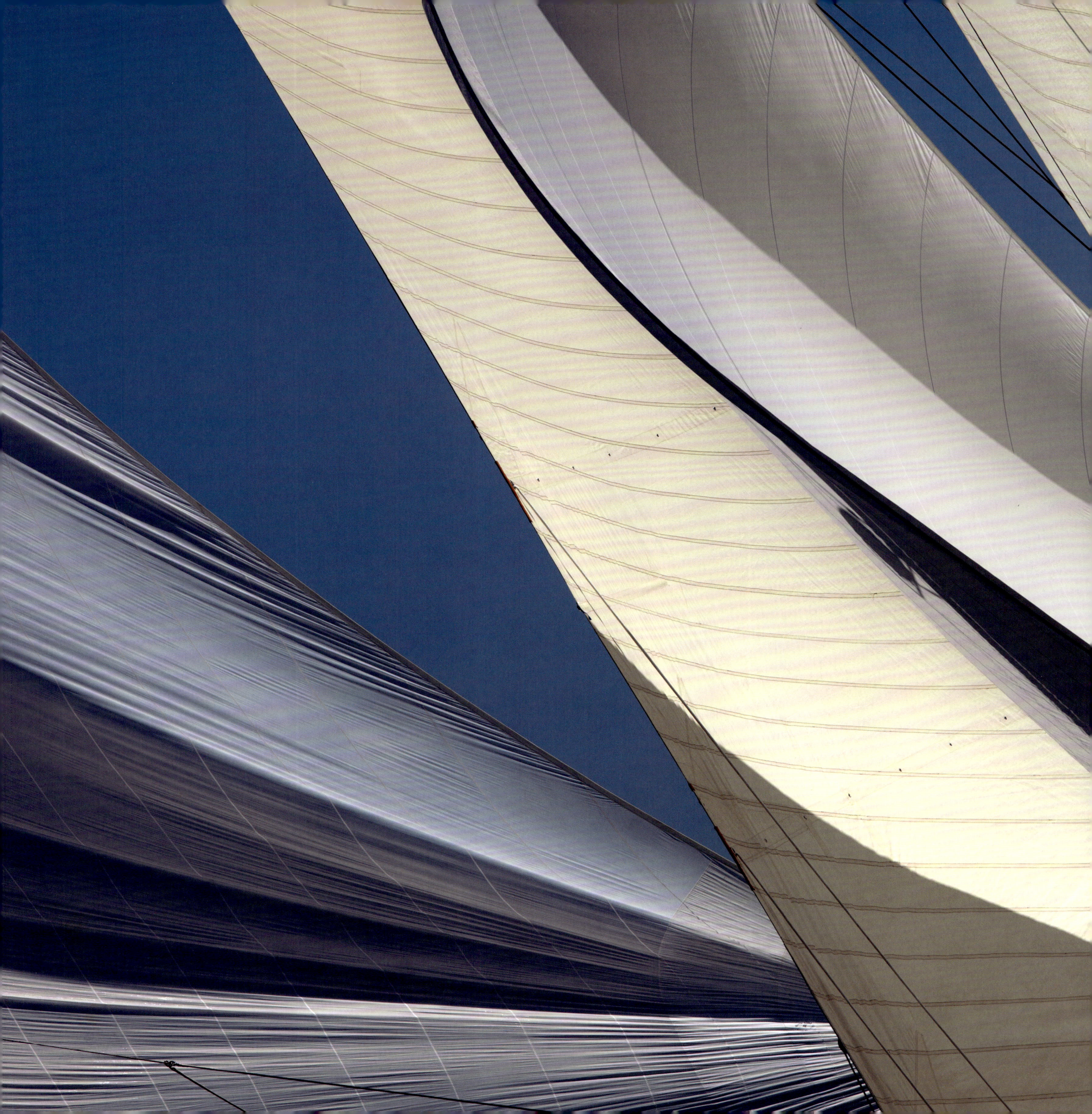

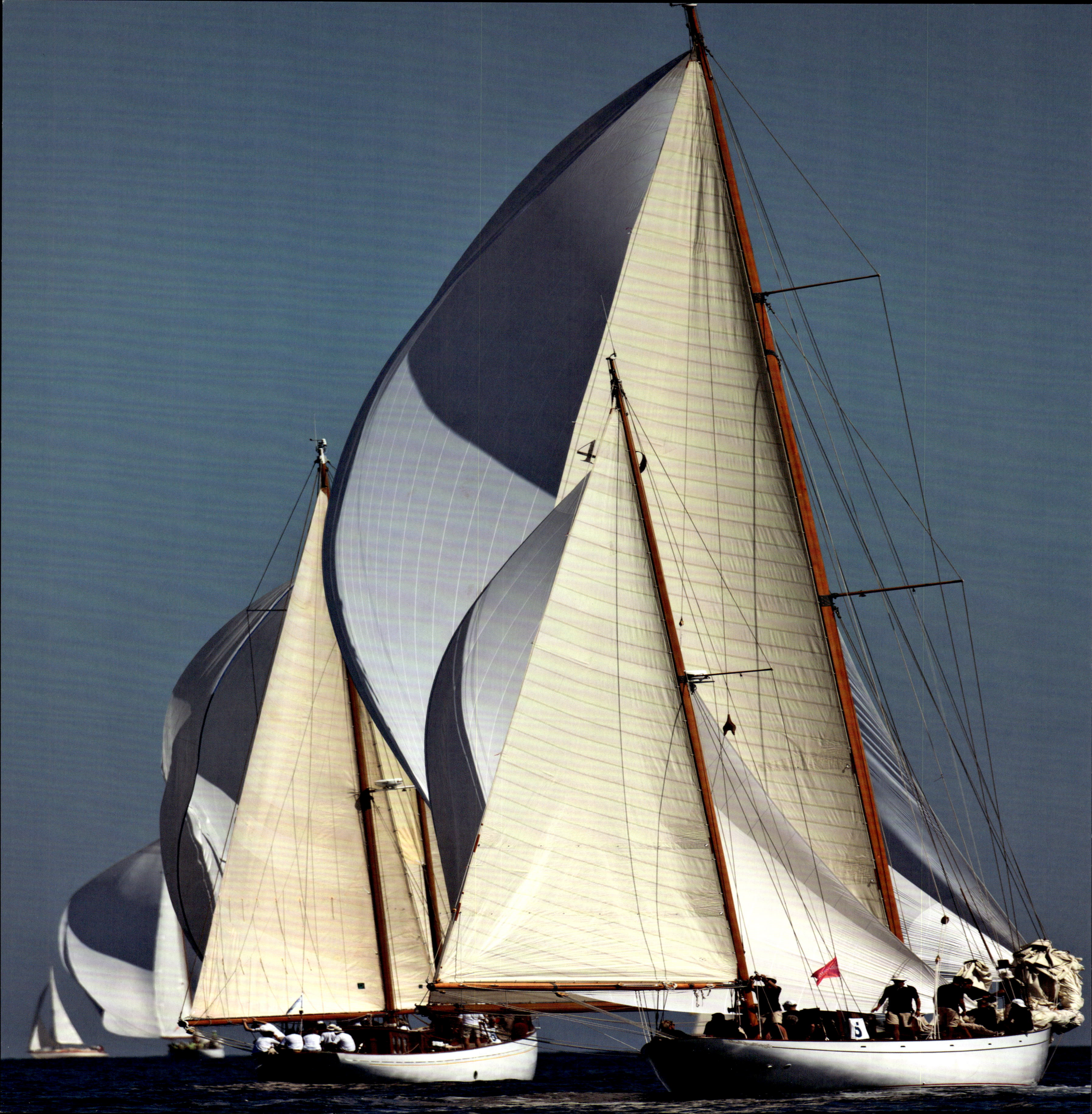

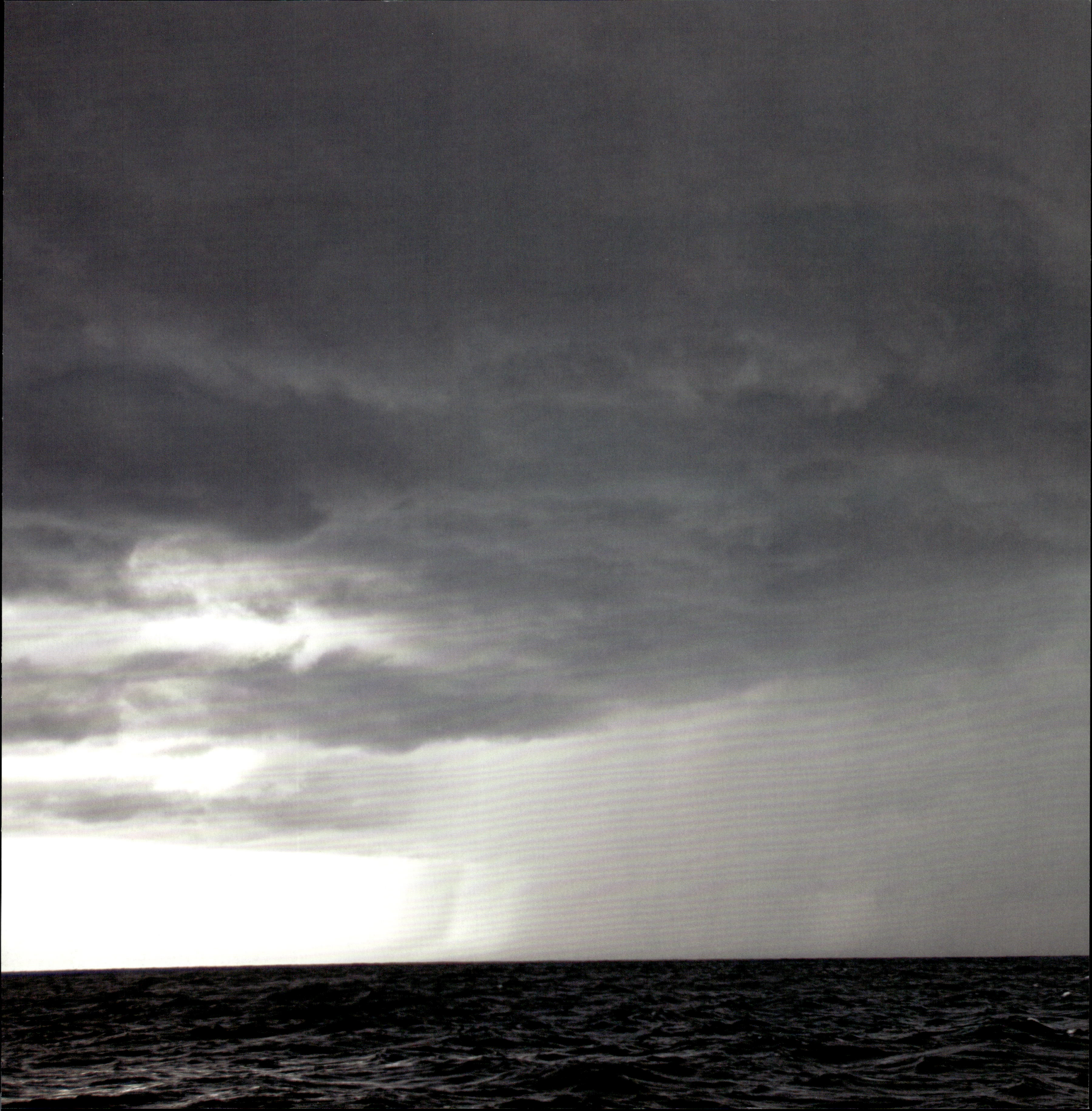

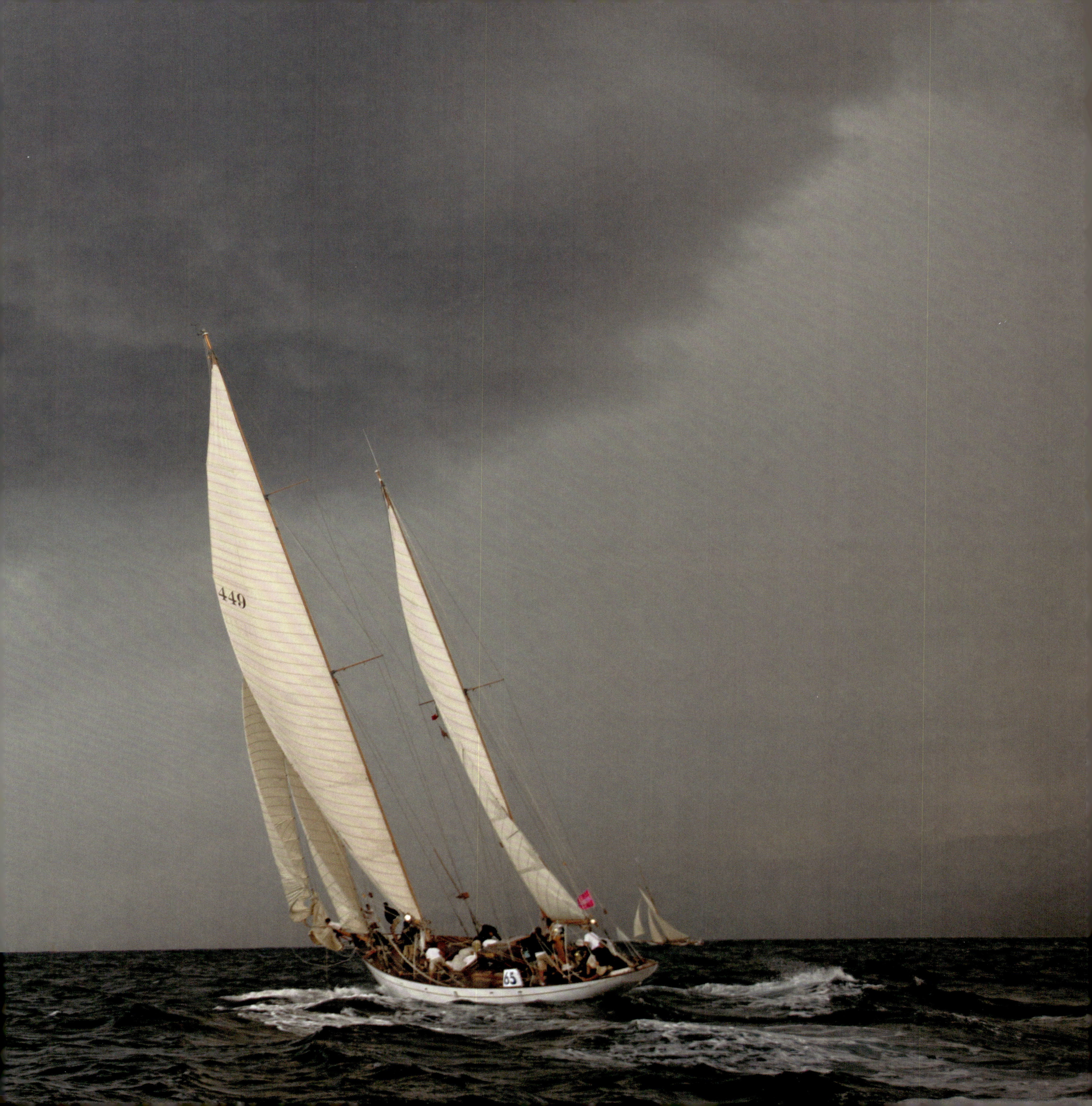
449
65

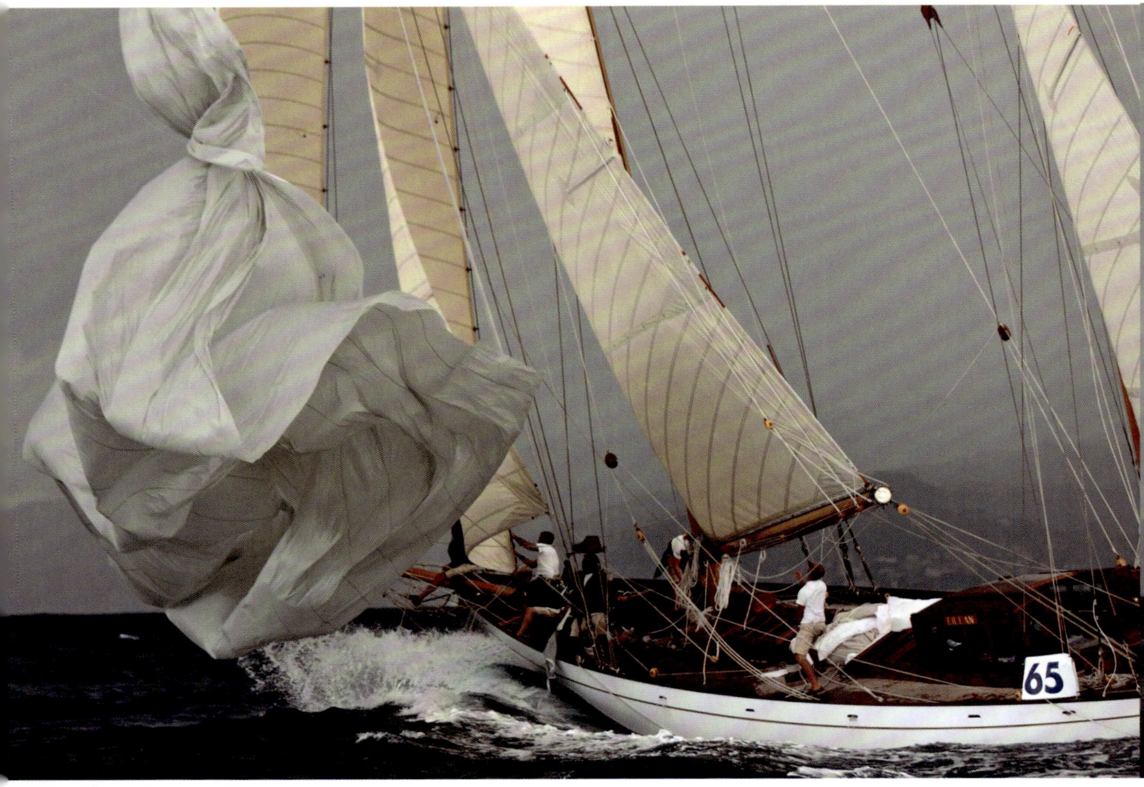
65

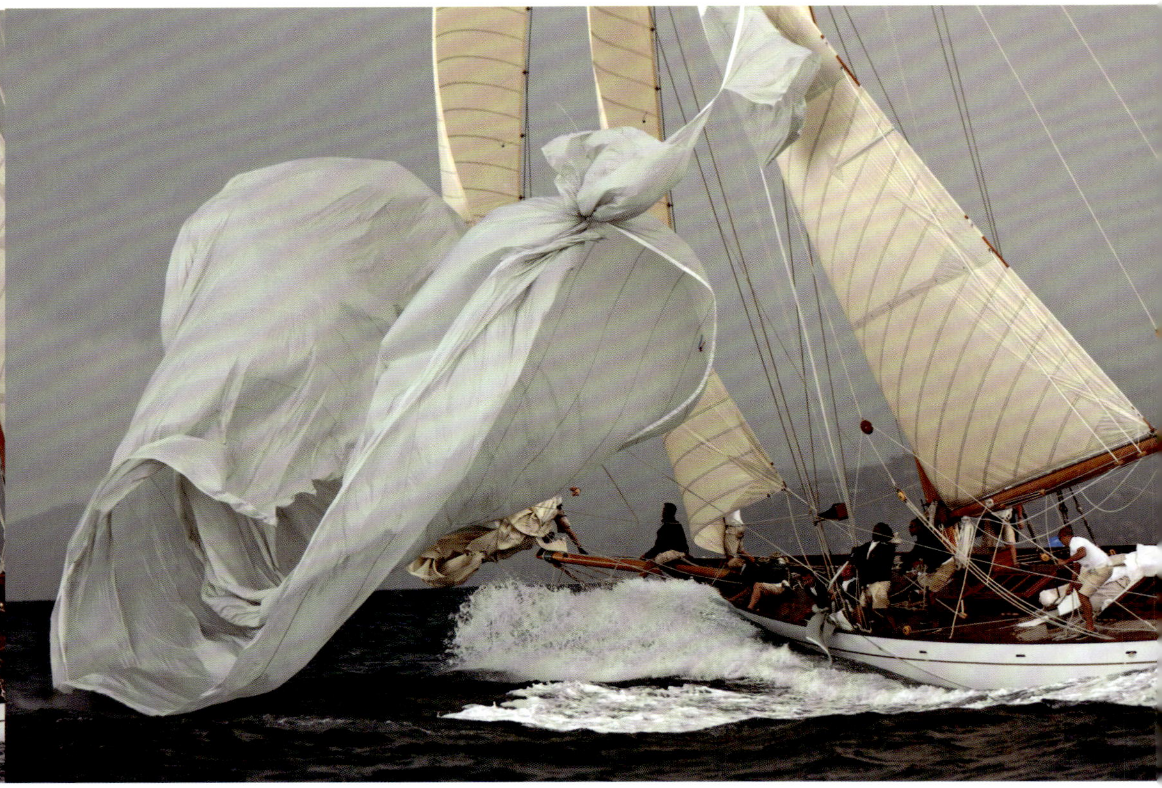

PAGES 184–187 Easterly squalls generated by a mass of clouds are particularly violent in the Mediterranean on the west side of the Riviera. This one is so severe that the coast behind *Eilean* is not visible; nevertheless, she faced the squall without taking in any reef.
The ketch has seen far worse storms and had no trouble sailing straight through them. Taking a torn sail down on deck is always a difficult operation, in particular when it is a downwind sail. The helmsman loses the ability to handle the boat and the wind holds the sail down to water level. The deckhands can only try to grab the sail if it has come down above the deck, which rarely happens. If the bowman can get hold of the tack, he has a chance to sort things out, otherwise the sail trawls and fills with water. In that case, it must be hoisted on board before it passes under the hull.

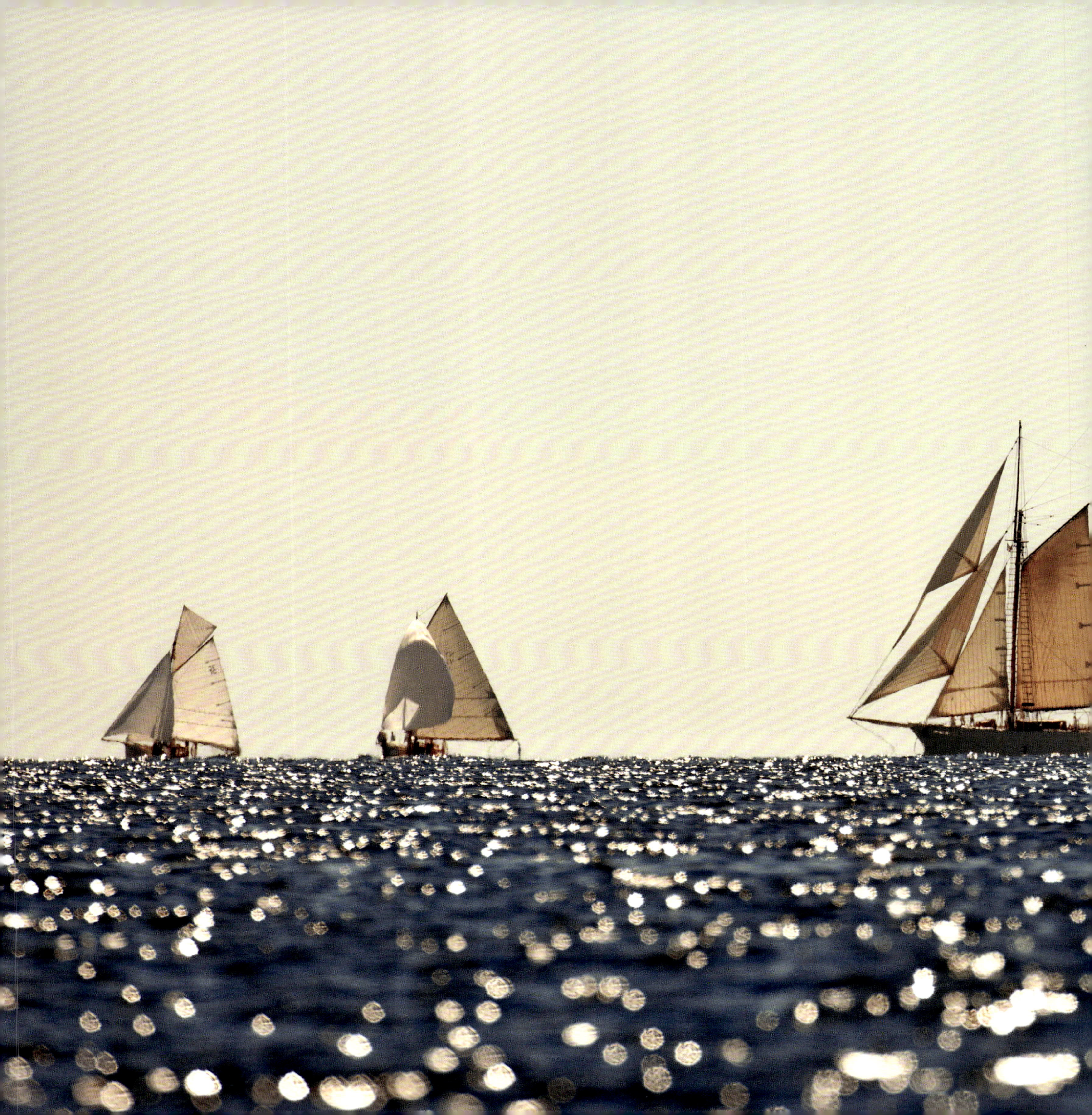

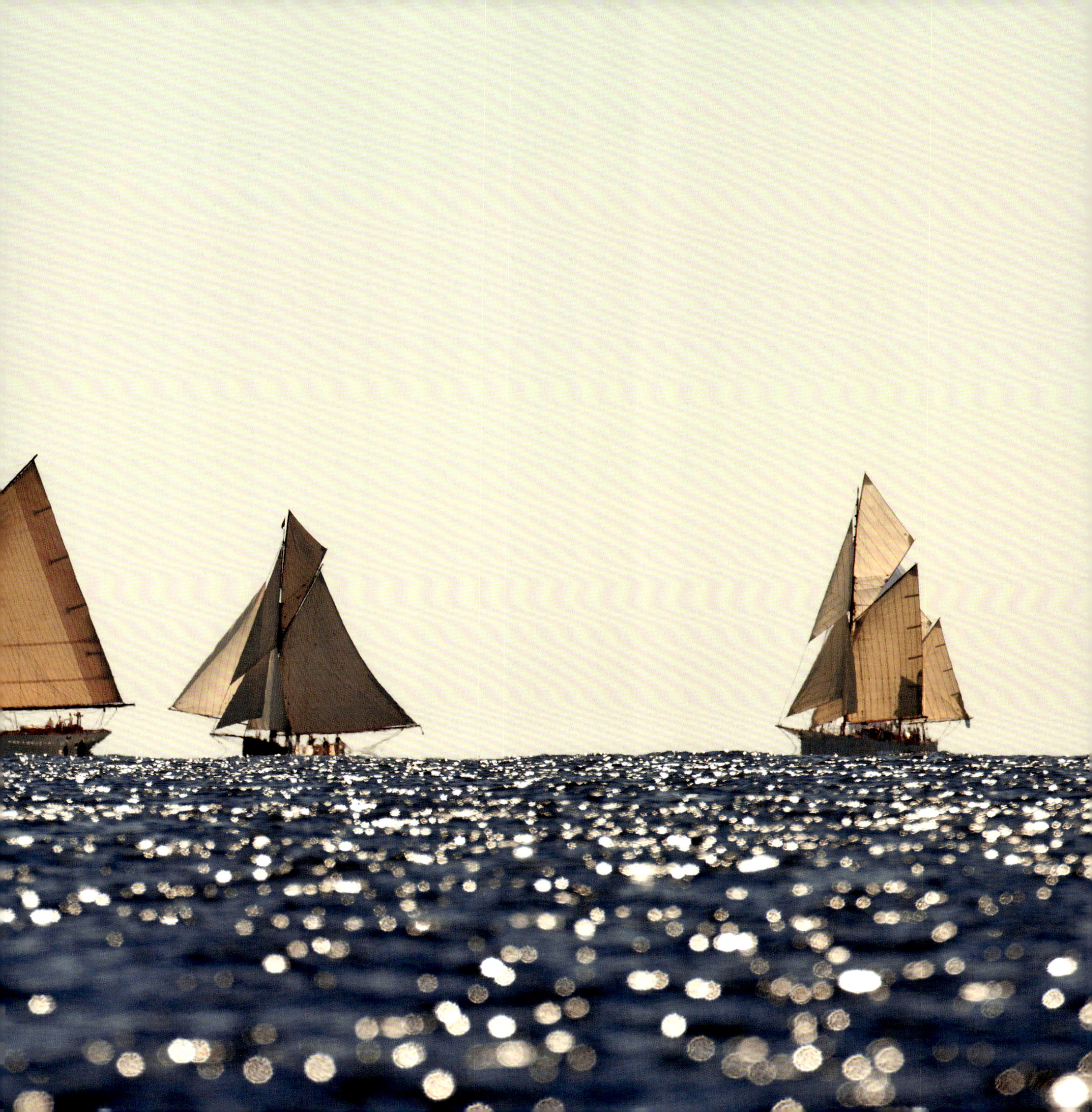

BIBLIOGRAPHY

Hunt's Universal Yacht List for 1869 (and next), London: Hunt & Co, 1869.
British Sports and Sportsmen, Yachting and Rowing, London: The Sportsman, 1916.
ALLISY, Daniel, *Les Plus Beaux Voiliers du monde avec voiles et voiliers*, Paris: Michel Lafon, 2004.
BARCK, Pekka and STREET, Tim, *The Six Metre - 100 years of racing*, Litorale, 2007.
BARNETT, J.R., CORDEROY, George, IRVING, John, KIRKPATRICK, J.B., LYALL, W., MACLEAN-BUCKLEY, J., MACLEAN-BUCKLEY, Major R., McC. MEEK, W., MARTIN, E.G., RICHARDSON, Leslie, ROGERS, H., SOMERSET, R. UNDERHILL, Sir Arthur, WAITE, Brian R., and WRIGHT, H.M., *Cruising & Ocean Racing*, London: The Lonsdale Library, Seeley Service & Co., vol. XV, 1945.
BELL, Helen G., *Winning The King's Cup. An Account of the ELENA'S Race to Spain 1928*, G.P. Putman's Sons, 1928.
BOBROW, Jill and JINKINS, Dana, *Yachts de tradition*, Paris: Gallimard, 1999.
BOWMAN, W. Dodgson, *Yachting and Yachtsmen*, London: Geoffrey Bles, 1926.
BRAY, Maynard and PINHEIRO, Carlton, *Herreshoff of Bristol, A Photographic History of America's Greatest Yacht and Boat Builders*, Brooklin (Maine): Woodenboat Publications, 1989.
BURNET, Constance Buel, *Let the Best Boat Win, The Story of America's Greatest Yacht Designer*, Boston: Solar, Houghton Mifflin Company, 1957.
CARRICK, Robert W. and HENDERSON, Richard, *John G. Alden and His Yacht Designs*, Camden: International Marine Publishing Company, 1984.
CHARLES, Daniel, *Le Yachting, une histoire d'hommes et de techniques*, Paris: E.M.O.M., 1980.
CHARLES, Daniel, *Histoire du yachting*, Paris: Arthaud, 1997.
CHARLES, Daniel, NICHOLSON, Ian, COLLIER, William, LEATHER, John, and WALKER, Dunkan, *Tuiga, 1909*, London: Yachting Heritage, 2005.
CHEVALIER, François, *Mythiques yachts classiques*, Paris: Éditions du Chêne, 2007.
CHEVALIER, François, *Classic Yachts*, New York: Abbeville Press Publishers, 2008.
CHEVALIER, François, *Legendary Classic Yachts*, London: Adlard Coles Nautical, 2008.
CHEVALIER, François, *Mythos Klassische Yachten*, Bielefeld: Delius Klasing Verlag, 2008.
CHEVALIER, François, *Veleros Clásicos de Leyenda*, Barcelona: Art Blume, 2008.

CHEVALIER, François, *Yacht Classici*, Novara: Istituto Geografico De Agostini, 2008.
CHEVALIER, François and TAGLANG, Jacques, *America's Cup Yacht Designs, 1851–1986*, Paris: 1st Ed. by the authors, 1987.
CHEVALIER, François and TAGLANG, Jacques, *American and British Yacht Designs, 1870–1887*, Paris: 1st Ed. by the authors, vol. I, 1991, vol. II, 1992.
CHEVALIER François and TAGLANG, Jacques, *J Class, Endeavour, 1934*, Fondettes: Éditions Van de Velde, 2001.
CHEVALIER, François and TAGLANG, Jacques, *J Class*, London: Yachting Heritage, 2002.
CHEVALIER, François, KNIGHT, Lucia del Sol, MacNAUGHTON, Daniel Bruce, and TAGLANG, Jacques, *The Encyclopedia of Yacht Designers*, New York: W.W. Norton & Company, 2006.
CRANE, Clinton, *Clinton Crane's Yachting Memories*, New York: Van Nostrand Company, 1952.
DAHEN, François-Jean, *À bord des plus beaux voiliers du monde*, Paris: Gallimard, 1988.
DEAR, Ian, *Fastnet: The Story of a Great Ocean Race*, London: Batsford Ltd, 1981.
DIAPER, Captain Tom, *Tom Diaper's Log, Memoirs of a Racing Skipper*, London: Robert Ross & Co., 1950.
DIXON, Douglas, *The King's Sailing Master*, London: George G. Harrap & Co., 1948.
DUCK, Noëlle, *La Passion bleue, A Tribute to Owners*, Monaco: Yacht Club de Monaco, 2002.
DUCK, Noëlle, *Yachts classiques*, Paris: Gallimard, 2004.
EASTLAND, Jonathan, *Great Yachts and their Designers*, New York: Rizzoli International Publications, Inc., 1st Ed. 1987.
FIFE McCALLUM, May, *Fast and Bonnie, A History of William Fife and Son Yachtbuilders*, Edinburgh: John Donald Publishers, 1988.
FINLAYSON, W.J., *Yacht Racing on the Clyde from 1883 to 1890 (and next)*, Glasgow & London: MacLure, MacDonald & Co, 1890.
FOX, Uffa, *Sailing, Seamanship and Yacht Construction*, London: Peter Davies Ltd., 1st Ed. 1934.
FOX, Uffa, *Uffa Fox's Second Book*, London: Peter Davies Ltd., 1st Ed. 1935.
FOX, Uffa, *Sail and Power*, London: Peter Davies Ltd., 1st Ed. 1936.
FOX, Uffa, *Racing, Cruising and Design*, London: Peter Davies Ltd., 1st Ed. 1937.
GILCHRIST, Ian G., *Scenes and Sails on the Firth of Clyde*, Dumbartonshire, Windward Publications Ltd., 1946.
GILCHRIST, Ian G., *Call of the Wind, Leaves from my Sailing Album*, Dumbartonshire: Windward Publications Ltd., 1948.

GROUT, Jack, *C'était au temps des yachtsmen. Histoire mondiale du yachting, des origines à 1939*, Paris: Gallimard, 1978.
GUIDETTI, Laura and SWERLING, Gail, *Panerai, Classic Yachts Challenge, Mare Uomini Passioni*, Milan: Mandatore Electa, 2007.
HAGLIND, Henning and PALLIN, Erik, *Kungl – Svenska Segel Sällskapet – 1830–1930*, Stockholm: Ahlén & Akerlunds Förlag, 1930.
HAMILTON-ADAMS, C.P., *The Racing Schooner Westward*, London: Stanford Maritime Ltd., 1976.
HECKSTALL-SMITH, Antony, *Sacred Cowes, Or the Cream of Yachting Society*, London: Allan Wingate, 1955.
HECKSTALL-SMITH, Brooke, *The Britannia and Her Contemporaries*, London: Methuen & Co., 1929.
HERRESHOFF, L. Francis, *Capt. Nat Herreshoff, The Wizard of Bristol*, White Plains: Sheridan House, 1953.
HERRESHOFF, L. Francis, *The Common Sense of Yacht Design*, New York: Caravan-Maritime Books, 1974.
HICKEY, Captain John J., *The Life and Times of the Late Sir Thomas J. Lipton, From the Cradle to the Grave, International Sportman and Dean of the Yachting World*, New York: Officer "787", The Hickey Publishing Company, 1932.
HISCOCK, Eric C., *The Yachting Year, Volume I: 1946–7*, London: The Rolls House Publishing Co., 1947.
HISCOCK, Eric C., *The Yachting Year, Volume II: 1947–8*, London: The Rolls House Publishing Co., 1947.
HOLM, Ed, *L'Âge d'or du yachting*, Paris: Éditions Anthèse, 2000.
HUGHES, John Scott, *Harbours of the Clyde*, London: Christopher Johnson, 1954.
HUME, John R. and MOSS, Michael S., *A Bed of Nails, The History of P. MacCallum & Sons Ltd of Greenock, 1781–1881, A Study in Survival*, Greenock: Lang & Fulton, 1981.
IRVING, John, *The King's Britannia, The Story of a Great Ship*, London: Seeley Service & Co., 1937.
JOHNSON, Peter, *Boating Britain*, London: Nautical Publishing Company Ltd., 1973.
JOHNSON, Peter, *Yacht Rating, 170 Years of Speed, Success and Failure Against Competitors, and the Clock*, Lymington: Bucksea Guides, 1997.
KRAMER, Klaus, *Max Oertz*, Schramberg: Klaus Kramer Verlag, 2001.
LAMMERTING, Dr. Kristin, *Meteor, die kaiserlichen Segelyachten*, Köln: Dumont, 1999.
LANG, Luigi and JONES, Dyer, *The 12 Metre Class, The History of The International 12 Metre Class from the First International Rule to the America's Cup*, London: Adlar Coles Nautical, 2001.
LEATHER, John, *The Big Class Racing Yachts*, London: Stamford Maritime, 1982.
LIPTON, Sir Thomas J., *Leaves from the Lipton Logs*, London: Hutchinson & Co., 1932.
LIPTON, Sir Thomas J., *Lipton's Autobiography*, New York: Duffield and Green, 1932.
MAC BRIDE, MacKenzie, *Firth of Clyde, Beautiful Britain*, London: Adam & Charles, 1911.
MARTIN-RAGET, Gilles, *Yachts classiques*, Paris: Éditions Denoël, 1990.
NEGRETTI, Giampiero and BURTON, Simon de, *Panerai*, Paris: Flammarion, 2008.
NICHOLSON, John, *Great Years in Yachting*, Lymington: Nautical Publishing Company, 1970.
PACE, Franco, *William Fife*, Paris: Gallimard, 1998.
PACE, Franco, *La Dynastie Herreshoff et la coupe de l'America*, Paris: Gallimard, 2006.
PARKINSON, John, Jr., *The History of the New York Yacht Club. From its Founding Through 1973*, New York: The N.Y.Y.C., 1975.
PARVULESCO, Constantin, *La Belle Plaisance, 100 ans de yachting classique*, Paris: Éditions ETAI, 2010.
PARVULESCO, Constantin, *L'Heure en mer, une histoire de chronomètres*, Paris: Éditions ETAI, 2010.
PHILLIPS-BIRT, Douglas, *British Ocean Racing*, London: Adlard Coles Ltd., 1960.
POOR, Charles Lane, *Men Against the Rule, A Century of Progress in Yacht Design*, New York: The Derrydale Press, 1937.
ROGERS, Andrew, *IDUNA. The Restoration of a Classic Dutch Yacht*, Naarden: Van Klaveren Maritime, 2004.
SCIARRELLI, Carlo, *Lo Yacht, Origine e Evoluzione del Veliero da Diporto*, Milan: Mursia, 1988.
SCOTT HUGHES, John, *Sailing Through Life*, London: Methuen, 1947.
SERAFINI, Flavio, *A Band of Brothers, Vela d'Epoca a Imperia*, Cavallermaggiore: Gribaudo Editore, 1994.
SHOETTLE, Edwin J., *Sailing Craft. Mostly Descriptive of Smaller Pleasure Sail Boats of the Day*, New York: The MacMillan Company, 1928.
STEPHENS II, Olin J., *All This and Sailing, Too, An Autobiography*, Mystic: Mystic Seaport, 1999.
TABARLY, Éric, *Pen Duick*, Paris: Éditions Ouest-France, 1989.
VANDERBILT, Harold S., *Enterprise, The Story of the Defense of the America's Cup in 1930*, New York: Charles Scribner's Sons, 1931.
WARD, Captain A.R., *The Chronicles of The Royal Thames Yacht Club*, Arundel: Fernhurst Books, 1999.
WAUGH, Alec, *The Lipton Story, A Centennial Biography*, London: Cassell and Company, 1951.

ACKNOWLEDGEMENTS

The author and the publishers particularly wish to thank Angelo Bonati, CEO of Officine Panerai, who gave us free access to his archives and other documents relating to the story and the restoration of the ketch *Eilean*.

We also extend our thanks to those people without whom this book could not have been written, as well as to the museums, libraries, universities, administrations and yacht clubs who all contributed extensively to the research concerning this beautiful adventure.

Philippe Abalan, Daniel Allisy, Claudia Arsié, Pierre Banyuls, Mike Beal, Gérard Beauvais, Jol Byerley, Nathalie Chapuis, Claire Cocks, David Cook, Andrew Cully, François-Jean Dahen, Bernard Deguy, Nathalie Dupuis, Giorgio Ferrazzi, Christian Fevrier, Joseph Flores, Christopher Franck, Julie Frankl, Gil Frey, Robin L.V. Fulton, James Gilmour, Tim Henderson, Betty Hendry, Paul Kaplan, Chris Kennan, Tove Knight, Robert and May Fife Kohn, Lord Lang of Monkton, Sharon Lawler, Ian P.C. Mackenzie, Howard Morrison, Michael S. Moss, Ian Nicolson, Chiara Panozzo, Ruth Parker, Mario Pirri, Stavely Roberts, Carla Salicini, Ombretta Schinetti, Annie-Laurie Shearer, John Shearer, William Shawcross, Joy Sulitzer, Jacques Taglang, Nerys Tunnicliffe, Christophe Varène, and Emma Yan.

The UK Local History and Genealogy Gazetteer, House of Lords, Inverclyde Libraries, Mitchell Library, Glasgow, Mudhook Yacht Club, National Media Museum, National Register of Archives (NRA), Royal Gourock Yacht Club, Royal Highland Yacht Club, The Royal Photographic Society, Royal Western Yacht Club, St Andrews Sailing Club, Scottish Maritime Museum, Irvine, University of Glasgow, Archive Services, and Watt Library, Greenock.

Officine Panerai wishes to thank Cantiere Navale Francesco Del Carlo, Enrico Zaccagni, Officina Meccanica Navale Petrozzi & Rossi, Elettro Naval Impianti, their staff and all the institutions, consultants, suppliers, friends or simple enthusiasts who, through their passion and commitment, have contributed to returning *Eilean* to its true element, the sea. Officine Panerai's special thanks for their invaluable collaboration also goes to Agostino Tanchis of RINA Spa, to Commander Fabrizio Ratto Vaquer at Viareggio Port Captaincy, to Riccardo Valeriani, to Michel De Joie and Francesco Rastrelli for having documented the most important moments of the refurbishment with their splendid photos, to Antonio Falchetti, and to May Kohn Fife of the Scottish Maritime Museum for having kept the glorious memories of the Fife Boatyard alive through exemplary dedication.

PHOTOGRAPHIC CREDITS

Pages 6–11: © Photo Gilles Martin-Raget / page 12: © Courtesy of Enrico Zaccagni / pages 13–14: © photo Gilles Martin-Raget / page 15: © Courtesy of Enrico Zaccagni / pages 16–17: © photo Gilles Martin-Raget / page 18: © Courtesy of Enrico Zaccagni / pages 19–22: © photo Gilles Martin-Raget / page 23: © Courtesy of Enrico Zaccagni / page 24: © photo Gilles Martin-Raget / page 26: © photo Gilles Martin-Raget / pages 29, 30: © photos Gilles Martin-Raget / pages 31, 32: © Courtesy of Enrico Zaccagni / page 33 (left and right): © May F. Kohn Collection / page 34 (top and below): © Courtesy of Enrico Zaccagni / pages 35, 36, 37, 38, 39 (top and below), 40 (top and below), 41, 42, 43: © Courtesy of Enrico Zaccagni / pages 44–45: © photos Mannelli, Anchise & C., Alinari Archives-Mannelli Archive, Firenze / page 46: © Panerai Archives / Page 47: © photo Mannelli, Anchise & C., Alinari Archives-Mannelli Archive, Firenze / page 49: Panerai Archives / Page 50: Panerai Archives / Page 53: Panerai Archives / page 54: © Courtesy Ufficio Storico Marina Militare / page 55: Panerai Archives / page 56: Panerai Archives / page 58: Panerai Archives / page 59: Giuseppe Toja / page 60: Giuseppe Toja / page 61: Giuseppe Toja / page 62: © photo Beken of Cowes / pages 65, 66, 67, 68: © Collection François Chevalier-DR / pages 69, 70: © photos Beken of Cowes / page 71: © François Chevalier / page 72: © photo Beken of Cowes / page 74, left: © Courtesy of William Shawcross / page 74, right: © Courtesy of David Cook / page 75: © Courtesy of Christopher Franck / page 76: © Courtesy of William Shawcross / page 77: © photo Bernard Deguy / page 78: © Annie-Laurie Shearer Collection / pages 81, 82, 83, 84, 85, 86–87: © Annie-Laurie Shearer Collection / pages 88–89: © photos Gilles Martin-Raget / page 90: © photo Francesco Rastrelli / page 93: © photo Francesco Rastrelli / pages 94–97: © François Chevalier / pages 98, 99, 100, 101, 102–103, 104, 105, 106, 108–109, 110, 112, 113, 115, 116, 117, 118, 120, 121, 123, 124, 125, 126, 128, 129, 131, 132, 133, 134, 136, 137: © photos Francesco Rastrelli / page 138: © photo Max Ranchi / pages 141, 142–143: © photos Franco Pace / page 144: © photo Gilles Martin-Raget / pages 146–147: © photo Franco Pace / page 149: © photo Gilles Martin-Raget / page 150: © photo Franco Pace / pages 152–153: © photo Franco Pace / page 154: photo Franco Pace / page 155: © photo Max Ranchi / pages 156–157: © photo Cory Silken / pages 158–159: © photo Max Ranchi / pages 160, 162, 163, 164–165, 166, 167, 168, 169, 170, 171, 172, 173, 174, 175, 176, 177, 178, 179, 180, 181, 182, 183, 184-185, 186, 187, 188–189: © photos Gilles Martin-Raget.